HAVELOCK ELLIS
Philosopher of Sex

(Frontispiece) Havelock Ellis in his last years

HAVELOCK ELLIS
Philosopher of Sex

A Biography

Vincent Brome

ROUTLEDGE & KEGAN PAUL
London, Boston and Henley

First published in 1979
by Routledge & Kegan Paul Ltd
39 Store Street,
London WC1E 7DD,
Broadway House,
Newtown Road,
Henley-on-Thames,
Oxon RG9 1EN and
9 Park Street
Boston, Mass. 02108, USA
Photoset in 11 on 12 Garamond by
Kelly and Wright, Bradford-on-Avon, Wiltshire
and printed in Great Britain by
Unwin Brothers Ltd
The Gresham Press, Old Woking, Surrey
A member of the Staples Printing Group
Plates printed by
Headley Bros. Ltd, Ashford, Kent

British Library Cataloguing in Publication Data

Brome, Vincent

Havelock Ellis.
1. Ellis, Havelock
2. Authors, English – Biography
3. Sexologists – England – Biography
301.41'092'4   PR6009.L8Z/

ISBN 0 7100 0019 7

To bear all naked truths
And to envisage circumstance all calm,
That is the top of sovereignty.
                    – Keats

The only indecorum known to science is
the concealment of truth.
                    – Westermarck

Contents

Illustrations

Preface

My interest in Havelock Ellis really began when I read a review of Ellis's autobiography, published in 1940, which described it as the greatest literary disappointment of the age.[1] Reviewers in both America and Europe voiced their dispraise with a rarely achieved unanimity.

My Life was received gloomily as a book not worthy of the Master. Its two main shortcomings sprang from a similar source. Ellis devoted too much attention to his relations with his wife, reproducing letter after letter. It was not so much their intimacy, as the sentimental treatment of all the details which became embarrassing. Devoted to Edith, Ellis allowed her to dominate the book in such a way that it virtually stops with her death in 1916 and is overwhelmed by her throughout.

There had been two earlier biographies, one by Dr Isaac Goldberg published in 1926, which need not delay anyone anxious to discover Havelock Ellis. A eulogistic study of a limited kind, it suffered from the fact that two-thirds of Ellis's life could not be told at that stage. Houston Peterson's book, *Havelock Ellis, Philosopher of Love*, published in 1928, was of a different calibre. An excellent study of Ellis's intellectual pilgrimage, it stopped at 1927, but suffered once more from the impossibility of revealing Ellis's private life. Re-reading Peterson's book is rewarding to any student of Ellis and I acknowledge the part it played in preparing my own biography. As to Ellis's autobiography, clearly, for many purposes it was indispensable. Many of my basic facts and a number of letters come from it. There remains a strange book by Françoise Delisle which appeared in 1946. The first half of *Friendship's Odyssey* recounts the early days in the life of Mme Delisle, and the second deals with her very intimate relations with Havelock Ellis over the last twenty years of his life. The account is confused. Once more a surfeit of letters overwhelms the narrative and it is difficult to distil the facts from the mass of sentimental reminiscence, but again, the book places on record unique and invaluable evidence without which certain serious gaps would have appeared in my own account. There remains

Arthur Calder-Marshall's biography in 1959 which is a very effective and useful piece of work on which I have drawn.

Many years ago I approached Mme Delisle and explained my intention of writing a life of Havelock Ellis. Considerable correspondence developed. After some months it was indicated to me that I was a suitable person to write the book and could proceed. I visited Mme Delisle, underwent a number of very long conversations with her and her son – in the course of which they were most enlightening about Havelock Ellis – and presently came away with a trunk-load of material including:

1. Unpublished diary beginning April 1875 (from the ship *Surrey*) ending 16 March 1890.

2. Commonplace books and notebooks dated:

1875–7	1877–80	1878–9
1880–1	1880	1881
1881–3	1883–5	1885

3. Eleven unpublished letters between Radclyffe Hall and Havelock Ellis from 1928 to 1930.

4. Unpublished letter from Olive Schreiner dated 1919.

5. Unpublished letter from Olive Schreiner dated 30 June 1912.

6. Ten early letters from Ellis to his father and mother, between 7 May 1877 and 14 December 1892. An eleventh letter in childish handwriting with scalloped edges, being the first letter from the ship *Empress* dated 29 June 1867.

7. Twenty-two other early unpublished letters and a number of postcards.

8. A hundred and twenty-nine – mostly unpublished – letters from Havelock Ellis to F. H. Perrycoste between 1901 and 1927.

9. A hundred and fifty unpublished letters and postcards from Edward Carpenter to Havelock Ellis between 1876 and 1922.

10. A number of unpublished sexual histories from Edward Carpenter.

11. Two unpublished letters to Winifred Horrabin dated 17 November 1935, and 2 August 1937.

12. Unpublished letter from Reginald Reynolds to Havelock Ellis dated 20 October 1933.

13. Two unpublished letters from John Burns, 27 October 1934 and 20 November 1934.

14. Seventeen unpublished letters from Jules de Gaultier between 1918 and 1935.

15. Nine letters from Thomas Davidson to Ellis beginning 1883. Three unpublished.

16. A number of Havelock Ellis's early manuscripts – some unpublished – St Paul, the Organic Unity of Humanity – Death – Woman of Samarra – Translation from Alfred de Musset – Translation from

Heine – Translation of Song of Songs from the French of M. Renan – A Few Words about Shelley – The Intellectual – The Tea (a humorous sketch) – A Fragment – Analysis of 'In Memoriam' Dedicated Not by Permission to A. M. Mackay – Three Visions of One – a number of early poems – Books I have Read – A Prayer – A Patriotic Song – Essay on the Comic Dramatists of the Restoration.

17. Ten letters from Max Ferrars.
18. Twenty-five other poems and fragments.

With the approval of Ellis's literary executrix, notices appeared in the *Times Literary Supplement* and *Manchester Guardian*, asking for letters and reminiscences and a long chain of correspondence began. This and the writing of the book extended over nearly three years. Difficulties developed between Mme Delisle and myself which made it necessary to suspend publication and only now in 1977, after her death, have I returned to the manuscript to revise, re-edit and bring the material up to date. The present biography is an independent study and re-assessment of his life and work which does not set out to be definitive.

I am grateful to the following either for many letters or their patience in answering questions:

Olaf Baker, Clifford Bax, Dr C. P. Blacker, Montgomery Belgion, Captain Bloodworth, Dr Vera Buchanan-Gould, Mrs B. Burgess, Alex Craig, Anna Freud, Captain Green, Mrs Lily Herbert, Winifred Horrabin, Lord Horder, George Ives, Dr Ernest Jones, W. G. Lawry, J. Mare, Harold Picton, Reginald Pound, Bernard Sleigh, Marie Stopes, Lady Troubridge.

In the second year of writing this book research switched to America and my appeals in the *Nation* and the *New York Times Book Supplement* brought some interesting material. Among my correspondents I am especially indebted to Robert Craven, William Galt, Jane Himmelein, Marie McCall, Basil Mitchell, Florence Mole, Albert Mordell, Houston Peterson, Margaret Sanger and Joseph Wortis, either for scores of unpublished letters or for their explanation of relationships with Ellis.

In particular Mrs Sanger's intimate knowledge of Havelock Ellis was invaluable to me. In a different sense the work of Basil Mitchell, then at Columbia University, was very helpful. I was aware that Mrs Ellis had given a number of lectures to certain unnamed newspapers during her two lecture tours in the States, and that they led to serious trouble with her husband. Tracing where the interviews appeared was a long and troublesome process, since every one of the 51 States had several newspapers. Mr Mitchell undertook and accomplished the task.

Beyond the material made available by the literary executrix I have examined over seven hundred other unpublished documents which included:

1. Thirty-three letters from Ellis to Edward Carpenter.
2. Six pages of notes and two sexual histories prepared by Edward Carpenter for Havelock Ellis's early *Studies in the Psychology of Sex.*
3. Ten letters from Ellis to Radclyffe Hall.
4. Seventy-four letters from Ellis to Dr Herbert.
5. Fifteen letters to 'J. R.'
6. Five hundred letters from various people concerning the 'Andrew Scott' or Hugh de Selincourt incident.
7. A copy of *Friendship's Odyssey* especially annotated by one of the chief people mentioned in the book.
8. Twelve letters from Ellis to Clifford Bax.
9. An interesting dossier compiled by Alec Craig on Ellis's library.
10. A newspaper dossier maintained over twenty years by a national newspaper.
11. Nine letters from Edith Ellis to Edward Carpenter.
12. Two letters from 'Paula' to Edward Carpenter.
13. Thirty-five letters from Ellis to George Ives.
14. Six letters from Ellis to Dr Trigant Burrow.
15. Sixteen letters from Ellis to H. Picton.
16. Ten letters concerning Josephine Walther and twenty-five from Ellis to Josephine Walther.
17. Eight letters from Ellis to Marie McCall.
18. Ellis's first letter to F. A. Davis signing his original contract.
19. The extensive correspondence between Ellis and Hugh de Selincourt.
20. Correspondence between Françoise Delisle and Hugh de Selincourt.
21. Twenty-five letters from Ellis to Bernard Sleigh.
22. Two letters from Margaret Sanger to Hugh de Selincourt.
23. A hundred letters from Olive Schreiner to Karl Pearson.
24. A number of letters from Olive Schreiner to Carpenter, 1886–1914.

There was also a fifteen-page unpublished manuscript on Havelock and Edith Ellis by Florence Mole, a four-page unpublished manuscript on Edith Ellis by Olaf Baker, ten letters from Mrs Margaret Sanger to the author, four letters from Houston Petersen, and a number of letters from Lawrence Lader, biographer of Mrs Sanger, Harold Picton and Montgomery Belgion. I am also grateful to Vera Buchanan-Gould for indicating something of the contents of another group of some one hundred love letters addressed by Ellis to Olive Schreiner, to Mrs V. R. Dernier for documents relating to Olive Schreiner and Ellis's early Australian days and to Mrs Olive Renier for some interesting information about Olive Schreiner and Alice Corthorn, including two letters of Olive Schreiner's. Arthur Calder-Marshall was helpful in several ways, especially in allowing me to see the Carpenter – Ellis and

Carpenter – Edith Ellis correspondence which he had lodged with the London Library. Edward Carpenter left a large collection of personal papers, now held by Sheffield City Libraries, Yale University Library and the University of California; Los Angeles also have some Havelock Ellis material, and the Karl Pearson archive in University College, London, was useful.

Obviously, Havelock Ellis's *My Life* was indispensable for many basic facts and a number of letters.

In psycho-analysis I should like to acknowledge the help given by Dr Ernest Jones, and in literature the enlightening criticism undertaken by the late Philip Henderson.

Ernest Jones was helpful in establishing the nature of the correspondence and relationship between Sigmund Freud and Havelock Ellis. A number of letters between Ellis and Freud have escaped the destruction which overtook so much of Ellis's general correspondence. Interpretation of the will made it necessary to relinquish many letters written to Ellis, and these letters were burnt, but the Freud–Ellis chapter of my book is my own responsibility and differs from the interpretation held by Dr Jones.

One of my most difficult photographic problems was solved by Mrs Olive Renier.

In its original form the book threatened to become unwieldy. It was decided to sacrifice historical references and background to the strict matter of biography, and the present volume makes no attempt to recreate period.

Inevitably, with Ellis, normal canons of biography collapse. His clinical examination of general sexual behaviour makes it necessary to examine his own in detail. To understand his preoccupation with one, it is imperative to probe the other.

Finally I would like to thank the staff of the British Library and particularly that part of it operating the North Library, for their continuous help in producing a multitude of books.

Acknowledgments

The author and publishers wish to acknowledge with thanks Professor François Lafitte's permission to quote from the works of Havelock Ellis and Françoise Delisle. I must also thank the executors of Edward Carpenter, Radclyffe Hall and Olive Schreiner for permission to quote from their letters. My thanks also to Olaf Baker, Jane Himmelmein, Winifred Horrabin, Florence Mole, Houston Petersen and Margaret Sanger whose replies to my inquiries are embodied in the text. Janet de Selincourt kindly gave me permission to use her letters and the contents of her husband's Hugh de Selincourt's letters. The trustees of the Estate of Miss E. A. Dugdale and Messrs Macmillan allowed me to reproduce a letter from Thomas Hardy. The Author's Society made available a letter from George Bernard Shaw and Rache Lovat Dickson some letters of Radclyffe Hall. Thanks also to Messrs Ernest Benn Ltd, for permission to quote from *The Letters of Olive Schreiner*.

Prologue

In his fifties, Dr Havelock Ellis was known to a select circle as a distinguished writer, but the outside world still regarded him as a purveyor of pornography, condemnation varying in proportion to ignorance of his work. He had by then behind him the *Studies in the Psychology of Sex*, a seven-volume work which had grown volume by volume over a period of more than thirty years. Books continued to multiply, sometimes at the rate of one a year: *The New Spirit, The Criminal, The Nationalisation of Health, Affirmations, The Nineteenth Century, A Dialogue in Utopia, The Soul of Spain, A Study of British Genius, The World of Dreams, The Task of Social Hygiene*. Some were 'strewn with innumerable findings bearing on practically all sound modern doctrines in the sciences of the human mind, human society and the human body'.[1] When asked how many he had written he replied characteristically: 'For the life of me I cannot remember. But I must go on writing; it keeps me alive. I fear, though, I am beginning to disappoint those who expect nothing from me but sex.'[2]

The humanist and literary critic were brushed aside by the mass of middle-class parents who still whispered his name with revulsion. Sex, after all, was only a highly undesirable interruption of other more noble pursuits, and any man who wrote books about it must be depraved. Two of his books were those Dr Inge boasted of having burnt,[3] and Marie Stopes read his *Studies in the Psychology of Sex* and felt 'choked and dirty for three months'.[4]

Inevitably, most people had to base their personal opinions of Ellis on the flimsiest evidence. So little was known about him. There was nothing of H. G. Wells's or Shaw's spectacular behaviour in this self-effacing person who had never given a lecture in his life, shunned public functions of any kind and, when a dinner was organized to celebrate his sixtieth birthday, was too shy to attend. There were no headlines in the newspapers. His movements were not 'copy' as were the movements of Wells and Shaw. People did not clearly know whether he

1

was married, had half a dozen children, or as many mistresses, but they were fully prepared to equip him with every possible depravity. Even his whereabouts were unknown. He attended no first nights or fashionable restaurants and, when his wife subjected their household on one occasion to something resembling a party, he found it so distasteful it drove him deeper than ever into his shell.[5]

His life was of the simplest. When alone he rose early, sometimes at six, prepared his own breakfast, wrote part of another chapter or article, and later cooked his own lunch. Sometimes a walk in the afternoon was followed by a cup of tea, and then back he went to his Brixton flat, largely unaware that his magnificent figure caused heads to turn. More work was followed by another spell in the kitchen where, quite alone, he sometimes prepared an evening meal of great delicacy. Perhaps there was a glass or two of wine on those occasions when he could afford it but, granted the wealth he never achieved, a natural sense of moderation would still have stopped his drinking at the second glass. Later in the evening he deliberately ceased work and surrendered himself to complete relaxation. If he worked far into the evening he could not sleep, and sleep, as necessary to him as long periods of isolation, began with rhythmic regularity at ten to ten-thirty. Sometimes, for days on end, he faithfully fulfilled this round without speaking to a soul, reaching those inner recesses of self-absorption from which he only retraced his steps with difficulty and occasionally, when a friend knocked at the door and broke into his retreat, came to the surface in some bewilderment.

Removed from many formal contacts with life, he still contrived to remain at the heart of it. Letters flowed from his Brixton flat to anthropologists, scientists and doctors, papers were written and exchanged, and an answering tide poured back from people like Hirschfield, Freud, Francis Galton, Bertrand Russell and George Bernard Shaw. Overwhelming the great names were the nonentities, hundreds of men and women who turned in distress to a man whose reputation for Christ-like omniscience had mysteriously spread. Sometimes the accumulated letters were piled high in odd places of his workroom and sometimes it was a month or so before he replied, but in the end anything remotely worthy of a reply received one.

The proportion of his 'patients by post' who called upon him was small, but his correspondence became enormous, and in the end, their number was considerable. Weeks would go by without a visitor and then someone, baffled by the savage contradictions in man-made laws and his own nature, would take courage to knock on the door, confronting a man to all intents and purposes barely recovered from a mystical trance.

Francis Watson was one such visitor. He always remembered, as the door opened, the sunlight falling upon a man nearly six feet tall, with a cathedral calm in his bearing, a beard silken white in the sunshine, and a magnificently handsome head. Ellis carried himself with a natural grace, so that a certain breathlessness attacked Watson; the splendour of this person was overwhelming. Yet the voice, when Ellis spoke, was high, slightly harsh, and the hand that took Watson's limp. 'Er – Come – in', he said with a shy gesture, and the flaws in the perfection were reassuring.

Books constituted the main furniture of the flat which Watson entered, and they were books not ranged along shelves in careful order, but rising in accidental accumulations from the floor, making sudden pinnacles which threatened every movement with an avalanche. Invisible pathways between them were clear to Dr Ellis who removed a heap from a chair and gestured to his visitor to be seated. There was a pause. Dr Ellis's eyes slipped over Watson's shoulder and settled on the distances. At last he said 'Ah – ' and then relapsed into silence again. The young man knew he should say something, but was paralysed by the proximity of the person whose name carried, for him, an almost religious significance, and the knowledge that here was the recipient of those intimate letters which he had written, and now, quite suddenly, regretted.

It had cost him great effort to enter the house at all. The home of Havelock Ellis sadly disappointed him. It was an impoverished apartment at Dover Mansions, opposite a police station in the grey desert of Brixton,[6] and he had paced back and forth before the house, trying to steel his resolution. Then at last he had knocked and entered.

Now the two men waited for some signal which would release them from their mutual shyness. Half a minute went by. The graceful immobility of Havelock Ellis gave a little as he permitted another half phrase to escape his lips. Watson's face brightened as he waited for the words to follow, but none came. The psychic knot tightened . . . 'So that I felt I was hopelessly lost and tongue-tied.'[7]

Then at long last Ellis said: 'Perhaps you would like some tea?', and without waiting for an answer disappeared into the small kitchen leaving Watson to the silence of what might have been a secondhand bookshop. The sofa, on close examination, revealed its secondary purpose as a gimcrack folding-bed, and the wicker chairs had obviously survived generations of owners.

Within a few minutes Dr Ellis returned with a flower-decorated tray, a pot of tea, two cups and some biscuits. Presently Watson offered a prayer to some divinity he had long ago abandoned that a winding sheet might come down from heaven and release him from this still mounting agony of silence, or that Dr Ellis might say something. Miraculously his prayer was answered. For suddenly Dr Ellis said: 'You don't need to worry you know – about homosexuality – every one of us is bi-sexual in some degree. Let me try to explain. . . .' They talked for nearly an hour.

Similar pictures of Havelock Ellis abound. His lack of small talk and tendency to fall into prolonged silences bothered many people. François Lafitte (son of Françoise Delisle), Margaret Sanger, Hugh de Selincourt, Edward Carpenter have all described Ellis's extreme shyness. Francis Watson found that two sustained visits still did not bring Dr Ellis to look him in the eye.

In and out of doors Ellis had quite remarkable powers of absorption. He passed friends without recognition and once unintentionally 'cut' the girl with whom he was in love. Yet he gave unquestioningly of his time and attention to anyone who called, and whenever the question of fees arose usually brushed it aside.

The clash between Ellis's 'primitive psychiatry' and psycho-analytic treatment was considerable. The true nature of his 'treatment', and its relation to modern techniques will appear in later chapters, but that many of his 'patients' went away reassured merely to have met such a man was indisputable. They included not only homosexuals, 'perverts' and adolescents, but ordinary married people, who believed that Ellis had special insights which could explain if not reconcile the conflicts in their lives. Whatever form it took – the 'treatment' of a 'patient', lending money or a book – the act of giving satisfied Ellis beyond the normal. It should, of course, be made clear that he did not have patients or carry out treatment in the Freudian meaning of those terms.

The minutiae of his appearance, personality and habits were contradictory. He was 5ft 10½″ in height but the splendour of his appearance made him look taller. His eyes, commonly called grey, were in fact green, 'that is to say, blue with brown circles round the irises'.[8] His hair began light brown, became dark brown, admitted patches of grey at forty and at fifty was a soft, glowing white. The hair on his head remained thick far into life but the beard became sparse and straggling. Of his face generally he wrote, 'It is rather a short face; the chin, with the large dimple in it (seemingly inherited from the Havelocks) is, I have been told, lacking in strength. . . . My mouth is broad and opens widely. . . .'[9]

Neglecting his teeth, at fifty he had false ones. He also wore glasses. It is interesting that I can trace no surviving picture of Ellis actually wearing the glasses. His head was 23 inches in circumference and he sometimes had difficulty in finding a hat to fit. 'There is', he wrote, 'a peculiarity in the profile of the lower jaw which is probably characteristic . . . in some aspects a slightly ape-like suggestion. Boys are quick to catch the faintest abnormalities, and my schoolfellows at Mitcham sometimes, quite good-naturedly, would call me Baboon.'[10] With an unusual burst of self-criticism, he thought this justified, both in his face and nature. It is difficult to understand what he meant by the baboon in his nature since he was far from being aggressive and even his sexual conduct appeared to lack that streak of 'animality' common to most men. It was a fellow-student at St Thomas's Hospital who first pointed out another and, in some eyes, far more flattering resemblance. He said one day with a dry asperity lacking in the woman who later repeated the remark: 'You know, there are moments when you remind me of Jesus Christ.'

The soft, gracious lines of the face unmarked far into life were partly the deliberate cultivation of an open countenance as well as an open mind, carried in boyhood to the pitch where he carefully observed himself in the glass to 'nip in the bud any wrinkling of forehead or contraction of lips . . . I felt, doubtless rightly, that the hardening of mind and heart had its outward expression in a tightly contracted face.'

In the practical tasks of everyday life his ineptitude as a boy became more pronounced in his fifties. He did not tie a very adequate knot, he preferred walking to driving in any kind of conveyance and he had not the slightest interest in card-playing or any form of gambling. 'All my instincts are in favour of *Justice*, and from the standpoint of Justice, *Chance* is the very Devil Himself, and as such an inevitable part of life which we need not seek to increase.'[11] Athletics of any kind wore for him a faintly ludicrous air. The spectacle of a healthy young man, bursting his lungs to complete a circuit in five seconds less than some formidable champion before him, always seemed to Ellis an incredible distortion of the human personality and an extraordinarily naive way of demonstrating prowess.

In restaurants it was common for him to wait until his wife had ordered something and then with a radiant smile, to glance at the menu, purse his lips, look over the waiter's shoulder, and order exactly the same.[12] He ate far too quickly and found difficulty in breaking the habit. He also experienced strain in conducting himself skilfully at dinner table as his wife – with her considerable flair for causing him distress – did not hesitate to point out. He believed himself congenitally left-handed and said his common use of the right hand was probably the result of artificial training, although he failed to see this as the explanation of the slight muscular unbalance which troubled him. He drank moderately but was never once in his life intoxicated. He smoked occasional cigarettes until he was sixty-two and then without apparent effort or trouble gave them up.

Practical decisions like practical tasks were always a torment to him. 'When left to myself in the details of life, I am apt to be cautious, nervous, self-suspicious, haunted by doubts when I have to choose between two courses of action, and tortured by the thought that the course I have rejected may have been the better. . . .'[13] He met the commonplace eventualities of life only with great effort and months of steadily accumulating resolution.

Beneath the external grandeur of his appearance there were mysterious forces at work, of which amongst his close friends he made no concealment. It seemed absurd that the man who had brought such grace into his everyday life should suddenly unbend and admit that commonplace indigestion troubled him badly. He was the epitome of the 'duodenal type' with its massively calm exterior never permitting stresses within to break through.

Stomach trouble rendered public life a torment. 'It would come on rather suddenly with intense pain and tenderness . . . in (if I remember rightly) the right side of the abdomen, . . . Vomiting always occurred. Eating and sleeping, any mental or physical activity, were alike impossible. . . . Sometimes the attack lasted for hours, sometimes for days. . . .'[14]

This acute stage later subsided into a chronic tendency to dyspepsia which made social functions of any kind difficult. A feeling of gastric swelling was likely to overtake him and to reach those paroxysmal proportions where he fell silent, feeling completely stupid with pain. The pressure on the heart from the stomach was liable to cause faintness. Once in a theatre he did in fact faint. When the attacks were very acute he would rapidly devise an excuse for escape, but being a very bad liar it sometimes left his host puzzled, sometimes hurt, while his already gigantic reputation as a recluse soon included hints of hopeless eccentricity. He remained far into life sensitive to the earliest signs of nervous stress. He knew that rest and change were necessities to him when certain symptoms appeared.

He clearly suffered from acute anxiety neuroses all his life which found substitute relief in a disorganized stomach. Certainly his choice of wife, his marriage and the psychic tensions which sprang so readily from his unconscious held rich promise for any analyst. His passivity frequently reached a pathological pitch, he could become outrageously sentimental and in his writings about sex the most extravagant grotesqueries failed to stir even a glimmer of humour.

Olive Schreiner exercised her own very special powers on him on one occasion. Extraordinarily, remembering his handsomeness when she first met him, she was so disappointed she burst into tears but later recorded:[15]

One side of your nature is like —s, and unlike mine. When I want to go to Trafalgar Square and fight the enemies of Freedom of the hour wildly and get my head broken, *you* say I am a fool, and you are *right*. . . . The man who sits quietly in his study, writing and working out a great scientific truth, while his little petty state is going to pieces, is greater, more human, more moral than one who, like myself, would rush out wildly and fight. *You* of all people I ever met (infinitely more than—) are a man of the study. You are perfectly dead on the other side. That is your weakness and your stength. That is why you will do great and useful work in the world. The world is crashing about you, your dearest friends are being dragged to prison, theories you have been interested in are being practically tested, cruel and wicked wrong is being done to innocent little children – and you look with astonishment and disapproval at another who is not untouched by it. . . . Your very medical work is not for its own sake, and give you £200 a year and you would curl yourself up in abstract study and thought for the rest of life. . . . Your *greatness* is your absolute absence of the enthusiasm of the market place.

Where Miss Schreiner exploded with anger when W. T. Stead revealed that girls in their 'teens could be bought in London for £3, Ellis regretted it in quite different terms but his understatement concealed a distress at least equal to hers.[16] Thought was for him a substitute for action but none the less full of concern. Like Roger Bacon he sat immersed in his cell writing great tracts in beautiful English which seeped unnoticed through the walls for nearly a generation before they took full effect. 'So as I watch the little casements in the valley below grow bright', he wrote on 21 December 1921, 'and as the huge beam of the Lizard revolves behind the heights, I softly repeat to myself those words of Coleridge which so often linger in my mind, "I am not fit for public life, yet the light shall stream to a far distance from the taper in my cottage window. . . ." '[17]

Far on into life he continued to enjoy, in discerning circles, a reputation for Christ-like serenity and was said to transform living into that art of which he frequently spoke. Those who knew him well did not disturb the legend. Deeper than the eye could see were signs which qualified the picture out of all recognition.

He had achieved that clear, impartial awareness which he believed inseparable from a fully realized life, but the Master was no match for life in the end.

Chapter 1
First beginnings

Turning the pages of *The Times*, already a month old, in Singapore, Captain Ellis at last found the brief notice: 'On the 2nd inst., at 1, St John's Grove, Croydon, the wife of Mr Edward P. Ellis, of a son.'[1] The year was 1859, the month February. Highly excited, Captain Ellis at once called together the officers of his ship, champagne was brought from below and the health of his son toasted 'with much jocularity' from the First Officer.

The pattern of short homecomings and immense voyages half round the world, extending sometimes into two or three years, was said to have established Captain Ellis and his wife in a state of perpetual honeymoon, and if this took no account of the enormous stretches of barren frustration which must have made up half of Mrs Ellis's life, the birth of a son delighted both. Captain Ellis was only to see that son, his wife's first child, for a few months in the first three and a half years of its life, and was similarly isolated from two daughters born three and four years later.

Havelock's had been a difficult birth. In his own understatement 'labour' became 'tedious' and the head was so large that forceps were necessary. In total contradiction to the outward personality he developed, the young Ellis, christened Henry Havelock, was born at 8.30 a.m., after 'a cold, tempestuous night', which the doctor remembered all his life. The birth took place in an ugly, little, semi-detached flint house in Croydon, then a small Surrey town near London, still unscarred by the multiplying tide of red brick and stucco houses which was to overwhelm London's suburbs.

A daguerrotype, the first picture of him, subsequently lost by Olive Schreiner, revealed a normal and happy enough baby boy.[2] Two years afterwards the self-satisfaction had vanished and a sad little boy appeared under a big hat, obviously chastened by the unexpected turn reality had taken. A third picture – revealing indeed – showed a tiny boy dressed in long knickerbockers tucked into stockings, a waistcoat, jacket and white collar, his stance extraordinarily mature, with one hand in the left pocket, the other splayed on the table. On his face was a look of melancholy apprehension, as though fighting the battle to look into the camera's eye, just as later he found difficulty in meeting the eye of any new acquaintance.

Everyone's childhood is fraught with incidents which have their echoes later in life, and it was odd in a man like Ellis, that he should recall some of these and underestimate their significance. He protested that his early relations with his parents were 'entirely free from any of those complications to which the child's affection for his mother is now supposed to be liable'. It is not only true that many memories are so deeply buried in the debris of the past as to remain incommunicable without the intervention of analysis; those recollected in tranquillity are often taken at a face value which is false. Ellis recalls in his autobiography that a nurse was wheeling his perambulator one day, when she suddenly stopped, a pause followed and then he 'heard a mysterious sound as of a stream of water descending to the earth'. This, he says, touched for the first time 'the strange mystery of woman'. He makes no reference to one of two abnormalities which he later termed urolagnia.[3] Several links in a long chain eventually led to urolagnia, but there were other far more normal childhood memories.

His mother might have recoiled in horror if she had discovered what lay hidden behind that barbaric word urolagnia, but she too had her part in what it is very important not to overstress as a minor 'aberration' in Ellis's make-up. Susannah Ellis, who came from East Anglian stock, sheltered a sensitive nature behind a tough façade, but her inner sensitivity did not prevent her having a strong persona. Her early years were spent at Suffolk House, Leyton, a district then capable of rustic seclusion, with an extensive garden, later obliterated by London's growing suburbs. She was just seventeen years old when she underwent an experience which she termed a 'conversion', and something very similar later overtook her son. Conversion, for Mrs Ellis, consisted in suddenly achieving serenity by accepting 'evangelical principles'. Contemporary evangelicism insisted that the Bible must be accepted unquestioningly and the evils of the outer world shunned as the devil. As Ellis later wrote, 'In the tradition of John Wesley she felt deeply the need of redemption through Jesus Christ and was quite indifferent to the rationalistic elements in religion.'

It is hard to accept Ellis's assurance that this 'inevitably cut' Mrs Ellis 'off from influences which might have developed her rich nature', when the face which looks out from the page opposite his statement achieves the acme of mediocrity, concentrating every commonplace characteristic from a shapeless nose to a tight mouth and stony eyes. Following her conversion, she was asked to accompany an aunt on a holiday in Paris, but she now saw Paris as a hotbed of immorality. Drink later shared the bedevilment of Paris, when she abandoned even the most moderate indulgence, and the theatre presently revealed similar shortcomings. In her later teens she considered the theatre too powerful a threat to her innocence, and never again risked contamination from even the most obscure seat at the back of the stalls. That it was her duty as a parent to discipline the children, she firmly believed, but she did not press her own austerities on them later in life. Perhaps family prayers was the one thing about which she remained consistently rigid and on Sundays she 'attended both morning and evening services', dimly hoping that her example might encourage stronger religious persuasions than were at first evident in her children. For the rest, 'Mrs Ellis played the piano as did all good Victorian ladies who had the proper admiration for Handel, and made quantities of fancy-work.'

Throughout Ellis's writings there are times when his inability to admit flaws in anything so wonderful as a mother, encourages him to juggle with words: 'Grave though with no formal solemnity, reserved if not exactly repressed, shy and nervous beneath the imposing presence. . . . Though she sought few friends, I doubt if she ever lost any. . . .'[4] The most he can bring himself to say against her in black and white is that her full development was arrested.

It was, to his grandparents, not his parents, that he owed his more remarkable characteristics. His grandmother, also named Susannah, was a very intelligent woman, with a sensitive, animated temperament and a considerable appetite for reading. With that precocity which marked his rapidly developing brain, he immersed himself in many of her books. He read from her library Rousseau's *Reveries*, Maria Edgeworth's *Harry and Lucy*, Rowlandson's *Doctor Syntax in Search of the Picturesque*, and the volumes of a series called *Nature Displayed*, in which Ellis's curiosity led him to a point where nature, it turned out, was heavily obscured.[5] At the age of twelve he was alarmed to find how many intimidating Latin labels could be placed in a region which statues and pictures had taught him to believe a barren and highly mysterious desert.

Like his mother, his grandmother also married a sailor but her passion ran so deep that when, following that marriage, Captain Wheatley desired to return to sea, she persuaded him to give up his command, and gradually he surrendered himself to life ashore. It was Captain Wheatley who said to his daughter Susannah, not long after she was born, 'Never marry a sailor.'[6] Not even Ellis's gift for euphemistic recollection could describe his mother-to-be as beautiful, but he was careful to point out that she had attractions other than those of being a ward in Chancery which were responsible for the number of men who became her suitors. The sole outbreak of insubordination she ever risked against her father was to choose a sailor amongst them as her husband.

At the early age of twenty-eight, Edward Peppen Ellis was already captain of his ship when he proposed to Susannah Wheatley, and if he sprang from a family of comfortable mediocrity unknown to excess or vice, and rarely throwing up anyone of distinction, he made a successful sea captain. Once again, the grandfather was so much more distinguished than the father, and there is every evidence to show that unusual traits from both grandparents were brought together in Ellis himself. Having in his physical make-up elements which could be said to be French, his grandfather combined a mild and sensitive nature with a considerable interest in the arts. His intelligence was an aesthetic intelligence and, like his grandson, he had very early shown an interest in lesser beauties like flowers, and his delight in music encouraged him to learn to play the flute. The roots of the Peppen Ellis family go back into the seventeenth century to the village of Wenhaston in Suffolk, but it is unnecessary to press beyond the grandfather to explain the grandson's qualities.

Havelock's father, Captain Peppen Ellis, spent more than thirty years as a sailor, acquiring a remarkable serenity which rode private and personal storms with the same equanimity as those he encountered at sea. He epitomized that type of handsome, upright, fair-dealing Englishman, with the rhythms of the sea in his gait, which was considered one of England's best products in the nineteenth century. In his worst periods he was never more than mildly indisposed, he did not need false teeth until he was seventy, commonplaces like headaches never troubled him and, unlike his son, he could easily digest the most indigestible foods. He moved through life with an easy tread, and wherever he went brought a sense of relaxation, which made him the most charming company. He had witnessed elemental upheavals in strange lands, he knew Valparaiso and Cuba and half the Americas, he had come through storms of appalling ferocity, played the priest and midwife, and faced death several times, but the mysteries underlying man and nature and the bewildering lack of purpose which appeared to distinguish the universe, troubled him not at all. The subtlest undertone he ever achieved in a divine simpleton's outlook amounted to nothing more than scepticism about the existence of God.

Health most certainly Henry Havelock inherited from his father and with it a splendour of countenance reminiscent of Leonardo da Vinci. Captain Peppen Ellis had fine brows, calm and beautiful eyes and a slender, perfectly proportioned nose. There was, unmistakably, in his bearing that graciousness so instantly apparent in his son, yet his own comparative dullness was enlivened in Henry by a fast-developing intellect. For the rest, his father contributed little. From his mother came a curious form of 'nerves', which rendered him highly sensitive to the slightest shock, but his real talents and inclination derived from his grandparents and behind them a long line of Suffolk ancestors.

In the wider British scene material progress sent steam engines uncertainly across the countryside belching smoke enough to choke their passengers, the electric telegraph had begun to annihilate space, ships made of iron were frowned upon as unnatural, textile machinery of a new and insidious design encouraged the early denizens of factories, and the prospect of swifter steamboats, taller chimneys and more intricate machinery was enough to sustain the glow of progress in men's eyes.

In this England, Mrs Granville's School in St James's Road, Croydon, played an insignificant part, providing the formally correct rudiments of an education when Henry Havelock entered it. Coming under the influence of a number of teachers who taught as well as their limited powers permitted, they left no very profound impression on him.

Inevitably he was a 'bright' pupil but there were many occasions when shyness and sensitivity frustrated the proper expression of his talents. Mrs Granville, proprietress and headmistress of the school, concealed considerable intelligence under a forbidding exterior, and showed no small insight into certain oddities in her new pupil. He had a tendency to break the rigid codes of class distinction laid down by Mrs Granville and his mother, and twice was reprimanded for mixing with working-class children. Once, inexplicably, a sudden burst of rage made him seize his boots and hurl them into the coal fire, constantly burning in the kitchen grate, and his mother had to rescue them as they began to smoulder. For the rest, his health seems to have been the chief concern of his parents in these small years, and under the physically robust exterior lay some mysterious weakness never clearly defined. A certain lassitude distinguished all his activities and he had no desire to cut the exuberant capers of boyhood. He escaped playing games at Mrs Granville's School whenever he could, although it was not in his nature to produce a point-blank refusal, but physical shortcomings were compensated for by immense mental energy of a kind which assimilated and ordered a mass of information.

Concern for his health grew rather than diminished. It was to cut short his first experience of schooling quite spectacularly. For presently his mother was persuaded to relinquish her beloved boy of seven, with his curiously dignified bearing, to the tender mercies of a sailing ship, The *Empress*, in which his father proposed to take him around the world. Mrs Susannah Ellis, long inured to those stretches of life which represented yet another voyage, must none the less have undergone considerable heart-searching before she surrendered not only her husband but her son to the caprice of a sailing ship embarked upon such a journey.

The voyage lasted a year and carried the boy to lands and places which remained with him vividly far on into life. The passengers included a group of Roman Catholic priests and nuns, and Henry's memories of the voyage were inextricably involved with the structure of the Roman Catholic faith. The Mother Superior unbent to talk to the boy at some length, Sister Agnes was charged with preserving some semblance of education in the confusions of shipboard life, and the irrepressible Father Doyle delighted in practical jokes. Sister Agnes was the object of his first recorded judgment of the opposite sex – he considered her 'very pretty'. Whenever the boy tired of Catholic dignitaries his instinct unerringly took him to the ship's library and there he discovered Hans Andersen and a book which became even more prized in his very early reading, Captain Marryatt's *Masterman Ready*.

But nowhere in any record Ellis left of the journey is there any hint of the excitements, the sheer boyish thrills which should, by all the laws of natural evocation, have overtaken a boy of seven setting forth upon the sea in a ship glorious with sail. Nor is it recorded what piratical fancies enlivened his mind on such islands as Chincha where they took aboard a cargo of guano, and an ancient coloured lady dispensed black grapes until a gorged Henry learnt to hate them for the rest of his days. The memory of the scent of guano always remained with him; he recalled Lima with its wonderful old patios dominated by sweeping Spanish arches; the gigantic Andes were still as fresh in his mind at fifty as when he first strained his eyes to see what moved so distantly upon their lower crests; and he remembered the young boy who shared a tiny boat with him to go exploring the rock pools and the caves, gathering a rich harvest of crabs, shells and starfish.

But the exhilaration of pure adventure in strange seas, of people myriad in their colour and habits, and a ship straining under a vast spread of canvas, does not break through any of the records he kept. Whenever his pen recovered the past there was a tendency for the detached, mature Ellis to dominate the scene and only once from early boyhood is there any sustained sense of powerfully recapturing early events; in *Kanga Creek*, a reminiscence written much later in life. Sheer precocity may have produced in Henry, at the age of seven, the seeds of that reflective calm which later distinguished his outer self, but it is hard to believe that even the most extravagant detachment could quite quell the quickening senses of a boy of seven confronted by such a rich, wild, fantastic passage. Deeper psychological forces were obviously at work.

The *Empress* carried him, at length, to Sydney in Australia, a country destined to play a powerful part in his adolescence. From Sydney they proceeded towards Callao, and there he met and played games with a tiny girl who solemnly took him through all the formal manoeuvres of keeping house on the ship's poop, helped by the sails, which provided walls to their imaginative home. With the girl there was no hint of sexuality, but the boy who went exploring with him explained one day how he had encouraged the growth of his genitals by a habit which Ellis later identified as masturbation. His own attempts to imitate, under

13

instruction, the exercise, turned out to be a dismal failure, and the problems and conflicts of masturbation did not trouble him at this stage.

The ship *Empress* proceeded on the then gigantic voyage through the dangerous waters surrounding Cape Horn. There followed an act, the incongruity of which would be startling to so gentle a person as Ellis, if psychology had not reconciled us to every anomaly. He saw the ship's cat slithering skilfully across the ship's stern one morning and, moved by a brutal impulse, he gave it the small touch required to confuse its balance and with a wild cry the animal disappeared overboard. It was never seen again. The episode disturbed Ellis much later in life, but it must have had deeper wellsprings than he perceived in a highly sensitive boy who disliked physical violence of any kind. Whether the cat represented the absent mother, he never unconsciously wished to see again, or whether it personified the growing sensuality of a small boy which had to be annihilated at any cost, we shall never know.

The voyage finished in 1867 and there returned home to the house in Addiscombe Terrace, Croydon, a bronzed, well set-up child, seasoned beyond his years, with an air of maturity which few town children acquired at so early an age. It was significant that, later in life, he had absolutely no recollection of his reunion with his mother but he remembered very vividly the house to which he returned.

Re-entering Granville's School he fell under the influence of the Misses Frowde, Cox and Bell, and while one fellow student tried to initiate Ellis into the correct enthusiasm for cricket these three ladies drummed into him the rudiments of English, arithmetic and a mysterious subject known as Deportment and Learning. On one occasion Mrs Granville, baffled by some indefinable difference in this shy, reticent creature, inquired whether his parents regarded him as quite normal, and was taken aback at the force of the indignant response. But Mrs Granville did save him 'from the cramping patterns of conventional education . . .' and acquainted him with that fundamental art – dancing – which became a favourite theme of his later life.

The whole Ellis family, now numbering six – three daughters were born in 1862, 1863 and 1867 – left the house at Croydon for another at Wimbledon in 1869. There it was decided to develop Henry's education at what was called the 'French and German College'.

The headmaster, de Chastelain, discovered nothing very distinctive about his new pupil except that his handwriting resembled the work of the kitchen poker. The headmaster's wife complained on one occasion that his manners were bad, and this influenced the report which de Chastelain sent to his parents, but Henry's introspective temperament produced gaucheries capable of complete misunderstanding. Later in life the glow in his eyes as he walked unaware past a life-long friend, wrapt deep in thought, induced in those without imagination considerable annoyance. For nearly three years Henry tried to come to some accommodation with the French and German College. He achieved a smattering of Latin and some French, and he dutifully went through the motions of playing cricket with quiet indifference. One of the masters swam naked in the swimming bath one day and Henry saw for the first time, with something of a shock, the fully matured sex organs. For the rest, nothing remarkable happened and he followed a course similar to that of every other shy boy whose talents did not seem striking.

If the French and German College did little to encourage Henry, privately his reading widened into a bewildering morass of books and rapidly assumed proportions which his mother presently considered morbid. Her protests were unavailing. Omnivorously devouring every printed word, Henry, too sensitive to respond to the coarse challenge of everyday school life, flowered in private, and reading gave him that special brand of delight which he completely failed to find in cricket or mathematics. There were times, in the holidays, when his mother insisted that he should go for a walk, so fearful was she that his health would suffer from his unnaturally sustained reading, and then she would come unexpectedly into his bedroom only to find him freshly ensconced with yet another book. Presently she recognized a force of destiny at work far more powerful than her own remonstrances.

If the family bookcase at first glance appeared well stocked, it soon revealed suffocating preoccupations with religion in every shape and form, from sermons and tracts to immense four-volume works of religious analysis. Henry tended to reject these in favour of the bound editions of the *Penny Magazine*, Scott's *Marmion*, and the little known but to him delightful Mrs Charles's *Chronicles of the Schonberg-Cotta Family*.

The discovery of his grandmother's books in the warped and capacious drawers of an ancient bureau which stood solidly in an upstairs room, completely revolutionized the scope of his reading. Here he found works like Rousseau's *Reveries d'un Promeneur solitaire*, whose contents might have distressed Ellis's mother had she troubled to investigate their true nature. Her astonishment at his literary preoccupations was increased when his birthday produced a demand, not for a model ship or steam engine, but for Macaulay's *Essays*, which he proceeded to annotate as well as read. He also bought the selected poems of Burns, Milton and Longfellow, at sixpence a copy, and conscientiously worked his way through each, loving the poems of Longfellow, but having serious reservations about the work of Burns and Milton. Once awakened, the intoxicating awareness of comparatively adolescent rhythms carried him through Alexander Smith's *Life-Drama* and Mrs Browning's *Aurora Leigh* with delight, but it was Longfellow who touched the real heart of his sweetly-sad puberty.

15

In prose he happened by accident on Scott. The family had retired to Shanklin in the Isle of Wight for a holiday and, desperate for reading matter, the landlady tentatively offered Havelock Scott's *Woodstock*, which at once fascinated him.

Soon the whole treasure trove of the penny pocket money which, at this stage, encompassed his total weekly wealth, was carefully saved until he could buy yet another Scott novel. Presently, the impoverished owner of the weekly penny found that his thirst for Scott far outstripped his income, and he was forced back on re-reading the same volume many times. Remarkably, this devotion to Scott persisted over many years, and did not seriously flag until he returned to Australia.

A third source of books dramatically different from Milton, Macaulay and Scott he found in an ancient sea chest still carrying a hint of the tropics in its fragrance, the survivor of many a long and arduous voyage. The chest contained, amongst other encrusted gems, *Robinson Crusoe*, now to hold Ellis enthralled. Nor was he immune from hypnotic concentration on *The Boys of England*, a penny weekly which sustained a drama as high and remote from reality as were some of its settings. When this penny dreadful gripped his interest, Henry read it while he was eating, while stumping the streets alone, and even sometimes while ostensibly sleeping. It was, he thought in later life, the result of unused motor energies demanding an outlet and vicariously finding it in the orgy of dramatic action which distinguished every tale.

Simultaneously there appeared the first stirrings of his own desire to write, in the form of a series of penny notebooks wherein he described the chief events of the week and religiously recorded quotations which fired his imagination. By the age of twelve, he already had one book of his own ready for publication. The manuscript has vanished but we do know that it was called 'The Precious Stones of the Bible' and condensed the accumulated information of many hours' reading about that book.[7] Solemnly and with never a qualm, young Henry, at the age of twelve, firmly desired to have the book published and made inquiries from his mother. She was sympathetically helpful. She quite understood that her bookish son should himself desire to publish a book, but the technical problems were outside her comprehension. Henry decided that he must not print too many copies in the first place and, assuming that costs fell in proportion to numbers, determined on a first edition of twelve which seemed sufficient to qualify for reduced terms. A letter went off to a large City firm of printers. They quoted the figure of £12 for printing twelve copies and at the very sound of such a sum his writing ambitions shrivelled. Wealth it seemed was the necessary corollary of literary expression, and publishers were either wolves in sheeps' clothing or quite unaware of a young writer's needs.

'The Precious Stones of the Bible' revealed the beginnings of a technique which was to persist throughout his life; the cool, impartial collection of widespread facts, their ordered presentation and critical examination.

In later years Ellis held the view, extraordinary in one so deeply versed in the literature of psychology, that he had 'never repressed anything'.[8] Such repression he believed would have given some sign of disorder in conscious life, ignoring the fact that his own personality was rich in neurotic symptoms. Similarly he claimed that infantile sexuality never troubled him on the grounds that he could not remember anything symptomatic of sex in his relations with his mother. Once again this ignored the inadequacy of adult memory. Childhood amnesia is a very effective and sophisticated device. 'There was no occasion for such repression or suppression', he wrote of himself. 'There was no need for it, not entirely because there was nothing to put away, but because the veil of impassive reserve with which I concealed the whole of my intimate personal life rendered repression or suppression completely superfluous.'

His childhood was on the surface smooth enough, but there is at least one experience, fully described by Ellis himself, which needs examination. One day, when he was twelve years old, Ellis accompanied his mother on an expedition to the Zoological Gardens, and suddenly she paused and Ellis heard a sound as of water hissing to the gravelled path. Later in life he knew that there was nothing involuntary about her action because the ladies' lavatory was not completely inaccessible and Mrs Ellis did not suffer from seizures of this kind. On another occasion they had visited an exhibition together and were strolling along when Mrs Ellis said that she desired to repeat the experience. She remained boldly standing, did not ask Henry to look away and 'before she had finished walked on a few paces and copiously recommenced, while I spontaneously played a protective part and watched to see that no one was approaching.' Something in the word 'copious' gave the clue to the erotic indoctrination which these episodes later revealed.[9] When he mentioned this episode to his sister Louie, she assured him that his mother had been flirting with him. In fact, she never seems to have met his constant yearning to be fully loved.

It would be difficult to establish with any psychological validity, morbid elements in Mrs Ellis's nature but, when at the age of nine Henry had thrust under his nose the urine-soaked napkin of a younger child, even the most psychologically inured might be justified in quailing. Not so the adult Ellis. He wrote, with that special pleading which distinguished all comments on his mother: 'a mischievous little trick played on her serious son, but also, I now think, with latently in it the challenge to accept this function as natural and sweet.' Later in life he was to build this, as so many other opposites, into an elaborate system of aesthetics, and to invent the term – 'urolagnia'. One of the

17

two 'abnormal' streaks in Ellis certainly sprang from these experiences.

Two other episodes now overtook him to sweep him a little nearer the realities of the outside world. The first was embodied in the short, eloquent person of the Reverend John Erck, then Vicar of Merton, a man full of Irish oratory. He had black hair, hypnotic eyes and a deep, rich voice. He would walk down the street towards his church, a shy, shut-away man apparently absorbed in the deepest reverie but, in the short time it took him to ascend the pulpit, he underwent a transformation. The memory of the dusk coming down, the lights and shadows patterning the pulpit and the Reverend Erck ascending the steps in the half-light to speak of the prophet Elijah, his periods mounting, his voice booming on a sonorous note, remained with Ellis far into life.[10] He remembered too the day when some tradesmen practised a small deception and the waves of the Reverend Erck's eloquence rose in their fury to carry the words, thunderously echoing out of the church into the street: Repent! Repent! Repent! Or – and this most of all remained in his memory – the rich voice softening, as it moved through Evensong, and came to the last muted words, 'Lighten Our Darkness'. Whatever orthodox religious beliefs remained with Ellis in his teens they were reinforced by the vision of the Reverend John Erck dominating the congregation of the small Merton church. He was also responsible for the many sermons Ellis wrote and delivered to his sisters.

There followed the second and even more deeply remembered episode. It involved a girl of sixteen, who went to stay with the Ellis family at their new home in 1871, and quickly struck up a friendship with the shy, serious, handsome Havelock. Agnes was at once still a child capable of unrestricted romping, and a growing woman with a hint of feminine allure. They played together and Henry did not feel sensuously attracted, but a shining boyish passion in the delight of her presence grew in him as they wandered across the fields, hand in hand, or played hide-and-seek in the hedgerows. Sometimes she was just a child sharing a game of hopscotch; sometimes she became a great lady demanding knightly attentions, and he selected the most expensive café in the town to buy her a lemonade. More frequently she did the buying, because Henry's powers of taking charge of any situation were slight. When the time came for Agnes to leave he exchanged Keat's poems with her for a copy of *The Wide, Wide World*, and she went her way and vanished from his life, but her image remained vividly in his mind. Indeed, in *My Life* he wrote: 'for four years her image moved and lived with me. . . . I was devoured by a boy's pure passion . . . that she should become my wife. I would lie awake in bed with streaming eyes praying to God to grant that this might some day be. . . . I have often felt thankful since that our prayers are not heard.'

The boarding school which next absorbed Ellis at the age of twelve was dominated by Mr Albert Grover, a man who cultivated a big, bushy beard, made more striking by 'a blind eye' and 'a very bald head'. Mr Grover's school, the Poplars, which stood near Tooting Station, consisted of a brick schoolroom wherein an assortment of boys daily went through a form of elementary education. Mr Grover was much given to expressing himself in 'verse' and drove home his teaching in appalling doggerel.

On one occasion Grover's inspiration overran itself and some verses attacking Darwin's doctrines were regarded as immoral and had to be withdrawn. His eccentricities had their effect on the haphazard teaching of the school and if Mr Grover was not altogether ignorant of what he attempted to teach, he could not convey the excitement of intellectual discovery. It was left to a comparative nonentity in the school, Mr Angus Mackay, who taught English, to bring a quite new vision into a world where Ellis failed to master Greek, struggled with Latin and learnt to loathe much of the school routine. Joseph Stevens, the French master, also encouraged him to widen his reading of French literature and helped him when he determined to learn Italian and German, but it was Mackay, a poetic young man of twenty, reconciling in his make-up a quick, nervous intellect with a powerful physique, who left the deepest impress.

The new and very uncertain pupil of twelve had travelled widely, found his own way into literature and made many exciting discoveries about the nature of his body and the universe, but he had never known intimately a person he regarded as cultured. To talk with Angus Mackay, a man passionately absorbed in general literature, came to Ellis like the vision of a new world. Mackay introduced him to Mrs Browning, George Eliot and Shelley, and spoke of life and living in terms which outraged every precept in Henry's immaculate upbringing. In politics something of a radical, and in religion a broad churchman, Mackay read Carlyle and Ruskin and was more concerned with the application of Christian teaching to social and economic problems than with the mystery of the holy sacrament. He brought into his discussions a daring which totally confounded the conservative politics of Ellis's parents and Mrs Ellis's religious fundamentalism. Steeped in English poetry, he himself had written two small volumes of verse and fired Havelock to read Hardy's *Far From the Madding Crowd* as it appeared monthly in the *Cornhill*. Their relationship slowly grew from that between master and pupil to pupil and friend. Ellis later wrote, 'For the first time I realised that there were great questions and problems in life, great aspirations beyond one's personal longings, great ideals to be passionately fought for. A touch had awakened my soul and my intellect.' Ellis never forgot Mackay, or those first glimpses of a wonderful landscape open to special reaches of the mind and emotions.

In part as a result of this revelation, Henry presently began to keep a

19

series of notebooks which showed the swift growth of an enormous range of reading, if not a complete awakening of soul and intellect. I have examined ten of these notebooks in detail. Book One began in April 1873 with a reference to Charlotte Mary Yonge's *Heir of Redclyffe*[11] and proceeded to analyse one book after another, expressing in May of the same year a smug self-satisfaction at his expenditure of money on books instead of toys. As Houston Peterson said of him, 'at best he was a serious youth, apparently destined for an honourable career in a conservative church. At worst . . . a sententious, unworldly little prig too much concerned with God and duty. . . .'

Approaching sixteen, Ellis read Renan's *Life of Jesus* and developed the first beginnings of a radical scepticism about the divinity of Christ, which was to last and destroy for ever any ambitions he may have had to enter the Church.[12]

The spirit of scientific inquiry, partly awakened by that book, was quickly reconciled with a growing interest in the visual arts. Dimly aware that behind the outward evidence which his young eyes perceived lay a mysterious and exciting world, not to be entered without special knowledge, he began to buy semi-technical manuals which explained in dry-as-dust language the secrets of chemistry, botany and geology. He struggled alone through page after page. The 'cultivated graces' of Mr Grover's academy regarded science as a sordid interference with laws of nature and recoiled from any inquiry into the chemistry of the human body as sacrilege. Mackay, in turn, disliked the cold world of the laboratory, and Ellis's mother was far more preoccupied with teaching him to perform on the piano, but Henry's nature could no more find exclusive satisfaction in the contemplation of works of art than it could in playing the piano, and in complete isolation, with a drive and application alien to his gentle nature, he pursued a steady path towards some understanding of natural history. Already signs of scientific curiosity were apparent in his desire to measure the most unexpected things. Where other boys vied with one another in the range of their urinary performance, he desired to measure it to a precise eighth of an inch.

Incongruously he turned from this to discover the masterpieces of the Italian Renaissance painters. He visited one art gallery after another with mounting excitement, and spent long hours sitting before the paintings of Raphael. Half his life was later spent exploring the identities of opposites, and if for the moment it needed very special gifts to reconcile urinary measurement with the work of the Renaissance painters, it was later for Ellis a not impossible task.

Presently Ellis found himself rebelling against the mental slums created by Victorian prudery.[13] There were so many statues which lied, so many beautiful works of art which dwindled away in deformity. He wrote long and passionately in his private notebooks about Lesbia, mistress of Catullus, and the passages are interesting for two reasons. First, it is almost as if Henry felt himself guilty of impure thinking and had to pour out that guilt on the written page. He did not understand, he wrote, how youth could be corrupted by anatomical accuracy in a nude statue 'when it is that same youth who gloats and revels in that which in his hands is transformed into filthiness'. 'Oh! the disgusting filthiness of a schoolboy's mind', the dirtiness forever creeping out of his mouth which he scribbled everywhere, turned into filthy doggerel. And this of which he spoke, he said, was beyond the reach of legislation to eradicate. It was universal. It was in all alike . . . 'Yes, in myself, in you, friend', in the gloating schoolboy and the Frenchman smacking his lips with gusto. 'I know not how I came to write all this but it is all true and from my heart; and as it is solely for my own eye I let it remain. . . .'[14]

For a youth of fifteen the passage was a remarkable feat; it conveyed his inner turmoil in spontaneous language which renewed the experience for every reader, and it revealed the power of the conflicts which were developing in him.

They were now reinforced by an incident which had sexual wellsprings not unknown to Aristotle himself. Willie Orr, a boarder at Mr Grover's school, was the son of an Indian Army Colonel, who saw himself cutting a dash on a cavalry charger, but since the provision of any sort of horse was beyond the capacity of Mr Grover's Academy, he decided to substitute a human being. This was so literally realized that every time the urge overtook Orr, he thrust Henry down on all fours, mounted him and rode back and forth across the dormitory, digging into him heels equipped with home-made spurs, in which pins substituted the actual spurs. Extraordinarily, Henry put up no resistance. With a submissiveness which later gave his nature a feminine grace, he simply accepted the brutality, never breathing a word to anyone. In the end, Mrs Ellis noticed his distress, pressed him for an explanation, and at last dragged the truth from him. There followed a choleric talk with Mr Grover, and Henry was removed to a different bedroom where the boys were not so deliberately sadistic.

It could not at once heal the psychic wounds this strange abuse had caused. His spirit hypersensitively balanced, shocks of any kind affected him deeply, but the sexual characteristic of these assaults became plain when 'copious seminal emissions began to take place during sleep.' Such emissions persisted far into life, but where, at first, he felt a growing sense of uneasiness if not shame, later in life he viewed his early distress with amusement. This was the natural development of every other boy. Extraordinarily, in his autobiography Ellis completely refused to acknowledge sexual elements in his early experiences with the words 'nothing of the slightest sexual character ever took place' – a truly astonishing example of refusal to accept his own insights.

For the moment sexual and intellectual discovery proceeded hand in hand, but mental activity far outstripped sex. To see, in perspective, the considerable sweep of Henry's reading, it is necessary to stress that these were the days of giant controversies released by Darwin's *Origin of Species*. The discovery that life had evolved, by a continuous process, from the protoplasmic jelly remaining in the scum as the first seas of the world receded, to develop through the jelly fish to gigantic reptiles and, comparatively late in the story, to become the lemur-like creature, one branch of which evolved into anthropoid apes and the other man, was still a very serious shock for even the least religious among the Victorians. Darwin had advanced the theory that this vast unravelling of the skein of life was the result of a continuous chain of small variations in different species, reacting to material forces and developing according to ascertained laws. The laws were those of natural selection and the survival of the fittest, and the changes due to the steady accumulation over a vast time-scale of minute variations. Followers of the French biologist Lamarck strongly resisted this, maintaining that variations resulted from the efforts of individuals to adapt themselves to changing environments.[15] Lamarck looked upon the 'effort' as conscious, but many of his disciples saw it as unconscious. The origin of the causative chain was the change in environment, and the organism unconsciously adapted itself or perished. When asked what caused variation in any given species Darwin replied, 'accident', and the Lamarckians, 'the pressure of changing environment', whereupon a babble of voices arose in deepening conflict.

Ellis presently became deeply involved in these conflicts if he did not yet grasp their full implications. A quite different voice from Darwin's rendered such theories palatable to him in the years 1875-7. A bookseller and author named Robert Chambers had written a book called *Vestiges of the Natural History of Creation*, a quite unreliable but thoroughly readable account of the whole panorama of evolution within the boundaries of orthodox religion. Appearing in 1844, it stirred the admiration and strictures of the great Darwin himself and aroused considerable exasperation in T. H. Huxley. Its geology was shaky and its zoology illiterate, but for Ellis the book explained the 'principle of evolution in a benevolent light, stilling his orthodox suspicions by simply denying that there was any conflict between theology and science'.[16] In his Note Book for 1875 he developed the theme with a quotation from Bacon which put the ultimate reconciliation in the hands of God, showing that he was still at heart a Christian.

Another important book now came into Henry's hands, *Human Physiology: the Basis of Social and Sanitary Science* by T. L. Nichols, an American doctor living in London. Characteristic of the cloud which surrounded sexual matters in the middle of the nineteenth century, a biologist of T. H. Huxley's calibre had written a book entitled

Elementary Physiology, which went through many editions without explaining the facts of reproduction. Dr Nichols's book dared to include a long section which not so much explored this forbidden territory as represented it with scrupulous conventionality. Henry – true product at this stage of an epoch anxious to persuade young men that females were solid from the waist down, and convinced that any open talk of biological matters was not only dangerous but unquestioningly lascivious – recorded in his notebooks that he did not entirely approve.

Meanwhile his reading continued to widen. He read Molière's *La Jalousie de Barbouille, Le Medecin volant* and *L'Etourdi, Tom Brown's Schooldays*, Charlotte Brontë's novels and Keats's poetry, and somehow contrived to embark on a second book of his own, this time a novel.[17]

Entitled 'An Earnest Life', the hero, Walter Woodleigh, revealed habits of reading, thought and behaviour which were familiar, once superficial disguises had been penetrated. The first chapter dealt with the unexpected return of Walter Woodleigh to his ancestral home and a meticulous description of the hero followed, which bore some resemblance to Henry's idealized vision of himself.

Then came an expedition to the National Gallery, precipitously close on the heels of Henry's own visits. Here the reader was to meet the Hamiltons, neighbours of the Woodleighs, but heard instead a lecture on Raphael, Guido and the wonders of painting, all reproducing the precise opinions which could be traced in Henry's own notebooks. Even Walter Woodleigh's sense of vocation was not unfamiliar. Ellis had at one time thought of going into the Church, and now wrote of Walter Woodleigh: 'Yes, he said to himself on his way home, after shaking hands with the Hamiltons and congratulating Rosa on her recovery, yes, he said – the buoyancy of youth overcoming all difficulties – I will become a clergyman.'[18]

It would be extravagant to expect this first novel, written by a boy of fifteen, to have any great depth. It says pathetically little, but the vocabulary, style and lofty preoccupations are characteristic, and the sheer ability to sustain the narrative an ominous pointer to the massive volumes he was destined to produce.

Chapter 2

Australian interlude

Leaving Mr Grover's school at sixteen, Henry found himself without training for any profession and with a steadily growing conviction that the process of earning a living was a distasteful necessity which would soon force itself upon him. Living in a world where long bouts of adolescent melancholy troubled him and trying to face up to adult life, he preferred to slip back into the gentle vagueness of the immediate past. He was absorbed in fantasies of beautiful women, music in a minor key and the half light of living in which wistful patterns wove their insubstantial shadows across a world eternally sad. He wrote, in his deepest awareness, of the futility of life.

The intervention of the ship *Surrey* was one of those heaven-sent accidents which brought resolution into his drifting life, but Henry, already familiar with ships and the sea, did not welcome it. From his parents' point of view the voyage was intended to reinforce his still frail constitution, but he had no great concern with his health. He could not know where the voyage would lead and if it conveniently shelved pressing questions about his future, an uneasy sense of irresolution persisted long after the ship had sailed. The ship *Surrey* left London one spring day in 1875, called at Plymouth where 325 emigrants came on board, and set out afresh on the vast voyage to Australia. Captain Peppen Ellis had more or less connived with the emigration authorities to smuggle his sixteen-year-old son aboard disguised as the captain's clerk, because normal passengers were not permitted on such ships.

The first entry in Havelock's shipboard diary recorded the fact that he had managed to cope with a good deal of seasickness, but seasickness did not for long prevent great questionings from troubling his fast developing intellect.[1] Nothing short of gigantic postulates about man, the universe, God, religion, good and evil, satisfied his deeper reveries.[2] A boy of sixteen solemnly projected his own vision on the universe, a universe now at work to outwit the ever watchful Captain Peppen Ellis in this cockleshell ship with its beautiful sails. Henry had taken on

24

board a small library with Shelley, Spenser, Rabelais and Goethe among the scores of authors to be read, and a scattering of technical books, intended to help him prepare for matriculation.

He also had access to a harmonium on which he exercised his never very great talent, playing snatches from Schubert and Beethoven, but books, writing and thinking remained more important in the early days of the voyage. Not that life at sea was uneventful in those adventurous days. Mile by slow mile the ship sailed vast distances, and long stretches of utter boredom were relieved by the threat of storms as they approached the tropics.

The climax came one sultry July day. Gathering like a giant out of nowhere, an enormous sea suddenly leapt up and down upon the ship, almost halting her in her tracks, sending a torrent of water into the saloon, breaking a number of ports, smashing open instruments and sending passengers screaming for safety. Momentarily some cabins were two feet deep in water, and people rushed about the decks in confusion. The ship shuddered, lurched, righted herself and ploughed on. It was characteristic of young Ellis that he recorded this event in his diary with no sense of its drama, and revealed for the first time that self control in moments of physical danger which was later to carry him unmoved through events capable of disturbing hardened adventurers.[3]

For thirteen long drawn-out weeks the voyage continued, with intermittent calms, boredoms, bursts of merry-making and occasionally fresh threats from the weather. In that time Henry continued to read deeply. Many a warm afternoon was spent lying on deck, his head supported by a roll of sailcloth, a book in one hand and his eyes constantly straying from the page to stare through the rigging at the white summer clouds. Frequently he was lost in wonderment at the infinite curve of the sky, which sometimes, in the burning heat, became a deep purple. He read Macaulay, Shelley and Rabelais and 'through the veil of old, unfamiliar French amidst its violent, boisterous disclosure of the obscene, the obverse aspects of existence, he was astonished to find profundity, gentleness and beauty.' At night sometimes he lay on deck again and stared in awe at the brilliant mass of stars, some so vivid they seemed to be almost within reach, and the sheer immensity of it all revived the great questions which lay unanswered at the back of his mind. It was there, under the night sky, listening to the gentle groan of the rigging and the silken rush of water from the prow, that he determined to write a long study of Rabelais.

Then, at last, on Saturday 24 July they approached Sydney Heads, and the thought of a bed in an hotel on dry land which did not swing with the sea, became an alluring prospect.[4] Many years later, when Ellis came to write his autobiography, the next few weeks were dim in his memory. He remembered going to a concert where the violins did not appeal to him; he went to see two plays and visited the representative of

25

the company which owned his father's ship; but presently something occurred which was to have considerable consequences. They met Mr Alfred Morris, a friend of Captain Ellis, who had gone into partnership with a Frederick Bevill, to operate an agency with a name more resplendent than its resources – The General Educational Registration Association. The *Surrey* was by now due to leave Sydney for Calcutta, but the doctor warned Captain Ellis that his son's frail health might be sorely tried by the Indian climate, and as the time for departure drew near, Alfred Morris suddenly conceived the idea that the young Ellis should apply for a job as a schoolteacher in Sydney. Without more ado he sat down and, with the authority of an undistinguished headmastership which he had once held in a small school, eulogistically described Henry's talents about which he knew nothing. Spectacularly, Henry, who knew virtually nothing of teaching, became assistant master to Fontlands, a small school run by a Mr Hole in a Sydney suburb.

Ellis seems to have accepted the prospect of considerable responsibilities quite calmly and remained untroubled until the time for the *Surrey* to sail arrived. There is no record of the parting between father and son but, once the ship had sailed and Ellis senior gone, a terrible sense of loneliness came down on him. In the following weeks it reached overwhelming proportions. Poets and artists did not easily flourish in Sydney in those days and the tall, aesthetic, hypersensitive young man, still in his teens, recoiled from a large part of the rough life of the port, and found the blunt cameraderie of 'colonial' types anathema. In the first few weeks there was no one with whom he could share the infinite gentleness of his own Shelleyan spirit, or achieve anything resembling a sense of rapport.

Reading was his one escape from loneliness, and continually he sought solace in the printed page. One night he turned again to Scott, this time to his novel *The Pirate*, and settled down to obliterate the night, the loneliness and the anxieties inevitable to anyone thrown up in their teens on a strange new continent; but the words no longer carried their old force. They seemed, suddenly, without life or colour. And then, as the moths burred at the window, the alien city settled into sleep and he remained painfully awake, the sense of desolation grew like a physical presence, and he felt as if the sweet security of childhood had gone for ever. Without any reference to his lost childhood, in December Ellis wrote to his mother enlarging on the horrors of Australia – locusts, bugs, poisonous snakes, tarantulas – which people in England were, all unsuspecting, invited to travel 18,000 miles to encounter.[5]

He continued to teach over the next few months to the best of his not very great ability. He tried to accustom himself to the ways of Sydney and the harsh Australian voices. Steeling his over-fine sensibilities, he ventured to talk to an occasional stranger, but finding the effort exhausting quickly withdrew again. Slowly he erected a new system of defences against Australian life and within it settled down to a tolerable existence.

Internally the turmoil continued and was deeply aggravated by new and disturbing impulses. A storm had grown in his soul and body which he did not fully understand. Inexplicable physical impulses were troubling him and then it was, one October evening in 1875, 'walking up and down an avenue of eucalyptus trees on the school grounds at Burwood', that he came to a momentous decision. 'He would', he decided, 'explore the dangerous ocean of sex.'[6] This was not meant in any strictly personal sense. It was mankind as much as himself he desired to enlighten. The precise reasons which drove him to this conclusion are not clear, but the ferment of increasing sexual awareness common to adolescence must have been deeply disturbing to the young Ellis, and he was particularly baffled to understand why these stirrings seemed to be considered sinful. Suddenly, it appeared to him that a whole series of problems needed investigation. Perhaps he could throw some light on them if . . . but his adolescent mind boggled at the complexity of the problems.

In the following November, browsing through a Sydney bookshop, Henry suddenly came upon *The Elements of Social Science; or Physical, Sexual and Natural Religion*, and he immediately bought and read the book.[7] The adult Ellis made little reference to this episode in his autobiography and spoke disparagingly of *The Elements of Social Science*, 'the tone' of which 'was thoroughly uncongenial to me'. If by tone he meant style, his early notebooks agree with this judgment, but the contents were then very palatable, and the book seems to have had a much greater influence than he admitted later in life. Several times in his autobiography mature views are substituted for the first raw reactions but, style apart, there was much in Drysdale's book (the author's name was George Drysdale, a young Scottish physician born in 1825) of general significance. This pedestrian volume of 600 pages, first published in 1854 at the height of the conspiracy of silence about sex, anticipated modern attitudes to sex in a remarkable way.

It analysed the principle of Malthus which postulated an increase in population always greater than any increase in the supply of food, with the result that certain and sometimes catastrophic checks were needed to maintain equilibrium. Chief among these checks were famine and plague, celibacy and preventive sexual intercourse. Malthus, conditioned by the puritanical austerities of the day, inevitably chose celibacy or abstinence as the most desirable solutions. Drysdale not merely rejected these; he argued that it was possible to have both food and love – an equation quite insusceptible of realization to the Jeremiah-like Malthus – by the simple adoption of preventive intercourse. Today, Drysdale's heresies are commonplace, today Freud has developed and codified Drysdale's belief that repression involved physical and mental dangers of a serious kind. But 'Drysdale was not merely an honest propagandist elaborating a pet thesis; he was a trained scholar, rich in insights. . . . He saw that sex was to be a central issue of the coming century, that love is a necessity rather than a luxury, and that moral virtues are in the last analysis matters of mental hygiene.'[8]

Drysdale threw fresh light into the confused complexities of those deep stirrings which were troubling the seventeen-year-old Ellis, but within a month material difficulties suddenly overwhelmed everything. Mr Hole, headmaster and proprietor of Fontlands Private School, indicated that Ellis's teaching was highly unsatisfactory and that he could only countenance continuing to employ him by reducing his salary to less than £1 a week. It was a humiliating offer and with an unexpected rush of resolution Henry at once tendered his resignation.[9]

Driven by fear of unemployment, he swiftly advertised his not very developed skills in a local paper and to his infinite relief was quickly offered another job – a private tutorship with a family in Goongerwarrie. If his first assistant teachership had drawn him reluctantly into the responsible world of the adult, he had remained a divided person still in many ways adolescent; the private tutorship quickly achieved every characteristic of harsh reality, and with it he seemed to become, against his will, a fully adult human being.[10]

Goongerwarrie – it was a name of booming reverberations, and when Havelock Ellis in the year 1876 first entered Goongerwarrie the name carried an aboriginal ring which reinforced the misgivings left in his mind by a long and exhausting coach journey.[11]

The father of the family he went to teach was a Mr Platt, a retired civil servant with a brood of children, and even if one of these was destined to stimulate the confused sexual impulses which continued to trouble Ellis, Goongerwarrie remained a natural haven remote from the rush of modern life. Its seclusion encouraged that reflective serenity which, beginning on the high seas in his father's sailing ship, grew and developed until it sometimes achieved the characteristics of withdrawal. When he went walking in the early morning, with Main's *Anthology of English Sonnets* to concentrate his mind, there were times when strange impulses troubled him.

The sense of foreboding from the first coach journey echoed through the next two years. He taught Mr Platt's children in the mornings and afternoons, and then set off walking with a volume of Shelley, Goethe or Flaubert under his arm. He would fling himself down on the side of a great hill with a view which sometimes held him spellbound. He became steadily more aware of Australia's beauty; of the great tracts of wild virgin land with mountains brooding in the distance; of the extraordinary profusion of gum trees, wattles and a whole brilliant outcrop of strange plants crowding away to vast lonely horizons.[12]

But teaching, poetry and natural beauty were presently troubled by a renewal of those erotic stirrings, when the eldest girl in the family instinctively realized that her precocious person attracted Ellis. Minnie by name, she was much older than her years, and liked to stand very close to him, while disturbing impulses passed between them, until, almost irresistibly, his hand was driven into minor caresses. His attraction to Minnie had physical reactions which he promptly recorded at some length in his diary, struggling against a sense of sin.[13] So powerful did the disturbance become that there were times when he felt that death alone could solve these problems and, if not death, a rapid retirement into the life of a monk.

Asides about Minnie occupied several pages of his private diary,[14] and then, significantly, a gap of four months followed in which no entries at all occurred. By then, his melancholy had deepened, and he was still more full of the woe of the world. Whether Minnie and his sexual arousal played any part in what followed is not clear, but he suddenly decided that he must abandon his job as tutor to the Platt family.[15]

Sorrowfully he returned to Sydney to live in a depressing little boarding house. Bouts of neurotically defensive illness followed. In the middle of one interview for a third job, a mysterious sickness assailed him and he had to ask to be excused, but luck was with him and he became an assistant master in a school known as Grafton Grammar School. A remarkable sequel followed. It was some measure of the erratic nature of private education in the Australia of those days that Henry was offered nothing less than the headmastership of the school when the headmaster suddenly died. He wrote off to his father in February 1877 to tell him the news, and his father replied in a vein as nearly ironical as his open nature could countenance.[16]

But sudden and spectacular promotion did not bring any greater happiness. The school included thirty boys, no more or less obstreperous than one would expect of a breed reared close to nature, and the gentle Havelock, who had never quite succeeded in asserting his authority over anyone, quickly found them devils incarnate.[17] Fate had bestowed a remarkable favour on him, but he was inadequate to the occasion and in a burst of dismay he suddenly found fault with the school, the boys and the profligacy of the Australian countryside.

Yet, in the worst moments some inner core remained inviolable and he continued to read deeply, to commit verses of Shelley to memory, and even to know, when the disorderly pupils had returned to their scattered homes and he was left alone with the beauty of an Australian summer evening, a delight sometimes approaching exaltation as he read and re-read Main's poetry anthology.

It was now that he became involved with a young woman named May Chapman. Committing the experience to his diary, he revealed that at the age of twelve he had fallen passionately in love with a young girl whose physical and spiritual presence held him in childish thrall for three years.[18] Since that first 'indulgence' one other woman had aroused what he understated as his affections, Minnie Platt. Now a third woman, May Chapman, brought to life the beginnings of that profound capacity for love which in later life was so slow to arousal and so deep when finally matured.[19]

Twenty-year-old May Chapman was the second daughter of the Chapman family, in the grounds of whose house stood the Grafton Grammar School. The experience with May Chapman flatly contradicted what Ellis understood to be his true nature. He confided to his diary that it had come as a surprise to him to find himself half in love with Miss Chapman before he had any reciprocal assurance. Indeed, just the opposite was true. She preserved a friendly but distinctly cool attitude. Ellis tried to face up to the fact that his attraction was dominated by sensuality and attempted to redeem himself with the claim that affection always preceded such impulses.[20] However, so strong was his sensual attraction that on one occasion he had the wildest impulse to occupy a chair she had just left in order to experience the vicarious touch of her body—and only just checked its overwhelming power. Once again nothing came of his relationship with May Chapman.

Nearly a year went by. His pupils thinned alarmingly, fresh recruits were not forthcoming, and at last Ellis decided to sell his school with an effrontery which, later in life, amused him. He quickly found a buyer and the whole school, with whatever existed of its goodwill, was passed over to a Mr Mackintosh,[21] who failed, when it came to the point, to pay the sum of £50 agreed upon, and made what he referred to as a token payment. Once more unemployed, Ellis was freshly distressed. His capital was small and dwindling, his academic equipment still impoverished, and his future very uncertain. Anxiety drove him into another burst of intimate confession in his diary.

Making allowance for the pomposity of adolescent reminiscence, there was, already revealed in Ellis, not only a gift for words far beyond his years, but a streak of scientific objectivity clearly indicating the man he was to become. It showed itself in an independent attitude of mind, paradoxical in a person whose gentle temperament bordered on weakness. For here was a young man, surrounded by every known convention for controlling the physical expression of passion, who calmly announced that no small part of the private trouble in the world was the result of sexual distortion. In a burst of inspiration obviously sublimating his own mounting passion, he cried out against it. Twenty years later he wrote with that lucidity which distinguished his best writing:[22]

As a youth, I was faced, as others are, by the problem of sex. Living

partly in an Australian city where the ways of life were plainly seen
. . . I was free . . . to meditate many things. A resolve slowly grew up
within me: one part of my life-work should be to make clear the
problems of sex.

To this end, whenever he was in Sydney he spent long hours in the
public library and the range of his reading developed in all directions.
He read and studied writers as diverse as Stendhal and Brantôme,
Rabelais and Macaulay, Coleridge and Quetelet, widening every
possible horizon. Above all he read Rousseau who was to have such a
deep influence on his thinking.

Now came his last job in Australia. He was appointed schoolmaster to
the curiously named Half-time Schools at Sparkes and Junction Creek
for a fee of £108 a year plus certain allowances and free accommodation
in the school house. Momentarily, economic anxiety and the threat of
starvation receded.[23] There was another equally attractive factor about
the job. Its location would bring him once more within reach of May
Chapman and his eyes filled with tears at the prospect, but cynical
reflection quickly overtook romantic impulse. This welling up of
tenderness was all part of the biological device – some called it
trickery – by which nature ensured the preservation of the race, he
recorded in his diary.[24]

Unaware of the repercussions J. A. Symonds was to have on him later
in life, before he left for Junction Creek he read for the first time
Symonds's *The Renaissance in Italy*. Simultaneously he re-discovered
the Bible, full of delight in its splendour as literature, but no longer
convinced of its divine inspiration. Omnivorous as ever, in the same
period he read Allen's *Physiological Aesthetics* and Mills's *Essay on
Religion*, but the writers who now brought a new direction into his
reading and possible future were the literary critics Arnold and Taine.
As literary men, they should have reinforced his passion for literature,
but since he regarded both writers as essentially scientific, the scientist
in him re-awakened, and made him wonder yet again where his true
bent lay.[25]

The journey by train to Scone, the town nearest to his new school, was
comparatively simple, but it gave him a vivid foretaste of the isolation
which marked this last year of his life in Australia. At Scone he met the
tall, scrawny Australian who had held the job before him and was now
living in a rather sordid little house on the outskirts of the town.[26] The
Australian's high nasal twang sprang into life with exaggerated echoes
from Cockney London as they spoke of Sparkes Creek, its doubtful
amenities and the possibility of provisions. The Australian drew a
detailed and very unattractive picture of what life was like at the
Schools, but if the information depressed Ellis, he did not permit his
disappointment to show.

31

Walking away from the house half an hour later, he observed the great tide of burnt grassland pressing down upon the small huddle of habitations as though, at any moment, the next wave would overwhelm it and nature reassert itself. Even now, the grass shoots pressed up through the very street itself and a brooding silence came off the hills like an emanation out of the sky. In Burwood, the Sydney suburb he had known best, life was depressing enough, but there were always people, movement and the shrilling cicadas to fill the night air. Here one listened to the silence, the world seemed emptied of human beings, even the locusts had withdrawn and nature seemed full of foreboding. Suddenly, Ellis felt once more weary and unhappy. But there was no escape. He could not – as he suddenly wished to do – run away, find a coach and set foot again in the teeming life of Sydney.[27]

Up early the next morning, he ate a swift breakfast, bought a few stores, donned a new alpaca jacket, and was ready to penetrate deeper into the backwoods. The bush running off from the track was brittle and parched, a handful of trees huddled together along the track and prickly pears thrust their harsh limbs into the air. Joseph, his guide – the son of a Scone schoolmaster – rode on ahead, with Ellis following some yards in his rear, very aware of his new coat for which he had not yet paid. The sun burnt fiercely, the land became more dusty, clouds of big flies tormented every living thing and one line of sweat wiped from the brow was at once replaced by another. Permeating everything the silence deepened. There were occasional crude habitations built from wood and corrugated iron, but soon even they dwindled away.

The sun grew hotter. The unaccustomed saddle began to torment Ellis, but the pace was very leisurely – for his special benefit – and he presently fell into one of those half-mystical reveries which later set words pouring so fluently on paper. Late in the afternoon, they approached a farm owned by a man called Ashford, where Ellis expected to stay the night. Prematurely aged by the harsh pioneering life, Ashford had a brood of children overflowing the house, and offered Ellis accommodation, somewhat churlishly, on the settee in the downstairs room. There, Ellis tried for two nights to sleep in the utmost discomfort, and in the day set out to discover the valley and what was optimistically referred to as the schoolhouse.

Built from a strange agglomeration of rough slabs – some shifting under strong pressure from the hand – it consisted of four wooden sections, the front two adjoining a small verandah. One room was full of crude desks and obviously the schoolroom; the second front room held a rough wooden stool and an extraordinary contraption masquerading as a bed. There were a few cooking, eating and washing utensils, an axe and little else. In places the sun burnt through apertures between the stone slabs and innumerable flies buzzed in the sunshine.

Ellis sat down heavily in the schoolroom, clasped his hands and stared round. The silence became intense. So this was it: this was his teaching domain where he would enlighten Australia's young for the next year. Suddenly there was a little scurrying sound and a mouse ran across the floor. He thought it looked a very dejected animal. Another one followed. He sat there for some time, and then at last came to his feet and made his way outside again. The brilliant blue sky stretched away for miles and the distant hills were folded in golden silence. Tears hovered at the back of his eyes.[28] He had a sudden desire to be very, very young again, because then it would be possible to cry.

In the next few days he recovered something of his spirits and set out to try to adjust himself to the life of a schoolmaster cut off from what was normally considered civilization. He divided his attention between the schools of Sparkes and Junction Creek, walking, on certain days, from one to the other. Sometimes he left meat smouldering on a rock over a wood fire in the schoolhouse, and sometimes he returned in the evening to a lonely bread and cheese supper. He quickly came to enjoy the long trek across the hills to Junction Creek, and these long walks seem to have left a permanent impress on his developing personality. A whole year he fulfilled this journey without meeting a living soul, and fifty years afterwards he could still recapture the vast serenity of those days, with the hills deep in sunlit silence, the kangaroos incredibly graceful, the few lizards so skilfully camouflaged and the native bears half prepared to exchange greetings and then, at the last moment, turning tail and dashing away. Frequently, he walked deep in thought, occasionally so lost he hardly noticed that rain had begun cascading down the valley; sometimes several hours slipped away for which he could not account. He only knew that he had moved several miles from one point to another. One natural feature alone came to have a disturbing effect on him: the mountain at the back of his hut seemed to grow to menacing proportions and when a storm threatened, lowered down out of the clouds with a pitch-black, horrifying brow.

It is difficult to believe that any discerning hand of providence picked the still adolescent Ellis to fulfil this function in the primitive backwaters of Australia, but the vein of aestheticism in his make-up contained the isolation of his life, and the mystic in him found a pantheistic glory in his lonely walks across the hills. Sometimes, sheer beauty drove him to stop astride some eminence, look down over a great prospect of hills and valleys and suddenly burst out singing; sometimes he would slip to the ground and lie full length, his arms outstretched, holding the earth, as though it were a woman, in almost sensual delight. Recollection of it all inspired some of his most evocative writing later in life. Simultaneously, in his reading, Swinburne spoke to him of a love beyond love of nature:

Nothing is better, I well think,
Than love; the hidden well water
Is not so delicate to drink.

He was reading *Poems and Ballads* alongside a mass of miscellaneous books, but it was not Swinburne so much as spontaneous physiological reactions which first increased his wonder at the power of nature to break through every restraint and taboo. He did not dream. His fantasy life is unrecorded. But a renewal of sexuality emphasized in the young Ellis a scientific streak as he calmly proceeded to note the date and time of each new 'incident' in his notebook, for all the world as if he were observing the behaviour of a patient. Similar entries continued for some twelve years, and became part of the evidence concealed under W. K.'s story in volume one of the American edition of *The Studies in the Psychology of Sex*. What he solemnly referred to as nocturnal emissions had relaxed tension in the past, but now in the backwoods of Australia, reading the *Dames Galantes* of Brantôme one day, he suddenly felt erotic excitement gathering towards an ejaculation which had never before happened in daylight.[29]

Sparke's Creek had no attractive women. Later in life he reflected that fortune had deluged him with delightful women, but now in Australia, when their appearance would have seemed miraculous, none came, and he was left to wander the hillsides, seeing in the bounding of the kangaroo a female grace it might, at any other time, have lacked.

The full powers of manhood were developing within him, and if profound sensual desires occasionally broke into his insatiable craving for knowledge, a third and far more spiritual consciousness was about to surge up and obliterate everything, in a mysterious conversion which he struggled for years to clothe in words.

Words – not spoken words, but words conveyed to paper in all their myriad forms – continued to occupy a steadily increasing part of his waking life. Writing came to Ellis as naturally as breathing. Matters of the greatest and smallest significance were committed to letters, diaries, articles and poems. It is possible to recapture from them the mood of events long since dead, in a manner too often unrealized by Ellis in the rambling immensity of his autobiography.

In his early writing monotonous undulations of style carried a sense of earnestness brought to a pitch where it seemed that the continued existence of the universe depended upon the young Ellis reaching accurately into its very heart. He had read selections from Newman's work and, although Newman's thought found little echo in Ellis's mind, the music of his prose left memories to be taken up, repeated and brought into fresh harmonies in his own writing. For the moment, at nineteen, he filled page after page of a thick, black-covered exercise book with notes and comments, from which eventually sprang the spirit of *Impressions and Comments*.

If his style continued to suffer from the flow of equally modulated Atlantic rollers, it was later to become self-consciously musical and then to abandon literary overtones for direct attack upon significance with the exact, sharp word. His diary, at nineteen, holds hints of all these phases. Yet writing, scholarship and sex, gathering as they were in a quite new organization of his personality, were now overwhelmed by the event which filled whole pages of his diary.

Inevitably, it concerned religion. Brought up to accept, without question, the dogma of Christianity, Ellis quickly found himself troubled by its more extravagant assumptions and as his scepticism grew, one precept after another collapsed in confusion. There were to be many attempts, from the first entries in the diary, to *The Dance of Life*, an article in the *Atlantic Monthly* and *My Life*, to bring precise definition to the experience which now overtook him, but for all the sense of exaltation which springs from page after page, none gives a satisfactory explanation. He referred to the experience as a 'conversion' or 'revelation', and it was closely concerned with the arrival from England of James Hinton's book, *Life in Nature*. Ellis wrote in *My Life*:[30]

> I read it calmly, with no undue expectation of personal profit; then, if I remember rightly, I read it a second time, this time more significantly. And then, as I read, I became conscious of what I can only call, in the precise and full sense of the word, a revelation.

From what followed this seemed exaggerated, and all his attempts to qualify it, failed. Two sides of his nature, he said, had striven to reconcile themselves:

> one . . . was the divine vision of life and beauty which for me had been associated with a religion I had lost . . . the other the scientific conception of an evolutionary world which might be marvellous in its mechanism but was completely alien to the individual soul.

Hinton now miraculously brought the two into harmony. In the same vague language Ellis said:

> It was as though there had been developing within me, with a painful sense of strain and division, two diverse streams of tendency which had now suddenly come together, each entering into the other to form a fresh stream of a new potency wherein the qualities of the two original streams were at length harmoniously blended. . . .

James Hinton (1822–75), the source of this revelation, was a man hostile to the mechanistic philosophies of the nineteenth century, who applied his medical training, knowledge of higher mathematics and mysticism to abstruse speculation about the nature of the universe.[31]

> What is the world that science reveals to us as the reality of the world we see? [he asked.] A world dark as the grave, silent as a stone and shaking like a jelly. That, the ultimate fact of this glorious world? Why you might as well say that the ultimate fact of one of Beethoven's quartets is the scraping of the tails of horses on the intestines of cats. . . .

A man much given to vivid metaphor, Hinton's pages overflowed with colour and life, and if the substitution of poetic images for logical thinking did not automatically unlock the secrets of the universe, Ellis had little regard at this stage for logical concepts. He too recoiled from anything mechanistic and disliked Strauss's picture of a universe elaborately geared to whirling wheels and shuttles, full of dim engines and quaking forces, compelled to behave in the manner of a factory.[32]

Page after page in Hinton launches tremendous assaults upon the emotions, and even if none is particularly convincing to a mind aware of the linguistic niceties of the twentieth century, and any 'thinker', in the exact sense of the term, would be more amused than enlightened by his words, Ellis was deeply stirred by the language of metaphor and swept along with it.

Much later in life he attempted fresh explanation of his 'conversion' in *The Dance of Life*, but it remained unsatisfactory. 'My self was one with the Not-self, my will one with the universal will. I seemed to walk in light; my feet scarcely touched the ground; I had entered a new world.'[33] There was also a passage which spoke once more of reconciling 'two opposing psychic tendencies', but it read like a mystical evasion.

The force which gave this experience the power of a revelation could easily have sprung from the damned up tides of sex suddenly breaking through as, indeed, he admits they broke through at this time. There is a correlation between revelatory experience and that period of adolescence when tides of unused sexual emotion threaten to burst. Starbuck showed, in *The Psychology of Religion*, that the majority of conversions appear to occur in adolescence, and Ellis himself later understood the connexion between sex and religion, remarking that one can pass its unexpended energy to the other.

Perhaps it remains a contradiction in terms to try to interpret such an experience rationally. Suffice it to say that Ellis had now achieved a set of 'beliefs' which deeply satisfied him if they evaded definition. Certainly his new faith would have sadly distressed the orthodox Christian. There was no personal God, he envisaged no future life, Christ lacked divine origin, and original sin, in the strict theological meaning of the term, had no place. There was a sense in which his rejection of the myth and ritual, developed over centuries by the

Christian religion, and the realization that these belonged to a superstitious past no longer capable of reconciliation with the spiritual life of modern man, represented a powerful part of the 'conversion' which had overtaken him. Modern man could not accept primitive rituals as adequately expressing the higher forms of spiritual belief. Whatever the precise mechanism of Ellis's conversion, in spiritual terms his new personality remained unchanged for years. He also claimed that from that time on, some core of his nature remained untouched by all the shocks which life brought against it. Deep beneath the surface, his inner serenity became inviolable. It was, of course, an illusion.

First sex, and now religion, both firmly faced and resolved against the desolate background of Sparkes Creek, that valley where human beings were dominated by the seasons, the hills, the cattle, and men subsided into pastoral life.

Close upon the heels of his 'conversion', in the same natural wilderness came the third great resolution. Once more Hinton played a leading part. Ellis recorded it all in his diary. Lying on his hammock-bed one hot, lazy afternoon reading *The Life and Letters of James Hinton*, Ellis suddenly reached a passage which forced him to sit upright.[34] He threw down the book and came to his feet. The young Hinton, equally uncertain which profession to follow, recorded in his *Life and Letters* that his family doctor had recommended medicine to him as a career, advice which he at once took, becoming a student at St Bartholomew's Hospital. Immediately Ellis knew that this was his career too. A doctor! He would enter the medical profession and become a doctor. At one stroke all the practical confusions of five years' tortured thinking were resolved, and he knew at last what it was he wanted to do in the world, with absolute certainty. Once more a sense of exhilaration overtook him and he paced the wooden floor of his 'bedroom' in near excitement. And then as reflection deepened he became aware that he did not want to be – just a medical practitioner.[35] It was a necessary part of the apprenticeship to the kind of life he desired to follow, a life still not quite clear but having wider boundaries than medicine itself. In the event the wisdom of his choice was unquestionable. Without medical qualifications his work on sex would have suffered worse attacks than were eventually launched against it; without technical knowledge of anatomy and midwifery, many of the problems he subsequently faced might have baffled him.

Within the next few weeks he began to grow impatient with the desolate life of Sparkes Creek and the handful of rustic children he taught. The magnificent landscapes, the simple life close to nature, could never bring him any nearer to the career which now dominated his thoughts. Simultaneously, a letter from his mother was full of a desire to see him again, and his father said he hoped he would be able to book a return passage for him on a ship whose captain he knew. Several weeks later Ellis completed his full year at Sparkes Creek and one beautiful day, when the sun was hot on the hills, he packed his few belongings and began to say goodbye to the people and the children he had come to know so well. Then he rode off on horseback towards Scone and stopped for a while to look back at the deep valley, its crazy old schoolhouse and the brooding mountain still forbidding in the afternoon sun. He had a disturbing feeling that he would never see any of it again.

In Scone he paid a number of visits and spoke to the schoolmaster Roberts. To Ellis's surprise Roberts congratulated him on surviving a whole year in the desolation of Sparkes Creek. There were even those who thought that it was wicked to exploit a youngster like Ellis by subjecting him to such an outrageous job in so remote a place.

Exploit him. It seemed to Ellis absurd. The desolation of Sparkes Creek had given him self-knowledge, a sense of vocation with deeper wellsprings than he realized, and an awareness that science was to him at least as exhilarating as literature. It also reaffirmed the mystic in him and revealed that inner self into whose core he always hoped to retreat whenever the outer world became too threatening.

Chapter 3

Medical training and Olive Schreiner

Late one April afternoon in 1879, Havelock Ellis returned to his family's new home at No. 24, Thornsett Road, Anerley, London. Mrs Ellis was sitting in the drawing-room, with her daughters – there were now four – full of feverish expectation, when a knock came on the door and there stood a tall, earnest-looking young man with a sunburnt face and straggling, yellow beard, his lean form draped in a big, brown ulster. With a quite new assurance he proceeded to kiss everyone in the room except fifteen-year old Louie and turning to her, he said, 'I am sure I have no idea who this young woman is.' Louie had been a mere child when he left for Australia.

It was like establishing friendship with a number of strange young women, so crucial were the years he had missed in their lives. A wonderful sense of intimacy arose, and Louie in particular stirred a response not altogether free from sexual attraction. Later in life it gave Ellis deeper insights into the problem which puzzled anthropologists – exogamy.

The years which followed (1879–89) were crowded with a profusion of interests. They began with teaching at Clifford House College School, embraced a complete and leisurely course in medicine, the production of two books, several articles and the editorship of a new literary series. Somehow amidst it all Ellis contrived a considerable correspondence. Teaching, the natural extension of his life in Australia, provided Ellis with an income in the beginning, but held very little real interest for him. His restless mind was ever pressing into fields far beyond the realms of teaching, and presently he became absorbed in a fresh study of the books of James Hinton. Houston Peterson wrote in his excellent study of Ellis:[1]

Returning from Australia with high reverence for Hinton, he wrote a letter of inquiry to Ellice Hopkins, editor of *The Life and Letters of James Hinton*, who sent it on to Mrs Hinton; the latter replied and

39

soon he was on friendly terms with the whole Hinton family, including the remarkable Caroline Haddon, Mrs Hinton's sister. They were all charmed with this handsome young admirer of their dead hero, and gladly turned over to him quantities of Hinton's unprinted manuscripts. The early books and Miss Hopkins' emasculated biography had left Ellis ignorant of the fact that the last five or six years of Hinton's life, tragically cut short in 1875 by brain fever, were devoted to brilliant pioneer work in the field of sexual morality.

Certainly Hinton anticipated modern attitudes to sex in a way startling to the reigning defendants of conventional morality. Inevitably the selection of his writings which Ellis proceeded to make under the title 'The Lawbreaker', was considered outrageous. Any passage, chosen at random, simply invited trouble from a society where even the biological facts of reproduction were elaborately cloaked. This, for instance, from Hinton, disturbed even the most emancipated: 'a chastity maintained by fear is as unchaste as harlotry . . . a kind of *anatomical* chastity; a feeling as if some physical relations of things were in themselves pure and others impure, which seems to me the most intense and profound of all possible impurities. . .!'[2]

Juggling with paradox, Hinton produced considerable pace and sparkle in his writing but there were times when even Ellis craved a hint of hard fact amongst the welter of words. Later in life he tended to underestimate the influence which Hinton had on his work. Frequently Ellis confesses in his autobiography that he has not checked back with contemporary evidence, and whenever one turns to it, the picture emerges considerably qualified.

'What is Pureness?',[3] his second article to achieve print, was little more than an exposition of Hinton's definitions. Hinton had concluded, long before Ellis, that sex was at the very heart of human happiness by reason of the cant, humbug, ignorance and waste which ill-advised divines and their secular counterparts, had so elaborately created around it. Indeed Hinton went further. He saw many Christian homes, 'reeking with respectability' as 'the real dark places of the earth', and expressed a preference for a restrained form of polygamy, more extravagant than anything Ellis advocated. He inspired Ellis at all points, but Ellis's thinking was to flow far more deeply and richly, bringing ordered thinking into his chaos.

In an article in *Mind*, Ellis wrote of Hinton:[4]

The selfishness of monogamy and the home, the cruelty of virtue, the rigidity of arbitrary rules and feelings in regard to all such questions seemed to him [Hinton] unparalleled before in Christendom, or out of it. In the Protean evils which are grouped around that part of life Hinton found a *reductio ad absurdum* of the present morality. . . .

It was as crisp and lucid a statement as the words from which it was derived were rich and obscure. It showed a considerable development in Ellis's writing and revealed the chief preoccupation of his still widening interests.

In his personal life he now found it wonderful, after all those long years of intellectual isolation in Australia, to move among a group of like-minded people, using the Hinton home as his base. However, he had far too few reservations about Hinton and Hinton's personal life. As Arthur Calder-Marshall has commented:[5]

> He did not see that women had been drawn towards Hinton either because their marriages had failed or because they had not succeeded in securing husbands; or that underlying Hinton's high flown theory of polygamy was a promiscuous sexual urge which demanded the justification of a sexual philosophy.

By 1880 Ellis at last launched into the medical studies which were to resolve the direction of his career for the next eight years. Sheer lack of money frustrated his purpose at first – one almost wrote ambition – but with Ellis he was never concerned exclusively with success as such, but with which task he could most adequately perform. Then his mother offered him the £100 she had lately inherited, convinced that medicine was a fine and worthy career, and blissfully unaware of the confused motives which drove Ellis along this path. In consort with Miss Caroline Haddon, his mother emerged at this stage as a most generous and understanding person. Miss Haddon, sister of James Hinton's wife, first discovered the financial difficulties which threatened Ellis's desire to become a doctor in his letters to Mrs Hinton. She promptly 'permitted him to borrow' another £200 from her which opened doors implacably closed to the impoverished.

In order to eke out his small capital Ellis also sought literary work from John Fougler, then editor of the magazine *Modern Thought*. It was in Fougler's office that Ellis met the Marxist politician H. M. Hyndman, John Burns the working-class propagandist and Belfort Bax, 'a lion in the jungle of theory but too frightened of the working class to walk through' a slum. Foulger was a middle-of-the-road reformer, highly congenial to Ellis, and when he formed the Progressive Association Ellis became its secretary. In the beginning he was full of ideas at committee meetings, but as his work threatened to drag him into the public eye, he slowly retreated and refused to speak or even sit on the platform during discussions. 'His position', Calder-Marshall wrote, 'was at the table placed at the entrance of the hall in a howling draught, receiving subscriptions, selling literature and catching colds. . . .'

At the Progressive Association he also met Percival Chubb, a clerk in the Local Government Board, and they became close friends, meeting to share sausage-roll luncheons and immense discussions about the nature of good and evil, man, God and the universe. It was Chubb who introduced Ellis to Thomas Davidson and Ellis came away from his first meeting with 'the Philosopher' feeling that Davidson was 'the most remarkable man, the most intensely alive man, I had ever met'.

Immense arguments sparked between the two men, with Ellis expounding the gospel of St Hinton with unrelenting commitment. It maddened Davidson to find that having undermined all the principles by which Hinton lived and exposed what he took to be the fallacies in Ellis's arguments, Ellis returned to exactly the same position when next they met, with the same cool logic. Davidson at last was driven to write a letter from Rome on 18 February 1884:

> I grieve deeply that you should so uncompromisingly assume the position that you do, a position which I cannot distinguish from a rather elevated securalism. To confound the eternal with the phenomenal seems to me the worst of heresies. It is one too in which you in your best moments don't really believe.

Secular or not, at this stage of his development Ellis would have no truck with absolute truths, believing that what logic killed by precision, could better be apprehended in metaphor and analogy. Growing suspicions of vast systems conceived by metaphysical philosophers crystallized with Davidson. He 'cut me adrift for ever not from philosophy but from philosophers'. It was Chubb, Davidson, Ellis and a handful of others who next formed a group with the ambitious title of the Fellowship of the New Life, an organization destined to introduce Ellis to a person who would dominate the most important years of his life.

In October 1880 Ellis entered the grey jumble of buildings known as St Thomas's Hospital, on the Surrey bank of the Thames, and became a 'perpetual student' destined to outface innumerable odds in an attempt to become a fully qualified doctor. Every day, for seven long years, he caught the train from Anerley where his mother provided board and lodging free of charge, the £300 capital permitting no other arrangement. Every day he tried desperately to find a suitable lunch, heavy food reducing him to mid-day stupor, and would eventually make do with sausage rolls and a brand of thick, treacly coffee remarkable only for its cheapness.

In the evening he hurried home to the dinner which his mother kept over from the family's midday meal, retired to his room and immersed himself in fresh study until late at night. Week after week, month after month this went on. His determination swiftly to overcome the difficulties of medical study, drove him to exhaustive feats. Presently, his nerves were overstrained and for a week or two he took to sleeping draughts, but it was not only strain. Medicine had revealed many characteristics hopelessly alien to him. There were times when it seemed quite impossible to memorize the cold, hard facts of anatomy, and times when a sudden violent hostility to the technicalities of medical textbooks, to diagrams of the human body and lectures which appeared cold-blooded, made him feel like abandoning the whole business.[6] But he persevered and soon developed a certain proficiency in practical chemistry and comparative physiology.

He spent two years in the medical school proper and then began his clinical studies as an out-patient clerk to Dr J. F. Payne in July 1882. There followed an endless round of dissecting, dispensing and dressing, familiar in its monotony to any imaginative intern who has ever walked the polished labyrinth of hospital wards. Ellis desired above all things to hurry through the more boring and distasteful parts of medical training, but this was frustrated by the rapidly expanding nature of his interests and the cast of his own mind, which proved in the end hostile to the sheer materialism of medicine. Taken in combination and reinforced by a natural state of indecision, these characteristics produced a person plainly anathema to examiners and sadly alien to the world of examinations. In some academic paradise which took account of hypersensitive temperaments, Ellis might have flourished or even emerged triumphant. Now, instead, he worked away desperately at his books until shortly before the first examinations were due, and then abandoned himself to his fate whatever it might be. The written papers were within the bounds of toleration and enabled him to give a reasonable account of himself, but confronted by the viva voce, his immense shyness rendered every moment an agony, and his answers were full of hesitation. There followed weeks of anxiety, in fear for what might be the result.

And then one day, disguising the emptiness in his stomach, he walked towards the Examination Results in the hall of St Thomas's, swiftly searched the list of names, and felt his breathing begin again as he discovered his own name there among the Ees.

For the next two years Ellis lived in a world obsessed with hygiene, a world of discipline and regulations, of over-scrubbed floors and steaming sterilizers, of pink-cheeked nurses, bright, young, cheerfully unaware of the nuance which could shatter the sensitively sick. It was a world of long corridors dimly lit, of red night-lights and a doctor's mess full of the brassy materialism which springs from too much preoccupation with bowels and ganglia. It was a world which at once chilled Ellis's poetic spirit and gave the scientist, growing in him, considerable satisfaction.

In the permanent record of St Thomas's, Dr Ellis appears as the 'very good' in-patient clerk to Dr Bristowe for a period of six months. He treated in that time many patients, among them Arabella, a girl who lived in a London slum but retained a flower-like poise and beauty. Attacked by tubercular peritonitis she seemed certain to die, but under treatment from Ellis and other doctors, she recovered, and left such an impress of natural grace on Ellis's mind that one night he sat down and wrote a simple poem about her, reconciling the horrors of illness with literature. It was not a very successful poem, but it served its immediate purpose of helping to satisfy his starved aesthetic senses.

In the prolonged and painful years of Ellis's medical training, the one subject from which he emerged with honours, midwifery, now took him into the reality of London slum life, which came up like a festering tide to the south side of Westminster Bridge and retired upon itself as though not quite daring the final assault on that House of Commons empowered to banish impoverishment from the land and inexplicably impotent when confronted with the reality at its very feet.

Over a period of three years, he undertook obstetrical duties and found himself for the first time intimately in touch with poverty. Known as the Acting Midwifery Clerk, he slept in a small room remarkable only for the size and power of a bell over the door. Trousers and jacket were placed close to hand together with a torch beside the black bag containing the routine equipment. There was a Satanic certainty that the bell would choose the moment of deepest sleep to ring, and its vibrations held a sort of malignant joy which always distressed Ellis who desired to smother it with his jacket in case the first harsh summons was repeated. Somewhere out of the night a distraught husband had materialized to mutter anxious words at the porter who had impeturbably pressed his bell. Dr Ellis rose from bed, slipped on his clothes and went down. Sallying out into the summer night of 1883 with a 'strange glimmering half light over the Thames', gradually came to hold a grim poetry for him. Writing to his father in November 1882 he said that he had finished his midwifery in August with more than thirty-four cases in a fortnight and on one occasion was called out eight times in one night.[7]

There were occasions when he had to remove bugs from his clothes after he returned from delivering a child, and once, during a delivery, Ellis was drenched in a stream of urine, and recorded the case in some detail.[8] It was to form part of his theory of urolagnia and seemed at the time to give him pleasure. On another occasion, a prostitute accosted him near London Bridge Station and he walked away, his mind busy wondering what motives lay behind the way of life she had chosen.[9] Later, he went to a famous London restaurant with a new friend, Walter M. Gallicahn, in order to meet certain 'ladies of the town', and Gallicahn recorded that Ellis was extraordinarily shy and tongue-tied.

The slums round St Thomas's Hospital became very familiar to the fledgling Dr Ellis. The struggle against the overwhelming power of poverty, the knowledge that most of the children born were unwanted, left indelible impressions; yet here, as always, he was not fired like Shaw or Wells to eloquent denunciation; he regretted it, and through the cool window of his detachment recorded those phenomena which bore upon the ultimate purpose of his life.

Scientific observation continued in the midst of operations, in witnessing small cruelties practised by frustrated nurses, and during those many moments which concerned lesser problems like modesty. If a doctor took undressing and urination as a matter of course, some patients would quickly accept these acts as natural and unembarrassing, while others – the younger girls in particular – remained inhibited and some even refused to remove their clothes at all.[10] From these observations, fourteen years later sprang part of 'The Evolution of Modesty', an essay quickly accepted as the most satisfying analysis until then published of a condition long misunderstood.

One among the men he met at St Thomas's remained a friend all his life. John Barker Smith was fourteen years older than Ellis, a simple, modest man of illegitimate birth, who had made a considerable study of natural science. Early economic hardship severely frustrated his career, and at one point he had undergone a nervous breakdown. Granted a phenomenal memory he could recite one poem after another with considerable verve, but his interests were wide and he was liable to sweep from Goethe to advanced analytical chemistry, from poetry to a minute analysis of peptic ulcers. Both in their very different ways were preoccupied with the problems of sex, but they shared many interests beyond medicine and biology. Often a frugal lunch in a cheap Soho restaurant preceded a visit to the National Gallery, the British Museum or the House of Commons, following the pre-Raphaelites in one, anthropoid apes in another and important debates in the third. On one occasion, they even attended 'a meeting at the hostel of the Y.M.C.A. where the members were engaged in discussing the evils of saying damn'.[11] Barker Smith was more important for the part his daughter was later to play in Ellis's life, but Amy was not significant at this stage. Another quite different woman now came out of the South African veldt to change his life.

In the first year of his long drawn-out medical training there arrived in England a small, dark, vivacious person, four years his senior, who had meticulously saved money from many years' work as a governess, to embark upon the same career as now revealed such shortcomings to Ellis. His ordeal extended over eight years and hers precisely eight days. In that time she became a nurse as a preliminary to more advanced medical studies, but was temperamentally alien to the disciplines involved. Driven by neurotic compulsions which explained half her brilliance, Olive Schreiner found England, after South Africa, depressing, and struggling with the conflict between a desire to write, which expressed itself in burning messages flung down on the pages of her journal, and the half understood urge to probe the mysteries of medicine, she moved restlessly from one address to another brilliantly committing her thoughts to paper.

Unaware of the elemental powers which possessed her, Olive Schreiner looked out on the world with her tormented vision and saw what seemed to her a bleak prospect. The daughter of a German, Gottlob Schreiner, and an Englishwoman, Rebecca Lyndall, she was the sixth of twelve children born in the mud-floored room of the Wittenbergen Mission Station. While the lofty Gottlob Schreiner poured the wealth of Christian dogma before the bewildered eyes of the infidel, she largely educated herself, plunging into every book available and emerging at the age of thirteen as a 'free-thinker' to the disgust of her very pious sister. Spencer's *First Principles*, stumbled on accidentally, restored some sense of religious equilibrium to Miss Schreiner, but simultaneously began the attacks of asthma, which were to haunt her all her life and to cause Havelock Ellis such distress.

From the earliest days Olive Schreiner committed thoughts, ideas, reflections to paper with that immediacy which distinguished one brand of born writer, and while barely into her twenties at least two novels were half conceived and in process of writing. Then, at twenty-two, she launched with considerable precocity into *The Story of an African Farm*. Messrs Chapman & Hall received the manuscript from the wilds of South Africa and were somewhat taken aback.

In the midst of renewed and increasingly fierce bouts of asthma, the collapse of her medical ambitions and an appalling sense of drift, Olive Schreiner learned that Chapman & Hall were ready to publish the book. However, the conventions of the day saw something unladylike in the spectacle of a young woman possessed not only by creative fire, but such passionate fire as this, and since critics were likely to recoil from feminine authorship they said she must change her name. Writing years later to Havelock Ellis, Olive Schreiner said:[12]

> Yes, Chapman & Hall *did* send my MS. back to me, and Chapman asked me to call and see him. When I came he said he wanted to publish the book, but he wanted me to make an alteration in it, just to put in a few sentences saying that Lyndall was really secretly married to that man, as if she wasn't married to him the British public would think it wicked, and Smiths, the railway booksellers, would not put it on their stalls! Of course I got in a rage and told him he could leave the book alone, and I would take it elsewhere. He climbed down at once, and said it was only out of consideration for me; I was young, and people would think I was not respectable if I wrote such a book, but of course if I insisted on saying she was not married to him it must be so. . . .

She had already compromised by choosing a pen name bristling with virility – Ralph Iron – but there, she felt, compromise must stop. The story of a passionate mind, born in the isolation of the rolling veldt, desperately trying to achieve a new kind of personal salvation was described as highly original and very bold when it finally appeared. People began to ask about Ralph Iron. Who was this man and where did he come from? Already one publisher had overcome the shock of discovering that the small girlish figure who entered his office was none other than the redoubtable Mr Iron, and now the wider public learned, to its amazement, that the author of this very daring book was a young woman some would consider strikingly beautiful.

There followed an article by Henry Norman in the *Forthnightly Review*, 'Theories and Practices of Modern Fiction' which named *The Story of an African Farm* as one of the outstanding novels of the year.[13] Ellis read the article and borrowed the book. There was some contradiction in what followed. With that cool detachment which made him on occasion a good critic, he wrote: 'The African Farm was not to me, then or ever, what it seems to have been to many, a revelation, a new gospel; nor was I able to accept it at all points either as fine art or as sound doctrine.' None the less he determined to write a letter to Ralph Iron. In due course came this reply:[14]

> St Leonards on Sea. My Dear Sir, on my return from a visit to London I found your letter which my publisher had forwarded here. Had I received it sooner I should have written to tell you of the pleasure your expression of sympathy with the little book *An African Farm* gave me. Thank you for having written. . . .
>
> There is too much moralising in the story but when one is leading an absolutely solitary life one is apt to use one's work as Gregory used his letters, as an outlet for all one's superfluous feelings, without asking too closely whether they can or cannot be artistically expressed there. . . .

There now commenced an exchange of letters which was to extend over thirty years and bring as much happiness as distress into their lives. Within three months of the first letter they met.

Ellis invited Miss Schreiner to accompany him to a meeting of the Progressive Association. It was not altogether a success. He called for her at her rooms and according to Olive Schreiner she had to hurry to her bedroom to conceal tears of disappointment at his appearance. This becomes explicable against the background of her recent experience. When she first came to England she went to stay with one of her brothers in the Isle of Wight and there fell in love with a man who was a sadist. To her horror she discovered that powerful masochistic impulses in herself responded to his sadism and gave her the most acute sexual pleasure. According to Arthur Calder-Marshall:[15]

> It ran utterly contrary to all her ideas of the equality of the sexes and

it made her feel ashamed of herself. . . . She despised the man who had found this flaw in her character and yet she wanted him more than she had ever wanted anybody in her life.

As a result she ran away to London, began training as a midwife nurse and received her first letter from Ellis. When he suggested meeting, she hoped – desperately – that his personality would match the vigour and boldness of his writing and opinions. Confronted by the shy, retiring Ellis who hardly dared to look her in the eye, she was so bitterly disappointed, she wept. Ellis, for his part, drew a sweetly conventional picture of this first meeting and gave no hint of the volcanic nature of her personality. Neither seems to have said very much. The meeting of the Progressive Association went off uneventfully. They parted with formal hopes of meeting again, both unaware that a profound relationship had begun.

Presently Olive Schreiner wrote again to Ellis:[16]

7, Pelham Street

My Dear Mr Ellis,

I enjoyed going with you to that lecture so much. Thank you for coming for me. If you are not too busy and do not feel it would be a waste of time I should be glad if you could sometimes come and see me. It would be a help to me.

I have made up my mind not to leave town yet. I shall remain here till Friday, then my address will be 32, Fitzroy Street.
Goodnight,

Olive Schreiner.

Correspondence grew. Dear Mr Ellis changed to[17]

Dear Havelock:

Come tomorrow afternoon, if you can, because on Friday I may have other visitors and then we can't talk so well, and I have much I want to say and you to hear. Don't think of, and dwell upon, Hinton *too much*. I think it is not well for any of us to allow another personality to submerge, in any way, our own. Do you?

I have been walking about in the quiet part of Regent's Park all the morning.

It was a remarkable tribute to Havelock Ellis, still only twenty-five years old, an unknown medical student with little money, less influence and shy beyond endurance, that the most brilliant young author of the day should now select him as her confidante and friend. Once over initial disappointments, their relationship flourished. They were the products of similar upbringings, one springing from the wastes of Australia, the other the wilds of South Africa, but subtler affinities gradually drew them together until presently she referred to him in her letters as 'the person who is like part of me'.

Soon another step was taken. He went to tea at Fitzroy Street one day. She had poured the tea, talked spasmodically and was putting strawberries on his plate when she suddenly changed the direction of her words, and confessed to him that she was trying to recover from a deeply disturbing emotional experience. She then told him the story not only of her sadistic English lover but of an earlier and equally disastrous love affair at sixteen.

He was at Fitzroy Street again a few days later. Evening came down before he left, and as she opened the door, imperceptibly, she drew towards him. He hesitated . . . looked shyly away and went. On the third visit, as he stood in the doorway once more, she came close to him and this time gently embraced him.

There is still some mystery about the precise nature of the relationship which developed between two such fundamentally different people. Olive's dark, passionate nature understood Lawrence's wisdom of the blood, and Ellis, aware of similar wellsprings could easily respond, but there was in Olive a burning, primitive sense of being which demanded a physical counterpart very different from the gentle Ellis. In the beginning she was 'warm, tender, impulsive, with an air of helplessness that made men want to protect her', but he suddenly discovered her capacity for both passion and splenetic outbursts. Such were the power of Olive Schreiner's sexual fantasies that she was driven to frequent masturbation and even took large doses of potassium bromide under the illusion that this would dampen what Ellis sometimes referred to as her 'ardour'.[18]

Presently she went for a brief holiday to a small cottage near Matlock drawn there by her friend Eleanor Marx, the daughter of Karl Marx. She remained in daily correspondence with Havelock who finally decided that he must join her on 1 August. There are at least three versions of what followed. According to Ellis, he suddenly realized just how difficult a person Olive Schreiner could be, and found himself bewildered by her mercurial moods. Asthma sometimes rendered sleep impossible, and she would pace up and down the small floor of the cottage bedroom, talking to herself until the simple couple who owned the cottage were driven to complain.[19] Sometimes, in the mornings, Ellis saw in her large glowing eyes that hypnotic look which presaged another outburst. Sometimes, they came close to final intimacies – if they did not actually reach them – and unsuspected difficulties arose.

Later in life Eleanor Marx once said to Olive, 'What you need is a nursemaid', but there were also times when she had no difficulty in completely dominating an assembly with her diminutive person. One such imperious moment broke through now. She suddenly swung on Havelock and called him 'Difficult! Difficult! Difficult!' in a voice as imperious as her manner. When he mildly remonstrated with her, she simply redoubled her attack.

Over the next few days they moved from place to place in the Derbyshire area, sometimes driven to accept separate rooms at opposite ends of a village (Bole Hill) to satisfy conventional morality.[20] On another occasion, when Ellis took the room next to Olive, it drove the landlady to ask them to leave on the grounds that it was all too much trouble for her.[21] Finally at Matlock they booked two rooms with a Mrs Thomas and suddenly everything turned sour, they were overcome with sadness and on one occasion driven to tears. Conscience forced Olive to protest that she felt guilty about their relationship and she told him – with her usual vehemence – that one day he would really fall in love and look back on this episode as regrettable.[22]

In the middle of this holiday Ellis was forced to return to London and drew a picture in his diary of kissing Olive's tears away as he left. She stood at the window and they blew each other kisses until he was out of sight.[23]

They met again shortly afterwards and this time there were explicit references in the diary to sexual encounters which did not seem to achieve penetration.[24] The morning following their secondary love-making Olive had an attack of asthma.[25] Ellis clearly did not want to get too deeply involved at this stage. He hoped in fact to achieve a degree of healthy detachment, from sheer familiarity. The relationship was good for him in many ways he thought, but he was afraid of too complete a surrender.

If all this conveys the impression of a tormented fortnight in the country, that is not true. There were periods of happiness, periods when merely to be in each other's company was sheer joy. Moreover, since they had both experienced solitude against the wildest natural backgrounds and shared some aspects of intellectual development – Herbert Spencer's *First Principles* and feminine emancipation – they were never at a loss for stimulating talk and discussion. Both were absorbed in the problems of sex and religion and Olive frequently came back to her struggles with atheism.

Mme Delisle in her book *Friendship's Odyssey* stated: 'Olive Schreiner . . . in my humble opinion, refused a lover relationship with him because he was not sufficiently virile. . . .'[26] Certainly the first glimmerings of a very interesting characteristic in Havelock Ellis were concealed within this relationship.

There was already another woman with whom he was involved whose role remained unmentioned in any biography or in his own *Life*. Born in the same year as Ellis, Alice Corthorn also became a medical student and was now as much in love with him as Olive Schreiner. In the end she played no very great part in the story since Ellis did not appear to return her love, and for the moment sheer enchantment with Olive put this out of his mind along with every other complication.

Years later, Ellis wrote of those days with a deep nostalgia for memories which were deeply imprinted. They were to know many experiences together. They were to read, write and travel, to visit Paris and Italy, but the small moments recurred with a peculiar sweetness of their own, and he wrote of them in detail. The smell of hay coming in at the cottage window, walking hand in hand through the moonlit countryside silenced by the power of feeling between them; watching through a microscope the ferment of a minute speck of spermatozoa; listening to Beethoven's *Ninth Symphony* with no more than fingertips entwined; Paris and the boulevards and the interminable talk far into the night.

Chapter 4

His writing career begins

It was surprising that the power of his relationship with Olive Schreiner did not wreck his medical studies. Instead his interests seemed to widen. Already deeply absorbed in literature, science and medicine, anthropology revealed fresh fascinations and he continued to write one article after another.

These were quickly successful. The first article appeared in a small magazine called *PEN* (1880) and took the form of a book review without much significance. In the following year came 'What is Pureness' published in *Modern Thought*.[1] Provoked in answer to a puritanical essay from a woman writer steeped in a mistaken sense of conventional saintliness, 'What is Pureness' appeared and passed without much comment. Influenced by Hinton, Ellis simply remarked that the time had come to re-define the word pureness, since it was no longer synonymous with virginity or sexual restraint. Derivative in style from John Henry Newman, the paper made a determined effort to reconcile what was commonly considered good taste with revolutionary statement.

There followed in April 1883 'The Novels of Thomas Hardy' (*Westminster Review*), the first long literary essay based not only upon a meticulous reading of Hardy's works, but an Easter spent in Dorset, where Ellis steeped himself in the atmosphere of Egdon Heath.[2] He had thought of asking to see Hardy himself before finally committing his thoughts to paper, but abandoned the idea for reasons of taste, timidity and a belief that Hardy would resent any intrusion on his privacy. 'The Novels of Thomas Hardy' gave him many harrowing moments, and revealed to him all over again, the infinite subtlety of the English language. He grappled with the opening paragraph for hours, consecutively rejecting wit, allusion and irony, and finally achieving a simplicity of statement not unlike the very first sentence which had occurred to him.

The essay was read by Thomas Hardy himself in his Wimborne home and he at once sat down and wrote to Mr Havelock Ellis:[3]

My dear Sir,

I have read with great interest your article in the 'Westminster', and can inadequately express by letter my sense of your generous treatment of the subject. I consider the essay a remarkable paper in many ways, and can truly say that the writing itself, with its charm of style, and variety of allusion, occupied my mind when first reading it far more than the fact that my own unmethodical books were its subject-matter. . . .

If novelists were a little less in the dark about the appearance of their own works, what productions they might bring forth, but they are much in the position of the man inside the hobby horse at a Christmas masque, and have no consciousness of the absurdity of its trot, at times, in the spectator's eye.

However, I cannot complain of any invidious remarks thereon in my case. The keen appreciativeness which the article discloses sets me thinking . . . of the writer. . . .

As to certain conditions and peculiarities you notice in the stories, I may mention that many are the result of temporary accidents connected with the time of their production, rather than of deliberate choice. . . .

I hope to read some more of your critical writings in the future, and believe I shall discover them without a mark. . . .

In the following year Ellis made his first contribution to the reviews of the day. He wrote a paper, 'The Present Position of English Criticism', which the editor of the *Fortnightly Review* accepted. Unfortunately Escott had already fallen into that eccentricity which later compelled him to relinquish the editorship, and Ellis was bewildered to have the paper back three weeks later with a fulsome explanation of its sudden unsuitability. Almost a year passed before 'The Present Position of English Criticism' appeared in a small periodical called *Time*.[4] Four other papers were printed in 1884, a review of Maxime du Camp's *Souvenirs littéraires*,[5] Hinton's *Later Thought*,[6] a review of A. Bebel's *Die Frau in der Vergangenheit*,[7] and an introduction to James Hinton's *The Law-Breaker and the Coming of the Law*.[8]

The *Indian Review* article analysed recent tendencies in English fiction and made this comment:

William Morris, who looks back yearningly to the popular art of the Middle Ages, deals out scorn to the novel; he fails to see that fiction *is* our modern popular art. After all it is the human soul in its myriad and everchanging aspects which is the one permanently interesting thing; it is of little consequence what art it chooses for its expression. . . .

The human soul in all its myriad aspects. Lofty commotions of this kind were common to the period and Ellis was no exception.

Considerably occupied with philosophy at this period, Ellis had read many histories of philosophy and closely studied the work of Spinoza. Schwegler's *History of Philosophy*, Kuno Fischer's *History of Modern Philosophy* and Ribot's *Schopenhauer et sa philosophie* all came under scrutiny and several volumes of Schopenhauer were later 'placed among [his] sacred books'.[9] There followed a careful study of Lange's *History of Materialism*, a book which appealed strongly to Ellis. Metaphysics, it said, were nothing more than a form of poetry. If Ellis at once saw the gulf between poetry and metaphysics proper, the idea opened the way for the later assimilation of the doctrines of Jules de Gaultier. He also read at this time Edward Carpenter's *Towards Democracy*, dismissing it at first as 'Whitman-and-water'. Characteristically thorough, he came back to the book a second time, rejected his first view and wrote: 'we have here a distinct individuality, with, indeed, points of contact with Whitman, and using the same mode of expression, but a new and genuine voice, nevertheless. . . .' Simultaneously Ellis wrote a letter to Carpenter and a warm correspondence developed between them, their devotion to Shelley and Walt Whitman reinforced by a mutual desire to unravel the darker mysteries of sex.

They first met in 1886 at the Fellowship of the New Life – its idealistic gatherings were rich in people destined to be important. Within a general framework approaching realism, the Fellowship wanted to encourage manual work alongside mental work, to reform education and supplant the spirit of self-seeking by that of unselfish regard for the general good. 'The subordination of material things to spiritual' was to be linked to 'the cultivation of a perfect character in each and all'. Shaw, a leading member of the society, later wrote 'Certain members of that circle . . . [believed] that the revolution would have to wait an unreasonably long time if postponed until they personally attained perfection.' If Ellis could ever be said to have an organized political outlook it assumed greater coherence at this stage than any other. It combined a belief in Fabian gradualism with individual self-cultivation and found inspiration in the work of Ibsen. In the event the dissidents of the New Fellowship led by Shaw broke away to join the Fabian Society proper while the Fellowship pursued its idealistic aim of realizing a vaguely defined New Jerusalem by genteel-liberal means.

Listening to Nicholas Tchaykowsky speaking to the Fellowship one evening, Ellis heard the door creak and there, peering round it, was the soft, beautiful face of Carpenter which was to become so familiar over the years. They remained friends for forty-five years, until Carpenter's death, but in the early days Ellis had no suspicion of Carpenter's special temperament.

The New Fellowship also introduced him to Ernest Rhys and Will Dircks, both on the staff of the Walter Scott publishing company, Dircks in some mysteriously undefined capacity, and Rhys as editor. Both quickly appreciated Ellis's literary talents and presently he was invited to edit Landor's *Imaginary Conversations*, to be followed by a selection of Heine's prose writings. Some of the essays in the Heine volume which he translated himself still survive critical examination today.

Ernest Rhys described Ellis at this period as:[10]

> a shy, silent, meditative-looking, bearded young man . . . with a voice of curious, thin, high-pitched tones. He was not at all diffident, however, but keenly alive to art, poetry, the drama, etc. He used to sup with me now and again at No. 59, Cheyne Walk, Chelsea (Holman Hunt's old house) and discuss books and plays. . . . He translated Heine's prose and edited Landor too, for my old Camelot series. He was already a convinced devotee in the sort of philosophical empiricism to be inferred from his books; but he was a quiet advocate, not at all vocal or dogmatic. He had a vein of humour, and I think, took a sly pleasure in the aberrations of men, their endless tricks, vanities and the rest. He observed closely, endlessly. He loved a good play, a good talker, a pretty face, and loved the sun, the south, travel and the sea. . . .

Ellis extended his editing to include Ibsen's *Pillars of Society* and other plays, preparing them for the Walter Scott company. As in so much of his literary editing, the Camelot Series represented a piece of pioneering which introduced the man in the street to highly original and disturbing plays like *Ghosts* and *An Enemy of the People*. The first Ibsen book sold over fourteen thousand copies, and became almost a best-seller for those days. There followed another literary adventure when he introduced Vasari's *Lives of the (Italian) Painters* to English readers, a development of that preoccupation with the visual arts which he reconciled with the growth of many other conflicting interests.

As if to demonstrate his versatility, he presently launched into yet another considerable undertaking, which many literary men might have considered a full-time occupation. From early schooldays, the plays of Webster and Marlowe had interested him, and many a precious penny had been expended to buy a special cheap edition. Now, at the British Museum, he re-read and developed his knowledge of the Elizabethan dramatists and something in the spacious robustness of the age, the spontaneous vitality and lack of prudery, found an echo in his mind and set him poring over Marlowe, Ford, Webster, Heywood and Porter. The urge to resurrect these forgotten dramatists suddenly grew strong, and sent him happily to his reading desk on Row H whenever he could clear a small space in his very busy life. If the roystering days of the Mermaid Tavern, the cut and thrust of debate and the swashbuckling life of Merrie England were alien to Ellis's gentle and abstemious nature, to sit, read and recollect those days, delighted him. Soon he launched eagerly into his first great task of literary reclamation with a letter to Henry Vizetelly suggesting the re-publication of unexpurgated volumes of the Elizabethan dramatists under the title, the Mermaid Series. Considering himself incompetent to edit the series, he made no such suggestion, but Vizetelly thought otherwise. Once a well-known journalist, Vizetelly had entered British publishing and quickly achieved notoriety by producing French novelists like Zola and Flaubert, then considered frank enough to border on the immoral. Vizetelly welcomed Ellis's proposition and replied at once, asking how much he required to edit the series. Dazzled by the invitation, Ellis determined to achieve, in the shortest possible time, the literary background which he thought he lacked and replied to say that he thought three guineas for each play reasonable. It was a sadly impoverished estimate, but money did not gravely concern Ellis. One of the more inspiring features of his life was that he never succumbed to the routine of *earning* a living, and found such close identity in work and pleasure that one automatically enlivened the other.

An almost Elizabethan zest distinguished the way he plunged into the Mermaid Series, selecting individual editors and embracing at one sweep Middleton, Ford, Marlowe and Porter for his own attention. Unexpected trouble arose over the publication of Marlowe and left him with an uneasy sense that scholarship should not founder on such spurious rocks as decency. His volume of Marlowe's plays appeared in 1887 and sold well, but he was courageous enough to publish as an Appendix, the original Harleian manuscript which levelled every kind of accusation against the poet. Little known to the average reader, it is worth reproducing in part as an early revelation of Ellis's heresies:[11]

> Contayninge the opinion of one Christofer Marlye, concernynge his damnable opinions and judgment of relygion and scorne of Gods Worde. . . .
> He *affirmeth* That Moyses was but a Juggler, and that one Heriots can do more than hee.
> That Moyses made the Jewes to travell fortie years in the wilderness (which iorny might have ben don in lesse then one yeer) er they came to the promised lande. . . .
> That the firste beginnynge of Relygion was only to keep men in awe. . . .
> That Christ was a Bastard, and his mother dishonest. . . .
> That Christ deserved better to dye than Barrabas, and that the

Jewes made a good choyce, though Barrabas were both a theife and a murtherer. . . .

That the women of Samaria wer whores, and that Christ knew them dishonestlye.

That St John the Evangelist was bedfellow to Christe, that he leaned alwayes in his bosom, that he vsed him as the synners of Sodome. . . .

That one Richard Cholmelei hath confessed that he was perswaded by Marloes reason to become an athieste. . . .

With a calmness only matched by his courage Ellis commented: 'I see no reason to question the substantial truth of these accusations.'[12]

In the embalmed correctness of Victorian literature such cool effrontery left a deep and horrified silence. It was bad enough to print these blasphemies, but openly to endorse them with such quiet certainty at the great age of twenty-eight was to invite disaster. A whole train of activities followed. An unknown woman first objected to the Appendix, and Vizetelly immediately cut out the offending passages in the remaining copies, but considerable numbers escaped unexpurgated. J. A. Symonds wrote to say he found the Appendix most distasteful, and Swinburne was relieved to hear that 'the horrible and disquieting passage in your appendix' had been suppressed. . . . 'I greatly regretted to find these monstrous abominations made public.' Years afterwards scholars still skirted around Ellis's comments, refusing to believe that such blasphemies could have any validity, and it was not until 2 June 1921 that the *Times Literary Supplement* published a complimentary document endorsing Richard Baines's view of Marlowe.[13]

The fourth and fifth volumes of the Mermaid Series – a group of Massinger's plays – were edited by Arthur Symons. An essay by Symons on Mistral, the Provençal poet, had first attracted Ellis who wrote to him and discovered that 'he was working on the Shakespeare facsimiles issued by Quaritch.' They met shortly afterwards and another friendship began which was to run on for thirty-five years. Symons, a self-educated man like Ellis, had also chosen the life of the solitary scholar, and if his poetry never rose above mediocrity he became an effective critic in the terminology of the day.

The Mermaid Series was widely read and prospered for some years. Then, suddenly and unexpectedly, came further trouble. The dramatic prosecution of Vizetelly for publishing what were described as the indecent books of Zola created havoc. Vizetelly was sentenced to a term of imprisonment, and the fate of the Mermaid Series seemed sealed, until Fisher Unwin came along and offered to continue publishing less objectionable plays in a similar format. To his astonishment Ellis was not asked for his opinion at any point, the work of transforming the series went ahead, and the first book which appeared under Fisher

Unwin's imprint did not so much as mention his name. Presently, the series dwindled away and publication ceased: but the original 'Mermaids' which Ellis edited remained one of the most stimulating pieces of literary reclamation which had happened in English drama for a century, even though his methodology in terms of modern scholarship remained crude and his emendations would today be regarded as somewhat reckless.

Complications now entered Ellis's relationship with Olive Schreiner to disturb his literary work. In 1885 a Mrs Elizabeth Cobb introduced Olive to that remarkable man Karl Pearson, a person who appeared to possess all the virility which she so much needed, without any slackening of intellectual power. Indeed, Pearson, as Professor of Applied Mathematics at London University, was supremely intellectual. He and Olive became members of the Men and Women's Discussion Club, an emancipated group, which made a point of talking about sex with the same directness as eugenics. From the minute book it is clear that Olive attended many meetings between July 1885 and November 1886, but Ellis, so much more interested in sex, did not, it seems, join. For the moment he was closer than ever to Olive and the spontaneity of her letters to him seemed to affect his style. His letters became quick with emotional life.

Olive Schreiner wrote to Ellis in April 1885:[14]

> You oughtn't to have been sad then at Croydon. You were so sweet and loving to me and made such little things so beautiful by being so lovely about them. . . . Just going to bed, my darling, my darling, you aren't going to be sad tonight, are you? I want to comfort you. Oh, if there were nothing to divide us! If we might be all in all to each other! If it were possible for one human being to make another human being *quite, quite, quite* happy!

These protestations notwithstanding, Olive Schreiner was presently involved in a web of relationships with one person at the centre who threatened disaster. Elizabeth Cobb, who first introduced Olive Schreiner to Karl Pearson, had herself formed a 'sentimental attachment' to him. Dr Donkin who attended Olive Schreiner for bronchitis simultaneously fell in love with her. Presently, with those volcanic symptoms which characterized her emotional life, Olive Schreiner was deeply in love with Karl Pearson.[15] In January Donkin proposed to her, and she wrote to Havelock:[16]

> I can't marry Henry, I can't and some awful power seems drawing me on. I think I shall go mad. I couldn't. I *must* be free, you know I must be free. I've been free all my life, Henry! Oh, they can't cut my wings!

From letters in the Karl Pearson Archive (February 1887) at University College London it is clear that Donkin pressed his suit, twice proposed to her and later accused Olive Schreiner of having ruined his life. She in turn protested – quite accurately – that she had never deceived him.

Another letter in the Karl Pearson Archive touches on her sexual relations with Ellis and Donkin. She had tried to feel sexual at different times with both of them she said, and retired hurt from her attempts. Ellis now suggested that Karl Pearson and Mrs Cobb were lovers in the full sense of the term, a statement which might have been based on that kind of jealousy which certainly troubled him later in life. Olive vigorously rejected any such suggestion and protested that Karl Pearson aroused in women that calibre of love which Beatrice felt for Dante.

When it became evident to Karl Pearson that Olive loved him, he at once made his own detachment clear. One of the greatest tragedies in his life, he said, was to be loved by a beautiful, single-minded nature and not to be able to return that love. His behaviour was immaculate, but its effect on Olive Schreiner shattering. Immediately she revealed little to him but wrote in December 1886:[17]

> when I look into the depths of my own heart I see a feeling that is deeper than the feeling I have had for any human being; but it is not sex love. I do not love you as a woman loves a man but as a soul loves itself. You will say 'Olive Schreiner, you are deceiving yourself that is sex love.' *I deny it*. Do you know what draws me closer to you than to any other human thing! It is that your mind works in the same way as mine, that your mental processes are carried on like mine, your brain works with its material in the same way. This is the case with no other human being.

Ellis in one of his wilder moments had entertained the idea of marrying Olive. Indeed for a brief spell nothing was more imperative, but now, with the appearance of Karl Pearson any such thought suffered severe qualification. As for Olive Schreiner, granted a profound capacity for suffering, she presently gave every appearance of mental illness. Mrs Cobb tried to see her but was met by a servant with instructions to admit no one. 'She was dreadfully ill, this morning', the servant said. 'Now she's walking up and down, up and down – I cannot bear to see her. . . .' Even Ellis was turned away, apparently by accident, but medical privilege carried Dr Donkin past the guard into Olive's room where he found her in a distressing state. She had given no hint in her letter to Pearson of the near madness which – according to Donkin – overtook her when she realized his detachment; now Donkin was in some alarm in case she injured herself. It was presently Donkin's opinion that Olive Schreiner must go away, and in December 1886 she left London one Friday morning accompanied by her landlady Miss Browne.

Inevitably, Havelock Ellis's feelings intensified as Olive Schreiner drew away, and there were moments when his remarkable powers of detachment broke and he cried out in language passionately alien to his normal self. From Italy she wrote in February: 'Havelock it was so strange when I got here last night, I had such a longing for you, almost like a child wanting its mother or a mother longing for her child. I felt as if I *must* see you. . . .'

These vivid letters continued to pour away for a whole year and then abruptly, in April they reached bursting point.[18]

Harry you must send me that letter of—. I shall be absolutely mad in a few days. I have not slept or really seen anything since I got your letter saying you had written to— after I had written begging you not to write about me. . . . Oh, my brain, my brain, my brain. . . .

Ellis himself was ill when he received this letter. He had by now made two attempts to practise the medical profession which had absorbed so much of his attention. In those days students who had not quite completed their medical finals were permitted to act as assistants to general practitioners, and in the winter of 1886 Ellis duly became assistant to a Dr Gray at Dalton-in-Furness. In the following winter he took a similar post with a Dr Aitchison in Blackburn, which led to his catching what seemed a cold. It rapidly turned into scarlet fever. Travelling down from Blackburn to London, his mother insisted on nursing him and, within a very short time, she too had developed scarlet fever, an illness far more serious to a person of her age. As Ellis grew better his mother grew worse, and when he was not sitting beside her reading or trying to comfort her, he wrote long letters to Olive Schreiner, still uncertain where this tortured relationship would end.

Some days later, well on the road to complete recovery himself, he had momentarily taken over care of his mother from the nurse and was sitting in his mother's room reading *Peer Gynt*. He had just come to the scene in *Peer Gynt* where Mother Aase dies – a powerfully written, moving scene – when he realized that his mother's breathing had changed. He went over to give her the small attentions which his medical training indicated, and a few moments later noticed an expression, close to anguish, momentarily distort her face. Almost simultaneously her breathing ceased. He gazed for a moment in stupefaction, then his medical training asserted itself and full of apprehension he tried her pulse, her eyes, her heart. It could not be. Dead like that in what had seemed a moment of recovery. With a great constriction in his throat he remained by her side staring down at her. Much later, moved by the recollection of a tremendous event in his life, he wrote: 'I had had many experiences of the diseases and sufferings of strangers in the hospital and elsewhere, but the first person whose death I had ever witnessed was the nearest person to me in all the world.'[19]

Whether she was still nearest, in any sense other than that of blood, remains doubtful. Havelock had grown so extravagantly away from the prim world of Mrs Ellis, and Olive Schreiner had so deeply invaded his feelings, it is difficult to believe that his mother still came first; but her death moved him deeply.[20]

It was in the year 1888, at the most crucial moment of his medical career, with his mother lately dead and his love for Olive Schreiner undiminished, that he conceived the idea of the Contemporary Science Series which was to play a big part in his literary life. Seasoned now in the intricacies of editing and fully aware that literature held an allure quite lacking in medicine, he put forward to Mr Gordon, manager of the Walter Scott publishing company, the idea of a modernized series to replace the then declining International Scientific Series. He did not hesitate to suggest himself as editor on this occasion. He could not have chosen a worse moment, since his medical finals were just about to take place.

Gordon leapt at the idea and, having no pretensions to scientific knowledge himself, he decided to give Ellis a comparatively free hand. A combination of luck and intuitive insight permitted Gordon to launch a series on a subject about which he knew nothing, with an editor totally unknown to the scientists of the day. Ellis, for his part, plunged into the undertaking with a remarkable alacrity for one who loathed haste, and quickly arranged for Professor Patrick Geddes, who had written the article on reproduction for the *Encyclopaedia Britannica*, to write a book which revealed the trend of his deepest thoughts. The field to be covered was daring indeed. In the last quarter of the nineteenth century many among the populace were prepared to admit the validity of Darwin's once abhorred theories, but some confusion of thought became apparent when biological inquiry remained respectable, while sexual research became repulsive. When *The Evolution of Sex* finally appeared, it revealed a balance between outspokenness and restraint, which permitted the most puritanical reader to purchase and read it without affront or fear of eternal damnation. The book was a considerable success and its readership wide. Gordon congratulated Ellis, and there was a wild moment when the harassed and almost qualified doctor began to wonder whether he could bring himself to face his finals after all. Fortunately he did, and in February 1889 at last completed his Licentiate in Medicine, Surgery and Midwifery of the Society of Apothecaries, eight long years after his first entry into St Thomas's. It was the lowest degree in medicine one could take, but it established him beyond doubt as a qualified doctor.[21]

Fast on the heels of qualification, Ellis visited the Savile Club to meet Canon Isaac Taylor, a man he had chosen to write *The Origin of the Aryans* in the Contemporary Science Series. Enthusiasm at first carried him away and he believed that one volume could be published each month, but chastening experience changed this view. For each of the following twenty-five years, the Contemporary Science Series paid him a sum hopelessly incommensurate with the work he put into it, but it was at least a regular source of income. As usual he was over-conscientious, not merely correcting already corrected proofs, and introducing elements of English into whole pages of highly eccentric syntax, but literally compiling the index of each volume himself. Once or twice he chose the wrong man and long and painful negotiations ensued; once a very dull semi-academic book, *Moll's Hypnotism*, translated by Ellis himself, surprised everyone and achieved the highest sales. For the rest, the Contemporary Science Series is chiefly remarkable in Ellis's writing career for the production of his own volume, *The Criminal*.

Combing the bookshops in the Leicester Square area one day, Ellis picked up a copy of Tarde's *La Criminalité Comparée*, decided that it was worth a shilling, took it home and devoured the book almost at a sitting. There he discovered for the first time the existence of criminal anthropology and the musical name Lombroso. As he read, the determination grew in him to write something in this field himself, and he decided on a book which would examine the nature of the criminal temperament from the anthropological point of view. He plunged in at once, reading widely in three languages, and devising a questionnaire to be sent to prison medical officers throughout the country. A mere handful troubled to reply, but over the next year he accumulated a mass of material and found the undertaking pleasant and satisfactory. The combination of research, writing and anthropological interpretation, appealed to three developing sides of his nature, and with an ease and speed unknown to any other book, he swung into preparation of *The Criminal*. Simultaneously he was at work on a series of essays, to culminate in *The New Spirit*, Tremendous literary activity made him optimistic that these essays might establish his reputation, a dash of confidence to be chastened in the next few years.[22]

Olive Schreiner encouraged him in both books, but a change had overtaken her. The long stretches when nothing but grey clouds blotted out the English sky and the air was damp and raw seemed to aggravate the ravages of asthma and the growing confusions in her own life, and presently she thought of returning to warm, sunny South Africa. They spent a last week in Paris together in March 1889.

Olive Schreiner was a primitive from the deepest caverns of creation, and Ellis found himself more and more in contact with that fury capable of expressing profound experience in savagely spontaneous language. She would stride quite naked into a room where he sat reading, carried on the impetus of a point she was making; talk brilliant heresies in the embalmed correctness of Victorian drawing-rooms; pace the garden, hands clapping over her head, lost in soliloquy; and when deeply moved release a convulsion of words which burst around Ellis, one of the few men who preserved his composure and survived intact.

Evidence given me by Winifred Horrabin, who later questioned Ellis, shows that the possibility of marriage between them was much stronger than anyone knew, but Ellis understood what it might mean with a woman like Olive.[23] Moreover, if they undoubtedly loved one another, Olive's greater love for Karl Pearson made marriage impossible. And now, as Olive suddenly resolved to leave England, they were both deeply distressed. Inevitably any association with such a passionately eccentric creature had led to stormy moments, but they were not all of Olive's making. Sometimes Havelock himself attacked strongly, and Olive wrote in February 1889:[24]

> Don't you pitch into me, Henry Havelock! I'm just learning you to do the damned fine horse! Wish you'd say the things a person wants to hear said about them, when *you* write, not all the things they don't! . . . The worst of this book of mine is that it's so womanly. I think it's the most womanly book that ever was written, and God knows that I've willed it otherwise! . . . I'm singularly well and strong; the dirty food here doesn't seem to do me any harm. . . . Goodbye, my old Harry Boy, the one person that ever quite truly loved me. I shall be glad when you marry, and yet, you know, something will be gone out of my life. . . .

When the time came for them to part he went down to the ship with her. She stood watching him as the sirens sounded and the engines began to throb. He always remembered her, very small and alone, clutching the rail, a look of utter desolation on her dead-white face. She did not wave or try to say anything. His own throat was choking.

Perhaps it was as well that she went when she did. She was rapidly growing into an extraordinary woman, subject to frenzies of denunciation when she seemed almost mad. She once denounced a famous traveller in distinguished company by saying that he had travelled Africa, but unlike Livingstone, had left a 'trail of slime and blood behind'.

In the end she reached a stage where she had no real consciousness of her own contradictions and would invent a whole row of imaginary incidents, as when she spoke of the destruction of a MS. entitled 'Women' which had never existed. But she was quite without humbug. Unreal people, events and places literally existed for her, so vivid did her imagination become, and trance-like states entered areas of her every-day life.

Fortunate as it was that she now went out of Ellis's life, she herself was very unhappy at the thought of leaving England. She said she must come back soon. She was quite unaware that twenty-five years stretched ahead before she would set foot in England for any prolonged period again. Neither did she know that her brilliant talents were to run chaotically to waste in a spendthrift temperament and asthmatic neurosis, one of the most painful spectacles which Havelock Ellis could witness. She was to live for forty years after the publication of *The Story of An African Farm*, without completing another sustained piece of creative work. She was to marry a man vastly different from Ellis who bred sheep and ostriches, was an accomplished athlete and, according to Olive's dubious evidence, could knock down seven men with one fist. But she continued to exchange letters with Havelock over thirty-six years, now beautiful, now explosive and, as the asthma increasingly gripped her, more despairing.

Perhaps, in the end, he never quite escaped this diminutive creature so capable of penetrating the burning core of life, so doomed almost from birth to desperate unhappiness. There were remarkable identities between Olive Schreiner and the woman who became Ellis's wife. Indeed it is possible to see the three most important women in his life as incarnations of Olive, each sustaining far too much of her eccentric heritage. And perhaps behind the complications that arose, lay the ghost of his mother.

Chapter 5

Meets his wife-to-be

One autumn day in 1887 a small, vivacious member of the Fellowship of the New Life noticed a newcomer on one of their country rambles, who aroused her interest because of his uncouth clothes. She inquired about him and with some pride another member of the Fellowship revealed that his name was Havelock Ellis. He introduced them and they fell into desultory talk. Walking side by side, each shyly observed the other, but Ellis did not like Edith Lees very much at this first meeting. He found something distasteful in this short, blue-eyed, over-energetic person, and not even her rich, musical voice could compensate for these first impressions.[1] Their walk took them towards a small church and as they opened the door and found it empty a wild impulse seized Ellis to pull the bell-rope and set the bell ringing. Edith Lees was annoyed by what she regarded as a piece of uncalled-for vulgarity. Their walk drifted to an end, they parted, and it could hardly be said that success had attended their first attempts to know one another.

Several years passed. Occasionally they met at New Life Fellowship meetings, once they recalled the prank he had played in the little church, once they exchanged a few bantering words which swiftly faded from their minds. The purest accident finally brought them together again. In July 1890 Edith Lees went down to Cornwall, a county to become dominant for much of her life, and Ellis simultaneously set out as a fledgling doctor to fulfil a *locum* for a doctor who practised in Truro. He intended to leave Truro at the end of a week to visit a friend he had not seen for some time, Agnes Jones, who owned a house in one of the most wild and beautiful spots in Cornwall, Lamorna. Unknown to him, Edith Lees and her servant-companion Ellen Taylor left Penzance and approached Lamorna on the very day Ellis was due to arrive. Precisely what followed has been the subject of considerable romantic speculation. The facts are these.

When they arrived, Edith Lees and Ellen Taylor were pressed by Miss Jones to stay with her, and they were busy settling into their room when

Miss Jones said that another guest would be arriving very shortly. Who was it, Edith asked, and heard the answer – Havelock Ellis – with mixed feelings. By now she had not only met Ellis in person several times, but had read and liked some of his writings. There seemed every reason why his arrival should not prove hopelessly uncongenial, yet eccentricities in her character permitted the memory of his ill-fitting suit and the momentary indiscretion with the bell, to overwhelm the deeper impression left by his work. For a time she thought of rejecting Miss Jones's hospitality and setting out afresh for a town on the coast. By another small detail which might, in all seriousness, have left Edith Lees unknown to Havelock Ellis – thus preserving the serenity of his life – Edith was persuaded to stay for no more impressive reason than that Ellen Taylor's feet were blistered. They stayed, and the tiny accident of the blistered feet was the starting point of a dramatic divergence in Ellis's life.

Towards half past five in the afternoon, the two women observed a man approaching the house incongruously wearing a tall hat – part of the professional regalia of the doctor of the day – and clothes which, Edith once again regarded as distinctly ragged. This meeting proved more fruitful than the earlier ones, and Edith's undoubted gift for establishing swift contact with people rendered the evening reasonably pleasant. The following day, Miss Jones and Ellis set out with Edith and Ellen for the first part of their journey to Penzance, and presently wished them God-speed and turned back. Ellis watched Edith's knapsack disappearing over the brow of the hill without any marked regret.

Superstitious people will be interested to know that 13 August was the date which first brought these two so opposite people together, but now the sense of unseen powers conspiring to enmesh them persisted as coincidence intervened to bring them together again. On the spur of the moment Ellis had decided to visit St Ives and was idling, enchanted, along a narrow alley overhung by ancient cottages, when he suddenly heard a rush of feet behind him, and then that voice, whose beauty was to haunt him all his days, broke into a babble of greeting. Edith Lees had seen him pass the cobbler's shop where her shoes were under repair, and had rushed out of the shop, down the road, after him. Some deeply unconscious motive may have driven Ellis to remember St Ives as part of Edith's itinerary, and taken him there as if by accident, but whatever mechanism governed this freshly fortuitous moment, they found, on the third meeting, a warmth not evident before.

While poor Miss Taylor was left to trail in silence behind them, they walked on together, Edith rapidly plunging into animated conversation, and Ellis becoming aware of a new quality in her. She possessed an overpowering spontaneity which swept aside his shyness more swiftly than anyone he had known. They remained together until they reached

Hayle Ferry, and became familiar for the first time with a name which was to head innumerable letters in future years – Carbis Bay. There they shook hands and parted. Edith's sturdy figure climbed into the boat and Ellis watched her cross the ferry. Once more he saw her dwindling away, stick in hand, knapsack rising and falling on her back, but now, for the first time, a small sense of loneliness broke into Ellis's serenity.

It was Edith Lees who took the next initiative and sent a brief letter from Condoldon, a village on her walking tour, chiefly remarkable for the proposal of marriage which she received from a butcher who lived there. The thought occurs that the butcher might have served posterity better by pressing his suit, but it was not to be, and Edith Lees could hardly be blamed for escaping him. Edith's letter invited Ellis to visit her if he ever succeeded in reaching Condoldon. Something persuaded him to keep what was the first trivial sentence or two she had put on paper to him. Edith, too, who destroyed correspondence with an almost morbid speed, made an exception of his reply.

Back in London, Ellis rented a house with his sister Louie, in Paddington, carefully arranging that certain rooms should be isolated for his use. Shortly afterwards, Edith rented a flat in Wigmore Street, and formed the habit of dropping in at No. 9 St Mary's Terrace, protesting that she had only a few minutes to spare and staying a whole hour. Once over the first restraints, her ebullient character broke out completely and fascinated Ellis. Mercurial, continuously in a hurry, she would release a cataract of conversation, suddenly remember the next pressing appointment, and then, like a fiercely animated sprite lately materialized from behind the wall, disappear again.

Presently they booked seats to see one of the racy music-hall shows which were then so popular; then she invited him to tea and supper, and she talked and talked. Sometimes she threw a handful of Christian names into the conversation and left a bewildered Ellis to discover which amongst them this so vital creature referred to when she said – 'But she's the loveliest person I've ever known – you must meet her – I will arrange it – tomorrow – or no – why not this evening – now – for tea!' Edith Lees was, above all, a social being.

Imperceptibly, friendship deepened. They were, from the outset, foils for one another, but some who remember them well, still wonder at the smiling calm with which the graceful Ellis suffered these not negligible intervals when Edith resembled nothing so much as a female bee, never still for a moment and equipped – whenever she chose to use it – with a devastating sting. The day when she suddenly confided in him the details of a previous love affair seemed to him a natural step in a growing and sympathetic comradeship.

Memories of Olive Schreiner were still rich in his mind. A deep nostalgia possessed him whenever an envelope arrived with the big, childish handwriting, and once at least he was moved to tears by a letter unexpectedly received; but Olive, in any serious sense, was gone forever and Edith's day begun.

It was her inability to believe this, which led to difficulties for Edith Lees. She had met Olive Schreiner and said that she liked her, but jealousy intensified as her own relationship with Ellis became more intimate. Soon there was talk of marriage and the ghost of Olive became more obtrusive. Then, at last, love broke into the open and with it fresh trouble. Ellis now wrote a letter to Edith which was rich in all his qualities. It showed sympathetic insight into Edith's problem, but like so many of these early letters, there was a sense of insipidity about it, a lack of virility which, from what he said, clearly had a physical counterpart. The letter was dated June 1891. 'We have never needed any explanations before, and that has always seemed so beautiful to me, that we seemed to understand instinctively. . . .' There was no need to be jealous of Olive Schreiner – 'it is true enough that for years, to be married to her seemed to me the one thing in the world that I longed for, but that is years ago. We are sweet friends now and always will be. . . .' Olive had not loved him enough to 'make the deepest human relationship possible'.[2]

He went on to explain that his relationship with Olive lacked the 'deep, mutual understanding' which was more important to him than passion. Passion for Olive had been there in some degree, and if it were absent for Edith, she must remember that she too had no passion for him either. As for marriage, he did not think they were suited to its legal complications. There was a union of body and soul which had to be established for years before people should consider accepting a life-long legal tie. But he loved her very deeply, and even his relationship with Olive had not seemed so beautiful and unalloyed as this relationship with her.

Edith treasured this and his next letter, and kept both of them all her life. Slowly correspondence between them increased and became more intense. Extravagant pictures have been drawn of the frictions which developed between Olive Schreiner, Edith Lees and Havelock Ellis and they need some examination in the light of facts unknown to the outer world. Vera Buchanan-Gould pieced together, in her interesting biography of Olive Schreiner, evidence to show that Olive's story, *A Policy in Favour of Protection*, disguised an interview which Edith Ellis had with Olive, in which she declared her love for Havelock, and more or less pleaded with her to abdicate. 'It seems likely,' she says, 'that the rift in the friendship between Olive and Ellis dates from 1887, the year in which Ellis met Edith Lees.'[3]

What Miss Buchanan-Gould did not know when she wrote her book was that Olive had fallen hopelessly in love with Karl Pearson. Her rift with Ellis was clearly due to her consuming love for Pearson, not to any jealousy of Edith. Yet the interview Miss Buchanan-Gould divined

68

probably took place and if it did, it concerned another younger person, who had become infatuated with Ellis, and was destined to play a considerable part in the story which followed.[4]

Edith Lees was now living at 29 Doughty Street, London, with a number of members of the New Life Fellowship group who were experimenting in communal living of a very restrained kind, and at this stage did not know the full emotional complications of Ellis's life. Genuine and eccentric characters came and went at Fellowship House: some like the Russian anarchist Frey quite saintly in their devotion to the cause; many like Captain Pfoundes drifting in Quixotic mists; and a few like Ramsay MacDonald destined to become towering figures in British public life. A number of Fabians attended the Fellowship meetings, but only one, later to become Lord Olivier, found any real sympathy with its principles. Edith Lees came to know Ramsay MacDonald quite well, but they were no more than passing acquaintances, and it was Havelock Ellis who mattered.

Presently Havelock set off on a brief holiday once more to Miss Jones's house in Lamorna. Miss Jones had gone away and left the house to Ellis and her housekeeper and now it was arranged that Edith should join him as soon as possible.

While waiting for her at Lamorna, he wrote one of those sweetly childish letters which delighted Edith and revealed the romantic streak in his nature. They were, in a way, remarkable letters, and it was as if he would not, or could not, commit himself emotionally. He had, he wrote[5]

taken a little house (rent free) made of granite and honeysuckle . . . the pillars of it are two huge foxglove stems. . . . I've got room in my house for a little wife – but she must be small – I've also got a nest in the rock right over the sea – and a very, very tiny sweet bird might nestle in close beside me there.

Edith reached Lamorna on 18 July. Years later, turning back over their life together, this moment stood out with a sacramental quality. It was to them more than a honeymoon. Forty years afterwards Ellis wrote of Lamorna in one of those simple sentences he could so effectively command: 'It is much changed now, but for me the wild beauty of that bridal place can never be changed.

His first important book, *The New Spirit*, appeared in 1890 and there at once arose a babble of protest which brought his name into that quickly forgotten prominence which accompanies the publication of any widely reviewed work.

What did the book in fact say? In the broadest possible terms *The New Spirit* was to be found in 'that scientific activity which centred around Newton', and had such profound influences in the French

Revolution. Darwin, a giant in the 'great and growing' tradition, had produced a 'conception of evolution' which 'penetrated every department of organic science'. 'Darwin, personally, to whom belongs the chief place of honour in the triumph of a movement which began with Aristotle, has been a transforming power by virtue of his method and spirit. . . .' This spirit was spontaneously spreading into ever new fields with the growth of sciences intimately bound up with the nature of man. Psychology, sociology, anthropology and that bristling child of an aged father, political economy, were slowly emerging from a jungle of hostility and suspicion. 'This devotion to truth, this instinctive search after the causes of things, has become what may be called a new faith.' Epitomized in T. H. Huxley, the faith admitted the same patience and humility as Christianity, without its myth and make-believe, substituting research into the causes of things for a faith in their divine origin. Ellis challengingly echoed Huxley's credo, with that ring of conviction which distinguished exactly opposite statements from religious leaders of the time:[6]

> To promote the increase of natural knowledge and to forward the application of scientific methods of investigation to all the problems of life to the best of my ability, in the conviction, which has grown with my growth and strengthened with my strength, that there is no alleviation for the sufferings of mankind except veracity of thought and of action, and the resolute facing of the world as it is, when the garment of make-believe, by which pious hands have hidden its uglier features, is stripped off.

It was possible, in those balmy days of late nineteenth-century England, to register no more than a mild protest against the mechanistic heresies of T. H. Huxley, but when Ellis spoke of the downfall of unrestricted competition, pleaded for fresh organization in industry, boldly saw one cause of war in rampant commercialism, and hinted at sexual allegiances of a remarkable kind, the critics reacted powerfully. Stripping away what one would now regard as inflated language, there were three straightforward elements in *The New Spirit*: the growth of the scientific method, the development of democratic processes aimed at enlightened education and a 'reasonable organisation' of life, and the encouragement of the rise of the Women's Movement.

Perhaps, after all, the attacks on the book which followed were intelligible. In an age when captains of industry were stamping their values into society, brazenly to support social re-organization, trade unions and factory legislation was bad enough, but when Ellis pressed on to anticipate the basis of certain twentieth-century socialist theories, it became outrageous to the complacent Victorian mind.

There are very few things in our daily life which this spirit of social

organisation is not embracing or promising to embrace [he wrote].
The old bugbears of 'State interference' (a real danger under so many
circumstances) vanishes when a community approaches the point at
which the individual himself becomes the State. . . . As it becomes a
State function, commerce will cease to absorb the best energy and
enterprise of the world, and will become merely mechanical.

These were disturbing sentiments to anyone enjoying the privileges of
middle- and upper-class Victorian society, convinced of their timeless-
ness. Ellis spoke in the preface of *The New Spirit* with the voice of a
socialist, but he would have recoiled in distaste from any such
description of what he regarded as his non-political self.

Some passages in *The New Spirit* read ironically today: 'all those who
care for humanity, view with satisfaction the growing influence of Russia
in the East, an influence which, we may reasonably hope, will
overspread the continent. . . .' And Ellis shared that calm, nineteenth-
century optimism which believed that Right would in the end prevail
against the forces of evil when he wrote, 'We may observe the
approaching disappearance of war. . . .'

The book was in some senses hopelessly contradictory. At one
moment it extolled the virtues of the new sciences, and the next
revealed Ellis's deep religious preoccupations, it spoke of the
emancipation of women and showed the dangers of democracy, it
believed enfranchisement to be a necessary part of the new spirit but
said that 'the enfranchised are capable of running in a brainless and
compact mob after any man who is clever enough to gain despotic
power.'

None of this roused the critics quite so much as the chapter on
Whitman. Not even Ellis's belief that there persisted, for all men, a
timeless religious awareness which touched the deepest fibres of our
being, could save him from the scathing comments which this chapter
invited. Whitman, whose significance Ellis considered it hard to
overestimate, Whitman who brought into fresh embodiment the
aspirations of all the others, representing 'for the first time since
Christianity swept over the world, the re-integration, in a sane and
wholehearted form, of the instincts of the entire man . . .', Whitman,
Ellis maintained, was a writer who reconciled mind and body in a new
synthesis, and was quite prepared to enter the dark places of sex.

For irrational disgust, the varying outcome of individual idiosyncracy
[Ellis wrote], there is doubtless still room; it is incalculable, and
cannot be reached. But that rational disgust which was once held to
be common property, has received from science its death-blow. In the
growth of a sense of purity, which Whitman, not alone, has
communicated lies one of chief hopes for morals, as well as for art.

Sex in these terms came close to purity and who, in those repressed days of the late nineteenth century, could acknowledge such a wild paradox?

Written in that crisp, flowing English which he had long sought to master, *The New Spirit* anticipated much of Ellis's literary work, and remains a pleasure to read today. Certain chapters have dated heavily, and there are also times when the prolonged solemnity of the book presaged that humourless treatment of certain extravagances in human behaviour which made later books irritating; but the book remained a considerable feat for its day and age.

The critics did not think so. The full effect of the chorus of condemnation was not apparent to Ellis until his publishers gave him a collection of press cuttings to read one day. There, he came upon extraordinary things. The *Spectator* opened its review with the mysterious comment: 'Mr Havelock Ellis – if "MR" be the proper title, of which we have considerable doubt. . . .' The review then mounted in hostility until it reached the words: 'We cannot imagine anything of which it would be more necessary for human nature to purge itself than the New Spirit of Havelock Ellis.' The *Nation* could not countenance the liberalization of sexual morality implicit in the book and wrote: 'one comes upon remarks that suggest a paean upon sex, scientifically, philosophically and poetically.' The *Dundee Advertiser* was much more blunt:

> On such a writer advice is thrown away, and we only refer to this unpleasant compilation of cool impudence and effrontery to warn our readers against it. We deny that the new spirit of the age has so much of the fleshy element in it as he would have us believe. He enlarges upon the all pervading influence of sex in human affairs in a manner which is more than immodest and verges on pruriency.

Another anonymous reviewer wrote:

> If we are to confess our true feelings, we have to admit that in our view the publication of this book releases a poisonous stream into our culture, a stream deliberately calculated, by its spurious air of coolness and wisdom, to carry away many who would resist the more outspoken cant of the revolutionary. . . . It is a most distasteful book.

The *World* commented: 'A more foolish, unwholesome, perverted piece of sentimental cant we have never wasted our time over. . . .' Oscar Wilde when he came to review the book chose the title – The New Spirit – Not Intoxicating.[7]

There is no very precise record of Ellis's first reactions to the tumult of disapproval. He says, in the preface to the fourth edition of *The New Spirit*, that he 'emerged from' his 'reading dazed and breathless'. In later years he learnt to press on regardless, but even now, in his writing infancy, a resilience springing from sheer depth of intellectual conviction, helped to sustain him. The shock must have remained considerable. Read today, it is difficult to relate much of this vituperation to *The New Spirit*, which broke new ground in the most gentle and persuasive manner.

Not that all was attack. One or two admiring voices broke through, and when, to the surprise of its more savage critics, *The New Spirit* ran into a second edition, at least one eminent critic changed his mind about the book. Perhaps, as Ellis suggested, it was the massive calm of his delivery which made outrageous precept seem, on the surface, wise and acceptable; perhaps it was the method of presenting in a number of men – Diderot, Heine, Whitman, Ibsen, Tolstoy – the new spirit which they epitomized, rallying support at the outset from these famous writers; perhaps too few saw that, by arbitrarily embracing such a galaxy in one book, Ellis did not concentrate a mere portrait gallery, but with subtle selection himself appeared in every picture and with it his philosophy. Whatever the reason, when the question of a second edition arose Messrs Bell were prepared to permit a different publisher to take over the rights without a qualm. A third and fourth edition followed over the years, and by then Messrs Bell had begun to regret their decision.

Fast on the heels of *The New Spirit* came *The Criminal* (1890), a very different, more scientific book, chiefly remarkable for the freshness of some of its conclusions today. There is no need to examine the book in any detail since it is not of great consequence in the sweep of Ellis's work, but anyone concerned for mankind's emergence from those traditions more venerated for their age than enlightenment must sigh to remember that over sixty years ago Havelock Ellis analysed the darker places of crime, and emerged with solutions still fiercely debated today.

In the interests of preserving the stability of the juridical system – one half of it still a confused inheritance from property rights – scientific and psychological evidence was excluded from courts of law, Ellis wrote. He claimed that[8]

> our courts are still pervaded by the barbaric notion of the duel. We arrange a brilliant tournament, and are interested not so much in the investigation of truth as in the question of who will 'win'. . . .
>
> It is entirely opposed to the interests of justice, and therefore of society, that the scientific conclusions in a case should be thrust into a partisan position. Experts will often differ as lawyers often differ, but the lawyer is no more competent to decide on the science of the expert than the expert is competent to decide on the law of the lawyer.

No matter how intelligent the judge, it was not in the interests of justice that he should pronounce on matters requiring specialized knowledge often beyond his competence. Necessarily, he fell into error. It was equally possible for one expert, representing nothing more than his own standpoint, to overwhelm another, representing a 'general body of scientific opinion', and the danger did not diminish with the multiplication of experts. 'Special points involving special knowledge' should, in Ellis's view, be submitted not to one arbitrarily selected expert but to a carefully selected 'commission of experts'. Its verdicts, on such issues, would 'be accepted by the court' subject only to 'an appeal to a supreme medico-legal tribunal'.

The Criminal has now passed into oblivion and certain aspects of the law have changed. There is not today the same emphasis on spectacular duels in court, and expert witnesses receive greater respect.

There remained in *The Criminal* some remarkably contemporaneous statements. All those years ago Ellis was eloquently protesting against the Macnaghten definition of insanity:

> whether a man is insane or not, is largely a matter of definition. Even with the best definition we cannot always be certain whether a given person comes within the definition, but it is still possible to have a bad definition and a good definition. The definition which lawyers in England are compelled to accept is of the former character. . . .

As succinct a statement on the matter as the best lawyers could make today.

The greater part of *The Criminal* did not deal with the nature of justice. Tarde's *La Criminalité Comparée*, which inspired Ellis's book, was not sympathetic to criminal anthropology, but a large part of *The Criminal* examined, on the one hand the cranial and cerebral characteristics of criminals, anomalies of hair, criminal physiognomy, the body and viscera; on the other, it analysed moral insensibility, intelligence, vanity and emotional stability. There were moments when Ellis's passion for statistical correlatives carried him to the verge of the ludicrous – he spoke of the amount of hair in the anus of female prisoners – but the book revealed an encyclopaedic knowledge of criminality gleaned in three languages, and its swift exposition was intelligible to the most obtuse.

The Criminal re-emphasized what was to become one main characteristic of Ellis's scientific approach. His theories of human nature were deeply rooted in the biological origins of human behaviour. Influenced by Lombroso, the Italian writer who analysed the innate nature of criminality, Ellis had some sympathy with the view that crime was an abnormality which could be treated like other illnesses.

With *The New Spirit* launched and *The Criminal* still on the press, Ellis left for Paris in the spring of 1890, travelling with Arthur Symons. Ernest Rhys later wrote of their departure: 'One evening, in the early nineties . . . [Havelock Ellis] asked me to sup with him and his fellow traveller . . . before taking the night train to Paris.' They talked eagerly of the young writers they hoped to see in France . . . 'and they carried with them enviable letters of introduction to several Paris illuminati. . . .'⁹ Ellis was determined to have a long holiday after the strains and stresses of the last two years.

They arrived in Paris as the life of the cafés and boulevards was beginning to brim over in anticipation of summer. Ellis came to it all as a man who had lately lost his mother, qualified in medicine, written two books, loved and lost a woman said to have literary genius, and was now involved in another relationship full of the promise of even greater anguish. Yet the sheer colour and vitality, the intellectual life of the absinthe-ridden haunts of the Left Bank, and the living presence of Verlaine, of Mallarmé and Remy de Gourmont, soon revived his spirits.

With Arthur Symons he stayed for twelve weeks at the Hotel Corneille near the Odeon. His sister Louie arrived from England in the early days, and the three so different people made their way from boulevard to café, café to gallery, extending their excursions into every corner of Paris. Houston Petersen has described the trio:¹⁰

the vivacious little blue-eyed woman strolling about the boulevards and galleries with her tall brother whose dark brown hair, reddish silken beard and golden moustache formed a striking harmony, and the precocious aesthete, Symons, with his delicate chiselled features, transparent complexion and brilliant searching eyes. On one occasion the three of them had cigars for the first time; Ellis threw his away, characteristically, half smoked, while his two companions finished theirs and felt rather ill. . . .

Presently Louie dropped out of the picture. Not merely a sense of holiday but a desire to discover what was happening in French medicine, anthropology and literature had brought Ellis to Paris, and now he went to a number of lectures. Although he met few men of medical note, he attended one evening a demonstration by a man whose name was to become profoundly part of psycho-analytic history. Charcot had, in one sense, inspired Freud, and it was to one of Charcot's demonstrations at the Salpetriere that Ellis now went. Later, he recorded his impression in volume one of the *Studies in the Psychology of Sex*. They were not very favourable.

Ellis and Symons rapidly widened their acquaintance, at first with the help of Mr Dyer, a painter from America, who seemed to know everyone, and later through Madame Darmesteter's salon. There, on one occasion, they had an appointment with the famous H. A. Taine, but confused the hour from nervousness and arrived just in time to see him leave.¹¹ Their meeting with Verlaine was more successful. Charles Morice, a man who had become a spectacular figure in the galleries and

salons of Paris, became the intermediary. It was a hot summer night and
'In the slow French fashion they strolled up the Boulevard Saint Michel
. . . café after café flaring with lights . . . the terraces were crowded
. . . students filled the pavements swarming to and fro with that noisy
pleasant gaiety of the Boul Mich after dark. . . .'[12]

At the corner they reached the François Premier, Morice pushed open
the door, and there was Verlaine, surrounded by young men. At once
he came forward to greet them. 'He was shabbily dressed, without a
collar, a white scarf round his neck, a grey hat pushed back on his head.'
He was 'all gesture: his hands, his arms, his whole body gesture, violent,
sudden, convincing, not French gesture at all'.[13] Morice, flushed with
the excellent dinner Symons and Ellis had provided, effected the
introduction with a flattering elegance which left the two Englishmen
delighted. Verlaine, painted in savage colours by his contemporaries,
and said to be an absinthe-sot, appeared to Ellis in a quite different
light. He found the poet 'very nearly a gentleman' – and certainly his
talk and behaviour proved absorbing. At one point Verlaine spoke with
admiration of Tennyson and Swinburne, and then turned ironically to
the English Sunday – 'so religious', he said and began to pull an
imaginary bell rope.

They called on him three days later at the Hotel du Mines. They were,
as Symons wrote,

> rather late and enquired of the concièrge for Chambre Numero 4. M.
> Verlaine. . . . The woman's face darkened; she evidently had no
> regard for the inhabitant of Chambre No. 4. Non, she said, jerking
> her head away, non. Monsieur is n'est pas ici. Somewhat surprised
> [they] turned away and began to stroll down the boulevard. [They]
> had not gone far before [they] saw him dragging himself along,
> leaning on the arm of the honest-looking shabby little man who
> seemed to look after him.

They greeted one another, and all four went back to the hotel and
climbed the stairs once more.

> The room was small and mean: the few things that were in it were in
> disorder. . . . The little man lit two candles. Verlaine confided to me
> that he had just been getting some money, a rare event with
> him. . . . 'I have got money; I will have pleasure,' he said in the
> difficult accentuated English into which he dropped.[14]

The companion went off to buy a bottle of rum, and ten minutes later,
they were all drinking and talking together. According to Symons,[15]
they

> noticed that he sipped his rum very slowly, often raising the glass half
> way to his lips and holding it there while he finished his

sentence. . . . He was by turns argumentative and explosive; his facial pantomime was more frantic than ever; and now and again he would get up, perhaps to show me his Bible, which he did with great unction . . . assuring me what an excellent book it was, and what a religious man he was himself. 'Je suis Catholique,' he said over and over again, 'mais,' he added fondling the Bible with the hand which did not hold the glass of rum, 'Catholique de moyen age!'

Arthur Symons and Ellis both remembered their meeting with Verlaine far into life, but Symons wrote the best account of it.

It was in Paris that Ellis suddenly received a letter from Olive Schreiner:

I got your journal-letter and liked it. Isn't it curious that I only wish to be with you in Paris? I never feel the least desire to see London again. . . . The only French writers I know for whom I feel sympathy are Renan and George Sand: the others I only admire, I don't like or enjoy. . . .

Ellis was too busy to sustain any lengthy correspondence but he at once replied to Olive. Still in company with Symons he now met Mallarmé, a man whose behaviour and abode contrasted sharply with Verlaine's. If the literary world which Ellis came to know was saturated by the Symbolists, and he regarded Verlaine and Mallarmé highly, someone else now left a deeper impression.

It was Huysmans rather than Verlaine or Mallarmé who remained most powerfully in his memory. A tall, thin person, given to a cultivated brand of civility which could, in its complexity, become stultifying, Ellis met Huysmans several times, and each new encounter deepened the conviction that here was a man who, for sheer personality, was without peer.

Sometimes they met in Huysmans's civil servant office – he was then a government official – and once at a restaurant he drank several aperitifs under the pretext that it would cure his acidity. Ellis later wrote a description of Huysmans which revealed his power to combine music, insight and feeling in one rolling sentence.[16]

If the man of genius is the supremely well-tempered man who yet has working in his constitution a strange ferment which produces on the physical side a certain fragility and on the spiritual side a new creative energy; and if – as I would also say – he is one who, with a temperament which thus freshly blends morbidity and health in hitherto unknown proportions, is set at an angle to the world and mankind at which no man was ever set before, so that he sees everything anew, then I think that genius is well illustrated by Huysmans.

77

Ellis, of course, had resemblances to Huysmans which even included persistent indigestion.

His devotion to Huysmans led to some confusion with the exotic refinements of living for which Huysmans stood. Some considered Huysmans the complete decadent; some thought him personally repulsive. He consorted not merely with men of letters, but also with women of the town, occultists and practitioners of Black Magic; he made an elaborate ritual of attending Black Mass, only to succumb in the end to Roman Catholicism. It was not difficult to misunderstand the delight which Ellis found in Huysmans's personality, for complete acceptance of his way of life. In fact, Ellis recoiled from many of Huysmans's habits.

There were other remarkable men Ellis came to know in Paris in the summer of 1890. It was there that his friendship with Remy de Gourmont began, a friendship destined to last, largely through correspondence, until de Gourmont's death in 1915. The range of Ellis's acquaintances in those brief three months was remarkable for a man constitutionally incapable of normal social life. In truth, his withdrawal became more marked in later years. For the moment, in Paris he approached a state which bordered on the gregarious.

But at last the holiday came to an end. Full of pleasant memories and new vigour, Ellis took the cross-Channel boat and reflected as it left Calais, that the England to which he returned held, for the first time, rich promise. Past his thirtieth year, with two books launched, at least three careers were open to him – literature, medicine and sexology. It was characteristic of him that he found himself involved in all three and professed a mastery of none.

Chapter 6
Marriage to Edith

On 19 December 1891 Edith Lees and Havelock Ellis were married at the Paddington Registry Office. Ellis was thirty-two and Edith thirty. Neither thought ecclesiastical sanctions necessary, but the experience of their friends Dr Aveling and Eleanor Marx, living discreetly in sin, had not encouraged them to try a similar experiment. Ellis went through the marriage ceremony without quailing, repeating the ritual phrases in a voice powerful enough to cause some disquiet to Edith, never quite free from the memory of an authoritarian father. What followed was not surprising to their friends, but to that leviathan of correct behaviour which drowsed happily over the Victorian scene, outrageous. In an age of matrimonial solemnity demanding complete conformity, Havelock Ellis and Edith Lees set the whole motif of their marriage by leaving one another outside the registry office and going their separate ways to different homes. There was no announcement in *The Times*, no elaborate exchange of presents, no previous agreement among relatives. Ellis, indeed, would rather have slipped away quite unnoticed to Paris, whence they had planned to carry through something resembling a honeymoon, but Edith sufficiently acknowledged the social sanctions to arrange, on the afternoon following their marriage, a small gathering which did not deserve the name of a reception, at New Fellowship House, whither Ellis repaired, late enough to escape the worst effusions of her numerous friends. They had resolved upon three vows, two of which would have struck horror into the heart of even the most liberal-minded Victorian. They were to remain economically independent, they were to recognize complete mutual frankness and not to live permanently under the same roof. How these resolves worked out was revealing. On 28 December Ellis wrote to his father saying that he had safely married Edith on the 19th and come to Paris the following day. Edith added a footnote expressing her surprise that Havelock seemed happy.[1]

Immediately, the combination of marriage, Paris and a love able to express itself fully and freely, gave Ellis a wonderful sense of liberation, and presently, sitting beside Edith in the Chatelet Theatre, listening to Beethoven's *Ninth Symphony*, a sudden exaltation overtook him. It was not Edith's love alone which transfigured him. 'In the exaltation of that solemn hymn to Joy my own new personal life seemed to blend harmoniously with the vision of my mission of work in the world. . . .' There was missionary zeal in his words. Ellis remained, throughout his life, as deeply married to his work as to any woman.

Edith plunged excitedly into the life of Paris, delighted with the restaurants, the museums, galleries and people. At the outset they appeared to share similar values, but apparent identities did not go very deep. Despite the romantic gloss carefully drawn over their marriage by biographies written within their lifetime, temperamentally they were aliens. She was intensely social, he almost a recluse; she was full of bursting impulses, he calm and reflective; she delighted to hear the telephone ringing, he convinced that the telephone was one of the more ingenious devices of the devil; she was ever ready to plunge into unpremeditated adventure while he liked to plan activities days ahead; she recoiled from those scientific sureties which Ellis required in any intellectual currency not to be considered counterfeit. At the outset, these differences held the attraction of novelty. They were foils to one another, her ebullience stimulating his calm and his calm giving her the reassurance which she badly needed.

Yet Paris cannot be accounted a complete success. It seems likely that Ellis married Edith in full awareness of the lesbian streak in her make-up which might have ruined any marriage, and would automatically have led him to the first volume of his life's work, *The Studies in the Psychology of Sex*, which dealt with homosexuality.

From talks with Françoise Delisle, who later became his mistress, I understood that he married Edith partly in order to protect the sensitive girl now masquerading as a mature woman; partly for other reasons. Certainly, from what later became clear, any straightforward consummation of their marriage must have been difficult. When the question of children arose, Ellis discovered that he had no irresistible paternal urge and Edith, fully aware of the possible satisfactions of motherhood, was correspondingly evasive. They consulted their Harley Street friend Dr Birch, whose medical insight detected in Edith's psychology, symptoms which, before the question of marrying Ellis arose, forced him to warn her of a number of dangers. At the time, Dr Birch's warnings meant little to Havelock Ellis, confronted by her sturdy, animated and distinctly lovable person. No one could then have foreseen the change which overtook her as the demons in her nature grew steadily more restless. It is also necessary to remember her early beginnings to understand the nature of the appalling confusions which quickly entered their marriage.

Born in 1861, she was the daughter of Samuel Oldham Lees, described by Ellis as a 'landed proprietor' who lived in Newton, Cheshire. His wife, Mary Laetitia Bancroft, also came from Cheshire, but her family was said to have Celtic blood which Ellis thought to be the source of Edith's mercurial nature. Physically a Celt, she disliked the idea of Welsh origins, preferring to think of herself as half Irish, but the other side of her nature came from the solid, slow-speaking Lancashire Lees. An unpleasant accident led to the premature birth of Edith two months before the normal term.[2] Thus, Ellis believed, her hypersensitivity and over-nervousness were the result of a not completely matured organism forced to face the rigours of the world before its natural time, and the streak of arrested infantilism in her nature may have been explicable in those terms.[3]

Within a few months of Edith's birth, her mother suddenly died and the overwrought young girl was left to the mercies of a father who presently became a hypochondriac. The disciplines which ruled her early life were continually reinforced by every form of punishment, and several times she was brutally overwhelmed by sheer physical force and made to submit, crying hysterically, to whatever course of conduct her father considered right. Somewhere in the lop-sided head of Samuel Oldham Lees lay the unshakeable belief that in order to produce in this unruly child the resemblance of a good woman, she must be broken to his will. He never succeeded. Instead Edith became an abnormally high-spirited person, with violent and irrational prejudices towards the male sex which, within a few years, passionately inverted her whole nature.

When her father remarried, his second wife diverted his outbursts against her on to Edith and frequently delivered cutting sneers which at first deeply disturbed her. However, Edith learnt to protect herself by retaliating in kind, and the psychological torments to which she later subjected Ellis probably had their origin in this early conditioning. Given normal love and security she might have become a quite different person and changed Havelock Ellis's life, but deeply hidden psychological motives may have driven him to search out just such a person as she became.

Her early meetings with Havelock Ellis convinced her of his gentleness, his lack of brutality, and it is possible that marriage to such a man was a reassurance against any repetition of her father and mother's abuse. Only one kind of man would she ever risk marrying, she said: he must be sensitive as a woman, poetic in outlook, capable of understanding her infantile moods and quite incapable of physical violence. Just such a man was Havelock Ellis. From his point of view it was all very different. With a dash of cold-bloodedness rare in his writing or make-up, he wrote much later in life: 'At the outset it seemed to me – though never, I think, to her – as possibly only an experiment. It was an experiment to such an extent that to many if not most people it might seem no marriage at all.'

Certainly this was a unique form of marriage. Edith told a close friend in one of those bursts of mischievous confidence which sometimes outran truth. . . . 'On our wedding night, the first thing my husband did was to measure me from head to foot!'[4] A friend who appeared much later in Ellis's life, Janet de Selincourt, told me that they married each other partly in the hope that Ellis would cure her incipient lesbianism.

For several months after their marriage they lived apart from one another, and during the remainder of the time they were sometimes together, sometimes 'not far away' from each other. It was a semi-detached marriage which fulfilled their vow not to face the hazards of daily confrontation.

There were four reasons why they had both embarked on the marriage with some hopes of success. Ellis could not afford to support a wife, and Edith possessed a private income roughly equivalent to his earnings. Indeed as late as January 1893 Ellis was driven – for the last time – to become *locum tenens* to Dr Bonar in Probus, to earn more money. He did not want children and nor did she – at this time. Ellis did not passionately love her, felt sexually insecure and shared her view that sex was not necessarily of paramount importance in marriage. On the other hand his marriage to her seemed odd when one remembered the remark of James Hinton's daughter Margaret. She had been to play the piano for the insane patients in Bethlem Hospital and when asked what they were like she replied 'Like that Miss Lees'.

Certainly their semi-detached relationship preserved a freshness and vivacity in their relationship, but no two such antithetical natures could long survive even the 'freest' association. The insatiable demands of Edith's extrovert nature necessitated, among other things, a constant stream of friends and visitors, who eddied about her in constant talk and gaiety, slowly wearing down even such monumental patience as Ellis possessed. They would burst in, with a slightly false exuberance, to embrace Edith, rush into frothy conversation, and could not be stopped from breaking into the flimsily protected sanctuary where Ellis sat, grappling now with the beginnings of *Man and Woman* and *The Nationalisation of Health*. It was not in his nature to growl and eject them. Nothing of the bear ever appeared in his make-up. He suffered with dropped eyes and a confused smile, and when they had gone painfully made his way back down the corridors of thought to that remote cell from which he only recalled himself with considerable effort. There came a time when the tide of visitors reached a climax. Nothing ever snapped in Havelock. His nearest approximation to an outburst of temper expressed itself in a mild protest. But suddenly, one year after their marriage, in the heat of a midsummer day, he made it.

1 The Young medical student

2 Olive Schreiner in 1879   *3 Olive Schreiner as a young woman*

*4 His wife, Edith Ellis, shortly before
her death*

Instantly Edith girded, turned and attacked him. Every gentle remonstrance of his was matched by vehement retaliation from her. It went far beyond that. She seems to have been thrown – with the same superficial ease as she later recovered her equilibrium – into a state bordering on despair. A few days later came a letter, vibrant with indignation, complaining bitterly of his conduct. The mildest protest had become in her imagination a cruel attack.

It must have been something of a shock to both. Immensely rational and emancipated beings, launched into a way of life unconfused by convention, it was not pleasant to find their utopia subject to upheavals not dissimilar from those which distressed suburbia. For the moment the upheavals were short lived. On the very next day, Edith wrote a letter full of apology and contrition.

It was some measure of the quality of Havelock's personality that he did in the end love her as much for her faults as anything else, and found his feelings deepening not only as the scenes became more frequent, but as quick reconciliations lost something of their validity from sheer repetition. It is difficult to recall any other exercise in marital saintliness to match him. Psychologically it all pointed in one direction – he was a practising masochist of a high order.

It would be a mistake to convey the impression that in all this tumult there were not, in the first two years, stretches of happiness sometimes approaching that marital bliss which Ellis knew to be so elusive. Indeed, a marriage which seemed mistakenly involved with legal ties, an affectionate arrangement in which neither made possessive claims on the other, was destined to grow into a bond of profound proportions. But one woman among Ellis's friends said that she 'saw through' Edith Lees from the beginning. Alice Corthorn disliked Edith intensely and severed her relations with both after their marriage.

In these early days, as if to clarify her own disillusioned view of marriage, Edith wrote a pamphlet, 'A Novitiate for Marriage', which explored a daring analogy between the novitiate nun, undergoing the probationary ordeal to test her sense of vocation for the church, and the young woman embarking on marriage. In this pamphlet she did not intend to propagand for free love. She merely wanted to reaffirm a more rational and enlightened form of marriage. She desired to substitute the deliberate attempt to keep the two parties in sustained ignorance of one another's true nature, by a period of self-discovery capable of assessing their sense of vocation in marriage. It was unfortunate that she chose a nun for her analogy since a nun's preliminary experience was full of the very sexual abstinence which Edith desired to remove.

Overestimating her audience, she had far too many copies printed and when fewer than a hundred were sold, her energetic salesmanship notwithstanding, she was bitterly disappointed. That it sold so few copies and yet was one of the crisper and more lucid documents among her scattered writings, was unfortunate; but then, most of Edith's writing was unfortunate. Her letters alone preserve their value, partly because of their spontaneity, partly because they throw such shattering light on her relations with Havelock. It seems for instance that some sort of physical intimacy must have taken place during their pre-marital visit to Lamorna, because a letter written a year later said: 'I was shy and frightened and cried over my wee babe that was never to be. . . .' Against all her emancipation she obviously desired a child at the time and indeed she was never entirely free from what Ellis solemnly referred to as the maternal impulse.

In April of 1894 Ellis went off alone to Italy for a holiday. The sun shone in a cloudless sky, the hotels were excellent and everything ran smoothly. He made his way to Rome where a great International Medical Congress had begun and there Lombroso – impressed by his book *The Criminal* – called to pay his respects. In Roman medical circles Ellis had already achieved a certain distinction, and now he quickly became one of the Secretaries of the Psychiatric Section which included men like Marro, Kurella and Ferri. But Rome, unfolding every morning in steady sunshine, Rome with its ancient buildings, museums and wealth of history, drew him away from the Medical Congress, and there were times when his secretarial duties suffered as he wandered, ecstatically lost, through one street after another, and gave himself up to a past vividly evoked by names, signs and monuments. When, at last, he broke away from Rome, inevitably it was with deep regret. From Rome he made his way to Naples and presently found himself walking through Pompeii, re-living once more the horror and beauty of the past with that special imaginative capacity which sometimes made living a doubly painful process. Returning via Venice he experienced a special pleasure in stepping from a stuffy train into a waiting gondola, the property of an Englishman, Horatio Brown, a close friend of J. A. Symonds. Lying back on beautifully embroidered cushions, they talked easily, lazily, as the gondola glided through the Venetian canals towards Brown's villa on the Zattere. Momentarily England seemed flat and uninspiring, and Edith Ellis very remote.

Within the joys and sorrows of the first year of his marriage, Ellis continued writing, and completed *The Nationalisation of Health* which appeared in 1892. In direct line of descent from *The Criminal*, it was swarming with little-known facts about international health services and anticipated some of the conclusions of Aneurin Bevan.

I have . . . urged [wrote Ellis], that the present time is peculiarly favourable for taking in hand seriously the organisation and socialisation of the elementary conditions of health. We have long left this primary duty to the spasmodic and confused action of

charities, and to the interested action of individuals and
corporations. . . .

If the year 1892 was favourable, another fifty-five years were to pass
before the House of Commons carried out the ideas foreshadowed by
Havelock Ellis in his book.

Until 1947, *The Nationalisation of Health* remained a very relevant
document. Only then were many of its ideas implemented. Ellis
discussed the establishment of a Ministry of Health, saw the advantages
of a chain of Health Institutes, thought that the dentists should be
brought into a State scheme at a time when they were considered an
inviolable stronghold of individualism, and wrote:[5]

> We scatter medical men across country and town, giving them
> perhaps a dispensary with a miscellaneous assortment of drugs and a
> few instruments (sometimes so old that the possessor cannot use
> them, or so new that he does not know how to use them) and we
> expect from him, and even feel that we are entitled to expect from
> him, all the skill and resource of a fully equipped hospital. . . .

But *The Nationalisation of Health* was less important than another
book upon which he worked simultaneously – *Man and Woman*. Not
published until 1894, the book had roots extending back over twelve
years. Developing from *The Criminal* and *The Nationalisation of
Health*, the growth of the most important of his anthropological themes
reached its first maturity and conveyed a new sense of confidence in *Man
and Woman*.

> A leading aim in this book . . . [Ellis wrote in the preface] was the
> consideration of the question how far sexual differences are artificial,
> the result of tradition and environment, and how far they are really
> rooted in the actual constitution of the male and female organisms.

Microscopic research subsequently removed this question from the plane
on which Ellis discussed it. Investigation of intermediate sexual types in
the chocolate moth and the fruit fly revolutionized the view held then
of the work performed by chromosomes, but the range of Ellis's inquiry,
from the growth and proportion of the pelvis, the head, viscera and
hands, to the intellectual impulse, metabolism and morbid psychic
phenomena, revealed an encyclopaedic compression of technical
knowledge, and developed revealing comparisons between male and
female. If no one could question its scientific character, the crisp
lucidity of its style made it palatable to the average layman. Advancing
role distinctions acceptable to the Victorian frame of mind but not to
the modern women's movement, Ellis said that women's child-bearing
destiny could be deduced from her different 'nature'. Reproductive
organs apart, women were smaller, more emotional, more childlike and,

for some reasons not rigorously thought through, this made them, in his view, more appropriate companions for children. Implicitly *Man and Woman*, in keeping with the mores of the day, said men were designed to make history and women to make children, a relationship which he poetically expressed as being a perfect equipoise. Rooted in the positivist biological approach of the nineteenth century, his analysis would have produced apoplexy in the extremists of the modern women's movement. None the less *Man and Woman* was among the more popular of his writings with six editions launched between 1894 and 1926.

Thorough, lucid and well documented, its reception disappointed Ellis. He always believed that one reason why respectable reviewers who had fought so fiercely over his earlier books now chose to ignore this one, was the frank discussion of menstruation in the book. Iwan Bloch, the German sociologist, described it as a classical work, 'the foundation for all later researches', and whatever strictures the few reviewers produced, in the end it ran into no less than eight editions. *Man and Woman* became the source for more specialized investigations, encouraged Professor Pfitzner to deepen his researches in Strasbourg, and stimulated fresh anthropological inquiry. Anthropology was still a young science and revolutionary advances were destined to be made outstripping Ellis's ideas, but in his day his book fulfilled a need.

Professor Karl Pearson, attacked the book and Ellis wrote a sarcastic riposte in a letter dated October 1897, which said among other things that Pearson's arguments were futile. In December of the same year came another sustained attack on Pearson's criticisms. Ellis had arrived at the conclusion that civilization was the result of mentally and physically 'abnormal' persons. Since he found more men than women fitting that description he drew the dangerous conclusion that civilization derived its inspiration from men. Pearson subjected this to fierce mathematical scrutiny and found it a very dubious doctrine. Whereupon Ellis wrote to say that Karl Pearson's methodology was more effective than his findings. Laboriously exposing a number of minor fallacies Pearson had fallen, Ellis said, into another major one.

Man and Woman led Ellis into his first and only public controversy. Once more it concerned Karl Pearson. Ellis had concluded, in the tradition of Darwin, 'that there is a wider variational tendency in men than in women', and Karl Pearson violently attacked this 'pseudo-scientific superstition'.[6] Ellis disliked polemic. Consistently he avoided public debate for the simple reason that it exhausted nervous energy which, he felt, would better be employed perfecting one's books. It was in fact several years before he brought himself to take up Pearson's challenge in print. In the Appendix to the fourth edition of *Man and Woman* he wrote: 'I think that any one who will take the trouble to follow the elaborate assault with which I have here dealt will agree with

me that it may fairly claim the attention I have bestowed upon it.'
Houston Petersen later wrote:[7]

> He then commented on the misleading precision which the
> mathematician is apt to achieve, when lost in the complexities of
> biological phenomena. Pearson had arbitrarily selected size as the
> only safe criterion of variability, although Ellis had already objected
> to it because of the unequal effect of the pelvis at birth on male and
> female children.

Ellis himself added:

> Professor Pearson's earlier excursions into the biological field were
> chiefly concerned with crabs; in passing from crabs to human beings
> he failed to allow for the fact that human beings do not come into the
> world under the same conditions.

Perhaps this was excusable, he said, in someone who was not a medical
doctor, but Professor Pearson also failed to take sufficient account of
environmental factors, and that was inexcusable. The whole long
appendix in *Man and Woman*, from which these quotations are taken,
was a considerable example of Ellis's powers as a polemicist. Remarkable
in one who denied all aptitude for public argument, it unfolded a
complex and subtle counter attack enlivened by ironic asides and
written in a style which Pearson could not match.

No answer came from Karl Pearson. His silence was not the result of
any inability to produce one, nor was it influenced by the emotional
complications with Olive Schreiner in which he and Ellis had recently
become involved. It was due, very largely, to his interpretation of the
word science. In the strict sense of the word he believed that Ellis could
not be regarded as a scientist, and looked upon his excursions into fields
requiring statistical analysis as those of a not very inspired amateur. In
applied mathematics Pearson was supreme; it seemed to him idiotic to
challenge a man in a language he did not understand, and later his lack
of faith in Ellis drove him to withdraw his *Grammar of Science* from the
Contemporary Science Series.[8]

But *Man and Woman* remained an important book if only because it
led the way to Ellis's major work which was to occupy thirty years of his
life, involve him in calumny and the public courts and take him into
fields as yet undreamed of.

Chapter 7
Studies in sex begin

Wintering together in Cornwall in 1894, Ellis and Edith shared the Cot, a minute cottage near Carbis Bay, but Ellis preferred to write out of doors whenever possible. Edith quickly found him a tiny shack at Hawkes Point, a short walking distance from the cottage and overlooking the sea. Once part of an ancient mine working, it was small, primitive, utterly isolated and from Ellis's point of view, ideal. Below him a fine sweep of sands gave on to the sea and St Ives appeared mistily on the horizon. Sometimes he wrote in the shack and sometimes in the broken ruin of a boat, with its bows forming a precarious shelter propped against the hillside. There, in the open air, with stones carefully placed to prevent his papers blowing away, Ellis would sit for hours, working on the mass of material about sexual behaviour he had by now accumulated. Sometimes he surrendered himself to the silence, and that awareness of the singing heart of nature which as he lay there could suffuse and illumine his person with a glow which set words flowing lyrically on paper. Winter after winter, he went daily from the cottage to the boat and wrote, book after book maturing in that half cockle-shell surviving from some fisherman's life at sea.

An early breakfast at eight o'clock, a quick farewell to Edith and he sauntered along the cliffs to the shack, sometimes working for an hour or two, sometimes not stirring from the upturned boat until it was time to go back for the midday meal. Never a man to inconvenience anyone, he was ready to prepare lunch himself and eat it at the shack to avoid causing Edith any trouble. Occasionally husband and wife made their separate ways to St Ives and had lunch together, Ellis returning in the afternoon to the boat and his writing. Every word of many hundreds of thousands he wrote in ink, his writing not easy to decipher, and sometimes in its sprawl showing every sign of spontaneous inspiration. There were times when he paced to and fro outside the shack searching for a phrase, waiting fot that sudden crystallization of half-emerged ideas, and then hurried back to the boat to complete another page.

Sometimes he wrote steadily, easily, with an almost judicial calm; and sometimes, but very rarely, nothing came at all. Whenever he could, he preferred to lie at full length, writing with the aid of a board. Writing, for him, was a considerable athletic feat, but in a long literary life he seldom varied his method.

Running through the steadily rising tide of books, articles, reviews and letters which poured from his pen, one undertaking came to dominate all others. Ellis had lately discovered a strain of homosexuality in several people he knew – John Addington Symonds, Edward Carpenter, and someone even closer to him whose behaviour sometimes puzzled him. The number of his own friends who were homosexual encourages speculation about his own preoccupations with the subject. For the moment, suffice it to say that he came to understand something of the subtleties of the invert mind by everyday familiarity with it. Presently deliberate investigation brought into his hands a mass of new data, and while he continued writing articles for the *Psychological Review* and the *Medico-Legal Journal*, steadily underlying it, the tide of his real vocation rose.

From the winter in Cornwall in 1894, he returned to London to share a flat with Arthur Symons in a beautiful backwater of the Temple, where they sometimes achieved a sense of total seclusion comparable with Ellis's Cornish sanctuary. Symons, at thirty, was considered one of the more inspired forces of the younger generation in that nostalgic, confused *fin de siècle* which had seen Aubrey Beardsley dismissed from the *Yellow Book*, Oscar Wilde imprisoned, Sir William Watson and Mrs Humphry Ward at the height of their powers, and Queen Victoria slowly and elaborately preparing for that most magnificent moment in a life become almost immortal – her Diamond Jubilee. When Symons took over the editorship of the *Savoy*, Ellis became one of his chief contributors among a gallery of names destined to achieve fame in British art and literature – Bernard Shaw, Max Beerbohm, Ernest Dowson, Aubrey Beardsley and Richard Le Gallienne. He wrote for at least six of the eight numbers which appeared before the *Savoy* was banned from the railway bookstalls. Late Victorian morals recoiled from Beardsley, who had dared to illustrate a subject as salacious as Salome and the whole Beardsley school, which began in 1886 with George Moore's *Confessions of a Young Man*, was inescapably French in its origins, embracing a literature not unaware that if the wages of sin were heavy, compensating raptures sometimes arose. Ellis, deeply familiar with French literature, preferred the far more robust and earthy works of Zola, and with Shaw stood in sharp distinction to the Beardsley school. It was Zola who became the subject of Ellis's first essay in the *Savoy*, and if there were biological preoccupations in his novels not to be confused with refinements of sin, Zola was no less anathema to the greater part of Victorian society.

Like Zola, Ellis had no desire to draw a circle around the middle of the human person and speak of everything there as the stomach. Coprolalia, placket holes, the digstive tract, bowels and the elemental impulse of sex, all crept into the essay on Zola and were observed with that disinterested calm of nature which stood outside conventional values.

Ellis knew his Zola well. He had, after all, translated *Germinal* two years before, partly to revive an enfeebled income, and partly to place an unexpurgated work of Zola's on record in the privately printed edition of Toxoira de Mattos. Evocative phrases – 'Zola – a barbarous and explosive name like an anarchist's bomb' – combined with scattered insights in his Zola essay to reveal the literary critic well in his stride. 'In spite of all his blunders, Zola has given the novel new power and directness, a vigour of fibre which was hard indeed to attain, but which, once attained, we may chasten as we will. . . .' To the dismay of those who picked up the *Savoy* under the impression that it was a gastronomic quarterly, Ellis appeared to applaud the disgusting Zola for those very failings which outlawed him from all decent English homes. Where other literary critics were preoccupied with English novels of a very different order, Ellis saw that 'The chief service which Zola has rendered to his fellow-artists and successors, the reason of the immense stimulus he supplies, seems to lie in the proofs he has brought of the latent artistic uses of the rough, neglected details of life. . . .'[1]

Criticism when it came anticipated modern attitudes. If novelists henceforth might find their inspiration in once shunned scenes, they would yet 'remain free to bring to their work the simplicity, precision and inner experience which he [Zola] has never possessed'.[2] Ellis was to look continually for this inner experience in literature.

His *Savoy* essays repeated the device used in *The New Spirit*, personifying the new morality in Nietzsche, Casanova, Zola and Huysmans. Casanova, said to trivialize sex and love, was put forward as an artist in love, a man whose moral code demanded detailed examination:[3]

> his book is a gallery of delightful women, drawn with an art that
> almost recalls his great contemporary, Goethe. . . . For if you would
> find the supreme type of the human animal in the completest
> development of his rankness and cunning, in the very plenitude of
> his most excellent wits, I know not where you may more safely go
> than to the Memoires of the self-enobled Jacques Cassanova Chevalier
> de Seingalt.

Ellis did not necessarily approve of all that Casanova wrote and did. He merely saw him as one fragment of the mosaic of morals worthy of examination. The *Memoires* were far removed from pornography. If literature was to represent life, the dangers of including aspects which approached obscenity were always present; they were dangers to which a number of great authors had readily succumbed. The *Memoires* had many other complex qualities and it was 'as a picture of the manners and customs of the eighteenth century throughout Europe', that they would probably survive. This, in his day, was an original observation.

Ellis's subsequent reading in books regarded as salacious became wide and there were times in the introductions he prepared for Restif de la Bretonne's *Monsieur Nicholas* and half a dozen others, when he mentioned in the same breath far greater authors and invited ridicule. He was more than capable of over-stating his case that these were literature and not pornography. Lamb wrote a more sober and effective justification of Restoration comedy. When Ellis stated that we had lost the orgy and substituted artistic licence, his case seemed sound enough, but he extended this view:

> under the artificial conditions of civilisation the contemplation of life and adventures of the heroically natural man is an exercise with fine spiritual uses. Such literature thus has a moral value; it helps us to live peacefully within the highly specialised routine of civilisation. . . .

When he came to publish his *Savoy* essays under the title 'Affirmations', the essay on Nietzsche was given pride of place. Ellis believed that Nietzsche did for moral philosophy what Zola did for fiction. Anyone so anti-Christian, anyone who attacked the substitutes placed between men and reality, anyone who had so much of the daemon in him, must remain hostile to the English, and only faint echoes of his thunder could survive the intellectual pall surrounding these islands, until Ellis, once again the pioneer interpreter, introduced him in the *Savoy* to a special British public. One of the few men capable of writing at a transcendental level, Ellis described him as

> the modern incarnation of that image of intellectual pride which Marlowe created in Faustus. A man who has certainly stood at the finest summit of modern culture, who has thence made the most determined effort ever made to destroy modern morals, and who now leads a life as near to death as any life outside the grave can be, must needs be a tragic figure. . . .

Like Nietzsche, Ellis launched an attack on modern morals but the word attack was too extravagant. He wanted to reform and re-vitalize morals. There were other similarities of ends and differences of means between Nietzsche and Ellis. It would be difficult to find in Nietzsche any empirical basis comparable with the methods which Ellis was about to employ, but *Thoughts out of Season* appealed to Ellis, and he responded to the idea of a race of supermen capable of leading the world to a new and splendid destiny.

91

He rejected Nietzsche's ruthlessness, he was incapable of venomous attacks on Christianity, he understood the necessity for pity and found at the root of so much confusion and evil that very compassion which Nietzsche hated. But 'However transitory Nietzsche's influence may prove as a philosopher, his place as an artist is assured, for he carried the German language to a new stage of perfection. . . .' And that touched a deepening preoccupation in the still developing personality of Havelock Ellis. In the last resort it was the artist he respected.

Meanwhile the first volume of his life's work was slowly moving towards birth. He continued to develop a vast repository of sexual information from his reading, men and women friends and investigation. This led to trouble with Edith. He began to ask her about her homosexual friends and she felt he was using her private life for his work. Whether by understanding her nature better he hoped to help her, or whether dedication to his subject overrode all niceties is not clear. Elements of both were inextricably mixed. Most helpful among other friends was Edward Carpenter, who provided a number of sexual biographies including a resumé of his own. He wrote:[4]

> For myself, I may say that since my earliest boyhood (eight or nine) it was always one of my own sex, that I thought or dreamed of – generally one of the same age, tho' when young I often felt also a strong passion and worship for some older boy or man. This passion has always been very strong with me, and perpetually present, making a possible romance in each new male acquaintance, and sometimes causing me the keenest anguish and suffering. It was quite congenital, for nothing occurred in my early life to encourage it, everything to discourage it. I was not a boarder at school, and never talked to the boys about such subjects. Home life was in an atmosphere of entire reserve on matters of love. I only knew that my feelings were entirely different from anything I ever heard mentioned at home or at school, and I looked upon myself as an outcast and a monstrosity. I dreamed of friends but I had none. The physical, emotional and spiritual desires have always been, with me, very intimately blended – almost inseparable. I have never contemplated with any *seriousness* a physical satisfaction apart from the psychical; on the other hand a spiritual relationship devoid of *any* degree of the physical has never really held me. I had six sisters mostly older than myself, among whom I grew up – and from whom I early learnt a pretty intimate knowledge of the female mind.

Similar précis, written by Carpenter, were prepared for Ellis, the material including an interview with a male prostitute. It concerned that venerable figure of homosexual humour, the young guardsman, but there was nothing humorous in the account. Deadly serious questions revealed that the guardsman preferred sleeping with women to men, that he didn't mind how his clients 'wanted it', that it gave him no particular pleasure, and that the 'fellows who mostly came to him' were 'swells – regular swells'. Carpenter adds . . . 'probably makes actual pederasty appear more frequent than it is'.[5]

A last document was a letter faithfully copied from the original by Carpenter, which carried a glow of feeling one would expect to find in a young woman desperately in love for the first time. The writer was in fact a working man and the letter addressed to another man.

It would be absurd to take too seriously these fragmentary notes as the real basis of the first volume in the *Studies in the Psychology of Sex*. They were the beginnings which Ellis, with detailed study and careful analysis, transformed into case-book histories. Nothing if not thorough, as the sex studies advanced, one history alone might grow over three or four years before he had organized the data satisfactorily.

However, it has to be said at the outset that Ellis's method was far removed from what would nowadays be regarded as scientific and did not match up to the empirical rigour of Freud. He rarely interviewed the subject of his case-histories in depth, unless they were close personal friends, and prolonged analysis comparable with Freud's did not occur. His material was frequently second-hand written accounts given by the 'patients' themselves without cross-examination and were really a form of literature. Worse still, in order to disguise their identities, details were sometimes deleted and even facts changed in what he regarded as the paramount interests of anonymity. Edith's own case under the cypher Miss H, made no reference to the absolutely crucial factors of the death of her mother and her father's cruelty.

Accident now intervened. It had always been Ellis's intention to proceed from *Man and Woman* to a book which would objectively survey normal sexual behaviour and prepare the ground for less conventional investigation. Now, suddenly, he received a letter from John Addington Symonds which changed his mind.

As early as 1873 Symonds had written *A Problem in Greek Ethics, an Enquiry into the Phenomenon of Sexual Inversion*, but England being England it was not until many years later that ten copies were printed and privately circulated. In 1891 another small book, *A Problem of Modern Ethics*, also appeared privately from Symonds's pen. He found his own strong homosexual impulse 'nobly justified in Greek literature' and suffering as he was from tuberculosis, conceived a plan to write a massive scientific study of the whole homosexual problem before he died. Symonds already knew Ellis as editor of the Contemporary Science Series, and the author of *The New Spirit*. Now the idea of collaborating with Ellis occurred to him and he wrote a long letter to him. As Phyllis Grosskurth commented in her biography of John Addington Symonds:[6] 'Nevertheless their subsequent collaboration was by no means the brain-child of Symonds alone, even though in both *Sexual*

Inversion and *My Life* Ellis creates the impression that all the overtures came from Symonds.' She pointed out that Ellis wrote to Symonds in July 1891, saying that he had heard from his friend Dr Tuke (editor of the *Journal of Mental Science*) that Symonds was working on the relevance of Greek love and morals to modern life. He hoped that they would meet when Symonds came to London.[7] Symonds replied warmly and in the course of his letter expressed the view that repressive legislation directed at homosexuals would never be changed so long as it was based on outdated medical theories. Mrs Grosskurth commented:[8]

> Was Ellis suffering from an old man's lapse of memory or was he anxious to dissociate himself from the notoriety that had persisted in clinging to *Sexual Inversion* when he stated in his autobiography that he had hesitated for over a year before committing himself to the collaboration?

In fact only three or four months elapsed between Symonds's first letter and his final agreement with Ellis. In that time their correspondence multiplied.

Symonds pressed Ellis to include *Sexual Inversion* in the Contemporary Science Series in order to invoke its scientific respectability, but Ellis was wary of risking the reputation of the series.[9] Opposing temperaments conditioned their different approaches to sexual inversion and these had to be reconciled. Symonds was emotionally involved in his subject to a degree which worried Ellis's scientific detachment. Symonds favoured a literary approach which Ellis resisted in his letter of 19 February.[10]

Symonds indignantly rejected Lombroso's theory that homosexuality was either a morbid or perverted condition, whereas Ellis included Lombroso's definition among a number of others. There was no doubt, Ellis maintained that sexual inverts were often neurotic people. Further letters analysed and argued the respective hereditary and environmental factors. Ellis said he did not want to get the emphasis wrong and appear to oppose current thinking among medical psychologists.[11]

Ellis now proposed that he should write the introduction to *Sexual Inversion*, and handle the clinical material while Symonds concentrated on the historical background. Symonds, according to Ellis, protested that Ellis had chosen the most interesting chapters for himself. No hint of this appears in Symonds's letters. Instead, he considered the arrangement very satisfactory.[12]

Symonds now turned over to Ellis a considerable number of documented cases, and Ellis added those entrusted to him by homosexual friends like Edward Carpenter. Hardly launched into full-scale collaboration, Symonds suddenly fell ill and within a few days died. By now doubts had arisen in Ellis's mind. He had come to view Symonds's cases with growing scepticism. However, Ellis consulted Symonds's literary executor, Horatio Brown, and was given permission to use certain material. In Ellis's autobiography he seriously underestimates Symonds's final contribution to the book, although in January 1893, he had written to Symonds that in terms of fresh material Symonds was the main contributor.[13]

In 1896 the first edition of *Sexual Inversion* was at last published, in Germany, under a title of which Ellis disapproved – *Das Konträre Geschlechtsgefühl*. In England Symonds's relatives suddenly panicked, objections were raised and the whole of the first version of *Sexual Inversion* was sold to the Symonds family for them to destroy.[14]

Years later Dr Magnus Hirschfeld wrote that the German edition

> was very important for the homosexual question in Germany. The spirit of this book was so noble and scientific that we have preferred it to Moll's *Contrare Sexualempfindung*. After this time the name of Havelock Ellis was very popular in Germany. The late Iwan Bloch was a very diligent author but not so deep as Havelock Ellis. A sexologist must have brains and heart together. —had brains (not much) Bloch heart, Ellis both together. On account of this we love him.

Two years before the appearance of the English edition of *Sexual Inversion*, Edward Carpenter had published his phamphlet 'Homogenic Love,' the first Anglo-Saxon attempt to bring homosexuality into the open. It too caused a stir. The pamphlet was beginning to reach a wide audience when the arrest of Oscar Wilde threw any attempt to discuss homosexuality sanely into confusion. Publishers carefully combed their lists to remove any mention of 'this horrible perversion'. Fisher Unwin at once refused to continue distributing Carpenter's *Towards Democracy*, and broke his contract to publish *Love's Coming of Age*.

The signs and portents were foreboding enough. The whole story of the struggle in Victorian England to throw off hypocrisy and illumine the dark places of sex was rapidly reaching a climax, but Ellis, as unlike a revolutionary force as any mill-pond, innocently awaiting British publication of *Sexual Inversion*, was quite unaware of the disaster which threatened. Prophetically, Edward Carpenter wrote 'Well done! I have received the German edition this morning. But it will make a sensation when *that* comes out in England – there will be silence in heaven for half and hour. . . .'

Carefully examining the list of possible English publishers, Ellis rejected at least six before his attention focused on Williams and Norgate. They had produced a number of semi-technical works quite unpretentiously and seemed to offer an admirable imprint for *Sexual Inversion*, but when the manuscript eventually arrived in their office, Williams & Norgate passed it to someone who knew Ellis.

Dr Hack Tuke (editor of the *Journal of Mental Science*) was sufficiently emancipated not to be shocked by the exploration of sexually taboo subjects; but confronted with the manuscript of *Sexual Inversion* his Quaker upbringing rebelled against such detailed analysis, and his report to Williams & Norgate was unfavourable. Frankly explaining his attitude to Ellis, he said that the medical mind was so different from the lay mind, and what might not injure one could conceivably harm the other – an attitude commonly adopted by those intellectuals who tried to reconcile emancipation and conformity in the late nineteenth century.

Undismayed, Ellis sent the manuscript to another medical publisher who replied in similar terms – a splendid scientific study but difficult to publish in England. It was F. H. Perrycoste, a scientist of sorts, who then put Ellis in touch with Dr Roland de Villiers, a man said to be concerned with launching a new publishing house which would concentrate on philosophic and scientific works. Perrycoste arranged a meeting between Ellis and de Villiers and presently an agreement was drawn up not only for *Sexual Inversion*, but for a novel Ellis's wife had by now written called *Seaweed*. The advance to be paid seemed reasonable, other books about to be published were reasonably scientific, and everything seemed dignified and normal, until Ellis suddenly discovered that the title of this new publishing house (Wilson & Macmillan) could easily be confused with that of a well-known and existing company whose reputation was irreproachable. Roland de Villiers was persuaded to change this, but his second choice turned out to be even less desirable than the first. It was now to be called the Watford University Press and since no university existed at Watford, the title invoked false academic credentials.

Presently suspicions multiplied. Whenever, with that infinite tact he sometimes misapplied, Ellis inquired about a certain wealthy Mr George Astor Singer, also a hidden force behind the scenes, he was either wintering in the South of France or busy enlightening backward South Americans with one or other of his more cultural books. It transpired that de Villiers managed Mr Singer's London businesses and was a member of the committee of the Legitimation League, an organisation founded to reform the laws of illegitimacy which published a periodical called the *Adult*. He shared a house at Bushy, Herts, with his sister who was – allegedly – Mr Singer's wife, and between them they ran the printing press at Watford. Edward Carpenter quickly warned Ellis that Mrs Singer was not the wife of Mr Singer but of de Villiers himself and referred to her as 'a puckered creole'. Singer himself never materialised in the flesh and seems to have been non-existent.

Presently, *Sexual Inversion* was published in a pleasantly printed volume and advertising strictly limited to specialists of one kind or another. Review copies went in turn to technical journals and not to the lay press. A handful of notices treated the book as a normal scientific production and a small chorus of faint praise made no particular impression on anyone. Honour, it seemed, had been satisfied, and the first child of a multiple birth quietly delivered into the world.

What was it in this book which, six months later, led to such appalling trouble? A brief recapitulation of homosexual writings is necessary to see the prosecution which followed in perspective.

In 1864 Carl Heinrich Ulrichs had apologetically challenged the social sanctions in Germany and written a number of essays about homosexuality which were developed more scientifically by Westphal. Ulrichs, himself inverted, later attempted to change the homosexual laws of Germany unsuccessfully, but Westphal, an eminent professor of psychiatry in Berlin, published in 1870 the detailed history of a young woman sexually inverted and threw open his journal the *Archiv für Psychiatrie* to further cases. 'Westphal perceived that this abnormality was congenital, not acquired, so that it could not be termed vice . . .', Ellis wrote.

In 1882 Krafft-Ebing published *Psychopathia Sexualis*, and became the leading authority recognized throughout the world. He acknowledged two forms of homosexuality. The first appeared spontaneously with the developing sexual life and was 'an abnormal modification of the vita sexualis'. This he regarded as a congenital phenomenon. The second 'develops as a result of special injurious influences working on a sexuality which had at first been normal, and must then be regarded as an acquired phenomenon. On what this mysterious phenomenon, the acquired homosexual instinct may rest, at present entirely escapes exploration and belongs to the regions of hypothesis. . . .'

In 1892 came Baron von Schrenck-Notzing's work *Die Suggestions-Therapie*, which resisted the theory of inborn inversion, and maintained that perversions were usually the result of suggestion, and that they were open to a similar cure. A physician practising hypnosis, he produced a number of cases in point, but his 'cures' had interesting characteristics. It was common for him to take a patient off to a brothel and there to persuade prostitutes to bring to bear all their erotic arts in an effort to achieve heterosexual desire, a method sometimes calculated, with highly sensitive homosexuals, to produce the deepest revulsion.

The term sexual inversion, adopted by Ellis from the French psychologists of the day, meant for him 'The sexual instinct turned by inborn constitutional abnormality towards persons of the same sex', and the phrase 'constitutional abnormality' resolved Ellis's position in a conflict which raged then and continues today. He held a balance between the findings of Krafft-Ebing, who believed that many cases of sexual inversion were inborn, and Schrenck-Notzing, who said that sexual inversion was largely acquired and open to successful treatment. ''There is, as usually happens', Ellis wrote 'truth in both these views. But in as much as those who represent the acquired view often emphatically deny any congenital element, I think we are especially called upon to emphasise this congenital element.'[15] This contradicts the modern Freudian view. Psychoanalysts today tend to share something of Schrenck-Notzing's views, but not his treatment, claiming that homosexuals are often examples of flight from infantile mother fixations, relationships which were normal enough in babyhood, becoming abnormal in adult life. Sexual ambivalence, Ellis argued, persisted in some degree in almost everyone, an element of femininity appearing in the male and masculinity in the female. Many men and women were 'potential homosexuals', but with the majority the impulse did not become overt.

Ellis commented:[16] 'How far the sexual instinct may be said to be undifferentiated in early puberty as regards sex is a little doubtful to me; I should not like to go further than to say that it is comparatively undifferentiated.' Anticipating one of Freud's main hypotheses, he added: 'we must regard the inversion of later life, if it persists, as largely due to arrested development.' Among thirty-three cases – many of which he admitted he had not personally cross-examined – four developed the homosexual impulse in adult life, three having suffered unhappy love affairs with women; in twenty-nine cases 'abnormal' behaviour 'began in early life without reaction to the opposite sex', and in nineteen of these the 'tendency began before puberty'. He found that inversion seemed to re-appear in different members of the same families and that produced what would now be regarded as the extravagant possibility that it could be inherited like many other inborn reactions. In the final revised version of *Sexual Inversion* he distinguished between 'homosexuality' involving any physical-or-sexual relation between the two people of the same sex and 'inversion' which had definite congenital origins. Liberal campaigners of the day tended to believe that inborn homosexuality was inescapable and therefore socially acceptable but acquired homosexuality might be open to cure and therefore not acceptable. Ellis escaped from the morass of moral complications this opened up by concentrating on *congenital* inversion. Another device intellectually dubious today which he employed in *Sexual Inversion* was to emphasize the respectability, distinction and special talents of many homosexuals, with thirty pages devoted to people like Michelangelo, Erasmus, Christopher Marlowe, Francis Bacon and Oscar Wilde. They tended to give the impression of a link between talent and inversion.

Until *Sexual Inversion* appeared, every printed case of homosexuality concerned criminals or madmen, the unimpeachable correctness of Victorian values insisting that anything so horrible must be abnormal if not criminal. Now Ellis revealed its presence in otherwise unblemished people. The first volume of the *Studies in the Psychology of Sex* was not only revolutionary to that extent. It brought a quite different attitude to bear on the whole problem.

Ellis of course was never trained as a psychologist. In the technical sense, it is difficult today to regard him as one. Modern psychologists consider him professionally naïve, and believe he would have benefited from a detailed university course. Perhaps there were times when he was naïve, perhaps his very isolation led him to accept some conclusions which highly trained groups pressing home research would have destroyed; but if their technical virtuosity could overwhelm him, he conveyed a continuous sense of apprehending the whole man, and expressed what he found in language outside the range of the average psychologist. He asked:[17]

> What, then, is the reasonable attitude of society towards the congenital sexual invert? It seems to lie in the avoidance of two extremes. On the one hand, it cannot be expected to tolerate the invert who flouts his perversion in its face and assumes that because he would rather take his pleasure with a soldier or a policeman than with their sisters he is of finer clay than the vulgar herd. On the other, it might well refrain from crushing with undiscerning ignorance beneath a burden of shame the subject of an abnormality which, as we have seen, has not been found incapable of fine uses. Inversion is an aberration from the usual course of nature. But the clash of contending elements which must often mark the history of such a deviation results now and again – by no means infrequently – in nobler activities than those yielded by the vast majority who are born to consume the fruits of the earth. . . . We are bound to protect the helpless members of society against the invert. If we go further, and seek to destroy the invert himself before he has sinned against society, we exceed the warrant of reason, and in so doing we may, perhaps, destroy also those children of the spirit which possess sometimes a greater worth than the children of the flesh.

Against the sombre background of Victorian England such statements were explosive, and not even the grace of his utterance saved him from shattering consequences. It was not desirable, Ellis felt, to attempt to convert a congenital homosexual into 'the mere feeble simulacrum of a normal man'. Far better to enable him to achieve self-respect by an appeal to 'the dignity, temperance, even chastity' of the Greek pederasts. Conceivably if a patient 'is still young and if the perversion does not appear to be deeply rooted', he might respond to treatment given his own willingness to respond. But, 'It is better that a man should be able to make the best of his own strong natural instincts, with all their disadvantages, than that he should be unsexed and perverted, crushed into a position which he has no natural aptitude to occupy.'

The Criminal Law Amendment Act of 1885 which made 'gross indecency' between males, 'however privately committed, a penal offence' was, in that clause, an anachronism, Ellis wrote. Merely the excision of two words 'or private' would bring it within the new and enlightened tradition. Indecency only occurred when those partici-pating considered whatever they were doing indecent, or an observer thought it so. Otherwise indecency did not exist. All this has a contemporary ring. The Wolfenden report of 1957 contained recommendations identical at some points and not far removed at others. Once again Ellis was in advance of his time, and it is difficult today to appreciate the full degree of his courage and daring against the savage sanctions of Victorian society.

However, it was not so much his view of homosexuality which shocked the self-appointed arbiters of the day; it was the detailed case-book histories, revealing the true nature of homosexual habits, and the blameless vacuum in which they were discussed.

Roughtly, volume one covered: The Study of Sexual Inversion, Sexual Inversion in Men, Sexual Inversion in Women, The Nature of Sexual Inversion and The Theory of Sexual Inversion. Serenely detached, Ellis told the story of 'Catharina Margaretha Lincken, who married another woman, with the aid of an artificial male organ. She was condemned to death for sodomy, and executed in 1721, at the age of twenty-seven. . . .'[18]

He explained – for the first time in print in England[19] – the sexual satisfaction a lesbian found

> in tenderly touching, caressing and kissing the loved one's body.
> (There is no cunnilingus, which she regards with abhorrence.) She
> feels more tenderness than passion. There is a high degree of sexual
> erethism when kissing, but orgasm is rare and is produced by lying on
> the friend or by the friend lying on her, without any special
> contact. . . .

Appendix D dealt with the Countess Sarolta Vay a woman born of 'a highly respectable Hungarian family', who lived as a man and indulged in one affair after another with women. A powerful personality, she experienced a compulsion to make love to good-looking women in their middle and late twenties and achieved satisfaction by masturbation or cunnilingus. Précis of this kind misrepresent the far more elaborate accounts which Ellis gave. The case of Countess Sarolta Vay ran to nine pages. Perhaps because he insisted on simple precision, the case-book histories detailed above were not as well written as the conclusions he drew, but they anticipated the findings of many later sexologists. The first volume lacked the crisp pace of later volumes. Ellis was still a long way from perfecting his scientific style.

Moreover, the work as a whole was derivative from Hirchfeld where it dealt with the effect of hormones on sexual differentiation and transvestism. Much less detailed than later volumes, it also suffered from conceptual inadequacies. Stressing as he did that male homosexuals were not effeminate he accepted masculinity in lesbians as frequently characteristic, a dubious position today. Against the findings of modern sexologists he also assumed that dildos were in common use and gave the clitoris a modified role.

The term sexual politics is current today but would never have occurred to Ellis, yet his book was fundamentally a plea for political intervention to change homosexual laws, and modified its aims with tactical cunning to anticipate possible objections.

Today the book would pass unremarked on any bookshelf. In those days it was no use pointing to the continually recurring technical passages describing 'abnormalities' in terms which only a doctor could translate. Volume I remained to the average Victorian mind, obscene.

On 27 May 1898 a disguised detective bought a copy of *Sexual Inversion* from the bookshop owned by George Bedborough. It was the climax to a campaign carefully organized by Chief Inspector Melville, not against Havelock Ellis, whose name meant nothing to him, or George Bedborough the unknown bookseller, but against certain groups of anarchists. George Bedborough was then secretary of the Legitimation League, distinguished by its determination to remove the stigma of illegitimacy and achieve divorce by mutual consent, both flamingly immoral proposals likely to bring fire down upon anyone's head. The publisher of the League's official organ, the *Adult*, was none other than the University Press of Watford, and once again the hand of the ubiquitous Dr Roland de Villiers became apparent. Ellis took no part personally in the activities of the Legitimation League, but it so happened that the League not only included a number of anarchists among its members, but somewhere on its book-shelves, hidden away from the public gaze, were copies of *Sexual Inversion*.

Detective John Sweeney wormed his way into a friendly relationship with George Bedborough for the express purpose of hunting down anarchists and it was quite by accident that his eye fell one day upon a copy of *Sexual Inversion*. Post-haste back to Chief Inspector Melville he went, convinced that here was the very weapon they needed. Chief Inspector Melville agreed, and they proceeded to try to stamp out simultaneously the Legitimation League, its journal and the anarchists by first attacking what was patently an indecent book.

The arrest of Bedborough took pace on 31 May 1898. Ellis received a dramatic telegram in Cornwall telling him what had happened. Badly shaken, he passed the news on to Edith, then staying with a friend, Miss Ellen Dakin, and on 2 June she replied cheerfully, with what Ellis regarded as lion-hearted courage; but when, presently, they met, she was momentarily in tears. She wondered whether this must lead to Havelock's arrest too, and there may have been mixed motives behind her anxiety. Edith hated what had happened to the man she loved, but at this stage she herself regarded this kind of book as 'rather horrid'. She did not desire to abuse or desert Havelock. She loved him dearly and she did many things to try to comfort him. She stayed with him in the worst days which followed, she spoke with happy indifference of the possible consequences and brushed aside, as of no moment, the fact that the publication of her own novel, *Seaweed*, had been overwhelmed in the spectacular troubles of *Sexual Inversion*, but the first seeds of repulsion about his work were sown. In the end she wanted her Havelock to be a great poet and philosopher, not a cold-blooded vivisector of sexual aberration.

Ellis returned to London and consulted a number of lawyers in June 1898. Bedborough, held in gaol for three days, was released on bail of £1,000 and de Villiers, after writing one letter to Ellis, promptly vanished. It quickly became clear that although Ellis was likely to suffer seriously from the case, he proposed taking very little direct action.

Similarly, many distinguished doctors and psychologists were prepared to offer a number of glowing tributes to his work, but not one was ready to risk his reputation as a witness in the case. Someone quite different presently burst into activity behind the scenes. Within a few weeks of Bedborough's dramatic arrest an anarchist of enormous energy, Henry Seymour, formed a Free Press Defence Committee drawn from brilliant and eccentric people like Edward Carpenter, Frank Harris, George Moore, Grant Allen, Frank Podmore, J. M. Robertson and Bernard Shaw. John Sweeney, the detective in charge of the case, described these men as 'a nice little gang of Secularists, Socialists, Anarchists, Free-lovers and others anxious to obtain a little cheap notoriety by defending Ellis's book on principle. . . .'[20]

Bernard Shaw rose in his wrath and wrote to Seymour:[21]

> The prosecution of Mr Bedborough for selling Mr Havelock Ellis's book is a masterpiece of police stupidity and magisterial ignorance. I have read the book carefully, and have no hesitation in saying that its publication was more urgently needed than any other recent treatise with which I am acquainted.
>
> Until it appeared, there was no authoritative scientific book on its subject within the reach of Englishmen . . . who cannot read French and German.
>
> At the same time, Englishmen and Englishwomen are paying rates and taxes for the enforcement of the most abominably superstitious penal laws directed against the morbid idiosyncrasy with which the book deals.
>
> It is almost invariably assumed by ignorant people that this

idiosyncrasy is necessarily associated with the most atrocious depravity of character, and this notion, for which there appears to be absolutely no foundation, is held to justify the infliction of penalties compared to which the punishment of a man who beats his wife to death is a trifle. . . .

I am glad to see, by the names of your committee that a stand is going to be made at last for the right to speak and write truthfully on a subject which every rascal and hypocrite in the country is free to treat falsely and recklessly. It is fortunate that the police have been silly enough to select for their attack a writer whose character stands so high as that of Mr Havelock Ellis; and I have no doubt that if we do our duty in the matter, the prosecution, by ignominiously failing will end by doing more good than harm.

Yours faithfully,

G. Bernard Shaw.

Significantly, no scientist, doctor or psychologist appeared on the committee, and if Seymour compensated to some extent by the gusto with which he threw himself into the fight, no amount of energy could repair the deficiencies of the solicitor selected to represent Bedborough. Perhaps it was inevitable that the League should attract a dubious brand of lawyer, but this one exceeded in shabbiness some of the League's more eccentric members. Unfortunately, everyone had faith in Bedborough's counsel. Mr Horace Avory, presently to become famous as Mr Justice Avory, was a man Ellis believed to be capable of changing the whole course of the case, but in the event he never had a chance. On 9 August Horace Avory tried to have the case removed from the Central Criminal Court to the High Court, on the grounds that *Sexual Inversion* was a 'technical and scientific work entitled to the careful consideration of a superior judge and a special jury'. The application was rejected. Two months now drifted by as the law prepared its elaborate machinery to crush Mr Bedborough and *Sexual Inversion* in one steam-roller thrust. Bedborough was formally indicted by a Grand Jury on 14 September, and the date of the trial fixed for the last day of October. In the fateful interval, Bedborough, eulogized by Henry Seymour and his Freedom Defence Committee as a man falsely made a martyr, underwent a complete change.

Of the versions of what followed, one was given by Havelock Ellis, another by John Sweeney and a third by Calder-Marshall. Whether Bedborough visited the Police Commissioner of his own accord, or received some mysterious summons from Scotland Yard, remains uncertain, but according to Sweeney:[22]

Bedborough countenanced the agitation willingly enough, and probably believed that Dr Ellis intended to give evidence on his behalf. As the trial drew near, however, this misconception ceased. A pamphlet came into our possession, in which Dr Ellis expressed his decision not to defend his own book nor to allow its continued publication. Bedborough's knowledge of this fact caused a breach in his relations with Ellis and his friends. . . .

From Sweeney's point of view, Bedborough's spectacular defection in the next few days was largely his own doing. The glories of martyrdom suddenly diminished when he heard the savage sentence which might be inflicted. He quickly decided to strike what was in the nature of a bargain. The Police Commissioner knew that the delicate implications of the case would be simplified by a plea of guilty, and 'without consulting his lawyers' or the Defence Committee, Bedborough played into the Commissioner's hands and abandoned all pretence to principles in the interests of securing 'the best possible terms for himself'. In exchange for his plea of guilty, it was indicated that he would be dealt with very leniently and might even have the whole case dismissed. This led to Bedborough's solicitor withholding the fee which should have been paid to Horace Avory, and Avory found himself forced, for reasons of professional etiquette, to withdraw from the case. At the last moment, it became appallingly clear to Ellis that Bedborough would not only appear in court without counsel, but would brush aside every other consideration in order to plead guilty. However, his own unwillingness to fight the charges must have seemed no less cowardly to Bedborough. Half the defence Committee was cheering Bedborough on to his splendid martyrdom, secure in the knowledge that they were most unlikely to come within sound of the gaoler's keys.

The trial began on 31 October at the Central Criminal Court of the Old Bailey. The Judge, Sir Charles Hall, was Recorder of London. Mr Matthews appeared for the Prosecution, Mr Tickel was Clerk of Arraigns, and nobody complained when the ill-equipped, intimidated and very contrite Bedborough appeared for himself. Somewhere in a back room Ellis and Edith waited, he apprehensive in case he was called, she bursting to tear Bedborough to pieces. Ellis had now brought his courage to the sticking point of at least waiting in the wings.

Mr Tickel opened the case and George Bedborough at once pleaded guilty on Counts 1, 2 and 3.

Mr Matthews: 'And the rest?'

The Defendant: 'I am not guilty.'

Mr Tickel: 'May the jury go, My lord?'

The Recorder: Yes, if Mr Matthews accepts that plea. Do you accept that plea, Mr Matthews?'

Mr Matthews: 'Yes, my lord: but I shall have something to say with regard to these counts to which he has pleaded.'

Mr Matthews then referred at some length to the third count in the indictment and went on:

104

May I tell your lordship that in the first instance when this prosecution was started it was conceived by those in authority, that the Defendant who is before you, was a chief offender. . . . But, my lord, on examination, I am glad to be able to tell your lordship, he has shown us that we were mistaken in this belief. . . . 'The person really in control' (says the Defendant) 'and the person who had the control of the Watford University Press . . . was a Dr de Villiers.' . . . My lord, Dr de Villiers has absconded. Against Dr de Villiers a warrant has been applied for, and granted, and if Dr de Villiers, who I am told is abroad at his moment, shall venture to return to this country, he may be quite certain that that warrant will be followed by immediate execution. . . .

With such an unequivocal plea of guilty, the case was brief. The Recorder gave judgment within twenty-five minutes.

I am willing to believe that in acting as you did, you might at the first outset perhaps have been gulled into the belief that somebody might say that this was a scientific work. But it is impossible for anybody with a head on his shoulders to open the book without seeing that it is a pretence and a sham, and that it is merely entered into for the purpose of selling this obscene publication. But it has been pointed out to me, as I say, that you have taken a very small part in this, and I am unwilling myself that you should suffer while others go scot-free. . . .

 The sentence of the Court upon you is that you be bound over in your own recognizances, in the sum of £100, to come up for judgment if called upon.

They brought the news to Ellis and Edith. Her indignation ran over. He remained quiet, wordless, resigned. An original and scientific work which was to pioneer new attitudes to sex and morality had been foully abused and brought into false association with publications quite alien to its author's pen; a Police Commissioner's plan to overwhelm a handful of harmless anarchists had unscrupulously become an assault on science. There was no one to raise a public voice against the verdict.

Even Massingham, editor of the *Daily Chronicle*, sympathetic before the trial began, now changed his mind, but the *Lancet* printed a reasonable leader. It was headed: 'The Question of Indecent Literature'. 'What decided us not to notice the book was its method of publication', it said. 'Why was it not published through a house able to take proper measures for introducing it as a scientific book to a scientific audience?'[23] Ellis at once replied. For him the letter was very nearly forceful. He explained the attempts he had made to secure a scientific publisher and the circumstances by which he had fallen in with de Villiers. It was of no avail.

When the trial was over, Ellis found himself as much distressed by the savage self-righteousness revealed beneath the smug Victorian scene, as by any damage to himself, and he immediately returned to Cornwall and plunged into work. What he did not reveal in his autobiography was the underlying truth of Edith's attitude to *Sexual Inversion*, an attitude temporarily suppressed but presently expressed with vehemence. She later told Margaret Sanger, the American birth control propagandist, that it was a worthless and unscientific book.

Immediately after the trial, a Miss Bacon, who had become deeply interested in Ellis's books, offered to help him with the second volume. Capable of taking shorthand at high speed, she encouraged Ellis to dictate a large section of the second volume of the *Studies*. He found the method uncongenial and never used it again, but now it enabled him to accelerate the publication of volume two considerably. It was almost as if, in justification, he was hurrying to repeat the offence he had given.

No one but the gullible Ellis would have offered de Villiers the chance to publish the second volume. He made one condition, that the second volume should appear exclusively abroad. If he had absconded from England – as stated in court – de Villiers was now back and anonymously at work once more. Ellis claimed that since de Villiers had promptly supplied all the 'financial aid needed for the joint representation of himself' and others and given him a free hand to control the defence he felt 'bound to him on this account'. In his naïve way he also referred to the 'suffering' de Villiers had undergone because of 'this book'. When the new German volume was published within a year, under the imprint of the University Press Leipzig, it did not at first arouse Ellis's suspicion, but presently even his gullibility was strained when he discovered, to his horror, that the book could be bought in parts of the British Isles. Ambiguous principles clashed once more. Arthur Calder-Marshall put it in harsher terms:[24] 'What moved Ellis to continue the association with de Villiers when . . . he had been exposed as a crook . . . is impossible to determine. Did the bold author of *Sexual Inversion* lack the moral courage to stand up to the cat-like Rhinelander?' Calder-Marshall developed his attack: 'In *My Life*, Ellis went out of his way to hide what had happened, to telescope time and so confuse events that he emerged with all the glory of a major prophet.' I think this over-states the case. However, an element of rationalisation does run through certain details of Ellis's account, some of which are questionable.

On 14 January 1902 a combined operation concerted by New Scotland Yard and the County Police led a number of officers to a well furnished, expensively rented house called Edenfield, situated in the best residential quarter of Cambridge, to find two extraordinary people posing as Dr Sinclair Roland and Mrs Ella Roland. In the next few minutes one melodramatic incident was piled upon another, and it is interesting to read Sweeney's vivid account:[25]

> Edenfield had been chosen for its security from observation, and its general utility as a hiding-place. There was an elaborate system of cupboards, and at the back there were secret passages by means of which the occupants could hide or escape. On this occasion every precaution had been taken, every exit was blocked, and after Mrs Roland made vain attempts at bluffing and the doctor had tried the secret means of egress only to find it closed and secured, a systematic search was made throughout the house. At length a secret panel was discovered, revealing a passage just large enough to hold one man. At the risk of his life Sergeant Badcock entered stealthily into the dark passage, and flung himself upon a man he found there. Dragged into the light, de Villiers faced his pursuers, a haggard fugitive at bay. Fortunately in the struggle a loaded revolver had been knocked out of his hands, and all his courage fled when the handcuffs were put on. He listened while the warrant was read to him, making no comment. . . . A few minutes later he seemed to develop sudden symptoms of a strange excitement. He called for water. One of the servants of the house ran and filled a glass which was standing on the drawing-room table. De Villiers swallowed a few drops of water which seemed as if it were choking him. A few gasps followed, and he fell dead. The most extraordinary criminal of modern times survived his arrest by about half an hour. . . .

This melodramatic account is full of false colour. The report of the inquest in the *Cambridge Daily News* in 1902 is a much quieter affair. All the flourishes of pistols and poison rings disappear in the verdict of the police surgeon – death by apoplexy. But Ellis at last knew his man. He was in fact George Ferdinand Springmühl von Weissenfeld wanted for years by Scotland Yard.

It was always his nature to trust people even when they abused that trust, and an all-embracing toleration still stopped short of anything resembling bitterness.

Privately published, *A Note on the Bedborough Trial* gave Ellis's personal reactions to one of the most painful episodes in his whole life. It had to be remembered, he wrote, that the act of bringing such a charge was sufficient in itself to damage an author.[26]

> The anxiety and uncertainty produced . . . on a man and on those who belong to him, the risk of loss of friends, the pecuniary damages, the proclamation to the world at large, which has never known and will never know the grounds on which the accusation was made, that an author is to be classed with the purveyors of literary garbage – this

power is put into the hands of any meddlesome member of that sad class against which the gods themselves are powerless. . . .

Arthur Calder-Marshall has a very different view of the whole affair. It transpired that George Bedborough's full name was George Bedborough Higgs, and Calder-Marshall wrote in his *Lewd, Blasphemous and Obscene*: 'Though Higgs confessed he was a coward at the time it was the consistent cowardice of Havelock Ellis at every stage after he had finished his bold book that turned a blow for homosexual freedom into one against it.' Whether it was cowardice or Ellis's consistent horror of public appearances, as we have seen, the Wolfenden Report in 1954 advocated reforms closely similar to those put forward by Ellis, and the Sexual Offences Act of 1967 legally enshrined them.

Three weeks after the Bedborough trial Havelock and Edith left Plymouth en route for Tangier on board an Orient liner. His last note on the Bedborough affair came in his autobiography. The judge involved died suddenly in the prime of life and Ellis commented almost vindictively: 'One might well believe the home truths he could not fail to hear concerning his part in it had struck him to the heart.'

Chapter 8

His wife's lesbian experience

Ellis was now nearly forty. Advancing years, aggravated by the tensions of four months' legal torment, had added grey streaks to his hair and presently he found it necessary to wear glasses. There were other indications of middle age, but in mind and spirit he was at the height of his powers, and those powers were about to undergo a supreme test. It was not only advancing years, the Bedborough trial and the life's work he had just launched, which left their mark on him. Edith also was on the verge of a dramatic metamorphosis. She too had gone grey, and her solid figure had become plumper, but there was still something boyish in her appearance which hinted at deeper wellsprings. Ironically, they first became evident as a result of the resolve not to spend their lives completely together, a resolve which may well have prolonged a sense of honeymoon between them but encouraged the tragedy which followed.

It really began in 1892. Edith had gone to stay in the cottage at Carbis Bay and left Ellis alone in London. Hating isolation herself, she invited to the cottage Claire, a friend of many years' standing, described by one of her relatives as the victim of a curious upbringing, but having far more interesting traits in her character.

There is little documentary evidence of the precise physical relationship between Havelock and Edith, but one witness from the 1950s believes that the clash between Edith's inborn abnormality and Ellis's lack of aggressiveness led to complications which can be variously interpreted. First, that Ellis was not a good lover, lacking that combination of virility and tenderness which Edith desired and, by his lack, unconsciously encouraging her to seek beyond him. Second, that the conflict arose purely and simply by reason of Edith's innately lesbian nature which drove her away from Havelock and undermined whatever confidence he had in his own powers as a lover. A third possibility, according to Hugh de Selincourt, was Havelock Ellis's impotence. Since Hugh de Selincourt did not become a close friend until 1915, his view may have no reference to earlier days, but it was interesting that Edith's lesbianism continued after two years of married life with Ellis.

For the moment, in Cornwall, the aroused and exuberant Edith found herself fatally attracted to Claire and very soon she was writing, with considerable anguish, to her husband, in fulfilment of their vow of mutual frankness. It was a letter which asked for understanding in words full of anxiety, love and a kind of bewilderment. It might have been released to some god-like abstraction lacking the subjective jealousies of any normal husband, but the first shock numbed Ellis in a manner all too human. 'I still vividly recall I restlessly paced up and down my study at Paddington with heart aching. . . .' The classic comi-tragedy, brought to a rare pitch of perfection, was now becoming apparent in the sweep of Ellis's vocation driving him towards a deeper study of sexual abnormality while his wife supremely epitomized the very obscurities he sought to illumine. Others might have found it savagely ironic. Ellis had no sense of irony in these situations. Deeply distressed, when he at last contained his feelings, he sat down on 8 March and wrote a letter full of attempted tolerance. It was typical of several such letters, simple, moving and in one sense false; false because at root he did not feel the way he wrote.[1]

> I read your letter ever so many times. Yes, nothing in the world or out of it will tear you away from my breastbone – unless you want to go. I am perfectly happy that you should be so close to Claire, I feel very tender to her. Give her my sweetest love. . . .

The threat that Claire was drawing Edith away from him recurred over the next few weeks until he began to read increasing detachment into his wife's letters. All efforts to prevent anxiety from entering his own broke down, and at last his pain became evident even to Edith's absorbed and newly enraptured gaze. What followed gave half the key to her erratic and passionately unbalanced character, a character quite capable of needlessly creating pain. Instead of sympathizing with Havelock – she had after all created the conditions which caused him pain – she turned and attacked him. She had fallen in love with another woman and when Havelock suffered, she attacked him for suffering! There remain qualifications. If Ellis married Edith in full awareness of her lesbian nature he should not have been surprised at what had happened.

As he grew older and wiser in the ways of his wife, Ellis came to understand the neurotic element which enabled Edith to twist events in the most maddening way. She summoned this skill to her aid now. He might also have seen that she was driven to angry attack because his suffering made her own guilt clearer. Yet Ellis, having received one blow, promptly accepted with meek apology another, and worse. With that submission which characterized so many sides of his character he shifted the blame back to himself: 'There was no doubt about the suffering I had caused her [he wrote]. 'In that realisation my obsession was dissipated, at once and for ever. I became completely repentant. I showered letters of remorseful tenderness on her by every post.'

If love enabled him to rationalize a false act of contrition, even he, in later letters, was not utterly convinced of his own guilt. Another long letter followed which revealed the philosopher hopelessly struggling to dominate the lover. 'My Sweet Heart, I am so pained at your letter, that I have hurt you so – and when it was only out of love. . . . That letter needn't have pained you so. It only showed that I love you a great deal more than is wise. . . .' 'That letter' was destroyed. Havelock happily believed that Edith only preserved letters which were beautiful. In fact she destroyed any which exposed her own shortcomings in terms too convincing to bear. Certainly some of the correspondence now became highly embarrassing.

The unique aura surrounding two lovers, differing in some subtle way from that of any other two lovers, makes the cold-blooded reproduction of love-letters hazardous and there are moments when such letters become grotesque: 'Love is funny and I am funny. It needs its wifie's little breasties every two hours like a baby, and if they seem far off – it do shriek!' There followed this phrase which put the burden of guilt in the right place with a gentle breath of remonstrance. 'But you know, my love, when the mother hears her baby, and knows that she has that within her to soothe it, she doesn't feel that she must yell too!' Later, the same letter became, for Ellis, very nearly vehement.

That Ellis's inadequacies as a lover had driven Edith into the arms of Claire is possible; but the choice of a woman established Edith as herself 'abnormal'. Edith did in fact complain about his love-making, but it is difficult to know how far it was part of her rich fantasy life, profusely peopled with creations intended to rationalize her own conduct. The evidence occurs in her novel 'Seaweed', which Ellis admitted to be autobiographical. She completed the novel – later called *Kit's Woman* – in 1898, and although the writing has a certain pace, and the theme a daring commensurate with her husband's beliefs, the machinery of the book reveals every sign of the amateur, and it is not surprising that it never achieved a wide sale.

Kit's Woman told the story of a wife married to a miner rendered impotent by an accident. The man sitting crippled in his chair, unable to satisfy his wife and watching jealously every move she makes, could easily symbolize Ellis – as he himself admitted. Whether literary transmutation sharpened deficiencies in love-making into impotence, or whether impotence actually existed, cannot at this point be established beyond question.

Seen in another sense, the book represented the transcendence of spiritual over physical love, the impossibility of one, more than replaced by the other, and if physical love was not impossible between Edith and Havelock, they certainly rose – or more exactly Havelock did – above their conflicts and achieved a devotion which remained unshaken. But presently, he admitted with disarming frankness that 'our marital relationship in the narrow sense was permanently brought to an end.'

At the time *Kit's Woman* was written they both remained highly original personalities in their own right. Edith's considerable gifts for swiftly establishing contact with people, had enriched her life with many 'friends', if they came and went with some facility. There were other sides of her character which dazzled and delighted the unconventional.

> It was her disconcerting frankness, a friend wrote to me, which sometimes spread confusion amid drawing-room amenities. . . . Not that she said things in a spirit of bravado, or with a desire to épater le bourgeois. It was simply that she believed in a direct and unblushing statement of matters usually considered unmentionable in polite society. She never, for a moment, considered the effect her shattering remarks were likely to produce. Nor did she care. With false modesty she had no concern. If her auditors chose to be shocked, that was their own look-out. *She* was all for Adam and Eve simplicities, and had no use for the conventional fig-leaf.

Such unconventionalities enchanted Ellis. Like her husband, she was more than capable of walking round the house naked while certain friends were present, and when she referred to the Holy Ghost some were horrified to find that she meant the male penis. She could be very earthy in her language and sometimes shocked the local clergy by references to God which – but for the matter-of-fact way in which she delivered them – must have seemed deliberate blasphemy. With endearing frankness there were times when she admitted any number of shortcomings, but bursts of such humility were a small part of her nature, and she was much more given to impish improprieties.

Resemblances to Olive Schreiner constantly came up from the past. Olive, who would step from the bath and enter the drawing room quite naked, her eagerness to talk overwhelming her lack of clothes; Olive, who stared fascinated at the agitation of spermatozoa revealed by the microscope, and burst into violent declamation in the most immaculate company. There were not only resemblances. Ellis was the fully-fledged incarnation of Freud's repetition compulsion. It was almost as if he had been conditioned to love only one type of woman, so true to pattern did some of them run. At least three of the most important women in his life were diminutive, behaved with extravagant unconventionality, talked explosively and shared dynamic energy: all three were more than capable of quarrelling, and shared a desperate desire to recapture lost childhoods. Edith concentrated these characteristics more intensively than her counterparts. If writing offers therapeutic treatment to many neurotics, it has, reluctantly, to be recorded that Edith's treatment was a poor shadow of Olive's.

Most of her writing was either published privately or on a limited scale, and she carefully preserved her married name. She could not quite bear all the glory to surround one head.[2] Moreover, as we have seen, she sometimes went out of her way to describe Ellis's sex books disparagingly. And she liked to tell the story of the visitor who saw them working together in the garden and asked a neighbour who they were. 'Mr and Mrs Ellis', the neighbour said, 'they're both writers.'

'Oh,' said the visitor, 'and what do they write?'

'He do write out of other people's books but she do write them out of her own headpiece', was Edith's version of the reply. The first half of the story was probably true; the second came from Edith's imagination.[3]

Where her own work was concerned she did not very much like it when he frankly gave her the criticism she craved, and her writing habits were devastating. There were times when she began at four a.m. still lying in bed with the light on, continued after breakfast and then rushed in to Havelock, saying 'Can I read this to you – *now*?' Having a literary critic, successful writer and philosopher always at her elbow, prepared to expend his fine sensibilities on everything she wrote, was obviously a supreme convenience. If there was no criticism she was cross, if the criticism approached severity she remained cross, and if he praised her work she threw her arms round his neck and said, 'Are you sure it's not just because you love me?'

As a person she was a terrifying mixture of warmth and generosity, bitterness and cruelty, love and hate. It pleased her, when she was ill, to have him wait on every small summons she made, and she would be brusquely rude to him in front of visitors saying, 'Don't worry – it does him good.' This was further rationalized by the explanation that she 'feared he would be injured by adulation or excessive praise, and took a Spartan attitude towards his work.'

Never very happy to be left alone at night, Edith found herself in the summer of 1893, without Claire, isolated in their Haslemere bungalow, and Ellis thought it would be a good idea for Amy to join her there. Amy was the daughter of Ellis's very old friend, Barker Smith, the man he had first come to know in his student days at St Thomas's Hospital. As a young girl she had fallen in love with Ellis but he had kept her at a distance. He now asked her to become a sort of companion to his wife, and this seemed to work admirably until Havelock fulfilled one of his routine visits to Edith, and did not think it necessary for Amy to leave.

She remained, and that was fatal. It is difficult to plead Ellis's blissful simplicity in extenuation of what followed. He became newly aware of Amy as a woman with qualities very different from Edith's, and presently, walking in the country together, he suddenly felt a compulsion to kiss her. At this stage physical relations with Edith were on the verge of collapse and Ellis, who combined a lack of sexual aggression with profound sensuousness, suffered considerably. It was not unnatural that he should be stirred by Amy, but the first kiss lay embalmed as a beautiful memory over many months before he made any fresh move. Meantime he confided in Edith. The vow of mutual frankness was religiously fulfilled throughout a considerable part of their lives, but now it led to recrimination and quarrelling. Reciprocal indulgence on the most refined and limited scale had no place in Edith's thinking. She wanted complete freedom to take, enjoy and possibly sustain any female lover she found irresistible, but when Ellis essayed a single kiss with Amy she flew into hurt and baffled rage. 'But why? Why? Why?' she burst out, pounding up and down the room. 'I do not understand. . . . Claire? . . . Oh but Claire is different. . . .' Some extraordinary twist in her thinking prevented her from getting to grips with the realities of the situation.

This time even Ellis rebelled. The affair with Amy developed partly because Edith's attitude was so unjust. Ellis became almost firm. He quietly insisted on Amy staying the full length of the time arranged. When at last she went, the friction continued. One factor in this episode can be said to excuse Edith's behaviour. She was afraid that Amy might completely undermine her marriage. In fact, Ellis turned to Amy precisely because he knew that she could never supplant Edith in his emotional life.

In the event, the appearance of Amy merely intensified Edith's love of Havelock, if her letters at this time can be taken at their face value. Protestations of love generally increase in proportion to the threat of losing the loved person, and if that person reconciles the role of lover, nurse, protector, philosopher and friend, such a combined threat might drive anyone into abandoned adoration. Certainly her letters now became excruciatingly sentimental. Occasionally she concentrated her feelings in a single evocative sentence: 'I am surged with love of you.' However, within a week of writing these words she had gone to spend a few days with Claire. It is hardly surprising to find Ellis recording towards the end of this period: 'Our marital relationship in the narrow sense was permanently brought to an end.'

Early in 1894, Edith suddenly revealed to Havelock that she had rented a country 'house' called the Count House, which was to become, intermittently, their home over ten years. It stood near the Cot on the Cornish coast of Carbis Bay. Once the 'office' of a near-by mine working, the Count House presented a depressing air of decay with the roof badly in need of repair and a grey cloak of dust over the whole building, but this was minor beside the cost of running the house. A

5 Portrait of Ellis in middle age by Bernard Sleigh

6 Olive Schreiner towards the end of her life

7 Deeply troubled in maturity

curious feature of their mutual vow to remain economically independent had now become evident. Edith, whose income was unearned,
indulged extravagances which frequently threatened her with bank-
ruptcy. The very expensive Count House was partly justified by Edith's
sudden and overwhelming desire to become a 'farmer'. Attached to the
Count House were some fields, a stable and outbuildings, and the
peasant streak in Edith's nature, which loved the smell of horses and
new-ploughed earth, suddenly produced such a boisterous eruption of
joy at the thought of farming the land, that Ellis stifled his misgivings,
and watched her plunge in to transform the broken-down buildings.
She had the gift for stamping her personality on any house or cottage
and now, in a whirl of activity, she swept and cleaned, repaired and
re-furnished, somehow contriving amidst it all, to set moving the
beginnings of a farm. First she bought a cow – Miranda – quickly added
two donkeys, and then, finding Miranda lonely, added two more cows.
Soon there were ducks, pigs, cats and dogs, and only Ellis's gently
restraining hand prevented her from experimenting with far more
formidable animals.

In the early dawn Edith, short, sturdy, gum-booted, strode about her
growing domain and multiplying subjects with a Napoleonic air. She
would happily act as travelling salesman to her many friends, soliciting
orders for parts of a pig about to be killed, and when the butcher
brought the beast to slaughter, chop the 'corpse' – as she called it – into
every variety of shape and size, at first crudely, but later with growing
skill. The profit remained negligible. Chickens, similarly, were
encouraged by every attention to outlay their neighbours, only to
relapse into miserably non-profit making habits.

Simultaneously, the farm extended itself in area. Without consulting
Ellis – she gloriously disregarded him in all those business matters where
his artistic temperament would have rendered him useless, although
common honesty and restraint made him far less dangerous – Edith
rented first one, then another and a third cottage, which, along with the
Cot, were duly let to a whole variety of tenants. A colourful motley of
people occupied the cottages at different times including men of letters
like Somerset Maugham and E. V. Lucas, and far more extravagant
types. In the beginning her 'farm and properties' were not unsuccessful.

Ellis now alternated between the Count House and a new London
home. In 1894 Arthur Symons pressed him to share his flat in the
Temple and Ellis, who had always wanted to live in that beautiful
backwater, was very happy to move. Presently, Amy – the source of so
much trouble with Edith – came to visit him in the two rooms in
Fountain Court, and there began some of the most serene and lovely
evenings of Ellis's life. A fountain played in the courtyard outside, and
a tree, which in summer burgeoned gloriously, spread its beautiful
shade under which they would sit, sometimes with Symons, talking far

115

into the evening while the traffic subsided, dusk came down, and the Middle Temple seemed to Ellis to grow steadily more satisfying. Sometimes Havelock sat alone with Symons, or with Amy: Amy who behaved so differently from the bustling, ebullient Edith, who could sit in gentle grace listening to the fountain, or gaze with adoration at Ellis, while Symons played a Mozart sonata and the notes poured out into the dusk to mingle with the music of the fountain. Here was a peace Ellis had not known in the company of a woman for several years.

Edith's feelings about Amy continued to fluctuate violently. At one time they reached a pitch where she encouraged an experiment in renunciation which proved as useless and confused as its origins were obscure. Whether Edith later pressed Havelock to give up the relationship, or whether Amy, becoming involved with someone else, distressed Havelock, is not clear; but at one point he did determine to end it all. Amy went off to Belgium and temporarily became a nurse and Havelock told Edith that he would write no more letters to her. Within a few weeks the resolve was weakening. As his sense of isolation grew an awful desolation came down on Ellis, and presently Edith relented again and agreed that they might at least write to one another. Once more she set out to make a fresh adjustment to the situation; alas, it did not work. Some sense that this magnificent creature who was her husband, shared the intimacies of his life with another woman, continuously troubled her, and not even the knowledge that she was now – after her sensitive and fastidious fashion – experiencing another affair with another woman, brought her to the sticking point.

She loved him, yes, desperately; her need of him fed on the danger of losing him; but when in 1899 she left Cornwall for a brief spell in London, and the question arose of Amy visiting Havelock from a village near Carbis Bay, he faithfully informed Edith, who at once wrote with that ironic venom which came to the surface whenever she regarded herself as victimized: 'Do cheer up, sweetheart, and if you *must* spoil Carbis Bay for me, why do. . . .'

Yet they never, at this stage, in any serious sense thought of parting. They no longer slept together, but Ellis protested that a deeper emotional and spiritual awareness had taken the place of sex, unaware of the irony of that remark coming from a man who had once insisted that sex was the most important problem of all.

He persisted with the belief that Edith's occasional bitterness and quarrelling was a small part of their warm, loving relationship, but the enigma needs further exploration. For here was Ellis, growing every year more deeply in love with a woman who no longer shared his bed, whose unbalanced behaviour merely increased his adoration, and whose attacks he rationalized in a way which suggested that he almost enjoyed them. Something in this relationship was irreplaceable to him. It was something not altogether explained by the ghost of Olive or his mother, or by the dismay which accompanies an emotional break for those who only grow slowly, over the years, into love of another person, and face, with the collapse of one relationship, a catastrophe of major proportions. Perhaps the boy ridden round the dormitory by another boy still haunted him, a masochistic streak intensifying his love in proportion to the pain caused. Perhaps ghosts of her brutal father haunted Edith, forcing her to attacks on the beautiful Ellis, convinced that she could drive the concealed parental likeness into the open if only she persisted long enough.

Whatever the true cause – and something of its real nature may appear later in this book – they survived many outbursts. Years later Ellis wrote beautifully about a relationship which – whatever else one said about it – was undoubtedly profound. He knew, he said, that

passionate love . . . may continue for ever . . . and stir the heart long years after the woman who inspired it is dead. . . . I know how it is that in old days when they expected to live again they said that love is 'eternal'. I can understand that threefold sigh of joy over a dead lover: 'Amavimus Amamus Amabimus.'

Chapter 9
Sex studies develop

Literary work continued unabated. There were times when the disruptions of his marriage broke into his writing, but always the tide of words recovered itself and crept slowly in again. There were times when writing offered a balm, an escape into a world of certainty where men, events and opinions ceased to fluctuate and answered the commands of his pen. In 1897 the essays on Zola, Nietzsche and Casanova were gathered together with those on Huysmans, St Francis and others, and published in book form under the title *Affirmations* in 1898. The preface explained:

> every man must make his own affirmations. The great questions of life are immortal, only because no one can answer them for his fellows. I claim no general validity for my affirmations. . . . If I can stimulate anyone in the search for his own proper affirmations, he and I may well rest content.

1897 was also the year of the famous mescal experiment. Finding himself alone in his Fountain Court rooms one Good Friday, Ellis decided to carry out an experiment with the drug (*Anhalonium Lewinii*) popularly known as mescal button. Used by the Kiowa Indians in New Mexico, an American had experimented with it in the United States, but no one in Europe. At 3.30 that afternoon Ellis dissolved three mescal buttons and drank them.

> From seven that evening until 3.30 the next morning he dwelt in his own private paradise.[1,2,3] [Before 7.30] the visions had become much distincter, but still quite indescribable, mostly a vast field of golden jewels studded with red and green stones and ever changing and full of delight. And moreover all the air round me seemed at one moment to be flushed with vague perfume – producing with the visions a delicious effect. . . .

'Later [Houston Petersen added] uniformly jewelled flowers and

118

gorgeous insects sprang up. . . .'⁴ Ellis went to bed at 9.40 and did not sleep for some hours. In the morning he rose feeling quite well apart from a slight headache, but not all the paradisal visions or the sense of having entered a world more beautiful than this persuaded him to repeat the experiment. It was important merely as a demonstration of the empirical streak in Ellis, always searching for the evidence of actual experience.

That summer he was invited to the International Medical Congress in Moscow and went with Arthur Symons. He had by now abandoned any idea of setting up as a general practitioner – his last locum occurred in 1894 – but he liked to keep in touch with general medical work and remained a member of the British Medical Association throughout the last fifty years of his life. En route for Moscow he and Symons dropped off at Bayreuth to attend an unforgettable performance of *Parsifal*. A tremendous heatwave unknown for many years held Moscow in a suffocating grip when they arrived and provided an excellent alibi for evading the more exhausting sessions of the Congress in favour of sight-seeing. Many expeditions at last brought Ellis to the monastery of Troitsa where thousands of pilgrims had assembled for the festival of the Assumption. As usual he wrote about it: 'There, at length, within the walls of that monastery fortress on the hill at Sergievo, they fervently kiss the sacred relics, and having been served by the dark-robed, long-haired monks with soup and black bread, they lie down and fall asleep, placid and motionless on all sides'. There were 'stolid great-breasted women of middle age, wrinkled old women decked in their ancient traditional adornments' – a tremendous many-coloured multitude who 'flung themselves down to sleep on the church steps. . . .' It was an 'orgy of a strong, silent, much suffering race, with all the charm of childhood yet upon it, too humane to be ferocious in its energy. . . .'⁵

Back in England he returned to the main stream of his life's work and took up the threads of revising the second volume of the *Studies in the Psychology of Sex*. It finally contained The Evolution of Modesty, The Phenomenon of Sexual Periodicity and Auto-Eroticism. Published in England in 1899, the American edition followed the next year.

When Ellis broke with de Villiers he had arranged for F. A. Davis & Co., already publishers of Krafft-Ebing's *Psychopathia Sexualis*, to produce the second volume of his own *Studies* as the first in America.

In a letter to the author Arthur Calder-Marshall described this as 'a lie'. It was not until 'after the police prosecution of 1899 that Ellis entered into negotiations with F. A. Davis. . . . But even then he did not withdraw his licence from Watford University Press or Leipzig.' However *Sexual Inversion* became the second volume in America in accordance with Ellis's original plan. The second volume in America confusingly carried the preface from the first volume in England, but since it is the key to his whole attitude it is worth quoting at the outset.

> The origin of these Studies dates from many years back. As a youth I
> was faced, as others are, by the problem of sex. Living partly in an
> Australian city where the ways of life were plainly seen, partly in the
> solitude of the bush, I was free both to contemplate and to meditate
> many things. A resolve slowly grew up within me; one main part of
> my life work should be to make clear the problems of sex.

That was more than twenty years ago, he continued, and since then the
resolve had persisted through every major activity.

Deeply launched into publishing the results of his findings, he was
now overwhelmed by the conviction that rather than solve the highly
complicated sexual questions which he posed, he had better limit his
ambitions to a proper definition of them. People argued that his *Studies*
were preoccupied with the abnormal, whereas he tried to plumb – as the
general preface said – not only the forbidden places of sex, but all the
facts he could muster about sexual behaviour and, having revealed
them, to examine them frankly as natural phenomena. He had only one
approach in these matters, he claimed, the approach of scientific
sincerity. His was by no means the first detailed inquiry into sexual
behaviour, but when Catholic theologians like Sanchez wrote their vast
treatises (*De Matrimonio*), he saw it like other Catholic theologians,
from the moral point of view, determining delicate differences between
morality and immorality, venial and mortal sin. Ellis considered that the
theologian brought undesirable preconceptions to the subject, steeped
as he often was in the doctrine of original sin. Considered sexually, man
had to be regarded as 'a naturally social animal', not a victim, of
original sin. Bluntly and boldly he went on to state:[6]

> I do not wish any mistake to be made. I regard sex as the central
> problem of life. And now that the problem of religion has practically
> been settled [sic], and that the problem of labour has at least been
> placed on a practical foundation, the question of sex . . . stands
> before the coming generations as the chief problem for solution. . . .

It was, again, a revolutionary statement in his day. Commonly,
reformers of the late nineteenth century wrapped their intentions in
cloaks of higher morality; Ellis, for the moment, dispensed with all such
pretensions.

Volume one of the first American edition opened with an
investigation into the nature of modesty and what had long been
assumed to be inborn, something intrinsically part of nice young ladies,
was revealed as nothing of the sort. There did not exist any inviolable
essence of modesty. Modesty in women, sprang he believed from a
complex pattern 'when [a woman] is not at that moment of her

generative life at which she desires the male's advances'. It was compounded of many other elements: 'Fear of causing disgust', since sexual and excretory organs coincided, coquetry seeking to allure, magical practices deep in the mists of the past, the conception of women as property and tensions created between the observer and the observed.

Modesty was interpreted in absurdly contradictory terms in different parts of the world. 'It is surprising how a Monbuttu woman of birth can, without the aid of dress, impress others with her dignity and modesty.'[7] Yet many Chinese women were 'as reticent in showing their feet to a man, as a European woman her breasts', and men of the Masai of East Africa 'considered it disreputable to conceal' the penis. Amongst the Eaupas people of the Amazon loincloths were obligatory for men, but women were without clothes of any kind, not understanding shame in relation to lack of clothing. The Naga women of Assam used very little clothing but 'I doubt whether we could excel them in true decency and modesty.'[8] Their belief that the breasts should be covered and nothing else, was based upon the indisputable fact that the breasts grew later and in privacy, whereas other organs were there from the start. Ellis gave seventeen detailed pages of contradictions. Fundamentally, he came to the conclusion that 'The sexual modesty of the female animal is rooted in the sexual periodicity of the female, and is an involuntary expression of the organic fact that the time for love is not now.'

This opening study set the pattern of Ellis's typical method of inquiry. The term modesty was defined, multiple illustrations from an enormous range of literature given, medical knowledge invoked, practical examples examined and carefully limited conclusions drawn. One flaw which distinguished much of Ellis's early work appeared in this study. He took his data too easily at its face value.

Included in the volume was his study of auto-eroticism which caused considerable comment. Already published in the *Alienist and Neurologist* (April 1898), this study defined auto-eroticism as 'The phenomena of spontaneous sexual emotion generated in the absence of an external stimulus proceeding, directly or indirectly, from another person.' Its typical manifestation was orgasm during sleep, erotic daydreams and involuntary emissions. He quoted the case of a woman whose sexual emotions were lost in self-admiration and this 'extreme form of auto-eroticism' Ellis termed narcissus-like. Within a year, his friend Dr Paul Nacke in Leipzig had translated his conclusions and, searching for the German equivalent of narcissus-like, fell back on Narcismus. Ellis later claimed:[9]

I seem responsible for the first generalized description of this psychological attitude, and for the invocation of Narcissus; the 'ism' was appended by Nacke. It seems correct to attribute to me the description of the condition as a normal state with morbid

121

exaggerations, but the *term* should only be attributed to me in association with Nacke. . . .

Freud also believed auto-eroticism to be that 'happy term invented by Havelock Ellis'.

Clearly the invention of terminology is not highly significant, but volume one was remarkable in other respects. In 1893 Breuer and Freud's first preliminary paper 'On the Psychical Mechanism of Hysterical Phenomena' stated that the manifestation of hysteria was not the result of heredity or degeneracy but in many cases of 'Psychic trauma'. Expanded into a book, *Studien über Hysterie*, published in 1895 – one year after *Man and Woman* and one year before *Sexual Inversion* – it made available to the medical world Freud's discoveries and the techniques he practised. In those difficult days when Freud's approach was still under attack, Ellis, in volume one, endorsed some of his conclusions and anticipated others. He endorsed the part played by sexual emotions in hysteria – indeed he traced clear origins of the theory back to a French physician, Charles Lepois, who flourished in 1618[10] – and saw some aspects of art and religion as involuntary manifestations of the sexual impulse. 'It would be easy', he wrote, 'to bring forward a long series of observations, from the most various points of view, to show the wide recognition of this close affinity between the sexual and the religious emotions.'

Starbuck had shown that conversion frequently took place between the ages of puberty and twenty-five. Indisputably 'early religious rites' were often 'sexual and orgiastic'. A wealth of detailed evidence followed from the early Christian Fathers to Spurgeon, who pointedly remarked in one of his sermons that 'by a strange, yet natural law, excess of spirituality [was] next door to sensuality.'[11]

For the moment Ellis did not claim religious sexuality as a discovery, acknowledging the priority of Swift's 'Discourse Concerning the Mechanical Operation of the Spirit': 'Persons of visionary devotion, either men or women, are, in their complexion, of all others the most amorous. For zeal is frequently kindled from the same spark with other fires, and from inflaming brotherly love will proceed to raise that of a gallant. . . .' The passage continues for a whole page, clearly relating orgasm to spiritual practice.

Beyond sexual influences in art and religion, volume one described infantile sexuality. It spoke of 'the practice of thigh rubbing in infants under one year' and quoted J. P. West's report 'of masturbation in very early childhood'.[12] Amongst a group of fifty prostitutes it was found that twenty-eight began masturbation 'between the ages of 6 and 11'.[13] Freud had, of course, anticipated much of this, and the evidence is now commonplace.

Providing some of the sources from which Freud built his postulates, at the outset Ellis did not share what he wrongly regarded as Freud's monosexual view of the universe.[14] From the beginning he misinterpreted Freud's view which, as Ernest Jones insists, was not monistic but dualistic. 'The sexual impulse', Ellis wrote, was not 'the sole root' of human emotions and attitudes, of art or religion. 'In the complex human organism, where all the parts are so many-fibred and so closely interwoven, no great manifestation can be reduced to one single source. But it largely enters into and moulds all of these emotions and aptitudes, and that by virtue of its two most peculiar characteristics. . . .' It was 'the deepest and most volcanic of human impulses', but unlike the nutritive impulse, the only other human impulse with which it could be compared, it could 'to a large extent, be transmuted into a new force capable of the strangest and most various uses. . . .'[15]

Victorian England reacted strongly to volume two. Ellis's opinions on matters like masturbation were considered by the moralists of the day positively libertine, and to suggest that it was far more common than alcoholism a flagrant violation of fact. How could he possibly know? He did in fact know a great deal, but occasionally he saw masturbation as the cause of illnesses now thought to have quite different origins. On the other hand, his evidence in favour of prolonged masturbation amongst the great men he named – Rousseau, Gogol, Goethe and Kierkegaard – has not been undermined.

Volume two was full of references to sexual behaviour which produced revulsion in many Victorians. To point out that 'riding, especially in women, produced sexual excitement and orgasm', that the innocent bicycle was capable of arousing sexual desire, and that 'savages' sometimes considered sexual organs beautiful, was bad enough; but to press on and pronounce that desire in women very often reached its most passionate pitch during menstruation, was not merely outrageous, it was, to that proportion of the lay populace unfamiliar with medical data, horrible.

Even some scientific men were dubious, but one amongst them remained untroubled. Indeed, the more outrageous Ellis's statements appeared, the more this man seemed to applaud. Away in Vienna, still as much an outcast as Ellis, Sigmund Freud was busy developing the refinements of free association. He had just uncovered infantile sexuality and his threat to destroy one more cherished illusion by which the world lived, had met with ferocious resistance. In January 1899 Sigmund Freud wrote to his friend Wilhelm Fliess:[16]

A pleasing thing which I meant to write to you about yesterday is something from [—] Gibraltar, from Mr Havelock Ellis, an author who concerns himself with the subject of sex and is obviously a highly intelligent man, as his paper in the *Alienist and Neurologist* (October, 1898) which deals with the connection between hysteria and sexual life, begins with Plato and ends with Freud, shows. He gives a good deal of credit to the latter, and writes a very intelligent appreciation of *Studies in Hysteria* and later publications. . . .

There were many senses in which Freud and Ellis competed as they strove to penetrate the clouds massed along their common path. It happened with infantile sexuality, with the sexual element in hysteria, art and religion. If the generalities of Ellis were sharpened and brought into a far more disciplined body of thought by Freud, the 'climate' of their sexual thinking was similar. In the end, of course, Freud's main work was based on his own cases; for the moment he took some heed of Ellis. In 1899 Freud was forty-three, his father had died a few years before and his monumental work *Die Traumdeutung* (*The Interpretation of Dreams*), was about to appear. In 1899 Ellis was forty, his father still lived, but two volumes of his life's work *Studies in the Psychology of Sex* were launched and another in process of writing. Each man was aware of, and interested in, the work of the other.

Close on the heels of what was chronologically the second volume of the *Studies in the Psychology of Sex*, came another important essay from Ellis entitled 'The Stuff That Dreams Are Made Of'. It was important because it appeared almost simultaneously with Freud's *Interpretation of Dreams* in 1899, and revealed once more unconscious identities in the paths they pursued.[17]

Intuitively aware that somewhere at the heart of every dream was locked a mystery which might reveal psychological secrets, Ellis had kept a record of many dreams from the days of his medical studies, and now he steadily worked his way through a mass of material, annotating and interpreting. If his view of dreams had points of coincidence with Freud's, their general approach differed widely. The study of dreams, Ellis wrote, 'reveals to us an archaic world of vast emotions and imperfect thoughts', anticipating Freud's principle of the primitive pattern in dream thinking. 'The psychic activities that are awake most intensely are those that sleep most profoundly', was again pure Freud; but there, very largely, coincidence stops, and Ellis, becoming much less clear than Freud, carries less conviction. Ellis could never quite bring himself to believe that every dream, no matter whether it involved pain or distress or sometimes murder, was really a wish fulfilment as Freud maintained. The detailed documentation with which Freud showed that guilt and horror at the dream of murdering one's father might conceal an active desire to carry out the deed, left him unconvinced. Eternally suspicious of the single sovereign principle capable of explaining the universe, Ellis believed that some dreams were wish fulfilments while others had independent explanations.[18] However he did write, 'A wish – and especially a wish for explanation – furnishes the motive force in the elaboration of the impressions and memories present to sleeping consciousness.' Strictly it was 'a *conation*, the movement of an impulse in a particular direction. But it cannot furnish an explanation of the dream itself or reveal its mechanism. It is, if we like, the fuel, but not the engine. That is in the sphere of reason, and though we may often (not always) find the reasoning bad – sometimes wildly or fantastically bad' – it was still, according to Ellis, reasoning.[19]

Ellis explored the correlation between states of stomach disturbance and dreaming, between flatulence and fantasy, terror and pain, and here his evidence was empirical because he suffered from continual and sometimes crippling indigestion himself. Such disturbances could throw a person into a state of agitation, 'a state of agony and terror' in sleep, quite abnormal to waking hours.[20]

> Sleeping consciousness, blindfolded and blundering, a prey to these massive waves from below, and fumbling about desperately for some explanation, jumps at the idea that only the attempt to escape some terrible danger or the guilty consciousness of some awful crime can account for this immense emotional uproar. Thus the dream is diffused by a conviction which the continued emotion serves to support.

As these two men grew into middle age the identity of the path they followed, split and divided, and if until their deaths the basic country they explored remained primarily that of sex, they were to correspond, to exchange papers, to become in a sense friends, but never on many major issues to agree.

There was so much more of the artist in Ellis than Freud. Later they were to discover what irreconcilably different interpretations the word artist held for them in their developing correspondence.

Chapter 10

A typical 'perversion' case

In the first few weeks of 1901, death overtook Queen Victoria, now endowed by the British public with the attributes of immortality. A great shadow, carefully sustained by all the machinery of mourning, moved across the country. An extraordinary age had not abruptly come to an end as some people emotionally proclaimed; the symbol which glowed at its centre had suddenly gone out and left a sense of gloom. On the surface our Victorian forefathers were very much the dummies of a correct and stuffy society, given to immense families, prudery, hypocrisy and humbug, but there were many contradictions. It was a society where wealth and poverty went uncomfortably hand in hand, where Charles Booth estimated that 30 per cent of the inhabitants of London lived in poverty while too many rich and indifferent people regarded their way of life as timeless.[1] The relationship between the sexes was governed by puritanical codes and in reaction the music halls remained vigorously bawdy, but Ellis had already explored some unexpected places and drawn a picture very different from the one conventionally accepted. Within the poverty and wealth, culture and illiteracy, a bigoted belief that the English were a superior people persisted; yet many distinguished Victorians were highly critical of their own time and deeply preoccupied with questionings which still disturbed the 1900s.

Matthew Arnold continued to attack the shoddy values he found in Victorian taste, John Ruskin and William Morris envisaged utopias unmarred by industrial horror, and that most sacred convention, the Family, suffered attack by Samuel Butler:[2]

I believe that more unhappiness comes from this source than from any other – I mean from the attempt to prolong family connection unduly and to make people hang together artificially who would never naturally do so. The mischief among the lower classes is not

great, but among the middle classes, it is killing a large number
daily. And the old people do not really like it much better than the
young.

An embarrassing solemnity too often distinguished the private life of
those intellectual revolutionaries so readily bred by Victorian England,
and few noticed the conflict between public heresies and private
practice. Critical at so many levels, they were prepared to risk censure in
many fields, but morally they presented impeccable façades. As to sex,
publicly they did not mention it, and privately, signs of frustration and
deviation multiplied. Constraint took its toll, driving William Morris
literally to bite the carpet on one occasion, making Ruskin and Carlyle
victims of occasional impotence, and Huxley, Tindall and Bagehot,
sufferers in different ways from headaches, indigestion and similar
maladies.[3] As for Havelock Ellis. . . .

Unsung in the histories of the day, unmentioned even in C. K.
Ensor's *Oxford History of England 1870–1914*, Ellis had several
apparent neuroses from constant indigestion to excessive shyness, and
was later believed by some Freudians to have achieved his own
psycho-analysis by leaving the respectable spheres of intellectual
rebellion and wandering for years in the labyrinth of sex. While his
contemporaries were busy resolving religion, economics and evolution,
Ellis continued to concentrate on sex. Yet Ellis, too, among the great
Victorians, led a life of immense sobriety as he came to the third and
fourth volume of his *Studies in the Psychology of Sex*. The third volume
dealt with the Analysis of the Sexual Impulse, Love and Pain, and the
Sexual Impulse in Woman.

Opening with an analysis of the sexual impulse, volume three pressed
on to produce a modified theory of contrection, tumescence and
detumescence. It showed that sadism and masochism were interrelated,
that the roots of many so-called perversions could be traced back to
instinctual bases, and that the sexual impulse in women was much more
widely diffused than its equivalent in men. Tumescence and
detumescence were defined as the vascular congestion and decongestion
that accompany orgasm and covered the complete process of sexual
arousal and release.

Ellis was among the pioneers of the theory of erogenous zones which
were specially sensitive to sexual stimulation and claimed that whereas
they were diffused over several areas of a woman, in men they were
centralized in the penis, a doctrine open to some qualification today.
Moreover, the conclusions he drew from this were, in modern terms,
unfortunate.

Sex played a very big part in a woman's life Ellis wrote, bigger
perhaps than in men's, because large areas of her body were involved,
and women were thus to a greater extent sexual beings. Then came a

127

statement astonishing in modern liberationist eyes: 'In a certain sense their brains are in their wombs.'

In his desire to overwhelm the old-fashioned doctrine that women were a-sexual beings he overstated his case and it could be argued that his revolutionary attitude helped to pioneer the way for the treatment of women as sexual objects. Nothing would have horrified him more because if anyone genuinely respected womanhood it was Havelock Ellis and one of his main objectives was to acknowledge and enrich their erotic personalities.

From the sexual impulse Ellis turned to love and pain. He was driven by its continual recurrence in the sexual act to accept forms of sado-masochistic cruelty with equanimity. It was only a 'slight counterpoise to that cruelty which has been naturally exerted by the female on the male long even before man began. . . .'[4] The male spider risked his life to impregnate the female and the Queen Bee quietly went her way after intercourse with the male bee, dropping its broken entrails and leaving him to die. Even the butterfly possessed 'a whole armoury of weapons for use in coitus' and in the papilionidae achieved an extraordinary combination of claws, hooks, pikes and knobs.[5] Freud was later to carry analysis of sado-masochistic motive into much more elaborate detail: Ellis, as usual, kept to simple statements. Despite his tolerance of the most contorted sado-masochistic behaviour, Ellis like Freud tended to believe that they were abnormal when they did not finally lead to intercourse but became a self-contained substitute for it.

Appendix B of volume three once more gave a number of personal histories under the title 'The Development of the Sexual Instinct'. They encouraged scepticism amongst Ellis's opponents who argued that half the details were fantasies foisted on him by highly erotic and repressed people. It may be true of some. But even if they were nothing more than fantasies, they represented mental facts and revealed a passionate preoccupation with the events which they described. Most, in any case, were rooted in something more than fantasy.

It is time to take one case typical of many others which illustrates Ellis's method and the aid he gave to casual 'patients', over the years without payment of any kind, beyond pleasure in the work involved. Most of his 'treatment' was without fees and he would not, in Freud's meaning of the term, have considered it 'treatment'. Primarily a natural scientist, he collected evidence and did not practise psycho-therapy, but if in the course of his research he could bring help or enlightenment to anyone he never hesitated to do so. One among the people who came to him for advice was Florrie.[6] She had read one day, in some unspecified journal, an article by Dr Ellis dealing with sexual aberration and like scores of people, wrote to him asking whether the case of a person named Florrie, which she enclosed, would be in any way helpful to him. 'There was no indication that the lady sending the narrative was herself identical with Florrie', Ellis wrote, but he soon saw through the camouflage. He replied to say that all cases interested him, correspondence between them developed, her deception quickly broke down and she revealed herself as by no means the illiterate person which her assumed name might imply. Ellis had a gift for 'naming' his cases in a way which helped to conceal their identities. Florrie was exceptional in choosing her own 'name'; she also had considerable powers of writing and could vividly evoke her case.

> As the outside world sees me, I am just an ordinary normal woman, fond of my people and my husband, and leading a good moral, if somewhat quiet, life. If I have to yield to circumstances in the planning of my life, no one knows it – or cares. . . . I still think, and know, that to love any man is for me to be his slave. It would give me sexual delight, thrills of pleasure, to be ordered about and punished. . . oh! what a woman suffers when she cannot indulge her particular sexual perversity! My brain has become powerless and my physical health lessened. . . .

More exactly Florrie was a woman of thirty-seven, married to a husband who did not satisfy her and obsessed with an elaborate desire for whipping. As a child her father had beaten her severely and memories of these beatings recurred so vividly that she had bought a whip and indulged self-flagellation, with wild erotic day-dreaming.

A correspondence in various newspapers next intervened. Florrie contributed and presently received a letter from a man Ellis referred to as N. She replied, the correspondence became more intimate, and one day N. suggested a secret rendezvous where they might attempt to realize their mutual obsession. Hesitating for several weeks, Florrie at last agreed and N. took her to an hotel, stripped and beat her, first with a cane and then with a thinner and more cruel whip which she specially craved. Commenting vividly about the experience she wrote: 'I wanted it, I craved it, and I got it! It was a terrific relief too, I enjoyed it thoroughly.' She was sufficiently a writer to be able to drop literary graces for direct colloquialisms when she chose and time and again most racily brought alive the anguished joy of her experiences.

There was a stage when her fantasy life became so obsessed with whipping and images of slavery, impossible of satisfaction with a very correct husband, that she began to wonder whether she was altogether sane. The terror of mental disturbance did not overwhelm her fantasies, and then she read Ellis's article and knew that here was someone in whom she could confide.

Several letters passed between them before she decided to visit him. Ellis was now living in Brixton and at the door of his flat her courage quailed. On the point of retreating, a renewed burst of resolution carried her back to knock on his door. Finally, confronted with the

129

handsome presence of Ellis and his reassuring words, she began to relax. Soon after their first meeting the knowledge that she was not alone in her obsession, and the sympathetic insight which Ellis brought to her case, helped dispel her fears of mental unbalance.

But presently 'the obsession came back' with renewed force and reached its height in the menstrual period, until 'she just had to roll on the floor and shiver with longing'. Day-dreams followed of a wildly erotic kind, 'in which she would imagine scenes of women seized by force and held down while men and boys performed coitus. . . .' Ellis commented: 'Imperfect connection with her husband, erotic reverie, actual flagellation, attempts at masturbation, none of these ever led up to actual orgasm, although there had often been a high degree of sexual erethism with much mucous discharge.' But one day Florrie deliberately touched her anus and at once experienced a flamingly passionate reaction. Clearly, for her it was a seat of tremendous sexual excitement.

For the moment her dreams erupted in fresh imagery. Ellis asked her to try to recall the detail of the dreams and to memorize them. This she did. One dream which recurred involved snakes. Ellis, aware that snakes might mean penises to Freud, also saw them as symbols of whips.

Her lover N. now wrote to Florrie again. His letter said that he passionately desired to see her and gave details of flagellation which so inflamed Florrie that she replied to say yes, she would meet him again. Then, in sudden revulsion, she sent another letter cancelling the first. But N., ignoring her second letter, kept the appointment and rang the bell one morning. Very angry, Florrie tried to dismiss him. The virile and dominating N. refused to leave until she had promised to see him again. Point-blank she refused. As adamant as she was, his voice grew loud as he repeated the demand. Simultaneously a tradesman came knocking on the door and Florrie, greatly agitated, smuggled N. into an upstairs room, came down again, opened the door, dealt with the visitor and hurried back upstairs where a very different N. was almost cowering in the box room. Presently he slipped out of the house unseen, she hoped, by the neighbours, and disappeared for ever. Months slipped by. She continued to write to Ellis, and sometimes saw and talked to him. Very gradually, over the next few years, her own intelligence, her interviews with Ellis and their lengthy correspondence brought some degree of relief, but it is important to emphasize one of Florrie's comments at this stage of the case. 'The whipping craze seems to have evaporated for the present after raging for four years, and, I suppose, I ought to be glad. I don't know that I am exactly, I miss it in a way. It has left me as sexy as ever but in a vague and more general way.' The 'treatment' in fact – if eradication of the impulse was intended – had not entirely succeeded.

However, Ellis never went so far as to describe his talks with Florrie as treatment. The motif running through them, he said, was an attempt to surround her with an 'atmosphere of sympathetic comprehension', to win her confidence, to encourage the application of her own intelligence. It 'became a process of mental analysis. . .', but it was Florrie herself who mainly carried out that analysis, 'and therein its virtue lay. There was little attempt to present to her relationships which were fairly clear, but which she had not worked out for herself; she would not fail to reach them, and sometimes . . . saw them first.'

It is difficult to establish the precise year in which Ellis began this 'treatment' but it had points of similarity with Freud's free association, transference and 're-birth of responsibility', if in the end it differed widely.

Had he accepted in totality the doctrine of psycho-analysis, Ellis might have made a supreme psycho-analyst. There were, of course, times when his shyness induced paralytic silences, when patients foundered in the sea of his own irresolution, but more often his very gentleness, sensitivity and patience, permitted them to yield up secrets long and painfully locked away. Ellis had considerable power to establish sympathy between himself and a 'patient', sometimes by the reassurance of his presence, sometimes by conveying an omniscient sense of understanding, which, when it met with reasonable response, was slowly heightened until, with some few patients, it resembled a state of love. This was specially true with women. Edith wrote long and glowingly of Ellis's understanding of female psychology.

Florrie's evidence confirmed Edith's. She knew Ellis over many years, and if presently she no longer wrote letters and finally ceased to call, she never forgot the sense of sanctuary in the broken-down Brixton flat and the luminous grace of his presence.

Florrie now vanished. Some years later, Ellis at last began the long and difficult process of inducing some pattern from the mess of Florrie's evidence. It matured for more than five years before he considered the details sufficiently precise. Then, at last he wrote the paper, but the story still was not quite complete. He met Florrie once more. She went through the paper he had prepared and said that no corrections were necessary – it was absolutely right. During the time Ellis knew her, Florrie married three times and in the last two marriages the mad obsession with flagellation dwindled away and died.

It was one of Havelock Ellis's distinctions that he wrote his case-book histories in a style which brought people alive. It happened with Florrie: 'She walks in light where formerly she stumbled in a darkness full of awful spectres. For years a mysteriously cloaked, terrible figure had seized her from behind in an iron clutch she could not shake off, threatening her with insanity and all sorts of dreadful fates.' Now she was able 'to discover with calm critical eyes what it is made of, and the iron clutch loosens and the monster dissolves into mist, a mist that even seems beautiful.'[7]

Neuroticism, Freud believed, was an inevitable concomitant of civilized life, but most people contained their neuroticism. In some it was invert, in some overt, in others not noticeable at all, but no one entirely escaped the scourge. Freud found too many identities in the dreams of 'healthy' and 'neurotic' persons to doubt this. Ellis equally believed that no small part of the abnormal was either normal or sprang from normal roots, and was subject, in most people, to similar 'containment'.

Whenever we, as the immutable products of nature, carried out an action it could not, by definition, be called unnatural, and our behaviour on so many apparently doubtful issues had its counterpart in other organisms, which were for some obscure reason considered even more natural than ourselves – as witness homosexuality among rats and mice. A preoccupation with scatology or flagellation was, as Freud agreed, an infantile fixation of the sexual impulse but it was only abnormal to that degree.

As we have seen, Freud and Ellis differed considerably in the emphasis they put on nature and nurture. Whereas Ellis stressed the innate constitution, Freud equally emphasized environment and upbringing. Neither completely excluded the other, but in Florrie's case Ellis wrote: 'When so definite an erotic symbolism as this . . . becomes constituted we suspect the existence of individual peculiarities rooted in the organism and specially fitting it to become the seat of that symbolism. . . .' There was in fact a pronounced development of the glutel region and thighs in Florrie's early years, he claimed. She was also to some extent 'sexually anaesthetic in the region of the vulva'. Orgasm did not occur from normal masturbation but from 'stimulation of the anus'.[8]

Freud of course would have questioned such an interpretation. It was not only the neglect of oedipal factors capable of thwarting or developing constitutional tendencies, which drove him to concentrate more attention upon nurture: at a moderate underestimate, one-half of human behaviour was, he believed, the result of an acquired Oedipus complex.

To clarify Ellis's considerable contribution to the pioneer work of analysis and his sharp divergencies from Freud, more detailed examination becomes necessary. Ellis frankly admitted that Florrie was in the end 'reconciled to "normal" sex relationships, *but they do not afford her any intense gratification*'.

The lack of any real abreaction in his treatment troubled Freudians. Merely to recapture repressed episodes from the past and to force oneself to confront them was not, in Freudian doctrine, enough. The recapitulation must be accompanied by an emotional force similar to that generated in the original experience. Granted abreaction, the terrible pressures of the long-choked psyche may erupt volcanically and release inhibited impulses in a new harmony. Without abreaction, the personality undergoes all the rational motions of change and fails to achieve primal re-adjustment. It was to be expected that Florrie eventually found no intense gratification because her cure was comparatively superficial.

Freudian purists also indicated the complete lack of positive or negative transference, but Ellis was persuaded that any analyst who aroused negative transference, should 'retire from the world for a time . . . to practise a little self-analysis'. Abusing the shortcomings of transference did not destroy a first principle in psycho-analytic doctrine. At some point, most patients resisted the revelation of secrets elaborately screened not only from the outside world but from their own consciousness. The most subtle process of revelation still did not overcome resistances which might spring from places far beyond the reach of reason, sympathy or understanding. More pertinent, most Freudian analysts were distressed if there was no resistance. Jung, in part, agreed with Ellis when he said that transference was not indispensable, but he did expect and sometimes invoke transference. The fact that Freud, in his brilliant paper 'A Child is Being Beaten', outdistanced Ellis, cannot be disguised. The lucid exploration of the three stages through which his own patient passed when obsessionally driven by fantasies of whipping should be read by anyone anxious to plumb the extraordinary complexities of a condition which Ellis seriously oversimplified.

Freud frequently found in masochists a hidden and incestuous love of the father which, when a boy child appeared, desperately desired that the newcomer should be beaten to demonstrate lack of love for the boy and continued love for the girl. There followed a need to expiate the incestuous impulse by the girl child herself being beaten. In Freud's own words:[9]

The little girl's beating-phantasy goes through three phases, of which the first and third are consciously remembered, the middle one remaining unconscious. The two conscious phases appear to be sadistic, whereas the middle and unconscious one is undoubtedly of a masochistic nature; its content consists in being beaten by the father, and it carries with it the libidinal cathexis and the sense of guilt. In the first and third phantasies the child who is being beaten is always someone else; in the middle phase it is only the child itself; in the third phase it is almost invariably only boys who are being beaten. . . . The unconscious phantasy of the middle phase had primarily a genital significance and developed by means of repression

133

and regression out of an incestuous wish to be loved by the father. . . .

Dr Stekel, who later became absorbed in the case of Florrie, paid high tribute to 'the brilliant therapeutic result' achieved by Ellis, but regretted that Florrie's luxuriant dream life had not undergone analysis. He proceeded to repair the omission, bringing to bear the whole dictionary of psychological symbolism in a way which revealed the immense detail of psycho-analytic interpretation in sharp contrast to Ellis's broad 'flow of feeling'. His analysis also took account of another considerable symptom of Florrie's condition, a symptom with which Ellis was very familiar, but translated differently – urolagnia.

Ellis continued to draw histories from real life, some tragic, some ironic, some unbelievably contorted, but no hint of identities was allowed to escape. Only once in a professional lifetime did a small indiscretion lead to trouble.

It concerned a man known under the pseudonym Mark Tellar. The first few months of his marriage had revealed characteristics not uncommon to many marriages involving correctly brought-up young English women. Sexual relations between them were unsatisfactory. His wife, in a word, disliked sexual intercourse.[10] When, on one occasion while in France, they revisited the spot at Fontainebleau where they had decided on their engagement, Tellar kissed his wife and becoming passionate made fresh advances, only to have her recoil in disgust.

Affairs developed in the life of Mark Teller in a desperate effort to compensate for the shortcomings of his marriage, and the whole relationship drifted into a morass of misunderstanding. Suddenly Tellar discovered the works of Havelock Ellis. Bursting with enthusiasm he sat down and wrote a brief narrative of his own sexual history – with false names – and posted it to Ellis. Within a month Tellar visited Ellis. Today, Mark Tellar has no clear memory of his visit, but what followed, with his wife, remained in his mind vividly. In a moment of misplaced boldness, Tellar suggested that she might supplement his 'case-history' with one about herself. She refused, but raised no objection when he audaciously suggested writing one on her behalf. Some days afterwards she made fresh inquiries and discovered that the account had already been written and posted. Another week passed and then suddenly, she disclosed that she, in turn, had called on Havelock Ellis and talked at length with him.

Many months afterwards, Tellar discovered what transpired between them. She had asked Ellis's permission to revise the history of her sex life as composed by her husband on the grounds that husbands were prejudiced.[11] Stipulating that she must return it, Ellis yielded up the all too dangerous document. This proved fatal. Following her visit to Ellis she suspected her husband's relations with a woman known as L.M. and had him watched. 'She found out', Tellar wrote to me, 'about other things including my adulterous relations with M— from the account of my own life that I had written for Ellis.' 'In my opinion,' Tellar commented, 'he acted improperly.'[12] However, she returned the account with a few negligible alterations which showed, Ellis said, what a faithful account he had given.

But the fat was now fully in the fire. Presently Elsie dramatically announced, 'I know all – a detective has tracked you and L.M. to a hotel. I am filing a petition for divorce.' Foolishly, Tellar had preserved the first draft of his account for Ellis in a cash box in his study which Elsie had broken open. In those days divorce required an appellant to prove cruelty as well as misconduct. The word being capable of endless misconstruction, the fact that Mark Tellar had sent such an account to Ellis was at once cited as an act of cruelty. Elsie Tellar won her divorce case.

The one indiscretion of a professional lifetime fraught with such dangers had certainly led to serious complications.

Chapter 11
Marital troubles

First one, then a second and third, and now a fourth valume of his *Studies in the Psychology of Sex* were distilled, with infinite care, from the living mass of material which, beginning as a small trickle, had become a tide, pouring every aspect of the sexual situation into his study, full of the bewilderment, ugliness and beauty which he strove to reconcile. In moments he still hoped that one day there would spring from these sprawling volumes that illumination of profound sexuality which would transform the experience for every other person, but the mass of evidence had begun to tower in all its confusions to the point where he sometimes feared it might topple about him in horrible caricature. There were times when even his magisterial disinterestedness blinked at the sheer ingenuity with which human sexuality contorted itself, but he had no sense of humour about those details amongst it all which became grotesquely funny to the average reader, and continued to record every tiny extravagance with immense solemnity.

As he prepared material for the fourth volume of the *Studies in the Psychology of Sex*, Ellis's own life entered a new and distressing phase. Inevitably Edith remained at the heart of it, but another person – a young woman artist – suddenly became very interested in Edith, and a storm gathered about his unsuspecting head. Living at St Ives under the watchful eye of her sister, Lily, as Ellis called her, painted with no great proficiency. She was a slight, delicate person with an elfin quality about her, but her lack of willpower was replaced by aesthetic discrimination. She quickly found in Edith a reassurance against the *ennui* of which she lived in perpetual fear, and discovered in her a stimulant which brought her wonderfully alive. However, the relationship was full of difficulties. Her sister kept baleful guard over all Lily's comings and goings, and at first their meetings were by stealth. Sometimes Lily would suddenly appear out of the night, hopelessly late for an appointment, very pale and infinitely thankful to reach sanctuary, explaining that her sister had been especially difficult that night. Once Ellis abandoned the studio in which he worked, for their use; once Edith begged him to speak to the sister in an effort to break the restrictions on her life. Intrigue and difficulties notwithstanding, their relationship ripened. Slowly it became apparent to Havelock that this affair with Lily was different. It began to enter into and illumine every corner of Edith's life, until suddenly one day there was one meeting which left a glow in Edith's mind for the rest of her life. It was characteristic of Ellis that he should romanticize every relationship in Edith's prolonged lesbian history, but Lily was certainly different from the normal run of her affairs. Once again she disturbed Edith's relations with Ellis, and if, once more, he said nothing, he was very aware of the difference. It was transparently obvious that Edith had fallen desperately in love with Lily, but their relationship was doomed to be short-lived. Within a year, Lily, overtaken by a mysterious illness, was found to be suffering from Bright's disease. The news threw Edith into great distress. Once the sister had Lily at her mercy in bed it became increasingly difficult for Edith to see her. Torn between a passionate desire to nurse Lily and horror of the sister's growing hostility, she was distraught.

Lily bore no resemblance to Claire for Ellis. She was in a sense not quite human. Peering out of her pale fragility as from another world, it was difficult for Ellis to feel jealousy of someone resembling a sprite. Month after month the queer, unsatisfactory relationship continued, month after month Edith became more deeply involved.

And then, in June 1903, Lily suddenly died. It was a terrible day for Edith. She lay prostrate in a state approaching coma. She simply could not accept the fact that Lily was gone for ever. However much heterosexual women recoil in distaste from the picture sometimes drawn of Edith 'the flaming Lesbian', eternally in pursuit of some fresh young woman, and however ironic Ellis's repeated references to Edith's 'new woman friends', it would be insensitive not to acknowledge that her love for Lily overwhelmed her. It appeared to epitomize for Edith all that exquisite delicacy, springing from emotional fibres more complicated than any male could know, which she eternally craved. There was something in this relationship which she found unrepeatable. Years afterwards, when other women, far more powerful in personality had come and gone in Edith's life, the memory of Lily remained.[1] Edith went regularly to her grave, and decided that she too, when the time came, would be buried at this very spot.

The middle months of 1902 had been bad enough for Edith. The weather never seemed to break free from cloud and rain, financial difficulties intensified, Miranda the cow collapsed one day, a dog she loved was put to sleep, and trouble with a knee joint reduced Edith to hobbling. Lily's death was the climax to a long series of lesser disasters. Edith became so depressed that her doctor advised her to get right away from the farm.

Despite the lack of money they somehow made their way to Aix-les-Bains, for an idyllic holiday lasting a month. Four days after their arrival Edith had recovered enough to desire to write again, and plunged into a short story. Finding the form attractive she persisted, and presently, through the influence of a friend married to the editor of the *Echo*, several stories appeared in that paper.

Edith had a private income of £150 to £200 a year and Havelock's earnings probably did not fall below £400. Surprisingly F. A. Davis & Co. printed 25,000–30,000 copies of the early volumes of the *Studies* at prices ranging from two to three dollars, and even though these were spread over several years, assuming a sale of 5,000 for the first year at two dollars each, a royalty of 10 per cent would have yielded £250, and 10,000, £500. Moreover there were second and third editions of some of the early volumes. Unfortunately F. A. Davis later relinquished the rights, and the actual royalty records were destroyed.[2] Until 1914 when the Contemporary Science Series ceased, Edith and Havelock might have commanded together £600. Any multiple is liable to be inaccurate but today a figure of £6,000 would not be too distorted an equivalent. It is difficult to believe that their penury was so pressing when Priscilla, a newly acquired maid, was invited to travel with them from Aix-les-Bains to Paris, but Edith, who followed no real profession from the day of her marriage, could not do without a maid. Ellis promptly treated her as a friend, and that led to the now familiar complications.

In the early 1900s – Symons having married – Ellis moved into a flat in Church Street, Chelsea, and began to spend his time between there and the Count House in Cornwall. Edith and Priscilla sometimes descended on him in London, and all three made do in his small flat, where presently the tangled skein of his relations with Amy, Edith and Priscilla came to a head. Another man had fallen in love with Amy, discovered her relations with Havelock, and become vengefully jealous. Without any warning, a lengthy document was delivered one day to Edith, revealing what the writer regarded as Ellis's flagrant infidelity with Amy.

Edith reacted dramatically. Either she collapsed in a genuine faint or successfully simulated that condition. According to Havelock there was nothing in the document which Edith did not already know, but it was written with subtle distortions which presented the whole story in a most unpleasant light. The author had in fact taken the trouble to have Havelock shadowed by a private detective and the report, in relation to Priscilla, read sensationally.

She had spent a day roaming London with Ellis and the detective recorded that they entered a certain hotel, which was untrue. One episode of spectacular unconventionality which would have added fresh colour to his report he apparently did not witness. Ellis and Priscilla had made their way up to the dome of St Paul's when the urge to urinate suddenly overtook Priscilla. There and then, she overcame her modesty, and in front of Ellis relieved herself.

The preoccupation with urination which began with his nurse and developed through his mother had now involved Priscilla, but some years later, writing a thinly disguised prose poem describing the act, he conveyed the transfigured beauty it achieved in his eyes. Edith, fully aware of this predisposition, was not in the least bothered. Nor, in the end, did the anonymous letter continue to trouble her.

In May of 1905 Ellis went to Spain. One vision of that holiday remained in his mind years afterwards. It was the vision of the beautiful monastery of Montserrat and the long and difficult pilgrimage up the rough road to San Jeronimo. One evening, he stood, at last, on the plateau sustaining the monastery and looked up at the mystery of the final mountain crest. Pacing to and fro along the wide, empty terrace, the air was intoxicating, the sky serene and down below the rocks fell away into caverns of nothingness as though the world he inhabited floated in a void. Suddenly he experienced a sense of spiritual exaltation which was to persist for many hours and to leave an indelible memory.[3]

In those high places where thousands of pilgrims came every year and the unceasing flow of people stretched back down history for five hundred years, he suddenly felt himself caught up in their company, and on the terrace, alone with the evening, a sense of ecstatic communion with something he could feel but not define, moved him deeply. Years later, in retrospect, the experience came to mean even more to him and as usual he conveyed it to paper.

Two weeks after he returned to England, Edith suddenly fell ill with pneumonia. It was the first of her more serious and progressively more demanding illnesses. Within a week she was out of serious danger, but partial recovery brought with it deep depression. Presently her apathy bordered on the pathological. She was no longer interested in people, plays or books, and slowly the sense of inertia spread until she felt her limbs as though weighted with lead and the slightest movement became a great effort.

There was now revealed in Edith all the signs of a manic-depressive. Ellis's devotion remained saint-like. No matter how demanding she became, he never complained. When the doctor urged Edith to pull herself together in order to try a short walk, Ellis went with her. Together, they crawled round Battersea Park, but she almost collapsed. They decided to move to new rooms in Reigate where a complete change of surroundings might stimulate Edith. To Ellis's astonishment the move worked with an alacrity which was remarkable. So remarkable indeed, that from then on Havelock no longer doubted the psychosomatic character of many of her illnesses.

However she had hardly recovered from one set of symptoms when the mysterious trouble with her knee joint became more acute. Once more she retired to bed. Complete rest might help, Dr Nichols said, but something far more profound than muscular rheumatism, lumbago or nerves – diagnoses variously achieved and abandoned by Nichols in a rearguard action against the mounting scepticism of his patient – was troubling the deeper places of Edith's spirit. With Lily dead, and no sign of anyone capable of filling her place, with her husband deeply interested in Amy and possibly much less so in Priscilla, she feared that one day, this god of hers, who could so magnificently reassure her, might show signs of defection, and then where would she be? It was the classic solution that she should render herself even more dependent by falling ill, thus making any thought of abdication impossible to Ellis. Such simple psychology did not give a complete answer to the infinitely complicated mental processes of Edith Ellis, for this illness continued and grew in a quite dismaying manner. Week followed week, and every week saw some fresh inroad on Ellis's time and patience. New duties were undertaken, their number slowly mounting to push his work into the background.[4]

Soon the nights were fraught with danger. As the illness reached its climax Edith tended to burst awake in the middle of the night in a state of delirium, and presently Havelock had to keep a night watch. Sometimes he was driven to stop her by force from rushing out in her night clothes and disappearing on the heath. Sometimes she woke in the night with horrible screams on her lips, and once she fought him savagely to try to escape from the room which had suddenly become a black prison.

Soon he gave up all thought of work. Day and night he nursed her. It was almost as if she desired him to add the love usually reserved for his work to his love for her, producing a very obliterative state of loving in which he ceased to be a person and became a slave. 'She had the idea that I was becoming successful and exposed to the demoralising influence of adulation which it was her business to counteract.' He understood this: 'there was no shadow of protest on my part when she treated me as a child who needs sharp correction in the small details of domestic life.'[5] Clearly the masochist was supremely able to take his punishment.

There were, indeed, times, when she exercised a sort of fascinated power over him, when she snubbed him with Priscilla in the room, ordered things only to brush them aside, made him run trivial and unnecessary errands. Ellis admitted that her behaviour could be embarrassing, but his embarrassment never led to rebellion. He was only distressed at the lack of peace for work. The saint-like Ellis, not content with stifling every selfish impulse, took innumerable photographs of her at this time and found them, even in recollection, the most beautiful portraits. Idolatry could go no farther than the descriptions he later gave.

As the winter dragged on Edith recovered sufficiently to leave her bed, but she could not use her leg and had to walk on crutches. Once downstairs however she mended quickly. Now, suddenly, she recovered so quickly that she abandoned her crutches and set out for London with a speed almost indecent in one so lately a delirious weakling.

It is easy to exaggerate Edith's shortcomings and the extraordinary uses to which she put Havelock, but she was, to some extent, the victim of a vicious up-bringing. Where the immutable laws of conditioning stopped and wilful abuse of love began, becomes even more difficult to determine when it is clear that Havelock accepted with undiminished love, if not enjoyment, the extravagant demands she made upon him. It is reminiscent of the boy ridden round the dormitory by elder boys, and the man who later quoted Queen Victoria after her husband's death: ' "Nobody contradicts me now, and the salt has gone out of my life." I am sure that Queen Victoria hated to be contradicted,' Ellis wrote, 'and I sometimes resented being scolded like a child, but no one treats me like a child now, and the savour has gone out of my life.'[6]

In 1906 they moved from the Count House into two cottages. Theoretically self-contained but part of the same building, they each took a separate room in a different cottage, and their semi-detached life was almost comically preserved. Ellis, still terribly anxious for Edith's health, wanted to build a connecting door but this was impossible.

An extraordinary ritual now developed. They slept in different cottages, Havelock never daring to overstep his wife's threshold at night and, under a curiously unconvincing pretext, Priscilla was in the habit of locking Ellis in before she went to bed. She did this, it was said, in order to return in the morning, unlock the door and set a match to the fire she had laid overnight.

Edith understood and enjoyed the comic element of this ritual. For his part, Ellis had become so overwrought about Edith's health that his anxiety continued long after she was better and sometimes he would become anxious in the middle of the night and stand close to the wall desperately trying to detect any sound of distress. He did not go down boldly, enter the cottage and find out, because he was afraid of causing what he described as 'unnecessary disturbance'.

Leaving the Count House meant closing down Edith's farm. Her career as a farmer and landlord had undergone the same spectacular flucuations as her career in writing and lecturing, and the intervention of illness – her heart grew more troublesome alongside neuritis – had forced her into the conviction that she had better employ her talents elsewhere. She refused to be parted from an amiable horse, rapidly ageing, and a donkey with an appetite for cigarettes, and she took a stable and a field, caring for them far on into life. Her devotion for the horse and donkey, even when in an advanced and diseased condition they became financially embarrassing, revealed the unshakeable loyalty she cherished for dumb and unprotected brethren of any kind.

In these two cottages Edith turned more and more to writing. Once again she was pouring words on paper at five or six in the morning, covering many pages before breakfast, and anxious to read them to Havelock before he was half awake. A collection of short stories was published in book form in 1906 under the title *My Cornish Neighbours*. 1907 saw a heavily corrected edition of *Seaweed*, under a new title, and two years later *Attainment* appeared. The name and standing of a publishing house may or may not mean anything. Masterpieces too often lie unappreciated by the most august publishers. The reader can draw what conclusions he likes from the fact that many of Edith's publishers bore names largely unknown in their day and age. Even Havelock did not think overmuch of *Attainment*.

Yet another illness now descended on Edith. This time it assumed all the characteristics of broncho-pneumonia, and once again Havelock became the devoted nurse. Sometimes he remained uneasily beside her all night, cramped on a couch, in case she should need him.

If Havelock's work suffered further interruption, illness did not quite stop Edith's. A burst of nervous energy was sufficient to convert a story from *My Cornish Neighbours* into a one-act play. Fearing the effect of constant rejection, Havelock warned her that theatre managers were a stony-hearted lot, and she must face the fact that the chances of acceptance were small. The play went to a Mr Otho Stuart, a young modern producer, connected with the Court Theatre. It came as a wonderful surprise to Edith to have Mr Stuart reply that he liked her play very much and hoped to be able to stage it. Momentarily, the excitement sent Edith's temperature soating, but success also raised a new and spirited resistance to illness. The play – it was in fact a very slight one-act playlet – had its early production as a curtain-raiser in several theatres, but the unlucky Edith was not well enough to be present.

The Subjection of Kezia does not require any very deep analysis. It is a theatrical cocktail, the subject of which, the imminent thrashing of a beautiful wife by a loving and sensitive husband, stirred many people who would probably have hated to know the true origin of their response. It showed some gift for dialogue, and admirably caught the Cornish dialect, but whatever qualities the first of its sixteen pages revealed were ruined by a factitious denouement. Here was Joe Pengelly, beautifully got up in the theatrical likeness of a Cornish peasant – corduroy trousers, hobnailed boots, blue and white shirt open at the throat – suffering untold misery because he had trodden something referred to as 'Crusties' into the kitchen floor and Kezia had snapped his head off. Here was short, stout Matthew Trevaskis, his friend, 'with bushy hair and a beard' telling him that the only possible way to deal with a recalcitrant wife was to 'wallop her just once'. Pengelly steels himself to thrash Kezia and buys a cane. Hiding it behind his back, he advances upon her, only to be told that she is in an interesting condition and then, as she sights the cane, Kezia expresses delight that he has so brilliantly anticipated the news by buying the cane to beat the child to be.[7] One of her closest friends thought the whole thing abysmal.[8] If it led Ellis to refer to her as though she had the potentialities of Marlowe, that was completely consistent with his unrelenting exaggeration of her talents.

Despite this small success, broncho-pneumonia left Edith tired and depressed. That and a weakening heart presently persuaded Dr Sansom to advise her to leave Cornwall altogether. Whereupon Edith moved out of the Moor Cottages into Rose Cottage, the last of the covey of cottages still in her possession, which was much closer to London. Ellis also moved to a new London address, a flat at 14 Dover Mansions, Canterbury Crescent, Brixton.

There were some wonderful negotiations about the new London flat, one room of which Edith wanted to keep for herself. She sent a letter in September 1909:[9]

> My Darling Boy, I think that the flat idea sounds splendid. Offer them £46 at first and let me one room for £10. Be in it before I come up and I will bring a bed and a few things with me. I should not disturb you a bit as I can always – as I do at the Club – cook my own breakfast. . . .

Later in the same letter she offered him a bigger rent for the room, but this was never paid; nor did she in the end cook her own breakfast. The letter was typical of her ambivalence towards him – wanting independence and never quite prepared to face its consequences.

It would be wrong to assume that illness, selfishness and insecurity consistently obliterated happier sides of Edith's character. There were many moods. Sometimes she would go roystering through the day giving every appearance that life had become a sustained and very exciting lark. These bursts of superabundant life when she suddenly felt completely well again exerted a magnetic influence on Ellis and certainly, in such moods, it was possible to understand something of his love for her. She could bubble with talk, whisk round the cottage in a flurry of gaiety, her beautiful eyes brimming with laughter. Or she lay beside Ellis in the Cornish sun and hardly said a word, absorbing the slow soft pulse of a summer afternoon. If she could never sustain contemplative interludes, bursts of energy suddenly shattering the calm and setting her off on some half-thought-out mission, against all the

143

abuse of his saintly self, there was no doubting that her love for Havelock had deepened immeasurably.

But her women friends continued to multiply. By the beginning of the summer her health had improved enough for her to go to Paris where she met and became 'very friendly with' an American woman who had once known Lily. The American lady, clearly a lesbian, had in fact meant rather more to Lily than Edith, but something now sprang to life between these two, and Edith spoke of caresses which passed from one to the other in words which were full of sensuality.

Chapter 12

Sex in relation to society

Between the years 1900 and 1904 Ellis had discovered the writings of the French philosopher Jules de Gaultier, who was to have a deep influence on him. At Remy de Gourmont's suggestion, Gaultier sent him in 1902 a copy of *Le Bovarysme*, which, amid pressure of work, he read with his usual thoroughness.

Born one year before Ellis, Gaultier was influenced by Schopenhauer, and coined the phrase 'Bovarysme', derived from Flaubert's characters who conceived 'themselves as other than they are'. This characteristic he later developed into a universal quality whereby men projected their own pattern on the universe and 'every expression distorts – at the same time that it evokes its object'.

Nietzsche, who later influenced Gaultier, already gloried in the power of 'vital lies', and Vaihinger's *Die Philosophie des Als Ob*, set out to solve the problem of reaching conclusions in harmony with nature through consciously false ideas; 'even the most sober scientific investigator in science . . . cannot dispense with fictions'; he must at least make use of categories, and scientific hypotheses were imaginative fictions which might be proved or disproved. Man's desire to project the organization of his own mind into an alien universe, probably subject to quite different laws, is now a cliché in modern thinking, but Gaultier drove it home in *La Fiction universelle* at a time when Ellis absorbed it eagerly. In the end, for Gaultier, the meaning of life and its deepest satisfactions were to be found in aesthetic experience which admitted no boundaries, embracing morals, truth and love.[1]

Absorbed as he was in philosophic problems of the day, Ellis had ceased to find technical philosophy interesting and concentrated more on aesthetic experience. In Gaultier he found subtle reaffirmation of his still developing ideas. Presently, these persuasions deepened and became more urgent until he gave them full expression in *The Dance of Life*. For the moment, however, he was absorbed in other books.

The fourth volume of *The Studies in the Psychology of Sex* appeared

145

in 1905. Generally entitled *Sexual Selection in Man*, it dealt with The External Sensory Stimuli Affecting Selection in Man and the four senses involved, Touch, Smell, Hearing and Vision. There was an Appendix on the Origins of the Kiss and the usual case-book histories. Under the chapter headed Touch, phenomena once considered perversions were analysed with the scientific calm native to Ellis's method, and once more revealed comparatively commonplace characteristics.[2]

There were repetitive elements in volumes four and five, but he had by now perfected the crisp style to be used for all future scientific writing and complex statements were made easily assimilable. Freud had once more anticipated many of the findings in volume four, but the real battle between them was delayed for many years.

Volume five (1906) followed close on the heels of volume four and dealt with Erotic Symbolism, The Mechanism of Detumescence and The Psychic State in Pregnancy. The Mechanism of Detumescence explained its psychological significance and gave a detailed study of sexual organs from the Testis and Ovary, the Sperm Cell and Germ Cell, to the Nymphæ Their Function and the Biological Significance of the Hymen. The chapter, 'The Psychic State in Pregnancy', dealt with the Relationship of Maternal and Sexual Emotion, the Pervading Effects of Pregnancy, Changes in the Nervous System, the blood circulation, pigmentation, and thyroid, the longings of pregnant women and their general mental state. Every chapter was immensely more detailed and subtle than this abstract of sub-headings conveys.

One chapter, 'Erotic Symbolism', revealed a fantastically rich variety of sexual fetishes from 'causes congenital, acquired, or both', whereby 'some object or class of objects, some act or group of acts, has acquired a dynamic power over the psycho-physical mechanism of the sexual process, deflecting it from its normal adjustment to the whole of a beloved person of the opposite sex. . . .'

Its most popular instance was shoe-fetishism. Because some episode, in early childhood, associated shoes and sex with tremendous force, a number of highly intelligent men were condemned to spend no small part of their lives searching out women who were prepared to make flashing play with high-heeled shoes so manipulated as to cause orgasm. Only under such extreme conditions was orgasm satisfactory, or, in many cases, could it be achieved at all. Others desired, with equal and quite immutable force, to have a woman urinate upon them or to witness the acts of defecation or urination, which, in themselves, as a sheer spectacle were liable to produce orgasm.[3]

Those who worked in birth control and marriage guidance often complained that Ellis's books concerned the flagrantly abnormal. Difficulties like impotence on the bridal night, contraceptives, hymen complications and fear of childbirth, never appeared in his pages. Indeed, as we have seen, the indefatigable Marie Stopes thought his volumes – 'like breathing a bag of soot',[4] and one reverend gentleman referred to them as 'cesspools liable to turn the uncontaminated nine-tenths of humanity into the same depraved state'.[5] 'They made me feel,' wrote Marie Stopes, 'that *abnormalities* are for experts only, and that what the world needed was knowledge about the normal and how to handle it rightly.'[6] Certainly Ellis did not deal with commonplace difficulties in the practical sense of the term. Whether half the psychic contortions he uncovered were not potentially part of everyone – in reality or fantasy – remains unproven. Certainly many seemed to flourish in the fantasy life of a considerable number of people.

As Lancelot Hogben has said:[7]

Apart from what we infer from the study of animals most of our knowledge of how the normal body discharges its functions comes from the examination of pathological conditions. In studying the body we find that the pathological condition is but an exaggeration of some aspect of the normal processes at work. . . . When a deviation from the normal has been labelled a crime or a perversion it ceases to be an objective of intellectual curiosity and is appropriated by the two professions most conspicuously devoid of it. Havelock Ellis was fortunate in escaping from one of them without irreparable loss. . . .

In his sixth volume, Ellis turned away sharply from the 'pathological' to the relief of some of his readers. He regarded the year 1909 as a tremendous year in his life. It brought to a close the huge undertaking which had occupied the greater part of his working life, with what he considered the most important volume of the *Studies – Sex in Relation to Society*.

The importance of the earlier volumes lay in their value as a comprehensive encyclopedia of physiological fact and sexual behaviour. In terms of sex they remained without parallel. In the tradition of natural history he had given an elaborately detailed picture of one side of man's nature – until then deliberately obscured – and had broken into a powerfully sustained conspiracy of silence. Now, in the sixth volume, he began to analyse social relations, and found himself involved in expressing at last his own philosophy. As the book grew it revealed a vision of the world freed from unnecessary laws and the web of blind tradition, liberated aesthetically and brought to that pitch of harmony where man realized and transcended instinctual appetites.

The six hundred and forty-five pages were given over to twelve chapters: (1) The Mother and Her Child (2) Sexual Education (3) Sexual Education and Nakedness (4) The Valuation of Sexual Love (5) The Function of Chastity (6) The Problem of Sexual Abstinence (7) Prostitution (8) The Conquest of the Venereal Disease (9) Sexual Morality (10) Marriage (11) The Art of Love (12) Science of Procreation.

A broad summary of his general approach occurred on page 417. It was a measured utterance the style of which made the sentiments expressed acceptable even to some among his enemies, and removed the questions he discussed from the confusions which analysis of sexual aberration had introduced into earlier volumes.[8]

> Sexual union, for a woman as much as for a man, is a physiological fact; it may also be a spiritual fact; but it is not a social act. It is, on the contrary, an act which, beyond all other acts, demands retirement and mystery for its accomplishment. That indeed is a general human, almost zoological, fact. Moreover, this demand of mystery is more especially made by woman in virtue of her greater modesty which, we have found reason to believe, has a biological basis. It is not until a child is born or conceived that the community has any right to interest itself in the sexual acts of its members. The sexual act is of no more concern to the community than any other private physiological act. It is an impertinence, if not an outrage, to seek to enquire into it. But the birth of a child is a social act. . . . The community is entitled to demand that the citizen shall be worthy of a place in its midst and that he shall be properly introduced by a responsible father and a responsible mother. . . .

The emergence of public morality with the birth of a child made it necessary to inquire into the nature of morals, and the issue was confused, Ellis said, by the conflicting attitudes of the early Christian Fathers whose voices so profoundly echoed in our day and age. Many early Fathers of the Church disliked the implications of sexuality, but 'some of the most distinguished' among them, 'especially those of the Eastern church who had felt the vivifying breath of Greek thought, occasionally expressed themselves on the subject of Nature, sex, and the body in a spirit which would have won the approval of Goethe or Whitman. . . .' Clement of Alexandria, for instance, protesting against the prudery which had begun to cloud his time wrote: 'We should not be ashamed to name what God has not been ashamed to create.'

Ellis believed that it was St Augustine, bred in the very different school of Roman Carthage who thought sin 'original', finding 'its special seat and symbol in the sexual organs'. He expressed his convictions with such force, passion and eloquence, as 'to make his answer prevail'. The final expression of this sense of sin, in modern codes of morality, needed close examination, but it was necessary to remember the violent fluctuations in the history of morals before attempting to define any such elusive word as sin. Up to this point, the facts in the chapter on morals were commonplace and but for the style it would have been within the capacity of many moralists and writers of the day to have written such an essay. Ellis now widened his inquiry and revealed a range of scholarship which took in half the world.

148

Back in the dim beginnings of early civilizations, ancient Egypt did not acknowledge illegitimacy, even the slave woman's child escaping any such stigma. 'Men and women were recognised as equal' in the Egypt of those days and as Amelineau had written: 'It is the glory of Egyptian morality to have been the first to express the Dignity of Woman.' Wide diversities in the morals of ancient Athens were too familiar to need examination, but there it was commonplace for high-born men to sleep with younger men and boys, and a classical correctness if not beauty invested what many now regarded with horror. Immense conflicts appeared in human morals, Ellis said, when the span of less than 2,000 years produced one society where – in Caesar's Britain – brothers shared several wives, another in Nuremberg where a man was permitted two wives in the middle of the seventeenth century, and a third, where monogamy was rigidly enforced, children born out of wedlock ostracized and adultery considered a crime. Regarded historically, whatever divinity shaped our ends, morals were definitely rough hewn. There was no absolute morality.

Ellis found two very different classes within what was generally known as morality: traditional and ideal. Traditional morality, a code of behaviour developed over generations, surrounded the child from birth, reaching a pitch comparable with indoctrination and becoming the voice of the child's conscience. It was both deliberately taught and accidentally acquired, it was the result of religious, private and school 'instruction'. Within it grew involuntary reflexes.

> Many persons, for example, who were brought up in childhood to the Puritanical observance of Sunday, will recall how, long after they had ceased to believe that such observances were 'right', . . . yet, in the violation of them, heard the protest of the automatically aroused voice of 'conscience'. . . .

'Ideal morality, on the other hand', was concerned with the future not the past. Nietzsche, in our society, represented its most ferocious champion, but the thunderbolts he had hurled down with such fine frenzies had conspicuously failed to destroy traditional morality. If the concern of ideal morality was not with how people behaved in the past, but how they should behave in the future, for Ellis there were complementary values in both. 'We have seen both applied to prostitution; traditional morality defends prostitution, not for its own sake, but for the sake of the marriage system which it regards as sufficiently precious to be worth a sacrifice.'

Belfort Bax had said that the prostitute who took less than the market rate for her wares – 'marriage for sexual services rendered' – became in effect a blackleg[9] Ellis however argued that it was the *wife* who undercut the market in comparison with the prostitute who surrendered her body alone.

Our sexual morality, Ellis wrote, was really the product of the laws of property and 'a primitive ascetic morality neither in true relationship to the vital facts of sexual life'. Christianity, which so deeply conditioned our own morality, envisaged sexual indulgence as 'a concession to human weakness', created a cult of chastity and virginity, and poured all its powers into spiritual dominance over what it sometimes seemed to regard as little more than animal appetites. Automatically, it assumed that without a whole system of checks and barriers, licentiousness was inevitable. Ellis did not believe this. He argued that, at root, there were *natural* restraints in nature itself, and that forms of behaviour simply needed liberating from the web of inhibitions with which civilization threatened to suffocate its finest potential.

In the last analysis, Ellis felt that many people, freed from the falsification forced on them by modern society, would behave far more virtuously than Christianity supposed. Indeed, the very fact of compulsion was capable of converting a virtuous person to the ways of vice. There was much truth in the picture Rabelais had drawn:[10]

> men that are free, well-born, well-bred, and conversant in honest companies, have naturally an instinct and spur that prompts them into virtuous actions and withdraws them from vice. These same men, when by base subjection and constraint they are brought under and kept down, turn aside from that noble disposition by which they freely were inclined to virtue, to shake off and break that bond of servitude.

But Rabelais's inscription in the *Abbey of Thelema* began with a long diatribe against the base, the hypocrites and the bigots, reserving the freedom of the Abbey for a carefully chosen élite. True, for them, 'Do what you will' became the accepted creed, but their numbers were strictly limited.

A Shelley-ean idealism, remote from the industrial worker burdened with a forty-five hour week, a wife, several children and the wolfish ways of competitive life, distinguished the whole of this chapter. It was a pity that Ellis did not press investigation into the origins of 'natural' morals deeper before so persuasively invoking their aid.

A long and carefully written chapter on marriage, followed. It began with the assumption that the marriage system of modern civilized peoples emerged from the later days of the Roman Empire, when

> there was no legal form of marriage. The Romans recognised that marriage was a fact and not a mere legal form; in marriage by usus there was no ceremony at all; it was constituted by the mere fact of living together for a whole year, yet such marriage was regarded as

just as legal and complete as if it had been inaugurated by the sacred rite of *confarreatio*.

The wife retained full rights over her own property, the restitution of conjugal rights was unnecessary, divorce a private transaction as much open to the wife as husband, and there was 'no . . . intervention of magistrate or court. . .'.[11] Up to that point, no one would quarrel with Ellis's interpretation; what followed was severely questioned by Christian historians.

It was Christianity, Ellis wrote, which gradually invaded this situation. A combined asceticism and hostility developed hand in hand under the influence 'of the barbaric Jewish marriage system', as propagated in the Bible, and the Germanic conception of marriage in which the wife was reduced practically to the state of a chattel.

'Among the Teutonic peoples generally, as among the early English, marriage was indeed a private transaction but it took the form of a sale of the bride by the father, or other legal guardian, to the bridegroom. . . .' If the Christian Church insisted on hallowing such transactions with a benediction, it was no more nor less than a similar ritual invoked to hallow the sale of goods under civil contracts. 'There was no special religious marriage service either in the East or West earlier than the 6th century.' It was simply customary to attend an ordinary church service after a private marriage. Not until the tenth century did the custom develop of celebrating 'the first part of the real nuptials' within range of the church, and presently the bride-mass was transferred 'inside the church'. In the twelfth century the priest began to direct the ceremony, in the thirteenth he literally presided, and slowly what had once held private validity for two human beings, was transferred to the church and through the growth of *custom*, not law, the rituals of ecclesiastical marriage achieved their dominance. Even so, Gratian's twelfth-century Canon Law, on which modern marriage ritual came to be based, accepted marriage by mutual consent, without demanding a religious ceremony and, as late as Milton, similar interpretations persisted when he regarded marriage as a personal matter open to private dissolution.

It was monogamy, not ecclesiastical marriage, which ran through the whole history of the human race, Ellis maintained, and human relationships must be built around the core of one man and one woman, freed, if possible, from unnecessary sanctions or penalties. This too lightly dismissed Lord Morley's statement that 'man is instinctively polygamous',[12] and underestimated other interpretations. Ellis accepted Lord Morley's statement if it was read to mean 'that man is an instinctively monogamous animal with a concomitant desire for sexual variation.'

The desire for sexual variety among women as well as men had grown to the point where they should be capable of having affairs gracefully and, providing husbands and wives frankly admitted their extra-marital inclinations if not affairs, jealousy should be kept within bounds. This was to have savagely ironic repercussions in his own life.

Despite his advocacy of legal, professional and political reforms for women, Ellis continued to emphasize the fundamental differences between men and women. Several reforms he advocated were an extension of his concept of their maternal role. Thus during pregnancy, childbirth and for a set period afterwards women ought, if necessary, to be supported by the State and even by their employers. Menstruation played so big a part in differentiating women from men that they should be granted four or five rest days every month. As for the claims of the leaders of the women's movement that menstruation caused them very little trouble, he received such statements with scepticism. The women's movement, he argued, should not be concerned with equality with men but social recognition of the special needs dictated by a woman's physical and psychological constitution.

Ellis did not accept the 'form' which monogamy took in contemporary cultures and he rejected the emphasis placed upon the contractual nature of marriage. Marriage was, for him, both a contract and an ethical sacrament but not more or less valid according to religious sanction.

If entry into marriage was beset by a remarkable legal jungle, exit from it was positively dangerous. Whenever a married couple found their lives becoming intolerable together and saw some hope of greater happiness apart, from every civilized standpoint it was better that they went their separate ways, with some sympathy and understanding.[13]

> The law ridiculously forbids them to do so, and declares that they must not part at all unless they are willing to part as enemies. In order to reach a still lower depth of absurdity and immorality the law goes on to say that if, as a matter of fact, they have succeeded in becoming enemies to each other to such an extent that each has wrongs to plead against the other party, they cannot be divorced at all!

When two people, incapable of adultery, cruelty or even simple disloyalty, came forward in all innocence and explained their incompatibility, they had no hope of enlisting the aid of the law to resolve their troubles because 'there must be a defendant'. Even adultery committed by both still gave no claim to divorce because 'there must be a plaintiff'. 'If only the wife' or husband set out to commit adultery alone, and the innocent party descended to 'the degradation of employing detectives and hunting up witnesses, the law is at their feet and hastens to accord to both parties the permission to remarry. . . .'[14] This, of course, exaggerated the facts for the sake of irony and made the case too symmetrical to be true, but Ellis, unlike Shaw, never prolonged his satirical displays and quickly returned to his main thesis.

Generally, Ellis favoured trial marriage before any final commitments were undertaken. This he felt to be free from the threats of corruption which were said to beset it. He quoted one instance after another from diverse corners of the world where trial marriages – as in 'enlightened' circles of the Middle Ages – still persisted without damage to the persons concerned or the stability of society.[15]

Since the law always followed lamely behind public opinion and any drastic reform of divorce remained remote, Ellis felt it better to increase the practice of trial marriage in a community where the dangers of sexual urges driving people into quick and hopelessly mistaken unions remained grave.

But with the appearance of children:[16]

we are approaching a time when it will be generally understood that the entrance into the world of every child, without exception, should be preceded by the formation of a marriage contract which, while in no way binding the father and mother to any duties, or any privileges, towards each other, binds them towards their child. . . .

Much of this has an old-fashioned ring today but was revolutionary in his time.

Defending the principle of divorce by mutual consent, Ellis felt that it was better for the children to be in the hands of one loving parent, rather than buffeted between two violently dissenting ones.[17] In the end, Ellis endorsed the plan of Paul and Victor Margueritte in which 'each party' to a divorce 'should choose a representative, and . . . these two should choose a third: and . . . this tribunal should privately investigate, and if they agree should register the divorce, which should take place six or twelve months later.'[18]

It came to this: socially sanctioned trial marriages were to take place on a widening scale, monogamy was not necessarily to have religious sanctions, marriage was to admit affairs and divorce by mutual consent. Meanwhile training in restraint, carried through 'a long series of generations' would prepare the way for the new freedoms.

The next chapter turned to the art of love. In Victorian days far too many newly married women found the bridal night almost indistinguishable from rape. It was Balzac's ape with the violin, who could so easily render the most beautiful instrument incapable of music for the rest of its life. Yet every available obstruction was put in the way of the young man or young woman who wanted to know more than the cold textbooks taught of the sheer artistry which belonged to this finest and most profound art of all.

It seems extremely probable [wrote Professor E. D. Cope][19] that if this subject could be properly understood, and become, in the details of its practical conduct, a part of a written social science, the monogamic marriage might attain a far more general success than is often found in actual life. . . .

SirJames Paget 'in his lecture on Sexual Hypochondriasis' was of the same opinion.

For Ellis, emotional and sexual life had to develop powerful aesthetic and spiritual elements before their true potential could be realized, and the introduction of aesthetics came close to the core of his philosophy of love. Love and art were inextricably involved for him, because morality in love was to be substituted by aesthetics. Codes of conduct imposed from without would be replaced by aesthetic discrimination from within. Whatever forms of love-making satisfied two lovers was their concern, but there remained an art in love-making, an aesthetic instinct which, once completely grasped and realized, could transform love, and in the transformation replace morals. It would be asked, not was it right, but was it satisfactory and beautiful to the two people concerned? He was to develop this aesthetic theory of love at greater length in the *Dance of Life* thirteen years later.

Ellis's attitude to sexual overtures in the sixth volume would dismay the modern women's movement. 'The art of love is based on the fundamental natural fact of courtship; and courtship is the effort of the male to make himself acceptable to the female.' Fundamental natural fact? Modern emancipation finds it very difficult to separate some aspects of nature from nurture in sexual relations but Ellis's biological positivism had no such problem. Ellis compounded his now old-fashioned views by quoting Vatsyayana: 'The art of love is the art of pleasing women.' Much more acceptable was this quote from Balzac: 'A man must never permit himself a pleasure with his wife which he has not the skill first to make her desire.' Ellis believed that the whole art of love was contained in that phrase excluding any possibility that a woman might herself take a similar initiative. The assumption that courtship patterns are an expression of inherent biological drives is regarded as somewhat reactionary today, but for Ellis it was one root of his radicalism. Paradoxically, he wanted to reform the relations between the sexes by means which had certain inbuilt limitations.

Sex in twentieth-century man had its own sovereign right, he said. It was no longer exclusively an act of procreation; in part because of the growth of psychic differentiation, in part because it had been freed from accidental pregnancy. No one had put it better, he felt, than Tarde: 'in place of a simple method of procreation (love) has become an end, it has created itself a title, a royal title.'[20]

Any condensation of volume six does it violence. It is impossible to convey the sweep of the twelve chapters without resolving to write a book within a book. Neither is it possible to do justice to the sometimes crisp, sometimes beautifully limpid style, which mounts so naturally to its moments of eloquence. But at last his immense undertaking was complete. At last the sixth and final volume was finished, and on 7 August 1909 Ellis put down his pen, the final sentence written. He sat in the tiny sun hut on the side of a Cornish moor and wrote in his diary a quotation from George Chapman: 'the work that I was born to do is done.' Later he spoke of it as if he had suddenly emerged in a very high place where an olympic vision granted him the illusion that he stood outside and far above the dark jungle he had traversed.[21]

> A deep calm joy possessed me, a serene exultation. I could enter the emotion that stirred Gibbon when he wrote the last words of his History in the summer-house at Lausanne. Certainly I had not, like him, achieved an immortal work of scientific art. . . . But I had done mankind a service which mankind needed, and which, it seemed, I alone was fitted to do.

Freud would have considered such words pretentious.

Chapter 13

Edith goes to America

Now a man of fifty, widely known in certain circles in Britain, America, Germany and France, Havelock Ellis still had not become a popular oracle like H. G. Wells or Bernard Shaw. The sales of his books had not made his name a household word, and he reached a different audience from Wells or Shaw.

A certain grandeur, always implicit in his person, had achieved fresh depth and assurance. The beard had whitened, the eyes were more deeply set, the brows craggy, but not all the pressures of work and emotional troubles had broken the glowing serenity which frequently suffused his face. As he entered a bus, or the Reading Room of the British Museum, the sheer spectacle of his figure set heads turning. He looked magnificently the part of the Messiah. Extraordinarily, to all outward appearances, there was still about his person that harmony so at variance with his private life. His belief that the measure of a man's civilization was his concern for every passing stranger, persisted, and forced him to place himself at the disposal of any casual person who came his way. He continued to give freely of time and books and advice to whatever anonymous person knocked on his door, and that was all the more remarkable because he deeply disliked people arriving without warning.

The feminine passivity of his nature, the awareness, sometimes to the point of clairvoyance, of what lay hidden in the feminine psyche, continued to make the company of women pleasant to him, and they so often found in him that negation of masculine rapacity which stirred their deepest responses. Several very close women friends had been added to the circle which now admired him.

Scores of others felt the breath of his graciousness in the large correspondence he sustained. He wrote in pen and ink to three kinds of person. There was the correspondence with psychologists, authors, anthropologists and sociologists; there were letters to friends and letters to complete strangers who wrote spontaneously from all corners of

156

Europe and America. Piles of letters accumulated in the Brixton flat: sometimes, answering them would occupy the whole morning, sometimes, a man in Australia who wanted to know 'the secrets of the universe' had to wait three months before Ellis attempted to elaborate them.

Destruction has overtaken some of the important letters, and some confusion surrounds their disappearance. His will made certain dispositions for his own letters but did not refer to correspondence addressed to him by other people. Legally, these letters were interpreted as belonging to the residue of the estate which passed out of the hands of the then literary executrix (Françoise Delisle). Bundles of correspondence were surrendered at the death of Havelock Ellis, and in the end it was decided that they were nothing more than old letters and were burnt. Fortunately, by accident, not all have gone.

The period 1900 to 1911 was immensely fecund. Deeply involved with the last volumes of the *Studies in the Psychology of Sex*, correspondence, articles and deepening trouble with Edith, Ellis yet contrived to write three lesser books – *The Nineteenth Century* (1900), *A Study of British Genius* (1904) and *The Soul of Spain* (1908). They were not important books, but *The Nineteenth Century* revealed the wit concealed within his scientific detachment. It took the form of a dialogue between two antiquarians of the future looking back on our forgotten civilization, and anticipated some chapters of H. G. Wells's *A Modern Utopia*. 'They knew all about the laws of what they called gravitation, but they thought it impure to ascertain the laws by which human beings are attracted to one another. . . .'[1]

As a piece of satire on the mid-Victorian scene *The Nineteenth Century* had sparkling moments and would be well worth re-printing today. Ellis attacked the press, poverty, militarism and the Bible. 'One-half of the journalists', he wrote ironically, 'could at most be right . . .', but understanding little more about the underlying facts than their readers, they formed 'decided opinions' 'at a moment's notice' and were thus enabled to express 'opposing views with much fervour'.[2] Since 'only one person per thousand had time to think for himself, the other nine hundred and ninety nine' simply accepted ready-made newspaper opinions 'for use at spare moments during the day'.[3] It was all very unexpected coming from Ellis. In personal relations he sadly lacked a sense of humour. In his books it was rare.

Of a very different kind, *A Study of British Genius* cost Ellis hours of weary work. It has lost its force today and even though well received by some critics of the day the book did not sell. Taking 1,030 people of supreme intellectual ability from the 66 volumes of the *Dictionary of National Biography*, Ellis set out to identify genius in terms of racial affiliations, geographical distribution, heredity, physiology and psychology. Genius, Galton had said, was the result of normal deviation from the average, contradicting Lombroso who thought it fundamentally a pathological state connected with insanity. Ellis differed from both. Houston Petersen, in his study of Havelock Ellis, remarks:[4]

> [*A Study of British Genius*] is a popular rather than a technical work and has by no means the standing, among scholars, of Ellis's sex studies. . . . For example, E. L. Thorndike and L. M. Terman have no great confidence in his conclusions and would not think of ranking him with J. M. Cattell as a statistical investigator in the field of genius. E. M. East doubts whether Ellis 'ever knew enough of statistical theory to pass a first course examination'.[5]

Petersen clearly saw one interesting portrait of British genius in the book. Men of brilliant intellectual ability, Ellis said, were often eldest children, revealing delicate constitutions, tending to suffer from shyness, having high-pitched voices and disliking social contacts. Add the difficult handwriting, a mother of marked piety, and a comparatively undistinguished father – all characteristics appearing in *A Study of British Genius* – and genius began to bear unmistakable resemblances to the subject of this book. Such a portrait was probably not intentional, and most psychologists would today consider his conclusions rubbish.

The Soul of Spain followed his fifth visit to that country in 1906. All that was old and beautiful in Spain came to life in these pages, with words woven like a tapestry into a pattern of something he loved. The sunlight burnt across the page and the gardens of Granada burst into brilliant life, until the reader stepped into the dark magnificence of Seville Cathedral, and presently it was almost as if – so vivid the writing became – he was breathing the exhilarating mountain air of Montserrat.

At least one Spanish scholar did not like the book. Nor did Olive Schreiner. Continuing to correspond with Ellis over the years she presently wrote from De Aar, South Africa:[6]

Dear Old Boy,
    Thanks for your two letters. You could write a book most engaging and splendid if you wrote more as you write letters, and more spontaneously. Any one of your letters to me where you've told me just a little about your travels in Spain, say, is worth the whole of your book. The letters *live*, the book seems artificial. You express in the book what you've really seen and thought but in a stiff artificial manner. There is not *enough* of *yourself in all your later writing*. If I were very ill and you knew that my life depended on my being amused and interested, and to help me you wrote an account of a fortnight spent in Paris, just who you saw, where you went and felt interest, what you felt about *your* food and *your* room: and how the

pictures impressed you, it would no doubt be splendid. Your short hurried letters even are 100 times more interesting than your books. . . .
Olive.

Sigmund Freud wrote his first letter to Ellis some time in the spring of 1907, and Ellis replied that he was very pleased to receive a copy of his new book. He had written a brief notice about the book, he said, a copy of which he enclosed.[7] Three months elapsed before Ellis wrote again thanking Freud for sending him a copy of *The Psychopathology of Everyday Life* of which he hoped soon to write a review.[8] A third letter from Ellis to Freud said that although he did not completely share Freud's ideas he always read his writing with admiration.[9]

This could hardly be justified by his review of *Ueber den Traum* which opened with the comment that Freud's views had not been universally accepted and concluded: 'the analysis of a few cases . . . hardly enables us to generalise.' Ellis gave a very inadequate account of *The Psychopathology of Everyday Life* in his review of that book, but successfully undermined some of Freud's examples, and showed that many everyday slips could be traced to conscious as well as unconscious causes. The case of the young man who met Freud while waiting for his wife, and later invited Freud to join them at breakfast, was relatively easy to attack. When Freud arrived at the breakfast table the young man had thrown his coat on the third seat. Freud interpreted this as a message that his company was no longer desired. Ellis wryly commented that he could easily have thrown his coat there because of a pre-occupation with the newly arrived wife and having nowhere else to throw the coat.

I have been unable to trace Freud's part in these early exchanges but later letters will be quoted and their relationship examined. A fourth letter from Ellis in August 1911 said he did not oppose the school founded by Freud, nor did he regard himself as a member.[10]

One letter from Freud does survive, for the year 1912:[11]

Wien IX., Berggasse 19
My dear sir,
    Your portrait in my study reminds me of a promise I made to reply to your gift. . . . I have decided to substitute a 6 years' old plaquette, regarded at the time as a reasonable likeness, for a photograph.
    You may accept it in token of the high esteem I have for your person as well as for your works.
    Yours very truly,
    (Freud)

In the same year Ellis wrote *The Task of Social Hygiene*, another full-scale book which developed his theories on eugenics. The chapter

'Eugenics and Love'[12] insisted that the time had come to concentrate upon the quality of the population rather than any equilibrium of numbers. It developed, in greater detail, the idea of a eugenic register which would show the pedigree, history and characteristics of whole families. This was not to be done compulsorily. People were to be persuaded to compile a brief summary of their family history voluntarily, until a eugenic aristocracy had been established.

Ideally, people possessing equal honours in the eugenics register would seek to marry someone of their own kind, producing children which, on the principle of probability, would have every chance of outdistancing the average. This, repeated over the generations, might go some way towards stimulating an increase in the 'right kind' of people.[13] In effect the register would bring about a scientifically reformed Debrett where the snobbery of birth, money and rank, would give place to health, intelligence and ability.

Ellis argued that this was no arbitrary interference with the laws of nature.[14] The widely accepted notion that luck and love brought people together without discrimination, was an illusion. Love did not altogether laugh at science, and passion was not blown by any casual wind. Certain types tended to be selected by certain other types when left to the random law of nature. On the surface, there was a dangerous contradiction here. If this happened 'naturally' why interfere with it artificially?

It was because socialism tended to subsidize the nation indiscrim- inately, encouraging the incompetent, weak and defective to multiply, that it seemed to Ellis to aggravate the problem it sought to solve. Steeped in the 'sympathy' of eighteen-century moralists socialism improved conditions of labour and pay, only to multiply the number of people who needed care and protection. The intervention of eugenics was necessary before the environmental school of socialism could be justified, but negative rather than positive eugenics was the first priority and would concentrate on trying to check the reproduction of the unfit. Here he became a pioneer advocate of abortion.

One big question remained unanswered. To establish beyond quibble those attributes most desirable in a human being, was a piece of subtle and complex analysis which too often led into a morass of doubt. Intangible qualities like generosity, imagination and sensitivity, insusceptible to scientific measurement, were as important as intelligence and might occur in the humblest stocks. It would misrepresent Ellis to say that he was unaware of these subtleties or to imply that he failed to see the value of poor relief, health treatment and unemployment insurance. In the end, he called for a higher synthesis of individualism and socialism, of eugenics and environment, of nurture and a new control over nature.

Edith Ellis preferred *The Task of Social Hygiene* to many of Ellis's books but she did not agree with its conclusions. Approaching fifty, she continued to be fiercely interested in all he wrote and thought, but there were signs of a new tolerance.

Among the new friends which her play, *The Subjection of Kezia*, had brought into her life, was a certain Mrs Cosmo Hamilton who lived at West Drayton. Early in 1911, Edith set out to visit Mrs Hamilton's country house, discovered a clump of cottages near by, and signed a long lease practically on the spot. Once again it proved disastrous. Known as Woodpecker Farm, the buildings had a superficial attraction from sheer age, but on closer examination revealed extensive dilapidation, colonies of vermin and tenants who were known in the village as oddities.

Ellis reminded her of the difficulties they had encountered with the Count House. It was of no avail. Edith affected astonishment. The past! The Count House! But they were different. She knew how things worked now. No cut-throat builder could any longer outwit her or intimidate her with exaggerated bills. When the last remnants of Ellis's objections still remained she protested that they could not honourably withdraw at so late a date. There would be no dishonour, Ellis answered. Oh well, Edith said, I suppose I'll have to get another backer.[15]

Realizing that this was impossible Ellis at last gave way. At the outset came a serious set-back. It was still not clear to Havelock that Edith's lesbian nature very often drove her to take cottages next to someone who either strongly attracted her, or had friends who shared similar persuasions. The people more than the property very often explained her enthusiasm for derelict cottages and decaying farms. And when the Cosmo Hamiltons now quarrelled with their landlord and left, it rendered half the venture purposeless. Bravely, Edith went through with the fumigation, and for a brief spell they actually lived together at Woodpecker. Delightful in the summer, Woodpecker became impossible as the weather grew wet and cold, and presently Edith accepted 'lodgers' in the effort to make ends meet. The rapidity with which people welcomed as friends, changed their fundamental natures once they became paying guests, dispelled Edith's enthusiasm for Woodpecker more effectively than mounting debts, but money matters grew steadily worse and soon even Edith had to admit that Woodpecker was beyond their means.

Their new friends now included a rich American who came to Woodpecker one day, thought the house delightful, and decided to buy it. Bubbling over with fresh optimism Edith embraced this salvation with a total lack of consideration for Ellis. Having almost blackmailed him into leasing the property and involved him in debt, when the American friend paid the purchase money, Edith promptly settled her own debts and ignored his. She would pay him back eventually, she said. He would, without fail, get his full share of the purchase price. Alas, he never did. There were extraordinary inconsistencies in Edith's monetary ethics: she would strain the last fibre promptly to pay any debt to a stranger, but with friends alarming intervals were liable to elapse, with close friends it sometimes extended into years, and with Havelock she appeared to work on the assumption that heavenly rewards were more commensurate with his lofty nature.

In 1912 she took a flat at the top of a doctor's house in Harley Street. There, once more, Havelock dutifully called to see her, laden with all the things she liked to eat. He gave her breakfast in bed, turned on her bath, and waited upon her in the familiar ritual. Still fresh duties thus fell upon Havelock's all too willing shoulders.

In September they travelled down to Carbis Bay together. Edith was reasonably well, the weather perfect and they relaxed in each other's company, but suddenly she launched an old complaint in a new form. She had become freshly conscious of 'a certain callousness' in Ellis. Love, for Ellis, remained a powerful presence running deep in the background, but it was a presence incapable of conventional expression. He was repelled by the ready-made love-responses which husbands so easily produced for doubting wives, and in a moment of comic inspiration he said to Edith one day when she was particularly distressed, 'if only I had a tail to wag'. It did not reconcile Edith. She needed constant reaffirmation of his love, and the more frequent the declarations, the more she needed them. On the day following their return from Cornwall, Edith wrote to him from Harley Street:

> Havelock – I think it is *because* I love you that I get so frenzied, or else I'm best dead. I feel I want to see you so badly and to kiss you well after my jig-jags. Please try and help me not to be like that. It is your apparent callousness to me sometimes that makes me want to put pins in you. . . .

Serious tensions not only remained between them; Edith's whole nature, still too easily subject to unreasoning fears, was about to take another and far more tragic turn. In the summer of 1913 she set off for a holiday in Switzerland and Ellis decided to spend a few weeks in Spain. The trip remained in his memory as full of minor accidents which culminated in a mysterious illness at Perpignon. Suddenly feeling unwell, he returned to his hotel, took his temperature, and found that it registered 102°. At a loss to account for this, he spent miserable hours trying to get simple food in an hotel which catered for enormous appetites and subtle palates. A fully qualified doctor, it was reasonable to conclude that when two days later he still felt ill, he would summon a Spanish doctor. Instead, Ellis dragged himself about, fell into an exhausted sleep every evening, and continued to make his way towards a rendezvous in France which he had arranged with Amy. At last reaching Nantes, he suddenly felt worse and took his temperature again. Still it stood at 102°. Hot and cold flushes were now raging over his body, he felt his weakness growing, and for the first time wondered whether he would ever reach Amy. At this worst point, a letter came from Edith:[16]

> My Darling One, I am very ill. Cannot get right at all somehow. . . .
> I feel the smash up I have dreaded for years has come at last. . . . Try
> not to let it spoil your holiday, but God only knows what it will be to
> see you again . . . if I die I shall leave all in confusion and what can I
> do? . . .

Emotional blackmail could go no further.

Both were unaware of the real situation. Edith did not know that Havelock himself was ill nor was her sense of physical disintegration entirely misplaced. A serious revelation lay a few months away.

I have not been able to trace Havelock's reply to Edith's letter, but he remained in France, met Amy, spent several days with her and then at last hurried home. Edith was away in the country. Once more her heart was engaged with what Ellis described as the 'dear friend of that period'. Her affairs were now numerous, but none could quite take the peculiar place Havelock held in her life and affections. Presently she wrote a letter which carried quite new significance. It was a letter from a sick, worried, distressed woman. It said that, above all things, she desired to be in his arms, her headaches were so terrible. She seemed to be such a hopeless human being one way and another. It was all . . . impossible – impossible. . . . And she was getting desperate. 'Write and tell me you love me, and don't always want to be away from me.' This was the first written evidence of the collapse of her desire for independence. As a result, for the next nine months they were mostly together.

The precise finances of Havelock and Edith still were not clear. For years they had made great show of dividing the expenses of theatre or food to such a pitch that Edith was fond of telling friends that even the bill for the wedding ring had been shared. In one sense Havelock was undoubtedly fortunate. A man living the hazardous life of letters, it was important to have a wife not in need of support. In another sense, Edith's extravagance sometimes threatened to make her a greater liability than any dependent relative.

The Lyceum Club for women, once a thriving challenge to its male equivalents, was now the headquarters from which she launched one fresh scheme after another. She sat on Club Committees, she wrote short stories, she lectured, organized dinners, flashed about the corridors and steadily became the Club's most indefatigable inspiration. Held in high regard by many of its members, and particularly by the Poetry Circle, each new step in her literary career was watched by a group of adoring friends given to raptures which sometimes proved embarrassingly premature.

Among the pioneers of the Poetry Circle in 1912 was Florence M. Mole who became a close friend of Edith's. She recorded interesting impressions from those days. She speaks of those rare evenings at the Lyceum Club when W. B. Yeats, Lawrence Binyon, Walter De La Mare, Drinkwater, John Masefield, Alfred Noyes read their poems.[17]

> On two occasions the Poetry Circle met at West Drayton – a little village close to Windsor Castle and Eton College, where Mrs Havelock Ellis had a cottage. The first meeting was in the summer time. . . . There were casement windows and bowls of roses, tall vases of 'Love in the Mist', delphiniums and Canterbury Bells and the scents of myriads of flowers wafted in from the open windows. Upstairs we gathered together to listen to a paper on the poet, Francis Thompson, with discussion . . . then we walked and talked in the garden till the tea-time hour. Imagine a long table with white napery and bowls of roses, laden with good things . . . Cornish cream and butter and cakes . . . waiting on the guests was Dr Havelock Ellis. . . . Tall in stature, leonine head and massive brow . . . the spirit of hospitality. . . .

In 1911 a collection of Edith's short stories appeared under a title – *The Imperishable Wing* – suggested by her husband. Moderately interesting as straightforward narratives, they drove poor Havelock, unmistakable victim of purblind love, into remarkable hyperbole about their humour, which, he felt, reached at times 'an almost Shakespearian quality'.

The peculiar quality of Mrs Havelock Ellis's mind can be judged not only by her love of the *Pathétique Sonata* above any other, but by the dedications she was dissuaded from including in book after book – 'Dedicated to a Healer by a Jester'. In this last book – against all advice – she included it.

As a lecturer she was much more impressive. If her first attempt to deal with homosexuality in a lecture given at the Eugenics Education Society did not lead to renewed invitations, the attraction of her platform personality remain unquestioned. She had a fine, rich, deep voice and once launched into her subject could talk fluently and at length, even if what she said did not rise above the superficial. There was an immediacy about her talk which gripped the attention of her listeners, as though the intensity which brimmed over in her large beautiful eyes poured out especially for each member of the audience.[18]

Mrs Ellis also ran a group described as the Higher Thought Centre at 10 Cheniston Gardens near Kensington High Street station, and there, for the sum of 1*s*. 6*d*. for one lecture or 3*s*. 6*d*. for three, she enlightened disciples of Edward Carpenter and James Hinton about their respective masters. If the extraordinary title given to the society and the strange nature of its literature repelled some people, once more the sheer power of Mrs Ellis's personality transcended the crank in her nature which was always waiting to caricature her more serious intentions.

Yet a growing disorganization in her personality, a continual foreboding of some mysterious force undermining her health, slowly drove her over the next two years to abandon half her work, commitees and lectures.[19] Since she was, in fact, not physically or mentally well this was sensible enough. But Edith being immutably Edith, she determined to interpret her withdrawal in portentous terms. 'I am resigning all Committees . . .', she wrote to Havelock, 'even the Poetry, so that I can at last live as an artist.'

The real blow struck one brilliant September afternoon in 1913.[20] Havelock was in the habit of waiting for Edith at the underground station in Down Street, which was close to the Lyceum Club. This was a concession to his distaste for meeting her with a crowd of fellow club members, now fascinated to get a glimpse of her famous husband. Instead, she would escape everyone, slip around the corner, and there, pacing gently up and down, usually a little ahead of time, was the ever faithful Havelock. That autumn day he paced as before. His face always lit up as he saw her, but today as he went towards her eagerly, he detected something in her manner which threw him into anxious inquiry. She had been to the doctor, she said. It was ironic that, in a roundabout way, she appeared to go to the doctor whenever she needed money. By determining her expectation of life and insuring it for several hundred pounds, she could offer the policy as security for a loan. One such policy and pledge for £200, already arranged, had encouraged her to approach the insurance company again. The pressure of another debt, the result of one of her illnesses, necessitated a second policy to cover a second loan. Just how the insurance companies would have regarded this double indemnity is not clear, but the risk of any such complication was scotched by the serious diagnosis the second doctor gave. She had diabetes.

The revelation shocked Havelock. They paced to and fro before Down Street station trying to get the measure of this utterly unexpected blow. Edith bubbled with questions. She had put the same questions to the insurance doctor, without believing his answers. Now Havelock tried to reassure her, but he felt a cold bewilderment. No one then knew of insulin and the complications of diabetes could be serious. It was some time before they ceased pacing and went home to Edith's flat together.

Over the next few weeks irrational fears multiplied. Edith's heart was getting worse, another disease of which at present she knew little or nothing, was developing in her system, and it seemed to her anxiety-ridden mind that the doctors gave the most unsatisfactory answers to all her questions. Everything simultaneously gathered against her. A sense of vulnerability to illness, a horror of loneliness in the night and the threat of mysterious forces waiting on the edge of life, combined to intensify her love for Havelock and drive her to seek his company more and more.

For Ellis, Edith had become part of his life in such a profound way that this bleak reminder of death waiting not many years away deeply dismayed him. Yet the discovery of diabetes did not so much draw them together in a new way, as suddenly make their love more articulate. They spoke of it more. A new range of expression, a new tenderness came into the letters they wrote.

But now, when Havelock looked into her eyes as he looked into the eyes of no other human being, there was suddenly a moment when he detected a strangeness there, beyond the reach of diabetes, or illness; a strangeness of spirit harshly alien to anything he had known before. It was a moment he could not understand and because it spoke of something beyond normal consciousness it left a sudden and worse chill. He saw it and said nothing, but when, a few days later the mood came back again, it troubled him greatly.

Far away in South Africa on 13 March of the same year, Olive Schreiner was approaching a similar crisis in her health. She talked constantly to her husband of a 'cure' Professor Carloni of Florence had effected in the case of a woman friend, and at last Cronwright Schreiner suggested that she should make the long trip via London to consult him. She left De Aar on 13 November 1913, very ill and unhappy.

She too had now reached a curious mental state. Like Edith, she was haunted by fears of dreadful diseases progressing unchecked in her system, like Edith, not a single doctor of the many eminent men who examined her, convinced her that he really knew what he was talking about; like Edith, she worried continually over the condition of her heart. Her midnight stumpings across the floor of her room, the states of trance when she still daubed words like splashes of paint on paper, the outbursts when she almost physically assailed someone whose behaviour appalled her, had grown worse. Sometimes she now created episodes in a life she never led. Writing to Ellis years later, her husband said:[21]

Yes, that account of Olive's about that long drive *is* interesting – *more so*, it seems to me, because it is untrue. Her imagination made things so real that she (unconsciously no doubt when once started) *invented* and related *just* such incidents as the one you mention. . . . Consider that . . . letter to Mrs Smith that she and I had turned vegetarians, that both us were much better (especially my non-existent rheumatism) and that I was living on macaroni and cheese – a thing I have never done at all! There is not a word of truth in the whole thing. . . .

Havelock left the cottage in Cornwall and travelled up to London especially to meet Olive Schreiner on her way through London. They spent a few days more or less together, but the old fire was no longer there. He was shocked at her appearance and spent hours trying to exorcize the strange fears which continued to haunt her. She, like Edith, found considerable reassurance in his presence alone.

On 29 December 1913, the Lyceum Club organized a dinner in Olive Schreiner's honour at which, inevitably, Havelock was not present. The occasion went smoothly enough until an admirer was unwise enough to repeat the piece of gossip that Olive had changed certain passages in *An African Farm* to meet the suggestions of her publisher. Immediately, Olive ceased to be the bright, friendly guest. She hit out ferociously, banging the table until the violence of her fist and denunciation made her almost incomprehensible. The august assemblage was embarrassed. Writers were eccentric – one accepted that – but such an explosion and in public. . . .[22]

Presently, Olive's asthma grew worse again, and she decided to make the long journey to Italy to consult Professor Carloni in Florence. From there she wrote letters to Ellis in an enormous pencil scrawl with three or four words to a line:[23]

> Dear Havelock Boy. . . . I'm so sick and faint all the time. . . . It seems I am not to get better anywhere. That little burst of betterness in England made me so hopeful; but when I go back there in May . . . I cling to the thought of – as my last hope. If I can't get better . . . I would so much rather die. The terrible thing is that I may not, and may live on year after year, to be a burden to others – I can't read or write a letter without exhaustion any more.

So lately parted from him, she desperately wanted to see Havelock again and asked whether he could possibly take a week off and join her in Italy. Edith was away at the time, and Havelock wrote to her explaining Olive's request. If she still seemed uncertain about Amy, Edith no longer feared Olive Schreiner and now, confronted with his letter, she encouraged him to go. It was a generous gesture. Edith had real evidence of her own serious illness and had lately committed to paper another letter across the envelope of which she scrawled, 'Open only after my death.' Several similar letters had been written before, each one scrapped as the years rendered its provisions superfluous, and she obviously enjoyed the power and importance which the threat of death creates.

Ellis set off for Florence shortly afterwards and at last joined Olive in an hotel which, instinctively, he disliked. She looked rather worse, he thought, than when he had last seen her in England. There was no questioning the awful ravages of asthma, the continual sleeplessness, the strain on heart, lungs and nerves, but Ellis was not overwhelmed as he would have been in the old days.

She was still an intimate friend, they corresponded closely and at length, but her place had been filled to overflowing by Edith. He found Olive, he wrote, with considerable understatement, 'in fair health'. Yet in January 1914 a letter to him had said:[24]

> I haven't written because I've been six days in bed. Those terrible internal pains came on suddenly as never before. I sent for an Italian doctor here; he said it was stone in the kidneys. For two days nothing but blood, due to the edges of the stone, he said, tearing the walls.

Returning to England, Havelock found Edith preparing for a great new adventure. American friends had encouraged her in the belief that she would find a responsive audience in America for any lecture she cared to deliver. Some revolutionary attempt to retrieve her fortunes had become imperative since her finances were now approaching a desperate state. The scheme for an American lecture tour simmered powerfully in her not terribly clear mind.

In August and September of 1913 they were frequently together in a small cottage near Stanwell, while the glittering mirage of America, awash with wealth, grew more and more persistent. The play based on *Kit's Woman* had its first private production in that year, but no one was prepared to launch it publicly. As a novel it had been tolerable; as a play. . . .

Presently, America loomed ever larger in Edith's inflamed imagination. She was well into middle age, diabetes had already taken its toll, she was not in any serious sense a seasoned lecturer, imponderables amongst American lecture audiences were immense, and the only proposals she could produce from the other side of the Atlantic were distinguished by an alarming vagueness; but her dash and daring were unimpaired, and with rather less than £12 to spare she plunged excitedly into planning such a sweep across the American continent as would bring dollars, prestige and renewed health at one stroke. Inevitably, the long-suffering Havelock was to be the subject of the first lecture. If Edith appears to have deceived herself into believing that she was equally important in her own right, it was Havelock Ellis, the philosopher of love, the Americans wanted to hear about, however curious they might be to know what sort of woman he had chosen as his wife.

She could now more easily face leaving Havelock in England, a vulnerable target to the several women who adored him, because the person once considered the most dangerous, Amy, no longer worried whether he would marry her. There had been many estrangements between himself and Amy, but their relationship had at last settled into a pattern in which all thought of marriage vanished.

And so one late April day, with spring in the air, Edith left for America and the break was agonizing for her. They parted in London in a state which Havelock described as 'sad exaltation'. He did not accompany her to Southampton, the honour of that final parting being reserved for her latest woman friend. In the following two days before she actually sailed, Havelock received six letters from her pouring out her yearning for his presence and re-assurance. Characteristically, when she finally left she had only £10 to meet her American expenses.

Olive Schreiner returned to London and wrote to Havelock a week after Edith sailed: 'Friday would suit me well dear. I'll meet you at Charing Cross. . . . I do hope you'll get a wire from Edith and good news; I'm anxious about you both . . .!'[25] They were to correspond almost until her death but this letter underlined the friendship, untroubled any longer by passion, which marked the remainder of their relationship. Unexpectedly, it was neither Olive nor Amy who was destined to disrupt Edith's sense of security yet again.

When a coded wireless message came indicating that Edith had arrived safely, Havelock felt great relief. Florence Mole travelled with her on the boat and the great event, she said, was a banquet held in Mrs Ellis's honour at which she gave readings from her book, *My Cornish Neighbours*.

Already Havelock had resumed work in his flat in Brixton, pressing on with half a dozen interrupted tasks. In the following weeks Olive was sometimes in London, but he saw relatively little of her. In June he left for two weeks holiday with Amy, and it was a holiday marked by fresh understanding.

Arrived in America, Edith threw herself into the life of New York, and the first shocks and difficulties were overwhelmed by the unceasing hospitality, the quick friendliness of the American people. She became the honoured guest of a Mr and Mrs Maclean, and presently many of the women stars of New York society were clamouring to meet her, the press telephoned and waylaid her and a whirl of invitations, sight-seeing and lectures swept her into torrential activity. She went to big houses, to lavish parties, to receptions and theatres. Everything she had ever written she read aloud to many different audiences; she delivered, in carefully varied styles, her plays, her stories, and lectures; she acceded to requests for future tours and readings; she drank, ate, made merry, did not get to bed until very late and delighted in every moment of it.

Diabetes and the dread of less tangible illnesses sank into the background. Her neurotic fantasies and tensions faded. Ebullient, given to total frankness and gifted with a golden voice which charmed everyone, she was a natural counterpart to the extravagantly extrovert

life of New York. Soon there were moments when she delighted
newspapermen beyond their highest hopes.

It was unfortunate that her desire to make an impression was
complicated by a complete lack of sophistication in interviews, which
led to appalling indiscretions about Havelock and her relations with
him. As they filtered back across the Atlantic he was very disturbed. She
had once expressed complete contempt for those members of the British
press who, in their eagerness to interview Havelock, strained at every
possible door into his private life. When his reluctance to talk about
himself broke down one day, and a most unobjectionable interview
appeared, she had recoiled in violent disapproval. But now she publicly,
and with apparent zest, gave intimate pictures of their private life
together, which not only disturbed Havelock but many of their friends.
He was driven to protest. He wrote three letters which do not survive
today. They must have been more emphatic than usual because they
created in Edith a renewal of that anger which, so inevitably part of her
character, always developed when she found herself in the wrong.
Penitence, in these moments, was alien to her. She complained that her
alleged crimes were created by her critics. They were not, in fact, crimes
at all. There was nothing wrong in giving newspapermen that dash of
personal spice which they so desperately needed to redeem their stories
from dullness. It was she wrote in one letter 'best for us both'.[26]

Best for us both. Neurotic people are sometimes unhappy without a
grievance. Superficially Edith had developed this gift to the pitch where
she suffered, even more intensely, the pain she caused in others, but
there were other tragic reasons for her highly irrational behaviour.

I traced some of the interviews which led to all the trouble. With a
prodigality excelling the most skilled publicity agent, Mrs Ellis
distributed interviews in some twenty of the forty-eight States, either
directly or indirectly.

In April 1914, there appeared in the *Evening World*, spectacularly
displayed across five columns, an interview decorated with vulgar little
sketches, illustrating the views and opinions of Edith.[27] Expressed in
essay form by Havelock, they had an original dignity of their own, but
delivered by his wife they read like indiscreet gossip.

Edith told the interviewer Marguerite Mooérs Marshall:

> I myself always vowed that I never would marry until I met a man
> who could accept thruppence from a woman for omnibus fare
> without looking like a fool. At last I met him! And I have gone on
> earning my own living just as I did before marriage. . . .

She had rarely 'earned' her living, but minor inaccuracies in this
interview were nothing beside the effect of another which appeared in
the *New York Tribune*.[28] There she revealed, with an attempt at
jocularity, the curious ritual of the Two Moor Cottages:

We took two wee stone cottages there . . . Mr Ellis's rooms and the kitchen were in one cottage; my rooms and the dining-room were in the other. Some of the good, narrow-minded Cornish folk were sadly shocked. . . . 'Her live in one house and him in the next house,' they gossiped, 'and every night the servant maid do lock the door on he and give the key to she!'

If the Cornish folk gossiped so did the New Yorkers. This was rich. The philosopher of love, the writer of that glorious rolling English, the man who understood the mysteries of sexual experience better than any American living or dead, the scholar and poet, locked up by the servant maid every night and the key given to his wife! It was not safe to let him sleep alone; he had to be locked in to sleep. It was not seemly to permit him to lock up his wife; she locked him up. Socialite New York buzzed with the paradox, and a brittle sophistication rich in sardonic undertones carried its implications into fields beyond the comprehension of Edith. The interview was probably more distressing to Ellis because it contained considerable symbolic truth. The women closest to him always appeared to dominate him.

New York did not know this. Nor were the New Yorkers aware of the subtle deceptions practised by Edith's exaggerated statements.[29]

My plays? [echoed Mrs Ellis]. . . . Oh, yes, I have produced several. 'The Subjection of Kezia' ran for six months in the best London theatres; then a stock company played it for a year. 'Kit's Woman' [published in America as 'Steve's Woman'] was produced by the Play Actors. Next fall Edith Craig, Ellen Terry's daughter, is to produce my new one-act play, 'The Pixie', at the Pioneer Players. I have another new play with me, a one-act melodrama, 'The Laughter of the Gods', which I hope to place here in America. . . . Yes, I write stories and novels, too, and I've lectured off and on for twenty-eight years. . . .

Desperately anxious to establish her importance in her own right, she overdid it all. It was difficult to detect the woman with a single one-act curtain-raising play to her credit, a number of lectures, some dubious short stories and an unsuccessful novel.

Presently words ran away with her and she became empyrean:[30]

Happiness to my mind is a definite art and not an accident, for it is beyond accident, even beyond analysis. . . . It is my firm conviction that women should be by spiritual and physiological laws a constructive agent in the world's work. She is a maternal force, and in the future we must give the maternal force full play, for we are badly in need of a new home and a new state. . . .

Perhaps it was the embarrassing attempts to philosophize in his own likeness which distressed Havelock as much as the lapses in taste and discretion.

But it all paved the way to success. Invitations to talk, to philosophize multiplied, and if they all came from highly unacademic quarters that was to be expected. Publishers inquired about her books, producers about her plays. All in all, the whole American interlude was, from Edith's point of view, a considerable success.

Chapter 14

Edith's attempted suicide and death

She returned to England in July, in high spirits, and almost at once set out with Havelock for the Stanwell cottage, changed by the break into a woman who could not pay him enough attention. Inevitably, he forgot the interviews. Everything connived at their happiness. The weather was glorious, she was delighted to be re-united to her old family, Nod the cat, Ricky the donkey and Tom the pony, and she told and re-told the glittering fairy tale of her American trip. Presently, there began the first stage of another honeymoon between them which was to run on for several months, undisturbed by old dissensions, until it achieved a peace of spirit they had not known for years. Her nerve endings had lost their rawness, she ceased to be pathologically sensitive and even her ebullience had quietened.

Day after sunlit day they spent in the park at Stanwell. Work, domestic and literary, occupied a large part of the morning, and usually, the afternoon brought more writing in the open air, followed by a break for tea, and then a drive in the most bizarre carriage which the village of Stanwell had ever seen. Edith considered the trap too much for Tom the ancient pony to pull alone, and she contrived to harness both pony and donkey to the traces. Thus they would drive through the late afternoon, Edith resembling a gypsy with a kerchief about her head, Havelock a rustic seer, his beard flowing in the wind, as donkey and pony attempted some accommodation in their two so different modes of locomotion. One warm glorious day succeeded another, the corn ripened, the grass lost its freshness and such a peace settled on everything that America and her memories seemed momentarily alien. They would sit together under a tree in the park for hours, silently savouring the deep satisfaction of simply being together. They were middle-aged lovers joyfully aware of each other's presence.

In August, a friend lent them a cottage for a month at Speen in Buckinghamshire and there the pastoral idyll continued. Sometimes, at weekends, they lay in each others arms in the sheltered end of the

173

garden; sometimes they wandered in the dusk through the countryside, or stood listening to the soft burr of moths and bat-wings as the light faded and the first stars glimmered. Many years later the images of those days had sharpened for Havelock because he knew them as unrepeatable. Many years later he desired, above all things, to recover their serenity.

The declaration of war in August 1914, the swift conversion of people into bloodthirsty patriots, the release of organized hate, struck a chill to their hearts, but the whole upsurge only served to conceal their own personal tragedy waiting two short years away.

At fifty-five Ellis was not called upon for any special contribution to the war. It might be said that both preserved a far too detached way of life in the face of threatened national disaster, but a man equipped as Havelock was, half mystic, half scientist, and so incapable of aggression, was ill-suited to war-mongering. As for Edith, she too did no war work, and was soon overwhelmed once more by financial troubles. In debt, with her creditors becoming more pressing every day, she thought of crossing the Atlantic again. Ellis himself had suffered a financial blow. With the War, the publication of the Contemporary Science Series ceased, and one of his steadiest sources of income vanished. Professionally, he saw the end of it without special regret, but it meant a sudden and very big drop in his earnings. Edith discussed and re-discussed the proposed American trip with Havelock, who remained uncommitted. For several weeks the subject criss-crossed their lives until at last she made up her mind. War or no war, she would go.

Their second parting was no less painful than the first. Edith always remembered Havelock's face going ashen as the sirens sounded and she quickly went to her cabin and at once wrote him a letter pouring out her pain. She had a stormy sea-sick passage and at one point felt quite desperately the need to take the next boat back to Havelock, but when she arrived in New York her friends were waiting for her, and within a few days she began to feel better. Again America rose to her and yet, caught instantaneously as she was in the rush of one reception after another, there were undertones in the comments about her way of life with Havelock. She wrote long letters back to Havelock and in the midst of her whirling life still desperately needed him.

In one reply Havelock spoke of the death of his father at the age of eighty-seven. Inevitably the experience was more moving to him than to Edith and the far greater depths of his personality realized that this was a big moment in the whole long history of the Ellis family. In sharp contrast to Edith's bubbling sympathy, he wrote in his private notes, in that flowing prose which came so easily to him whenever deeply moved:[1]

today, maybe, that rite has in this Kentish graveyard for the last time been paid to any of the males of my house, who in centuries of old showed themselves so faithful to its observance, and in beautiful old churchyards in Suffolk and Kent, counted it their high office to scatter the grace of this final Mystery over so many human things that now are woven afresh into the texture of the world.

Some of his letters to Edith continued in her own spontaneous vein. Small business details, the settlement of one debt after another occupied many pages, but by far the greater part of the letters was taken up with a loving concern for Edith's health.

Soon her letters were full of references to coughs and colds, to 'flu and the prolonged weakness which followed it. In the midst of minor illnesses she suddenly asked him to write a lecture for her. In response he completed the paper 'Feminism and Masculinism', and a very large audience listened to the lecture. Edith's letters now increased rather than diminished, one coming close on the heels of another full of love. She proved, at this period, an inspired letter writer, and many pages were bright with colour and immediacy. A sense of whirlwind activity broke into every other line. There were also wild impulses to rush home to Havelock whose protection she continued to crave.

Not until 4 February did the first serious shadow cross her delight. Then came signs of irritability, criticism in the press, followed by a sharp break in the constant flow of tenderness towards Havelock, and at last outspoken resentment. Nervous exhaustion and a change in the reactions of her American audience were not alone responsible.

Unwittingly, Havelock himself played a part in what followed. In December 1914, an American woman, visiting London under an assumed name for reasons which will presently appear, came to his flat.[2] It so chanced that Amy was away at this time, illness in her family demanding attention, and Havelock, comparatively alone, welcomed a person who at once struck a sympathetic chord. Temperamentally they were alien however. She was impulsive, mercurial, daring, inheriting these traits from Irish ancestors, and again it was as if the characteristics which he himself lacked were those which strongly attracted him in others. Writing to me, B. Watson, the name under which she travelled, has described this first meeting:[3]

> I went to call on him about December of 1914, and was invited to
> tea. That was when he lived in that sordid apartment at Brixton,
> across from police headquarters. He opened the door for me, as he
> always did for his guests – and with his great white lovely head and
> flowing beard he was truly God-like. I found him modest,
> tongue-tied in expression, never looking one straight in the eye until
> he knew you very well; and then his eyes seemed to look right

through you into the very depths of your being. His eyes were extraordinary sky-blue. He was a magnificently handsome man. But his shyness was rather forbidding. . . .

B. Watson had arrived in England in melodramatic circumstances. A convinced disciple of birth control she had begun a crusade for voluntary parenthood in the United States. Charged with distributing 'obscene, lewd, lascivious, filthy, indecent and disgusting information to the public', she was arrested and only released on bail. The attempts of a Mr Comstock to bring her prematurely to trial led her to jump bail and take ship, under a false name, to England, where she proposed to prepare her defence in detail. Very familiar with Ellis's books, it was inevitable that she should want to meet a man whose ideas had much in common with her own, but now, confronted with Havelock Ellis in person, unexpected reactions stirred. Whatever their differences, an affectionate friendship rapidly developed between them, and brought Ellis into close understanding with someone who believed him to be a greater man than he realised. B. Watson – whose real name was Margaret Sanger – had not only read his books, and found them highly sympathetic; she thought that his influence in Western Europe and many parts of America was far wider than he understood. She tried now to convince him of this, but found him fairly incredulous. She later claimed that certain people close to him, had contrived to keep him in his modest place so effectively that he could not adjust to her belief that he was a great man. 'I am afraid I hammered at that a good deal', Margaret Sanger wrote to me. 'I think I helped to break through that curtain of Edith's ashamedness, and made him believe it, too. . . .'[4]

It was by now difficult for any woman confronted with the handsome Havelock Ellis, to remain completely unmoved, but by reason of the very swiftness of its growth, Havelock made no immediate reference to his new relationship with Margaret Sanger in his letters to his wife.

Far into the night they talked over every quirk and cranny of human behaviour, and together analysed all those problems of sex which were still anathema to the great mass of respectable people. One of the questions discussed was impotence and this had a special bearing on Havelock himself.

Nowhere in his autobiography does Ellis refer to those occasions when he put a note on Margaret Sanger's desk in the British Museum Reading Room saying – 'come to dinner and let me pick your brains' – or to the long talks they had far into the night. Nowhere does he tell of the trips to the Clyde, to Ireland, the visits to museums and concerts and the walks through Hyde Park and Kensington Gardens, which meant so much to both of them. Faithfulness to Edith may have driven him to concealment. At all events, his first letter to America mentioning Margaret Sanger had arrived on the very day Edith was steeling herself for her worst ordeal. She was to deliver a lecture and re-read the paper 'Masculinism and Feminism' at one of the biggest halls in Chicago. Anxiety, tensions and adverse comments in the press had reached a freshly distressing pitch, and the one certainty she knew in a very uncertain world was the unshakeable love which bound Havelock and herself together. It was just that love which – suddenly – his letters seemed to question. Whether a morbidly exaggerated imagination forced Edith to read into the letters a significance they did not contain we shall never know, because, as with all letters which disturbed her, she destroyed them. In fact, she was, she said, forced to destroy them because the police had suddenly descended on the house.

The state of the posts in wartime enforced a gap of three weeks before Havelock received a reply and, in all innocence, he continued to write more letters, each one alive with references to his new-found 'friend'. Edith's reaction was strong. She clearly saw a rival assuming very serious proportions 4,000 miles away across the Atlantic where she was powerless to intervene. The situation once more illustrated their so different temperaments. For Havelock, Edith had become an immutable part of his life, but Edith lived in a jungle of anxieties where suspicion transformed every shadow into a threatening shape. At root, it was her own self she distrusted as much as Havelock. Her powers of holding this beautiful person in thrall seemed inadequate in face of his strong attraction for others. Self-distrust had persisted throughout her life from the moment when she began to hate her father, and now it rose with renewed force. She wrote a long letter on 4 February which said what a shock his letter had been to her and how she wanted to die now that there was clearly someone else.

Havelock referred to this as 'a long and sweet letter'. Certainly there were sweet passages in it, and she was obviously thrown into terrible anxiety, but there were also barbs of an unmistakable kind: 'I wonder how you spent your birthday, Dear One? Which of the . . . came, or did they come in relays? . . .' The letter ended with this P.S: 'I drank to you and your new – – in a cocktail last night.'[5]

Surprisingly her lecture met an enthusiastic reception. There were fresh dinners, parties and press interviews, but the great set-piece at the Orchestral Hall had taken more toll of her strength than she realized, and the coincidence of Margaret's appearance was hard to bear. The querulous note grew in her letters. Self-pity sometimes ran over. Writing of this episode many years later in his autobiography Ellis said: 'I speak more especially concerning my own attitude [towards Margaret Sanger] . . . one of calm friendship, even though there was a sweet touch of intimacy about it.' Nowhere does he state that in 1915 he told Margaret that he loved her, which makes Edith's violent reactions far more intelligible.[6]

Edith recovered somewhat in the following week, but on 24 February she sent Havelock a doctor's report and it was almost as if she wanted to increase his by now deep distress. Ellis, a tormented and unhappy man, wrote and sent off letter after letter in an effort to reassure her.

New resentments, jealousies and feuds were beginning to beat up in the brassy glare of the lecture world, and the elemental need to renew daily newspaper sensations drove some journalists into attack. One article was bluntly headed 'Mrs Ellis's Failure'. Even worse, Edith, incorrigibly indiscreet, had talked afresh to newspapermen, and speculation was suddenly rife whether she had in fact ever married Havelock Ellis. Other vaguely comic references to 'loving the woman one's man loves', were received with bewilderment in some quarters and derision in others. Interwoven into her letters the bright thread of Lily's name came and went, Lily her long since dead lover, whose haunting spirit seemed to come to her aid in those increasingly frequent moments when the sheer intensity of American life became intolerable. She spoke as if she were in communication with her, listening to supernatural voices, and this and the contradictions in her letters all pointed in a direction presently to become plain.

In the end, after many delays, the charges against Margaret Sanger were dropped and she made American history by opening the first birth control clinic in the United States in 1916. As we have seen there was more cause for Edith's distress than met the eye or appeared in Ellis's autobiography. He undoubtedly loved Margaret Sanger and they agreed not to mention any of their doings in letters to American friends for fear garbled gossip might reach Edith's ears. For the moment, Ellis sometimes read Edith's letters to another friend and shook his head over them saying – 'America has gone to her head.'

Her last letter from America came in April.[7] 'My darling Boy, I'm dreadfully weak and ill yet. I shall of course sail on the 8th, if able, and you'll get a cable, but I'm not fit to face anything. . . .' She had gone down with a badly ulcerated throat. The threat of quinsy poison drove people away from her, she said. Illness had drained her strength and the threat of Havelock's new-found 'friend' threatened to break her spirit. 'Hell – Hell – hell – it has all been. . . . Oh! Havelock – Havelock darling – I feel that the foundations of the deep have gone if you are merged in someone else. . . . I love you always and belong. . . .'

The eighth of May had passed when Ellis received her letter but no cable arrived. More distressing the news of the torpedoing of the *Lusitania*, an unarmed liner, in mid-Atlantic had just come through to shock the British public, and set the newspapers baying for intensification of the war effort. Deeply uneasy, Ellis rushed off a long letter to New York. 'My ever darling Wifie, I have been restlessly awaiting a cable to say you sailed on Saturday and it has not come. . . .' There was no real need, he said, to feel depressed: 'you have had great success not "failure". In the same way it is of course quite ridiculous to refer to me as "merged in someone else" . . .'. Margaret Sanger, he went on, was a pleasant companion, but without any true power to 'help comfort me'. When she went away it would make no particular difference. The letter ended, 'Always your belonging H. . . .'.

Reassuring as this might have been to Edith, it directly contradicted Ellis's letter to Margaret Sanger on 27 January in which he said he loved her, however universal the word 'love' had become for him. Moreover the letter reached New York after Edith had left.

The cable came at last. Edith had entrusted it to a friend who delayed sending it. Sensibly choosing the *Philadelphia*, an American boat, immune to attack since America still was not involved in the war, Edith found that the news of the sinking of the *Lusitania*, which reached New York the day before the *Philadelphia* sailed, drove scores of people to rush for greater safety from British to American ships. When the *Philadelphia* sailed, amid scenes of some confusion, it was hopelessly overcrowded and, but for the inevitable two women friends accompanying her, a nerve-wracked, unhappy, distraught Edith might even have turned back. The boat was overrun with cockroaches, most of the passengers terrified of torpedoes and one woman journalist hinted to Edith that Havelock would be waiting at the quayside – 'to break the news' accompanied by Margaret Sanger. When at last she landed and confronted Havelock, her first question was 'Are you alone?'

She took the morphia tablets one day in the Brixton flat shortly after she returned. Amy had been to visit her. 'I left them alone for a while, and Amy with kindly intentions but not happily inspired spoke of my care and kindness and hoped that would soon help her to get strong.' Havelock went into Edith when Amy had gone. Quite unemotionally, she told him what she had done. Havelock was horrified. He hurried away to prepare an emetic. Edith swallowed it without a word and the tablets were quickly vomited up. It was the inconsequential act of a child anxious to draw attention, to be reassured of love, but from that moment Havelock was never free from a quite new strain.

They went down to Speen together when she recovered. May spread into June, the summer grew warm and beautiful, and a false resurgence of energy almost led Havelock to hope that perhaps Edith's old self was not completely dead. But 'She was really enfeebled in body and mind as never before', and the book she had struggled to write for years remained hopelessly entangled. It was the book which led to fresh trouble. She had undertaken to prepare a life of James Hinton, before she went to America, and had accepted a considerable advance from her publishers. They read with some misgivings of her mercurial career as a lecturer in America and presently, on her return began to press their

179

claims. Where was this long-expected, paid-for, and what they hoped would be important book?

Havelock did everything possible to smooth away her difficulties. He talked endlessly of Hinton and his work, he offered a multiplicity of opening sentences and took enormous pains to place Hinton amongst the ecclesiastical eccentrics, so subtly as to make it easy for Edith to mistake the estimate as her own. But it was not merely his brain which he enslaved at her bidding and surrendered to her service. Automatically he undertook endless domestic duties, as before, and in the mornings would carry down her cushion – Lily's cushion – and her mass of papers to the revolving shelter on the lawn waiting for her to follow. A nature not normally acccustomed to the patience and discipline required by biography was, in its sickness, even less amenable to the morass of Hinton's paradoxical writings and she would puzzle over the papers, morning after morning without much result. Yet again Edith said she was restless if she could not look up at any moment and see him, and once more Ellis pulled his hammock chair within easy range of her, only rising in order to spin her shelter after the retreating sun. Half her moods he believed were the result of deepening diabetes. He knew how easily it could transform a personality and felt that every whim should be satisfied.

Still, in the evenings he always hoped a good dinner and a glass of claret or burgundy would revive her spirits, as it had infallibly in the past, but now diabetes had invaded her whole bloodstream and the two hours after dinner tended to become the most depressed period of the day. It was an ominous change. Even reading what she had written to him revived little of her old verve.

Presently another, and for Havelock more alarming, phase appeared. Suddenly her tenderness towards him was held in check. She would sit before the old fireplace, dejected for hours on end, and if conversation developed, it often centred around resurrected grievances from the past, and she spoke without the old feeling in her voice. She said that Margaret Sanger had spoilt him.[8] When she left him to go to America he was a philosopher and poet who wore his greatness with humility, but when she returned she found an egotistical, boasting person, proud of his reputation as a sex psychologist. Difficult as it was to see Ellis in the role of braggart, many of his friends found him little changed at this stage. Perhaps he had a new confidence, a new belief in the significance of his work, but Edith insisted that his American 'woman friend' had spoilt him.

Bouts of sleeplessness became more frequent. Soon she began to fall into long silences. Sometimes the once ebullient Edith did not speak for a whole afternoon, and once he caught her looking at him in an extraordinary way. As if to blackmail him, she now told him one afternoon that as the dawn was breaking she had risen, gone downstairs, made her way to the well beneath Havelock's window and tried to summon courage enough to throw herself down. There were those who said she never intended to do more than add fresh anxiety to his already overburdened life. In this she succeeded. His fears thereafter were re-doubled and his sleep broken.[9]

Next came a comparatively trivial event which caused both of them fresh distress. The pony Tom and Ricky the donkey had become so old and unhealthy, it was necessary to have them destroyed. Harnessing the two sadly incongruous animals together for the last time and driving over from Speen to High Wycombe one glorious summer afternoon the dog-cart was heavy with a sense of death and a strained silence fell between Havelock and Edith. She could not bear to hear the last shot and went into a distant stable, crying softly. Their death left a new mark on her for weeks. She had severed another tie with the happy past. She, like Ellis, was very aware of one tie after another dropping away.

A number of fluctuations followed and one day her spirits appeared to revive enough for her to talk of visiting America again. Sanguine, for a whole week that she could take up and develop her old success, she wrote to her agent: 'Everything is opening before me in quite a wonderful way. The moment the war is over I shall make arrangements to return to the States. Probably my husband will come with me. . . .'

Ellis had never said anything of the kind. Margaret Sanger and Olive Schreiner had both remonstrated with Edith when she tried to persuade him to accompany her. Significantly, to Edith's evident distress, he was still seeing Margaret Sanger. She, for her part, felt he would never be happy in the United States. Edith was not easily put off and even, at one point, suggested that he might sit on the platform beside her while she lectured about him, as a kind of caged and specimen Ellis. A moment later she was interpreting his horror at any such notion as lack of love. Querulously now, she often prefaced her words with the ancient phrase of every hurt and bewildered woman denied a specially craved privilege, heightened in this case by a disease very little understood in those days. . . . 'If you really loved me, you would do it for me.'

In the end he made half a promise that he would perhaps join her in Bermuda or California. On financial grounds alone he strongly resisted the whole wild idea. While she had been away in America he had simultaneously contrived to double his working output, live frugally, save money and find himself in a position where he could help her out of the financial scrapes which still beset her. Now, in any case, the whole notion of another American trip in her present state belonged to the realms of fantasy.

When Edith's friend arrived to stay with her at Speen, Ellis retired – circumspectly – to London. There now began a steady tide of letters full of love, anguish and continuous appeals for reassurance. In her manic states she was inspired to write some moving protestations of

181

love and, despite the plethora of embarrassing endearments her letters produced some of her most vivid writing. Ellis certainly did his best to re-assure her *in his letters*, but he was still seeing Margaret Sanger and Amy; in his autobiography he seemed unaware how disturbing this must have been to Edith. The persistence of women friends in Edith's life was paralleled by equivalent women in Havelock's. Pained references to Amy and Margaret recur in her letters: 'If you care to go with Amy for your week to Somerset *now*, do, or I can arrange for Y to return later.' On 26 June he duly left for what he described as his last holiday with Amy, choosing – from Edith's point of view – this most inopportune moment. Havelock claimed that 'not long afterwards Amy decided to marry which brought our intimate relations to an end', but many years later Amy was still very jealous of the woman who occupied the last quarter of his life. Edith arranged for her friend Y to arrive at Speen the day before Havelock left with Amy, partly as an insurance against loneliness.

Some days later she wrote another letter which concluded: 'I am very sad and feel that you are going up in health and wealth and I am not – only longing to die and can't.'

As the winter approached, the question of a visit to Aix again came under discussion but Carbis Bay seemed much more accessible and sensible to someone whose physical and mental condition was subject to such violent fluctuations. They still owned Rose Cottage at Carbis Bay and, when the couple renting it decided to leave, Edith, for the first time in months, succumbed to Havelock's persuasions and agreed that they should move down in the hope that it might improve her health. She went first with Y, but Y quickly retired to bed with a strained back. It was, in fact, some considerable time before Havelock joined Edith in Cornwall, the long gap being some measure of his reluctance to do so.

The tenants had left Rose Cottage in great disorder and, with her usual gregarious gift, Edith swiftly surrounded herself with workmen painting and distempering, a typist busily transcribing Edith's latest effusions, a new servant reluctantly taking her training and her girl friend Y lying luxuriously in bed, the idle centre of a pool of activity.

By November Havelock still had not arrived in Carbis Bay and she wrote a letter full of love and anguish which revealed writing powers not unlike the instantaneous transmutation of elemental forces which distinguished Olive Schreiner's outpourings in similar circumstances. 'Oh this awful gale', the letter began. Come at once because simply the sight of him would revive her. 'Oh I want you so.'

In the days that followed, her letters multiplied until sometimes she wrote two a day, veering between plaintive apprehension and overwhelming love. 'A new love is born in me of gratitude and understanding of how you've loved me in the most beautiful sense.' How far her schizoid or manic-depressive nature was intensified by diabetes is difficult to determine, but she certainly combined classic psychosomatic conditions.

Then, at last, Havelock arrived at Carbis Bay and for a time, all went smoothly.

Over the next few weeks their relationship fluctuated: one moment the old love in Edith dominant and everything harmonious between them; the next petulant suspicion and bursts of temper subjecting Havelock to the greatest tensions he had ever known. There were times when an inexplicable lassitude overtook him, an obvious defence against her moods, but they served only to increase Edith's fear that he had ceased to love her.

Priscilla's place as Edith's maid had been filled by a young woman called Millie, lately a housemaid at the Lyceum Club. Drawn to Edith as servants so often were she had agreed to go down to Cornwall with her, but soon after Havelock's arrival Millie began to find Edith's moods disturbing. Incapable of Havelock's inexhaustible tolerance, she took to snapping back at Edith and then one day she said something so flagrantly rude that Edith rounded on her and ordered her out of the house. Packed and ready to go, Millie went to the foot of the stairs and called something which very few people had yet dared to say to Havelock, 'I feel sorry for you', she shouted and walked out without another word.

In the past such an incident would have died with the day, but Millie, forced to live in an adjoining cottage until she found another job, became a torment to Edith and set fire to an imagination overwrought from disease, until she subjected herself to a whole battery of quite unnecessary persecutions. The neighbours she said were talking about her, they accused her of taking to drink, they wanted to rob her house, they were even, in their more venomous moments, planning an attack upon it. So vivid did these fantasies become that she abandoned burgundy and drank water for dinner in order to be in full possession of herself to repel any intruder. She gathered up her most precious treasures and carried them off to friends at St Ives, and took to looking anxiously out of the window at every approaching figure.

Havelock observed these growing abnormalities with alarm. An Irish doctor, voluble, explosive, but himself in such delicate health as to make his every diagnosis depressing, was indeed depressing about Edith, and over the next few weeks she worsened visibly.

Soon she was quite without the will to do anything and the household now fell completely under Havelock's care. Chopping wood and lighting fires in the morning was a pleasure to him; washing-up was not. He prepared breakfast, turned on Edith's bath, led her to it and left her sometimes sitting irresolute on the edge. Sometimes he came back half an hour later to find her still there, with the bath water gone cold. Dressing became an arduous and long drawn-out torment, fraught with fresh distaste for this or that garment because inexplicable dreads were associated with it, and even when dressed she often progressed no further than the head of the stairs, sitting there firmly and obstinately, staring vacantly down at the hall as though a number of unseen phantoms held her gaze. Sleeplessness added to her restlessness and through the thin wall which divided their rooms Havelock heard her twisting and turning far into the night. Endlessly, in the middle of the night, he rose and went to her, trying to comfort her. Sleep presently became even more difficult for him. Once or twice, worn out with anxiety and sleeplessness, he would hear her calling at three in the morning, and 'long failed to respond'.

The diabetes had gripped her deeply. There was a wildness in some of her moods indistinguishable from insanity. Dr Hamilton recommended moving her to the Convent Nursing Home and at last they persuaded her to go. There at first she was not allowed to see anyone. When Ellis finally visited her she persuaded him to lie on the bed outside the covers with his arms round her. This was bad enough from the point of view of the nuns who ran the Nursing Home, but when Ellis asked permission to sleep like that all night, in order to keep her from disturbing other patients, they rejected the idea firmly. Hence he frequently slipped away as she fell asleep only to hear her voice crying out his name in terror as she suddenly came awake and found him gone.

Ellis in *My Life* makes no mention of the fact that somewhere in this period Edith suffered the final humiliation of being in some way bound or tied down. The detail is revealed in one of Ellis's letters to Edward Carpenter.

The day came when Havelock suggested that her old friend Y should send her some fruit and flowers without disclosing their origin. It would be a pleasant gesture to have something come out of the blue from an unknown friend. Receiving the parcel, some disordered association clicked in Edith's mind. She opened it, sat staring for a moment, and then she suddenly said, 'So she has found me has she!' An hour later she threw herself from the lavatory window on to the concrete paving stones.

Her head was badly cut and her foot injured, but the mysterious alchemy of violence worked within her, and the shock dispelled the black clouds which had enveloped her thinking for months. She was lame for weeks afterwards, she did not recover her old vitality and independence, but her 'mental condition greatly improved'.

Nevertheless the Mother Superior felt that she had no alternative but to ask Edith to go, and at last the dreaded question came into the open – should she be certified and sent to a lunatic asylum?[10] No asylum, it turned out, would accept a 'voluntary' patient who had attempted suicide and the thought of carrying Edith off by some ruse and leaving her locked up a prisoner amongst mental patients was too

184

appalling for Havelock to face. For the moment he compromised by introducing a mental nurse. Astonishingly Edith took to her. She now realized that she was not completely sane.

In March 1916 Edward Carpenter wrote to Ellis: 'I don't know how you get through all the work you must have on your hands just now. . . . I am sending you dear Havelock, a little cheque – as I am sure you must be rather put to it just now – and I am doing well with my books. . . .'[11]

He also wrote to Edith. Previous letters over the last few weeks she had ignored. To this one she replied. At this unfortunate juncture the doctor in whom Havelock and even Edith had some degree of confidence came to treat her wounds one morning, walked out to his car, lit a cigarette and died. A new and unsympathetic doctor said that if Bethlem would not accept her as a *voluntary* patient there was nothing for it but to certify her. The mental nurse suggested a compromise. She knew of a nursing home which catered specially for convalescent mental patients. Edith entered this home under the illusion that it was concerned with general convalescence and when an American friend of Lily's came to visit her she liked her so much that she invited her to stay the night. Calder-Marshall described what followed: 'She rang the bell and told the nurse to get a room ready for her friend. The nurse said it was a nursing home not an hotel. Edith lost her temper and called for the Superintendent. There was a violent and acrimonious argument.' She left the home the following morning.

She next stayed with various friends, to their acute discomfort, but a false energy was reviving her will and driving her into fresh activity. When recovery seemed a possibility, her pathetic dependence on Havelock slipped into 'ostentatious independence' again, and, in great distress, he talked to Olive Schreiner, who believed it was normal for mentally unstable people to turn against their dearest friends. Havelock should go away Olive said, go abroad, go to Spain for six months. It was the only way of restoring their relationship. He hesitated for a long time and then at last went to Norfolk for three days. The rain fell steadily all the time as he walked the countryside nursing a continuous misery. For the first time in the whole of their lives together he had gone away without telling Edith. As if psychically aware of this, Edith reciprocated and herself went to Cornwall. Both expeditions proved disastrous.

In a sudden manic state, feeling much more her old self, Edith set out eagerly to meet old friends, to re-establish the reign of the magnetic Edith whose verve had drawn so many people close to her. Instead, she gradually became aware that people were eyeing her askance, keeping the children out of her way, mouthing polite nothings. Later, she discovered that the pessimistic Irish doctor had spread rumours about her mental state which had grown and multiplied until it became apparent that she was about to be locked away in an asylum, her husband having 'signed the necessary papers'. It was characteristic of the quirks of her mental state that she accepted these extravagant rumours and rushed back to London by the next train watching every fellow traveller suspiciously, surrounded by dark new threats which now included even her beloved Havelock. He had planned to lock her away. He had laid this terrible plot behind the semblance of his love. Even he, the one man in the world she knew she could trust, had at last cruelly and brutally betrayed that trust. A nightmare sense that the whole world was crumbling about her must have grown to a terrible intensity.[12] Nothing was true any longer. Everyone was plotting to shut her away from the world.

In the next few days a new solution recurred in her mind. She would separate from Havelock. She would make it impossible for him to interfere with her life, her movements or her love again. Yet in the very moment of conception the solution was deeply qualified. It was to be a legal separation only and did not necessarily involve living apart. Thus they went solemnly, one day, to the rooms of the Law Society and there signed a legal separation, which also stipulated that he must not 'use any force or restraint to her person or liberty'.

Within a few weeks Edith took a flat in North London and promptly, to the utter confusion of the whole situation, arranged a room for Havelock to occupy. This time, sorrowfully, he had to reject the idea. Her suspicions had proved too much, even for his Olympian tolerance. It merely served to increase the threatening shapes which were now beginning to crowd at the back of Edith's mind, until the simplest event was full of sinister undertones.

Since he would not use the room she had reserved for him she took to calling on him at Brixton. Usually she arrived unannounced and before very long the new morbid self overwhelmed the loving impulse which had brought her, and she launched the old charges of deception and cunning, claiming that she had absolute proof of his intention to imprison her. He bore these outbursts without a word of retaliation, knowing that her sick mind would never respond to reason, but it all left him 'crushed and saddened'. Once she attacked him in the presence of Y, her girl friend, and Y remonstrated with her afterwards. 'But think of the things he said to me!' she said, when he had said nothing.

A manic phase returned once again. Suddenly she was convinced not only that she was better, but that she had tremendous new powers capable of carrying through one hazardous project after another. Temporarily the delusions of grandeur common to some forms of madness seized her and thrust her into one wild scheme after another. Briskly, with a bright determination, she not merely arranged to give more lectures and readings, but suddenly launched into a publishing business of her own, the Shamrock Press. By sheer force of a delusion-driven personality she succeeded in persuading Marie Corelli to permit her to publish one of her pamphlets. Not content with this, she wanted to launch a car-hiring business and capped that with grandiose schemes for a film-producing company. It was the film-producing scheme which brought into her life a woman who was to become important in Havelock's.

Françoise Delisle was then a young woman who had just risked £5 of the only £20 she possessed in the world to join a Dean Street (Soho) class, where two actors had undertaken to reveal the secrets of screen success in the now familiar short and easy lessons. However, she had arrived at the studio to find that the two actors had fled and with them her £5 vanished. It came as a thunderbolt to someone struggling against a tide of misfortunes, but presently a friend introduced her to a woman who wrote plays and was thinking of launching a film-producing company of her own. Thus, in June 1916 Françoise Delisle met Mrs Havelock Ellis and later wrote of her: 'She was alive and vivacious, rather ugly I thought, in my pride of youth, when her face was in repose, for it was extremely wrinkled. Also she was rather fat. . . .' But her wrinkled face would suddenly brim with life, her whole personality burst into animation and 'She plunged so swiftly into my troubles that it took my breath away. . . .'[13]

The film company quickly revealed its very uncertain future, but almost at once Edith, who appeared not to mind incurring another debt in the wealth of her indebtedness, offered to pay Françoise Delisle if she undertook to translate her book *Three Modern Seers* into French. The book dealt with Edward Carpenter, James Hinton and Nietzsche, and the shrewd Mme Delisle at once pointed out that such a work in France had a limited market, but Edith, possessed by overpowering self-confidence, offered her £30 for the translation, irrespective of trivialities like markets. 'And,' she added, 'I shall go to Somerset House and send you a stamped agreement.' Mme Delisle protested that this was unnecessary but the agreement duly arrived.

Their acquaintance ripened into friendship. Mme Delisle became a frequent visitor to Edith's North London flat and Edith bubbled over in appreciation as the translation grew. Quite unaware of the black pits which had already so nearly overwhelmed her benefactor, Mme Delisle saw her full of animation and sunshine in contrast to her own poverty-ridden self. Twenty-five years her junior, Françoise Delisle found this driving, eloquent woman a wonderful companion and when she first brought her two children to visit her discovered that uncanny dash of divination which sometimes burst through the confusion of Edith's mind. 'This is a premature child, isn't it?' Edith said at once, quite rightly, of the younger child.

Imperceptibly the two women grew closer. Edith invited Françoise to spend an occasional night at her flat, and presently they arranged to meet one Tuesday late in August when Edith was to pay her £7. 10s. of the translation money. But when Françoise arrived no one answered the door. Persistent knocking brought no response, and at last in despair she turned away, only to remember that she could not pay her fare home. In the end she was forced into the humiliating expedient of borrowing the money from the lift boy. A letter came from Edith early in September full of apology and distress, saying there had been some confusion over the date.[14] Mme Delisle wrote to arrange another day. She never received a reply.

On 3 September 1916, a Zeppelin was hit by anti-aircraft fire over London and slowly sagged down, a roaring mass of flames. Standing in the doorway of her block of flats, Edith watched fascinated, as the twisted fabric ballooned earthwards, unaware of the cold wind chilling her. She sent a comparatively formal letter to Havelock the following day – ending – 'Yours as ever E.M.O. Ellis'. The signature was studiously detached for the first time in twenty years. That Sunday morning vigil at 3 a.m. led to a cold and temperature with consequences beyond anything even Edith's tormented mind could envisage. Havelock went to see her the following Sunday and found that although the cold had become an attack of pleurisy she was getting over it. She talked cheerfully enough and appeared well on the road to recovery. Indeed the ironic balance of personality had once more relaxed the stresses and confusions of her mind as tangible physical distress increased, and in spirit she seemed buoyant enough.

Havelock set off with Barker Smith for two days in the country. He arrived back at Brixton the following Wednesday, to be confronted with a telegram saying that his wife was dying. Stella Browne, an old friend, recorded on 7 September that she had found Mrs Ellis 'gasping and helpless' from a very severe heart attack. Deeply distressed, Havelock hurried over to her flat in Maida Vale. She was lying in bed semi-conscious, a nurse by her side, and when he entered the room she did not recognize him. He stood uncertain beside the bed, and the nurse told him in whispers what had happened.

Recovering from lung congestion, a diabetic coma had intervened and in the coma she had called many names, the nurse said – but especially she had called for someone named Lily.

After a while Havelock left her bedside and went into the room she had so lovingly prepared for him. A numbness held him safe from reality. Presently he was back again. She was breathing with great difficulty. Slower and slower it grew. Soon there were long pauses between the breaths and then she slipped easily into stillness. He stood close to her for a moment without tears. He could not yet face what had happened.[15]

Many people went to the cremation at Golders Green, amongst them Olive Schreiner. It was a still, autumn day with sunshine pouring into the chapel as the soaring notes of Handel's 'Largo' rose on the air. There were no words. Nothing was read or said. The flames grew in intensity and presently the coffin burst in one incandescent mass, and then a strange thing happened. The deep distress in Havelock suddenly broke in a flash of joy as the flames advanced and swallowed up the coffin. It was a moment of transcendence he never forgot, and he wrote of it movingly. He did not say what a relief it must have been that the whole tormented story was at last over.

He left the actual cremation still tearless. It was only later he wrote: 'Often, as I have walked the street, at some memory or some scene, I have felt tears brimming over my eyes, and even now – when it is ten years but a few days since she left – it is so still.'[16] Havelock Ellis did not believe in an after-life.

By November a letter to Perrycoste revealed that living alone had made it more difficult to cope with Edith's death and he had just spent a few days with one of his two sisters.[17] He abandoned the cottage in Cornwall and never went there again. Loneliness came down on him with a force he had never felt before. Fresh obliteration quickly followed. Olive Schreiner's health became worse, and she suddenly asked him to destroy all the letters she had written to him. For some time he resisted. But she wrote again, begging him to burn everything, and at last he destroyed some. Many more ghosts were consumed in the flames.

Another letter came from Olive in October 1918: 'I've been very ill. . . . My heart is twice the size and the point two full inches from where it ought to be, and the blood flows back into it with each beat through the defective valves. I have arterial sclerosis of the blood vessels, and a floating kidney. . . .'[18]

By February 1920 Olive was writing, 'I don't mind death, I am not afraid of it – but what's so terrible is silence. You can't get a word across; not one little word. The everlasting stillness has come between you. . . .'[19]

It came again for Havelock on 10 December 1920. Olive was found by the maid, dead in her bed, her glasses still on, her mapping pen in her right hand, the candle burnt down to the socket. There was no sign of any struggle. Someone who had known such intensities in life, died soundlessly in her sleep.[20]

They were all gone by 1920. His mother, father, Edith and Olive, the four people who had formed the deepest roots of his emotional life. He was sixty-one, his great work on sex almost finished, his energies slackening. Life, he felt, had not much more to offer him.

Chapter 15

A new love life

The roots of his renaissance can really be traced to 1917–18. The world about him was deeply preoccupied with war. The Allies' refusal to accept Germany's peace terms in 1916 had led to the unrestricted submarine warfare of 1917, scores of merchant ships were sunk in February and March, and 600,000 American troops poured across the Atlantic. Austria showed signs of breaking up, the German Western Front was threatened by the Allies and mutiny broke out in sectors of the German Navy.

In 1916 *Essays in War-Time* appeared, a collection of not very significant fragments. Not only the origins of war, but changes in conduct, morals and clothing brought about by war conditions now absorbed Ellis's attention. There was no correlation, he thought, between renewed waves of jingoism and relaxations in the moral codes, but as the later days of the war intensified, resistance to relaxations slackened. Woman were now accustomed to wearing trousers in munition factories, mixed freely with men, rejected the tyranny of parents, the Church and the more austere canons of respectability. A new independence created by paid work emboldened many young women once held in thrall to break out on their own, and the picture which H. G. Wells had drawn in *Ann Veronica*, now had many counterparts. One article by Ellis, originally published in the *New Statesman* in November 1914 at the height of bitter jingoism, was endearingly entitled 'Why the Germans Are Not Loved'. It was remarkable amongst the belligerent clamour to hear the voice of reason saying, 'We shall still have to live in the world with them and may as well try to understand them.'

Ellis had not yet finished with sexual behaviour. Indeed, to the end it continued to fascinate, and still in some cases to puzzle him. By 1917–18 the drag of Edith's death no longer checked the steady recovery of his work and as though the gigantic impulse, not yet fully extended, demanded further realization, another volume of the *Studies in the*

Psychology of Sex, the seventh, occupied more of his time.

In a letter to Perrycoste he told him that he had recorded a vote for the first time in his life – for Sidney Webb the London University Labour candidate.[1]

A row blew up with Dr Marie Stopes. He never seemed to get on with her and now they quarrelled over Ellis's theory of the rhythm of sexual desire in women. Ellis complained that she had grossly misrepresented his theory and then proceeded to attack her distortions.[2]

Now a venerable figure in British literature, psychology and sexology, letters poured in from a growing number of distinguished men and women. Some among the letters were from the mass of Edith's creditors. Since Edith had separated from Havelock he no longer held any legal responsibility for her debts, but he religiously replied to scores of letters and freely surrendered what little money he had in an effort to satisfy the most needy of her creditors. One very undemanding sympathetic letter came from Françoise Delisle, the young translator, who was in the process of fighting a desperate battle to bring up two children.

He sent her three separate £1 notes in the next few months.[3] Several letters passed between them and then they arranged to meet. It was 8 May 1917, a date to become memorable in the last third of Havelock Ellis's life. Francoise Delisle recorded the meeting in her strange book *Friendship's Odyssey*. She was, she wrote, overwhelmed by his magnificent appearance and but for their mutual shyness might have remained tongue-tied.[4] Presently she found herself talking freely, and something of her story emerged. It was the story of a person who had experienced those pits of poverty from which one never returns quite intact.

Born in France and named Françoise Lafitte, Françoise Delisle was young enough to be Ellis's daughter. Quickly absorbed by the very milieu which Ellis had helped to create, she became a socialist, feminist and pacifist, had no belief in a personal God, but regarded herself as naturally religious. Escaping from a claustrophobic family, she came to England and attempted to earn a living from teaching, odd jobs and occasional forays into journalism. Disliking conventional marriage in which the man ruled the family, she fell in love with an American and at the very point where the relationship showed signs of collapsing found herself pregnant. After the child was born another and more colourful figure, Serge Cyon, a Russian revolutionary exile, entered her life. In the account she now gave to Ellis the pseudonyms subsequently adopted in her book *Friendship's Odyssey* were of course stripped away. Delisle, her pen name, was an anagram of de Ellis, and Serge Cyon appears under the name Aleksei de Ritter in her book. When the October Revolution of 1905 split Russia apart, Serge Cyon had fled from Russia and joined various anarchist-socialist circles in Paris and London. Françoise Delisle rapidly fell in love with him and discovered that he too had a son from an earlier relationship. When he proposed that they should marry, share a common home and bring up their children together she readily agreed, only to find that Cyon's lofty devotion to female emancipation was more theatrical than real. Underneath the vivid person committed to personal freedom for both sexes lay a man with an implacable faith in bourgeois values which required a woman to devote herself to home-life and certainly not earn her own living. Nothing if not impulsive, against all inclination Françoise found herself pregnant again.

When war broke out Serge Cyon became a military correspondent to a London newspaper which clashed with Françoise's pacifist views and led to fresh friction. As their differences intensified Françoise decided that she must make up her mind whether to accept the economic security and comfort of a now intolerable relationship, or take her two children and strike out on her own. At this point a friend gave her £20, £5 of which she spent on the dubious course for actors, and Edith Ellis appeared with her translation commission. Edith's sudden death destroyed Françoise's last financial life-line and then she wrote to Havelock Ellis.

Now as she unfolded this story to him he saw her at the outset as a potential 'patient' and indeed his first reactions and subsequent treatment exemplified his method. First, the slow establishment of sympathy, then deepening confidences and – with women particularly – the growth of a rapport which successfully reconciled empathy and detached observation. What psycho-analysis saw as a process of transference, Ellis simplified into reciprocal response and understanding. What Freud believed re-activated earlier and possibly fixated levels of experience, Ellis reduced to imaginative insight. Lacking the rigorous methodology of psycho-analysis, Ellis none the less achieved some success, but he never seems to have dealt with psychotic illness and few of his 'patients' were deeply disturbed in the technical meaning of the phrase, if one excluded a limited number of homosexuals.

Now as Françoise Delisle finished telling him her story, his shy eyes made out the person sitting on his sofa more clearly. She was petite, vivacious, given to quick gestures, with eyes which sparkled with flashes of amusement as she saw a streak of humour in her long saga of disaster. Her clothes were poor, her shoes, which belonged to someone else, were ugly, her home-made coat, shapeless and, according to his own evidence, he wasn't at first sight strongly attracted to her.

However, the following week he suggested that she should come to lunch. It had astonished Françoise Delisle to know that Edith Ellis was married, but fresh revelations awaited her. It quickly transpired that this kindly man, with the handsome presence, had qualified as a doctor, was a cook of epicurean skill and appeared to have written enormous scientific books on the subject which she had found wrapped in obscurity. On this second occasion the talk turned back to her husband, and they discussed the possibility of reconciliation. Aleksei had suggested that they should go to Russia together and she had considered this reasonable, provided it was regarded as an experiment with certain understood conditions laid down before they left England. Ellis pondered the proposal. The evidence of what followed is conflicting. My own attempts to ask Madame Delisle a few sceptical questions about her recollection of these early interviews were usually met with indignation. Was I questioning her integrity? She had no wish to misrepresent anything. She recalled precisely what had happened. Arthur Calder-Marshall in his account says that Ellis refused to give her any concrete advice. Madame Delisle told me, however, that he said it would be sensible and indeed courageous to go to Russia with Serge Cyon for a six months' experiment. Their talk ran on for over an hour. Françoise Delisle left at last, convinced – as she put it to me in her colourful way – that Ellis was a 'born healer of the soul'.

It was never Ellis's intention in this new friendship to disturb in any fundamental way Françoise's relationship with her husband. According to Calder-Marshall in his biography:[5]

> He did not intend to usurp her husband's function but to open up to Françoise the continent of psycho-erotic personality which was terra incognita to [her husband] Serge Cyon. His desire at this time was to awaken Françoise [erotically] in the hope that she in turn could awaken her husband.

His success was duly recorded in his book *Little Essays of Love and Virtue*. 'Her new erotic experience has not only stimulated all her energies but her new knowledge has quickened all her sympathies.'

Fortunately perhaps for Françoise she never went to Russia with Aleksei, because the October revolution intervened and he was imprisoned in Finland. Escaping to Sweden, he wrote to say that he would return to England as soon as he could secure a visa. By October 1918 Aleksei wrote again explaining that he still could not get a visa, but was sending his son Boris who held a British passport. Unfortunately, he added, he was suffering from tuberculosis. Boris duly arrived looking 'immense as an asparagus gone to seed and as thin' with just £3, but he did not have tuberculosis. Another bombshell followed. Suddenly Françoise discovered that she was not Aleksei's first but his third wife, that he had legally married another woman somewhere in Eastern Europe, and that his divorce was a highly uncertain event for which her informant could not, with any conviction, vouch.[6]

Late in September she again met Ellis and, very distressed, explained the new development. He now changed his view of the whole situation and encouraged her to look for a job quite independently of anything her husband might do. Presently he wrote her a letter full of understanding. Whatever appearance of cheerfulness he may have conveyed to passing visitors – and he certainly conveyed it to many – a year after his wife's death it still moved him, but this letter, full of sorrow over the anniversary of Edith's death, did not fail to sympathize deeply with Françoise in her difficulties. However, the sense of decline and decay remained strongly with him and he now shared something of these moods with Françoise Delisle. They met again, he lent her books and slowly, in the winter of 1917, their relationship deepened. Simultaneously his bouts of depression lessened. By the spring of the following year she was writing a letter of several pages explaining that something tremendous had happened to her – she had fallen in love with him.[7]

He wrote a long, restrained reply in which he said that he had many women friends, some of them so close that there was nothing they could not talk about with complete freedom – 'But there is not one to whom I am a real lover. I don't ever want to be, and if they had a proper lover I should not feel that I had any right to be jealous.' He would, he said, like to regard Françoise Delisle in the same light, *because 'as a lover or husband' she would find him 'very disappointing'* .[8] The italics are mine. These phrases become important in the analysis of Ellis's character which will follow.

In the years immediately after Edith's death there were at least three women in love, in their different ways, with Havelock Ellis. One made a last effort to press her claims and then, accepting the finality of a situation which had fluctuated over a number of years, married someone else. The appearance of Françoise Delisle made this inevitable. Mme Delisle's declaration of love occurred on 3 April 1918, and within a fortnight she and Havelock met in much more intimate circumstances. Françoise Delisle later wrote; 'On the first day I foolishly expected the marital act I had so far known, but now with a man I truly loved. . . .' When it 'did not happen' a sudden fear overtook her. 'But instantly came the astounding assurance. . . . On that bed in broad daylight, his hands and his kisses, never jerking me with fear, tenderly brought me to this delight. . . .'[9] Three details from these events are interesting – as a lover or husband she would find him very disappointing – the marital act did not follow – and his hands and kisses 'brought me to this delight'. Once again this was obviously not straight intercourse. Apart from other complications there is some evidence to show that urolagnia played a part in their sexual relations, as indeed it did with many women in Havelock's life.

Françoise Delisle felt slightly dazzled that such a grand person could be so interested in a woman who was nothing more than a schoolteacher. She taught in an East End school, earned £160 a year and tried to provide for herself, two sons and a 'retainer' Bessie, who helped with the children. She had already pawned her wedding ring and, anticipating hostility from any secondary school towards a married teacher without such an insignia, Havelock promptly presented her with another. Symbolically, it set a seal on their relationship.

They continued to meet on Saturdays at the Brixton flat, to exchange books, to examine details of the dreams which she presently recorded to help him in his work, and love grew between them. Discovering a house within walking distance of her school, Françoise Delisle rapidly moved her family into it, but her pleasure at having more time to see Havelock was chastened when the summer brought bugs swarming from the skirting boards.[10]

Havelock's flat might be free from vermin but it was no less poor. The 'settee' in his sitting-room, was really a gimcrack folding bed, the chairs were worn contraptions of the wicker variety, and the rest of the furniture stained and old. Mme Delisle's clothes at one time consisted of lengths of corduroy cut from curtains, and Havelock too was sometimes forced, after settling most of Edith's debts, to face the world in a pair of cracked boots from the toes of which patches of thick woollen sock protruded. Neither had any very great concern for clothes, and if Ellis's fame was still spreading, his way of life remained simple. Mme Delisle disputed his fame at this time when she wrote: 'He was then practically unknown, and while the war lasted I did not even find him surrounded by friends, apart from dear Dr Barker Smith and faithful Amy'. This was not the view of other friends.

Françoise Delisle encountered Ellis during one of his worst financial periods. Convinced that the climate of opinion would resist two books he had prepared for publication, he had delayed releasing them until the war was over, and Edith's debts came at a doubly embarrassing time. Equally difficult were Françoise's occasional encounters with some of the women who had not only remained a constant part of Ellis's life, but still suffered from elementary forms of jealousy. Amy was one such. Calling unexpectedly on Havelock one day only to find Françoise in possession, she was about to retreat when the all-tolerant Ellis innocently insisted that his 'two dear friends' must get to know one another. The result was unfortunate. As Amy left she whispered fiercely in Françoise's ear: 'Don't think you'll keep him—you won't!'

As the war drew to a close Mme Delisle met many of his friends and anxieties grew. There were doctors, writers, dancers, painters, and a group of leisured young people whose emancipation dazzled her. Ellis saw each one independently, and sometimes, in the company of older people who had known him for years, blossomed intellectually in a way which disturbed the less widely read Françoise Delisle.

But they were now very close. Their letters had become intimate, with hers addressed to – Faun – and his to – Naiad. All those massive stirrings in Ellis which could lead to such engulfing love were beginning to get beyond conscious control once again.

Françoise Delisle made personally to me a claim about this stage of her relationship with Ellis for which we have little corroborative evidence, even though she repeated it in her book *Friendship's Odyssey*. Put bluntly, she claimed that she gave him back his potency. The incongruity of a man who all his life remained an incompetent lover in the fundamental meaning of that term, suddenly at the advanced age of sixty recovering his potency, is hard to accept without careful scrutiny. But Françoise Delisle's powers as a lover were fully vouched for by Janet de Selincourt who had the evidence from her husband as we shall see. Moreover Ellis suffered for a great part of his life from *ejaculatio praecox* or premature emission, a contributory cause of his impotence which would naturally, as he approached his sixties, trouble him less. Thus nature herself would delay detumescence and maintain any erection he might achieve.

One April day in 1918 there was no mistaking the full flowering of Ellis's renaissance. He wrote in that mystical-sentimental mood which came more and more to distinguish the entries in *Impressions and Comments*:[11]

> These years have gone by, I scarcely know how, and the heart has often been crushed and heavy. . . . Yet on the first days of spring, and this spring more than those of the late years that passed over us, soft air and sunshine lap me around and I indeed see again the solemn gaiety of the tulip and hear the message in the blackbird's low and serenely joyous notes, my heart is young again, and the blood of the world is in my veins, and a woman's soul is beautiful, and her lips are sweet. . . .

Some weeks later, sitting in the same garden Ellis wrote. 'To see the World as Beauty is the whole End of Living.'[12] It was an ugly world but wherever one turned, he said, it was possible with patience to discover, divine or create beauty – as romantic a conception of life as ever came from the pen of a writer, but one perfectly fitting his mood.

Early in 1920 the generosity of two friends made possible a long trip abroad, and for two months he travelled through Greece. Modern Greece and the smart Greek citizens who walked through Athens seemed to him disappointing,[13] and there were parts of Athens he found ugly and depressing. But the other Athens, the ghosts which lay beneath every stone of every street, the monuments and the museums drew and held his fascinated gaze. The beautiful reliefs of a daughter saying farewell to her mother, of a husband walking with his wife in an ancient street, of a craftsman mastering his masonry; these were the scenes the Athenians of the classic age saw as they emerged from the great Dipylon on the once crowded Piraeus road, scenes he now recaptured in vividly evocative language. This, he wrote, was 'one last swallow's glimpse over a world that I was leaving forever'.[14]

When he returned to England Ellis was pressed to write a biography of Olive Schreiner. After some thought he rejected the idea. It was finally undertaken by Cronwright Schreiner, Olive's husband, who promptly settled close to Ellis and bombarded him with so many questions that it interfered with his work. Beginning in February 1921, Cronwright was still, with intervals, interviewing Ellis two years later.

In March 1921 'The Play Function of Sex' appeared in the *New York Medical Review of Reviews* with a flaming headline extraordinary in a journal said to concern medicine . . . THE GREATEST ARTICLE WE HAVE EVER PUBLISHED. In the same month Ellis was busy writing an outline of 'The Meaning of Purity' on an odd scrap of paper. The back of a telegram, or bill, any fragment might receive the raw materials of the day's thought, later to form part of another volume of *Impressions and Comments*.

Illness now broke unexpectedly into his working life. Characteristically with some who preserve an outward calm, the stresses within Ellis multiplied. And now, when maturity made control seem effortless, when Françoise Delisle promised to fill the gap Edith had left and happiness had come back into his life, he was stricken down with a duodenal ulcer.

It was March 1921. He had gone to visit one of his sisters at Tunbridge Wells, felt suddenly ill and as the pain became intense went to bed and called a doctor. Immediately Françoise Delisle wanted to rush down and nurse him back to health, but he would have none of it, protesting that a sick man was not a pretty sight. Presently, first one sister and then another fell ill, and at last Françoise Delisle did go to Tunbridge Wells, to take over the house at 63 Woodland Road.

There was something very interesting psychologically about this illness as there was about every illness which overtook Ellis. At the apparent height of spiritual recovery, he was suddenly the victim of an illness said to spring as much from stress as any other source. Somewhere new stresses had taken the place of old. It was characteristic of duodenal trouble that pain disappeared when he ate the right food and re-appeared when he was hungry, and now there were many days of pain when he felt a wolf had taken possession of his viscera, but as recovery began he wrote on 12 March 1921: 'I find, I remain serene, even continuously cheerful. . . . Death is the final Master and Lord. But Death must await my good pleasure. I command Death because I have no fear of Death but only love.'[15]

Only love? Did that mean fear only of love, or love only for Death? And if fear of love, was that the cause of this inexplicable breakdown; the knowledge that, by loving Françoise as he had loved Edith, he

197

became vulnerable all over again? For now Ellis believed himself more deeply in love than he had ever been before, and found himself, a comparatively old man, exposed to dangers which usually beset the young, without their resilience.

Whatever the cause, by 20 March recovery seemed certain. There followed a minor relapse, but he quickly picked up again and early in April went for his first short walk. By May he had gone to Margate to complete his recovery and there met Harold Child, a member of *The Times* editorial staff, later to become part of the Shelly-ean circle at Sandpit.

Early in July a devoted admirer sent him a cheque in 'recognition of the enlightenment' he had given the world, and Ellis was encouraged to make an extravagant trip to France for the first time by plane. The expedition revealed a remarkable streak in his personality. Ellis and Françoise Delisle took their seats with ten other passengers, and Ellis quickly accommodated himself to engine-noise and plane-vibration. It was an ancient Goliath-Farman machine built to carry twelve, and eleven of the twelve passengers were unaccustomed to flying. Everything ran smoothly until they approached Boulogne. A wind of quite unusual force then rose and the single engine strove to fight its way through what presently took on the proportions of an atmospheric wall. The pilot climbed as high as possible; still the wind blew; he dropped almost to earth but could not escape the wind. By now the plane was dipping and wallowing like a ship at sea. Sickness overtook one passenger after another. The wind grew worse. It now bore all the characteristics of a hurricane. Paper bags for sickness were exhausted, every other passenger sat vomiting and a terrible stench filled the plane. When the pilot himself was suddenly sick, fear ran like a current through the bucking, jumping machine.[16]

Astonishingly, remembering his recent illness, Ellis alone sat without sickness and almost unmoved. An inner sense of security – quite mistaken whatever else one said about it – left him calm and he later wrote several pages in *Impressions and Comments* evoking the scene with an extraordinary detachment: 'the air seemed firmer than the calmest sea; one began to understand birds. As I sat in my chair my eyes would be fascinated by the circles of little pistons just outside the window, for there was something ferocious and yet almost human in the untiring energy and speed. . . .'

Two hours went by. They should by then have landed at Le Bourget, but Le Bourget was miles distant. At Abbeville the pilot did try to land, came within a few hundred feet of the ground, found it too dangerous and roared up again. With three hours gone, still the plane shook, the passengers slumped in their chairs, and the wind continued to rave. With the fourth hour, the last reserves of petrol were being used up, and something desperate became necessary. The pilot decided to try another landing, and at last close to Beauvais they bumped down to earth. Grey, sick, dishevelled, the passengers stumbled out into the field; all except Ellis who walked quietly from the plane, and still calm, enjoyed the fresh air and the surrounding country. There was talk of resuming flight when the wind dropped and fresh petrol arrived. The majority of the passengers would not hear of it. Travel by road seemed to them a blissful prospect, but Ellis determined to wait for the petrol and stood talking to Françoise Delisle. She, sick as she had been, decided to see the venture through with him. In the end all air passages were officially cancelled and they too travelled by road. It was interesting that the detachment common to his study should help Ellis to face physical danger with equal equanimity. It was reminiscent of Earl Russell, many years later, at the age of seventy-six, calmly swimming without sign of panic from a crashed plane, with the shore hopelessly distant.

Back in London some weeks later, Ellis briefly met Margaret Sanger, but it was a meeting handicapped by sore throats and other troubles. They talked far into the night. In September he saw her off from Plymouth and she had such a throat she could not speak. She wrote on a pad to Havelock in the train, 'You will have to hang a card round my neck and write on it in large letters – She is dumb.'

Sometime in 1921 the paper 'The Play Function in Sex' was presented to the British Society for the Study of Sex Psychology. Ellis, as usual, did not read it himself. It was not a revolutionary paper but its crisp language was distinctive beside the material usually delivered at these meetings. The paper said that we had to regard as limited the men who thought 'the procreative act' and the 'pleasurable relief' it afforded as 'the whole code of love'. Equally, the woman who passively accepted without richer response, was worthy of contempt. The art of love had 'nothing to do with vice, and the acquirement of erotic personality nothing to do with sensuality'. Expectations of mutual satisfaction were frequently unfulfilled but there were techniques which could be taught to overcome female unresponsiveness. More rapes had occurred inside than outside marriage.

It was far too easily possible, the paper continued, for a woman with a husband, children and an apparently deeply fulfilled family life, to remain sexually immature. 'The deep fountains of her nature have never been unsealed. . . .' In the 'divine play of love-making', Ellis said, something beyond passivity and aggression, beyond demonstrating manliness and inadequate orgasm was required. He saw the ideal lovers as 'passing to each other the sacramental chalice of that wine which imparts the deepest joy that man and woman can know'. It was another example of those poetic flights which seemed difficult to reconcile with the twisted realities of love on earth.

Chapter 16

The dance of life

The Philosophy of Conflict published in 1920 could be said to be distinguished by not too much conflict or philosophy. Both *Essays in War-Time* and *The Philosophy of Conflict* have passed into oblivion. *Little Essays of Love and Virtue* (1920) was more significant. It contained a chapter which developed Ellis's views on renovating the family. The decay of the family had long been a preoccupation with social Jeremiahs, he wrote, but the family stubbornly persisted, dismaying those who called for its disintegration. Sexual relations outside marriage had developed in many parts of Europe and divorce removed the crippling inflexibilities of legal marriage, both of which movements he applauded, but marriage and the family remained as institutions with considerable renovations. Divorce no longer had any necessary connection with lack of children and Ellis now believed it was quite appropriate to plan a marriage which deliberately avoided procreation. Commitment to parenthood in *Little Essays* still involved social as well as personal responsibilites, but his increasing concern with the problem of population control now drove him to accept the fact that some women could achieve fulfilment without having children. Women had won the freedom to assume work and responsibilities formerly considered exclusively male which could change a woman's maternal role. As for those who did have children, it must now be seen that they followed a vocation in which some training might be a prerequisite of success. Consistently with his almost utopian approach to some aspects of social planning he recommended the initiation of Schools for Mothers.

Ellis sometimes gave the impression of so desperately striving to reach a balance between opposing views that he spent his polemical life swimming between Scylla and Charybdis without ever reaching either. So it was now with the question of State subsidies for mothers and children: 'On the one hand there is a tendency to diminish the duties of the family and of the State towards each other to a minimum; on the

200

other hand the tendency to increase them to a maximum.' In general Ellis seemed to favour State subsidies linked with the development of contraception to control the population explosion, but the Labour Party had investigated and rejected a system of family allowances because it believed the enormous sums required would dislocate the wages system. Ellis also saw what he regarded as the danger of subsidizing the wrong kind of people, a concept which he well knew opened up intimidating perspectives of definitive confusion.

Books, papers, articles and reviews continued to multiply. *Impressions and Comments* were dashed down on the wing, and 'The Psychology of European Peoples' developed in the background. He had by now deeply revised and enlarged several of the early volumes of the *Studies*, developing them in the light of modern knowledge. The revolutionary discovery of the part played by hormones 'in the physical production of the sexual instinct and the secondary sexual character' was taken into account, and the work of many psychologists examined in detail, but if the volumes were widened and deepened there was little change in interpretation. Fresh case-histories, which Ellis considered more or less typical of sexual development were added.

In May 1921 the second volume of *Impressions and Comments* appeared and drew exalted praise from H. L. Mencken. It re-echoed through the United States, preparing the way for *The Dance of Life*. Mencken wrote[1]:

> There is something almost of Renaissance dignity in his chronicle of
> his speculations. The man that emerges is not a mere scholar
> immured in his cell, but a man of the world superior to his race and
> his time. . . . A fine air blows through the book. . . . If the test of
> the personal culture of a man be the degree of his freedom from the
> banal ideas and childish emotions which move the great masses of
> men, then Havelock Ellis is undoubtedly the most civilised
> Englishman of his generation. . . .

In the end there were three volumes of *Impressions and Comments* and they stand in that tradition of a literature peculiar to England – the journal written for private purposes which achieves publication.

Comments on every aspect of life multiply in these pages, moving abruptly from love to lunacy, sometimes concerned 'with the miracles of Nature', sometimes 'the Charms and Absurdities of the Human Worm, that Golden Wire where from hang all the joys and the mysteries of Art'. Yet 'they spring, even when they seem to contradict one another, from a central vision, and from a central faith too deeply rooted to care to hasten unduly towards the most obvious goal.'

There was joy, sorrow and pain in these volumes, expressed in a soft prose-poetry, sometimes sentimental, sometimes rhapsodic, but always instinct with compassion and a sense that somewhere at the heart of

201

what he wrote, however ugly its lineaments, lay that core of beauty which, if he refined his own powers to the right pitch, might yield at last its final essence. Several passages were written by a mystic surrendered to a cloud of words, hovering on the edge of life, aware of something beyond life, capable of inducing states of exaltation. In the last resort they were unsatisfactory to those who could not follow him into his clouds, but only the most philistine were unaware of the impulse to song which poured from some phrases.

In 1923, one year before the publication of the third volume of *Impressions and Comments*, there appeared what many regard as the culminating book in Ellis's literary-cum-philosophic work – *The Dance of Life*. It was, from many points of view, a remarkable book, but philosophic 'only in the simple sense in which the Greeks understood philosophy, merely a philosophy of life, of one's own life, in the wide world'. Certainly it rejected technical philosophy in the very image Ellis chose as the core of his attitude, an image admitting every kind of echo.

Ellis had long resisted the more extreme teachings of J. S. Mill and Comte, disliking the proposition that human knowledge had as its limits 'the reciprocal relations of observable phenomena'. He felt that these two philosophies had 'almost driven out all higher spiritual ideals', and he shared something of the desire of the South American philosopher Rodo for 'an individual awakening to higher possibilities . . . an indefatigable pursuit of the beautiful and the spiritual, not to be deceived or drawn away by the lure of utility or the hunger for material gain.' *The Dance of Life* was one step in this direction. It was also a powerful part of that climate of opinion represented by the Cambridge Apostles, led by G. E. Moore and Lowes Dickinson. Laying great stress on personal relations and beauty, convinced that the important thing was the modification of tradition by intelligent individuals rather than the revolutionary power of mass movements, it flourished in the 1920s.

The Dance of Life suffered from the diffusion of the chapters on dancing, religion and morals, written over a period of several years and now brought loosely together under a general title. The second half of the chapter 'The Art of Writing', was first published as early as November 1908, in the *Atlantic Monthly*. Not only a certain lack of cohesion rendered the book far less satisfactory than it might have been; the chapter on thinking too clearly derived from Vaihinger, the conclusion of chapter 6 was closely related to Gaultier's vision of the world, and the constant strain put upon the word 'art' in an effort to bring so much within its range, distorted its meaning.

'The art of dancing', Ellis wrote, 'stands at the source of all the arts that express themselves first in the human person',[2] but the chapter on the art of religion dispensed with the symbol of the dance. It was a re-statement and development of earlier religious beliefs and said that the quintessential core of religion – once more an art – lay in 'finding our emotional relationship to the world conceived as a whole'. Orthodox believers would at once substitute spiritual for emotional, but Christian theology could never accept quite so powerful a mystical streak as Ellis insisted belonged to the religious attitude. He knew mysticism as a word of ill repute, 'the common label of abuse applied to every pseudo-spiritual thing. . . .', but he defined it for his own purposes as: 'the relationship of the Self to the Not-Self, of the individual to a whole, when, going beyond his own personal ends, he discovers his adjustment to larger ends, in harmony or devotion or love.'[3]

Underlining the distinction between religion and church, he said that when 'Freud speaks of the probability of religion disappearing and socialism taking its place', he means not 'religion' but a 'Church'. We cannot speak of a natural impulse disappearing; an institution easily may.'[4]

If this chapter recapitulated his own spiritual pilgrimage, the influence of Rousseau was strong. 'There was not a single clause in' his 'religious creed', he said, which could be written into any code because he had in fact no creed. Theologically, of course, not only was Havelock Ellis's religion without a creed; it simply did not exist. Logically it was hard to explain, spiritually it achieved oneness with the universe through a mystical awareness which the ordinary, down-to-earth worker found it hard to understand, encased as he was in the sharp boundaries of his own flesh and blood. For Ellis there was no one true God, no immortality, no resurrection or absolute good or evil.

As a transcendent mystic Ellis found nothing particularly significant in salvation or for that matter in monotheism. What he did find significant was a relationship between science, mysticism and religion which brought apparent opposites into complete harmony. The whole of this chapter was shot through with a desire to show the underlying identity between this inimical trinity, but the evidence was strained beyond its true strength.

Science could now be shown to have accepted such diaphanous nothingness as the raw material of the universe – as in the wave and particle theory – that it merged into the intangibility of the spiritual world. Even those formidable materialists the physicists, said Ellis, had compromised, and now saw matter as something we had 'invented to account for our sensations'. Matter closely resembled 'an electrical emanation', and thus became almost as 'ethereal' as 'spirit' and indeed scarcely distinguishable from it.[5] Anyone who thought the analogy through in rigorous detail found this a false conclusion.

A chapter inquiring into ethics was called – 'The Art of Morals.' Aristotle remarked in his *Poetics,* Ellis wrote, that any moral judgment must take account not only of 'the intrinsic quality of the act' itself, but the motive, the circumstances and nature of the people involved. There was no appeal to rigidly formulated moral laws – 'it meant that an act must befit its particular relationships at a particular moment, and that its moral value could, therefore, only be judged by the standard of the spectator's instinctive feeling for proportion and harmony.'[6] In philosophic jargon, Ellis dealt in situational ethics.

Aesthetics became for Ellis the essence of morality. Derivative from Plotinus, the Alexandrian Greek philosopher, who lived and taught in third-century Rome, he shared his belief that beauty in the physical world had its counterpart in the moral world.

There remained the contradiction between the Greek belief in an 'aesthetics of goodness' and the Roman conviction that 'beautiful action' was 'honourable' action. 'The Greek was concerned with what he himself felt about his actions; the Roman was concerned with what they would look like to other people, and the credit or discredit that would be reflected back on himself.'[7] 'In Latin suavis is sweet, but even in Latin it became a moral quality. . . . In Sanskrit and Persian and Arabic, salt is not only a physical taste but the name for lustre, grace and beauty.' Ellis seemed to imply that if a situation *tasted* right it would be morally good, but that involved a moral palate which did not exist.

Clearly a Greek devotee, Ellis did not relate these metaphysical flights to the harsh realities of a contemporary city like London teeming with a population many thousands times greater than Athens, bedevilled by every industrial device and remote from that Aegean shore where beauty was an inescapable part of everyday life. Having limited application to the conduct of one human being in his or her relations to another, these subtleties of morality became impracticable when courts of law intervened to reinforce social sanctions devised for more complex groups. To those familiar with everyday realities and the shortcomings of the average citizen, it all read once more like a beautiful dream. Ellis himself realized this, but his attempts to answer the criticisms of the realists were not very convincing.

In conclusion, the chapter traced the Greek heritage into modern times through the third Earl of Shaftesbury. Ellis shared Shaftesbury's belief not only in aesthetic conduct but in 'natural goodness'. The famous dictum of Hobbes – *Homo hominis lupus* – had suffered contemptuous dismissal by Shaftesbury who wrote: 'To say in disparagement of Man' "that he is to Man a wolf" appears somewhat absurd when one considers that wolves are to wolves very kind and loving creatures.' Ellis applauded this and said that it was perfectly possible for 'goodness' 'to be as "natural" as the sweetness of ripe fruit'.[8]

Ellis fused something of Rousseau, Gaultier and Russell with many other strands, added interpretations completely his own, and drew a picture as inspiring as it seemed to many unrealistic. Aesthetics would, in the long run, govern our moral, sexual, social and even spiritual life, slowly overwhelming the cruder faculties of our ancestors, but an active eugenics must be practised to multiply those people in whom the potential appeared most strong. In the event, Ellis's faith in the 'new aestheticism' was hardly justified. Scientists, indeed, tended to regard it as romantic nonsense.

A cool common-sense blew through the chapter on 'The Art of Writing'. Ellis complained of too many rules in writing as in morals, he deplored the worship of dead writers from pure tradition, he said that men were always 'apt to bow down before the superior might of their ancestors'. Smilingly unhampered himself, he wrote: 'If he [the modern critic] would take the trouble to compare the average prose writer of today with the average writer of even so great an age as the Elizabethan, he might easily convince himself that the former, whatever his imperfections, need not fear comparison. . . .'[9]

Whatever age was isolated, one characteristic distinguished its critics – a desire to bemoan the corruption of prose whether in speech or writing, the critics 'sometimes . . . showing no more knowledge of the history and methods of growth of English than our academic critics show today.'

He pointed out that when Sir Thomas Browne wrote his *Religio Medici* he observed an 'obedience to personal law and abandonment to free inspiration'. He spoke of 'the beautiful incorrection' and underlined the heavy penalties of 'slavish adherence to mechanical rules'. None the less, Ellis himself preserved a style which seemed flawlessly grammatical.

But how to define such an illusive element as style? According to Bergson, 'the perfect expression is that which has come so naturally, or rather so necessarily, by virtue of so imperious a predestination, that we do not pause before it but go straight on to what it seeks to express, as though it were blended with the idea; it becomes invisible by force of being transparent.' Ellis commented, 'I do not feel that that is all there is to say. . . .'

At this point one expected an elaborate analogy with the rhythms of the dance to justify his title. It never came. In the end he wrote of style as the 'miraculous transubstantiation of a spiritual body, given to us in the only form in which we may receive and absorb that body, and unless its clarity is balanced by its beauty it is not adequate to sustain that most high function. . . .'

In short, he dissolved once more into mystically inexact statements. It might have been better to do what a man of Ellis's immense modesty would have found it heretical to do; refer the reader to the method and substance of his own chapter as an illustration of a style at once lucid, beautiful and highly individualized.

There were five main chapters in *The Dance of Life* – The Art of

Dancing – The Art of Thinking – The Art of Writing – The Art of Religion and The Art of Morals. Rarely did these lofty abstractions touch everyday life. Work, industry, economics, achieved very limited reference throughout the whole book, but in the Conclusion, Ellis came within sight of everyday reality. We had seen organized demands for more wages and 'diminished hours of work', but no 'desire to raise the level of culture' or to set moving an 'aesthetic revolution', 'yet, by "the law of irony" . . . that is the result which may be achieved. The new leisure conferred on the worker may be transformed into spiritual activity, and the liberated utilitarian energy into aesthetic energy. The road would thus be opened for a new human adventure. . . .' Once again it had elements of that false loftiness which went with so much nineteenth-century rhetoric.

The Dance of Life was a spiritual exploration of Ellis in search of himself, but the person he wanted to find above all others, the artist, was too often challenged by a man primarily a scientist.

W. E. Henley wrote of *The Dance of Life* that Goethe, that colossal sentimentalist, stalked through the whole volume. A literary agent in Paris said that the book was too sentimental to appeal to a French audience. Bertrand Russell who reviewed it was more instructive. Mr Ellis's main work, he wrote, was unobtainable to ordinary men and women[10]

> on the ground that no one would be virtuous except through
> ignorance, and that therefore the spread of knowledge must be
> illegal. It is true that a host of wise men, from Socrates onwards, have
> taught that wrong conduct always springs from ignorance, but that
> has never been the view of the police, who have always believed that
> people must be either ignorant or wicked, without telling us which of
> the two they considered themselves to be. . . .

With Ellis's view that life should become play, interrupted by a minimum of commonplace work, Russell theoretically agreed, but he saw the problems of sustaining any reasonable standard of living in such a society. Cold economics tediously intervened. Even the eight-hour day left hundreds of thousands in some poverty.

A man far more materialist, in the best sense, than Ellis, Russell found it hard to swallow the wholesale optimism and idealism which, he said, distinguished too many pages of *The Dance of Life*.[11]

> The present writer, as a devout believer in Satan, holds that in our
> age he is incarnate in the captain of industry, whether trust magnate
> or communist commissar [and] to say to the ordinary person: 'Remain
> a living man or woman; do not become an automatic machine', is
> equivalent to saying: 'Die of hunger, and do not attempt to earn your
> living. . .'.

The creed of Havelock Ellis needed either a private income to sustain it or talents commensurate with his own. Man was still, unfortunately economic man to a large extent, and without brilliant gifts. Moreover, the holders of power, supported by cohorts of clerics, backed in turn by professors, preachers and a host of minor dignitaries, were, Russell felt, so desperately determined to maintain the *status quo* of a world driven by inadequate motives, that the mystic-humanist, standing alone, had little hope of changing it.

How is one to say, in such a world [Russell wrote[12]] 'my will is one with the universal will'? Mr Havelock Ellis professes that his mysticism is free from dogma; but if he supposes that we have anything to do with a universal will other than that of organised mankind, he has adopted all that is essential in the dogma of theism. The only 'universal will' visible to me is that of human groups, which are all bent upon mutual destruction. With this universal will I am emphatically not at one. Agreeing with Mr Havelock Ellis as to the ends of life, I find it difficult to agree as to means. I believe that those who value these ends must temporarily submit to the yoke of organisation and co-operation, since otherwise they will be crushed in detail by clever energetic maniacs. If one could believe in some cosmic purpose, worked out through the folly and wickedness of men, it might be possible to wait patiently for the happy consummation. But if one believes that there is no purpose in the non-human world – at any rate in that part of it with which we are in contact – it is useless to look to anything but human effort to extricate us from the dangers of the time.

Chapter 17

Freud's relations with Ellis

Ellis was now sixty-five. The world about him had changed. The reading public was busy absorbing the works of H. G. Wells, Bernard Shaw, G. K. Chesterton and, less frequently and sometimes by stealth, Havelock Ellis. Modifications of sexual codes, clothes and habits encouraged the idea that a revolution in social behaviour was developing apace. Observing the scene in the 1920s Havelock Ellis had some cause for satisfaction when he remembered the iron-bound 1870s and the suffocating days of his own childhood.

There were more personal reasons for satisfaction. His health was still robust, his renewed spirit unquenched and a new recognition, beyond the group of specialists who had loyally read his books over the years, now spread throughout the United States. It reached what was for him almost embarrassing proportions. *The Dance of Life* sold poorly in England, but six months' royalties from America totalled £1,000, the sales developed over four years, and presently there was no questioning an unfamiliar distinction in the slow accumulation of honours which marked the last fifteen years of his life. Havelock Ellis was suddenly a best-seller. Soon, even the great newspaper tycoon, William Randolph Hearst was persuaded to ask about this modern sage who had inexplicably won a hearing for spiritual matters in a land whose thundering cannon pulse of materialism appeared the very antithesis of the creed he proclaimed. Hearst decided that his empire was incomplete without the services of such a writer. Cables flashed to and fro across the Atlantic; the literary agent of the great man was sought; but he had no agent; he stood alone, and he wrote letters in ordinary pen and ink. Moreover, at the outset, he turned down the idea of writing for popular newspapers as 'unsympathetic'. Later, Hearst made an offer which Ellis considered spectacular and simply accepted without question, only insisting that he must be free to write what he pleased.

At the current rate of exchange, his articles were worth £30 a week (perhaps £200 now), and for the first time a sense of wealth entered his life. There were penalties. The weekly articles, his growing fame and the power of mass communication brought a fresh surge of correspondence. His quality as a spiritual healer was magnified in some places out of all proportion; his personality occasionally granted characteristics of the Messiah.

It was said by his votaries that he had not only broken once and for all the conspiracy of silence which surrounded sex and accorded its study a rightful place in modern science, he had also laid the foundation of fresh ethical and aesthetic attitudes towards every aspect of modern life. Even the British Museum Reading Room now inquired after new volumes of the *Studies in the Psychology of Sex*, but when he stipulated that they must be made available in the general catalogue if copies were sent to the Museum, the Secretary refused to commit himself.

Still Ellis figured at no public functions, still there was never a paragraph about him in the papers; still the attempts to draw him into the lecture hall and public dinners were met in the same spindly handwriting with the same polite evasions. But in the privacy of his home sometimes he entertained, preferably one person at a time, and then there were glimpses of a man different from the saint represented in the writings of his more devoted disciples.

Hugh de Selincourt was invited to the Brixton flat at 3.30 one day in the summer of 1921 and exactly to the minute arrived to be greeted by a man whose face was drawn with anxiety. Visualizing a major catastrophe, Hugh de Selincourt made rapid inquiries and Ellis simply announced in the low, hurried voice of despair, 'Smith's here!' This was followed a second later by the whispered explanation, 'I didn't ask him and he's brought his woman, too.' Then, as though breaking the last word of disaster, 'he knows I can't bear her.'

Smith, of course, was his old friend Dr Barker Smith. Hugh de Selincourt was ushered into the sitting-room, swift introductions followed and Havelock at once sank on a cushion by the wall, with his legs crossed and a fixed smile on his face. Hugh de Selincourt found himself isolated in the middle of the room with Smith close against the window on the left, and a woman resembling a successful barmaid, seated on his right. Grabbing a small upright chair, de Selincourt sat down and, as he regarded the tableau afresh, an almost uncontrollable impulse to laugh overtook him. With immense effort he stemmed it. The silence continued and became painful but de Selincourt felt it was for his elders and betters to break it. By now, Smith's constraint expressed itself in a curious swaying motion of his body and at last, in a desperate attempt to overcome the spell, he began a highly irrelevant account of how he had known Havelock for fully forty years, held him in the highest regard and considered his work of the first importance. One painfully obvious cliché followed another. Ellis achieved the impossible; his smile became wider and more fixed. The bar-lady's silent demands for tea were now almost audible, but Barker Smith ploughed on. He knew too well how Havelock disliked seeing more than one person at a time he said, but passing by he could not resist the temptation to introduce. . . . Suddenly control burst in Hugh de Selincourt, a tide of laughter surged over and was quickly camouflaged in a coughing fit. Barker Smith's narrative evoking no other response, the smile on Havelock's face faded and the tensity of the atmosphere increased. At last Smith said uneasily, rising from his seat . . . perhaps they had better. . . . 'At the very first hint of . . . departure, Havelock leapt to his feet from his cross-legged posture (no mean feat) his hand stiffly outstretched, his smile appreciably wider.' As Smith found and grasped the outstretched hand Havelock said, 'Goodbye – goodbye', whipped his hand away and presented it, just as stiffly to the bar-lady who sat immovable until the hand helped her to her feet. A few quick strides to the sitting-room door, another to the hall door and they were swiftly and skilfully shepherded out. When Havelock returned he was sighing deeply, but the sight of de Selincourt helpless with laughter produced a half smile.

'Really Havelock,' de Selincourt said, 'The poor lady's tongue was simply hanging out for tea – why. . . .'[1]

Havelock interrupted firmly and angrily. Nonsense! The Brixton High was full of tea-shops where the pair would be much happier. Smith should have known better. He knew his dislike of surprise visits; knew even better his inability to appreciate anything about his lady friend. 'No! No! Far better that they should go off as soon as possible and enjoy themselves quietly in their own way.'

'He spoke angrily in self-defence,' Hugh de Selincourt wrote, 'justifying himself with the clearest reason for a situation which given even a touch of gumption on his part, need never have arisen.'

There was another occasion – they were rare – when Ellis asserted himself to overrule a situation. De Selincourt had gone to lunch once more at the Brixton flat and the gourmet-cook had exhausted his skills to produce a casserole with steak, onions, turnips and carrots, sauté potatoes and what was for him the pièce de resistance, a salad mixed with infinite subtlety, blending beetroot and lettuce in mysterious dressings. De Selincourt murmured – delicious – as they started eating, and began to talk about the latest batch of *Impressions* which Ellis had sent him for criticism. Years of knowing Ellis reassured him that he would never interrupt anyone launched on serious discourse, but now, firmly and unmistakably, he did. 'Forgive me but . . .', and he swept aside all light talk about writing to inquire into the subtleties of the casserole and its precise reaction on de Selincourt's palate. Then he turned to the salad. With his eyes searching de Selincourt's face to unmask any attempt at politeness he asked – 'What do you think of it?'

He hung on his reply. 'No child at a feast in the nursery could have been more anxious that his pretence dishes should be a success. . . .'[2]

Somehow de Selincourt satisfied the inquisition, only to be subjected to another. The choice lay between a bottle of Burgundy, a bottle of claret or a white Spanish wine largely unknown in Britain. Patently the guest had to try the Spanish wine. It turned out to be as good as the salad. Then and then only was the talk permitted to return to the batch of *Impressions*. With the clock approaching three, they went their separate ways, Havelock to reply to many letters, Hugh de Selincourt to write another review.

Ellis's correspondence had become immense. Letters poured into his letter box in several languages, and he complained to friends that there were weeks when he desired above all things to recover the obscurity he had for so long enjoyed. Letters came from publishers, editors, strangers, patients, friends, lovers and cranks. There were letters to and from Harold Picton analysing the distinction between the 'diseased' and the 'abnormal'; letters and meetings with Dr Herbert and correspondence with Dr Barker Smith. Far more important were the letters to and from Sigmund Freud and his whole relationship at one remove with the great Viennese analyst.

Looking back over the years it is possible to establish identities between these two men as remarkable as the differences on which they finally split. Socially and scientifically their backgrounds were opposed, but both came to medicine in the same decade with some apprehension, and both had no special sense of medical vocation. Where Freud frequently wished 'that he could retire from medical practice and devote himself to unravelling cultural problems', similar aspirations drove Ellis. The following extract written by Freud about himself, equally describes Ellis:[3]

> After forty-one years of medical activity, my self-knowledge tells me that I have never really been a doctor in the proper sense. I became a doctor through being compelled to deviate from my original purpose; and the triumph of my life lies in my having, after a long and roundabout journey, found my way back to my earlier path.

Influenced by Naturphilosophie, a pantheistic monism taught by Schelling and eagerly adopted by thousands of intellectuals in the Germany of 1794–1830, Freud passed through a brief phase as one of its disciples. It came close in some characteristics to mysticism, and saw the universe in terms not very different from those which Ellis at one time accepted. In Austria Naturphilosophie never gained much ground but, before he swung away to materialism, Freud, inspired once more like Ellis by Goethe, sympathetically embraced it.

Freud's early student days were little more distinguished than Ellis's.

Of his first rigorosum in chemistry, botany and zoology he said, 'I escaped disaster only through the clemency of fate or of that of the examiners',[4] and in general medicine he came through, like Ellis, as merely satisfactory. It needed a philanthropic patron – Breuer in Freud's case – to sustain him in his medical studies, as Miss Caroline Haddon had sustained Ellis. Freud's state of chronic poverty persisted for years, but if, unlike Ellis, it prevented his marrying the beautiful Martha Bernays for a painfully prolonged period, it was not in the end quite so enduring. A visit to Paris and the Salpêtrière in October 1885 deeply influenced Freud's medical career as Ellis's Parisian expedition influenced him, but their view of Charcot was very different.

Ernest Jones wrote in *Life and Work of Sigmund Freud*, 'In reading through the tremendous story I have outlined here one apprehends above all how mighty were the passions that animated Freud and how unlike he was in reality to the calm scientist he is often depicted. . . .' Once again there were equivalent stresses and passions in Ellis. The legend that Freud preserved a masterful grip on life, sailing serenely through every difficulty was as false as the story of Ellis's unfailing composure. 'However unpalatable the idea may be to hero-worshippers, the truth has to be stated . . .,' wrote Jones of Freud. 'There is ample evidence that for ten years or so – roughly compromising the nineties – he suffered from a very considerable psychoneurosis. . . .'[5] So in my belief, did Ellis. His extravagant shyness, acute indigestion, the case for a form of impotence and something beyond impotence, are not easily dismissed.

Each man read the works of the other over the years, and their early books followed close on the heels of one another. *Man and Woman* (1894) preceding *Studien über Hysterie* by one year, *The Stuff That Dreams Are Made Of* coinciding with *The Interpretation of Dreams* in 1899. Correspondence between them began in the late 1890s. Freud sent Ellis a plaquette of himself which enabled Ellis to visualize his physical presence. In the same year came *Three Contributions To The Theory Of Sex*, the preface to which commented on 'The remarkable volumes of Havelock Ellis. . .'. Later Freud said, 'The facts contained in the first "Contribution" have been gathered from the familiar publications of Krafft-Ebing, Moll, Moebius, Havelock Ellis, Schrenk-Notzing, Löwenfeld. . . .' Thereafter there were recurring acknowledgments to the work of Ellis. He remarked, 'to use the happy term invented by Havelock Ellis, we will say that it is auto-erotic.'[6] Speaking of the simultaneous existence of sadism and masochism in the same person, Freud continued: 'Instead of substantiating this statement by many examples I will merely cite Havelock Ellis (*The Sexual Impulse*, 1903): "All known cases of sadism and masochism, even those cited by v. Krafft-Ebing, always show (as has already been shown by Colin, Scott and Fere) traces of both groups of manifestations in the same individual.'''[7]

Another footnote said:[8]

Havelock Ellis, in an appendix to his study on the Sexual Impulse, 1903, gives a number of autobiographic reports of normal persons treating their first sexual feelings in childhood and the causes of the same. These reports naturally show the deficiency due to infantile amnesia: they do not cover the prehistoric time in the sexual life and therefore must be supplemented by psychoanalysis of individuals who became neurotic. Notwithstanding this these reports are valuable in more than one respect, and information of a similar nature has urged me to modify my etiological assumption as mentioned in the text.

This assumption was one of Freud's early statements of infantile sexuality, in which he said that no seduction was necessary 'to awaken the sexual life of the child' and 'that such an awakening' could arise 'spontaneously from inner sources'.[9] Developing the much-hated postulate that a boy child could desire his mother sexually, Freud placed the infantile sexual life mainly under the control of erotogenic zones. He referred once more to Havelock Ellis whose 'treatise on the relations between mother and child . . . expresses almost the same ideas. . .'.[10]

With Freud's eventual theory that a child between the ages of three and five selects one 'object' or parent on whom to lavish its sexuality, that a latency period ensues when the further development of sexuality is suspended, and that in puberty sexual selection renews itself again, Ellis was in substantial agreement. The conclusions Freud drew about homosexuality, Ellis strongly resisted. Freud believed that 'The object selection of the pubescent period must renounce the infantile objects and begin anew as a sensuous stream.'[11] The failure to make this adjustment left the person fixated at an infantile level, leading in some cases to homosexuality. In other words, a child who sexually desired its mother must break free from that desire before it could achieve normal relations, later in life, with an adult person of the opposite sex. In flight from the fixation on the mother, the young man chose a member of his own sex.

Freud stressed the acquired characteristics of homosexuality, Ellis the innate characteristics. Freud wrote:[12]

Only for the first and most extreme class of inverts, as can be imagined, has innateness been claimed. . . . [But] The fact of the existence of two other classes [1. absolute homosexuals; 2. persons sexually attracted by either men or women; 3. persons occasionally inverted], especially of the third, is difficult to reconcile with the

213

assumption of its being congenital. . . . In many inverts (even absolute ones) an early affective sexual impression can be demonstrated, as a result of which the homosexual inclination developed. . . .

Freud said that Ellis designated inversion as 'a frequent variation of the sexual impulse, possibly determined by inheritance and a number of external circumstances', but this apparent certainty was overthrown when many people who experienced just those influences in early youth – mutual onanism (masturbation), seduction or assault – failed to become inverts. Thus the alternatives congenital or acquired did 'not cover the circumstances present in inversion'.[13]

Havelock Ellis, Freud continued, frequently found a diminution of sexual impulse in the inverted, and even stated that some 'slight anatomical stunting of the organs' could be detected. If this was so, it did not occur often enough to be considered preponderate and we had to recognize that 'inversion and somatic hermaphroditism are totally independent of each other.'[14]

Ellis emphasized the occurrence in the inverted of the secondary and tertiary sex characteristics. Freud acknowledged a degree of truth in this but pointed out that those self-same characteristics frequently appeared in people who were not homosexual. Androgyny (having characteristics of both male and female in the same person) did not necessarily involve 'changes in the sexual object in the sense of an inversion. . .'. Spelt out, this meant that a man whose breasts resembled a woman's might easily be heterosexual and such an occurrence did not automatically create a homosexual.

If there followed an admission from Freud that psycho-analysis had not yet given a full explanation of inversion it was clear that he had thrown more light onto the complexities of its origins than Ellis. In every case examined by Freud it was found that persons who later became inverts went through a childhood 'phase of very intense but short-lived fixation on a woman (usually on the mother). . .'. If it was overcome they first attempted to make themselves their own sexual object. Subsequently they searched for 'young men resembling themselves in persons whom they wish to love as their mother has loved them. We have, moreover, frequently found that alleged inverts are by no means indifferent to the charms of women, but the excitation evoked by the woman is always transferred to a male object. . . .' This was coming dangerously near to undermining half of Ellis's interpretation. When Ellis read *The Three Contributions to the Theory of Sex* he saw its importance, resisted details of interpretation but found no serious threat to his own position.[15] As yet he could absorb Freud's thinking without any sense of being superseded.

Ford and Beach in *Patterns of Sexual Behaviour* summed up one modern view of homosexuality: 'homosexuality is not basically a product of hormonal imbalance or "perverted" heredity.[16] It is the product of the fundamental mammalian heritage of general sexual responsiveness as modified under the impact of experience.' According to this view, persons solely interested in members of the opposite sex were no less abnormal than the homosexual, and sexual morality as such had little validity. With much of this Ellis would have agreed.

The exchanges between Freud and Ellis entered a new phase with the appearance of *The Philosophy of Conflict* in 1919. In that book Ellis began by saying that Freud found his *Studies* helpful in the development of his doctrines, following 'the "Histories" of normal persons in the third volume of my Studies'. He then referred to an article published by Sanford Bell in the *American Journal of Psychology*. Taken together, Ellis said, these two sources encouraged Freud to persist in[17]

> the task he had already begun of pushing back the sexual origins of neuroses to an ever earlier age, and especially to extend this early origin so as to cover not only neurotic but ordinary individuals, an extension of pivotal importance, for it led to the Freudian doctrine becoming, instead of a mere clue to psycho-pathology, an alleged principle of universal psychological validity. . . .

Ernest Jones has since revealed that in 1896 – long before Ellis's third volume was published (1903) – Freud surmised that 'perhaps even the age of childhood may not be without . . . sexual excitation . . .', and in 1897, six years before he 'had discovered the truth of the matter'.[18] None the less it has to be remembered that Ellis was familiar with J. P. West's reports on infantile sexuality published in 1895.[19]

However, it was one thing for Freud to 'modify' his 'etiological assumption . . . in the text' and another to see this as the beginning of 'an alleged principle of universal psychological validity. . . .'. It was one thing to say that Ellis and Sanford Bell inspired Freud to follow a path of universal consequence and quite another to imply that without their inspiration his work might have remained 'a mere clue to psycho-pathology'.

But Ellis was in a critical mood and he went on to complain that the Freudians had perverted the term auto-erotism borrowed from his vocabulary. This was not Freud's fault. When Freud first adopted the term in 1905 he 'found its chief significance in the fairly legitimate sense of a sexual impulse which was not directed towards other persons and found its satisfaction in the individual's own person'. It was Freud's disciples who later used the term to indicate a sexual impulse which not only found its satisfaction within the individual's own person, but was actually directed towards his own person. . .'.[20] That was what Ellis meant by narcissism. In his terminology auto-erotism derived from

215

words like automobile, meaning 'moving *by itself*'. and not in the sense Freudians used it, *towards itself.*

In turn Freud complained that Ellis himself misused the term: '[he] spoils, however, the sense of his invented term by comprising under the phenomena of autoerotism the whole of hysteria and masturbation in its full extent.'[21] Generally it was not easy to substantiate Ellis's assertion of 'a frequent Freudian tendency to looseness in definition' if Freudian meant Freud, but usually he did not mean Freud.

More direct charges followed. Ellis revived the infantile sexuality dispute and accused Freud of exposing his whole position 'to unnecessary attacks by speaking of infantile sexuality' in terms of adult physical facts. The diffused sexual visions of the child were easily distinguishable from those of the adult – 'the leader's confused mistake has been followed by a sheep-like flock of Freudians, who have thereby copiously aided the unnecessary indignation of their opponents.'[22]

Freud had already shown that if the infant's sexual life was 'mainly under the control of erotogenic zones', other persons were often regarded as sexual objects which introduced reactions difficult to dissociate from the adult. But, Ellis said, blindly to fasten on the most familiar body object in a sexual manner could be said to be different from consciously desiring a person of the other sex with a rational understanding of its implications.

The incest-complex had long troubled Freud and Ellis and the publication of Freud's *Totem and Taboo* revived their differences. Both knew their Westermarck:

> that an innate aversion against sexual intercourse exists between persons who live together from childhood, and that this feeling, since such persons are as a rule consanguineous, finds a natural expression in custom and law through the abhorrence of sexual intercourse between those closely related.

Ellis largely supported Westermarck but disputed its instinctive character:[23]

> For persons who have grown up together from childhood, habit has dulled the sensual attraction of seeing, hearing and touching and has led it into a channel of quiet attachment, robbing it of its power to call forth the necessary erethistic excitement required to produce sexual tumescence.

This of course was nonsense. Tumescence could and did occur, but Freud had already summoned Sir James Frazer to demolish Westermarck and Ellis at one stroke:[24]

> it is not easy to see why any deep human instinct should need to be reinforced by law. There is no law commanding men to eat and

216

drink, or forbidding them to put their hands in the fire. Men eat and drink and keep their hands out of the fire instinctively for fear of natural not legal penalties, which would be entailed by violence done to these instincts. The law only forbids men to do what their instincts incline them to do; what nature itself prohibits and punishes, it would be superfluous for the law to prohibit and punish. Accordingly we may always safely assume that crimes forbidden by law are crimes which many men have a natural propensity to commit. If there was no such propensity there would be no such crimes, and if no such crimes were committed what need to forbid them? Instead of assuming, therefore, from the legal prohibition of incest that there is a natural aversion to incest, we ought rather to assume that there is a natural instinct in favour of it, and that if the law represses it, as it represses other natural instincts, it does so because civilised men have come to the conclusion that the satisfaction of these natural instincts is detrimental to the general interests of society.

This seemed unanswerable. Much less certain was the question whether incest was in fact harmful to society and Freud insisted that the dangers of inbreeding could could only be shown with difficulty in man. Similarly, the idea that the incest taboo arose because men realized its threat to the quality of their stock made nonsense to Freud. Such sophisticated eugenics would not have been within their range.

From a mosaic of sources – papers of William James, letters of Freud, talks with Ernest Jones and Ellis's own correspondence – I have pieced together the next stage in the differences between Freud and Ellis. For the most part they combined scientific detachment with vigorous exposition, and rarely fell into anything resembling bitterness. Throughout they continued to hold each other in the highest regard, but there was never, in any sustained sense, a close relationship. Organization of the evidence may give the impression of impassioned disputes between close friends. In fact, long years might intervene between one book or letter and another and they never became intimates. Indeed Ernest Jones believed that their exchanges were not significant to Freud.

When Albert Mordell's book *The Erotic Motive in Literature* appeared in the United States (1919) and came under attack, Freud wrote to Mordell: 'I would like to tell you that you should not take too seriously . . . unfavourable criticisms. At present we cannot expect anything else, and besides a good criticism by Havelock Ellis outweighs two dozen bad ones by the other side. . . .' Ellis paid similar tribute to Freud's defence of the book.

Early in 1920 Freud wrote what appears to have been a long letter to Ellis complaining about certain comments in *The Philosophy of Conflict*, and although destruction overtook the letter, to judge from

Ellis's reply, it must have preserved their usual amity.[25] In April 1920, Ellis wrote saying that *The Philosophy of Conflict* had not been written for a technical audience and indulged a certain literary licence.

If Ellis's mood was an approximation to penitence there followed, within a few years, a review of McDougall's *Outline of Abnormal Psychology*, tantamount to another attack on Freud:[26] 'it has been the unfortunate fact that at an early period Freud became the head of a sect, on the model of those religious sects to which the Jewish mind has a ready tendency to lend itself, as the whole Christian world exists to bear evidence.' A description of the troubles Freud encountered, Ellis wrote, had[27]

> lately been written by Dr Stekel, with all his profuse and complacent candour, and it is a distressing narrative. Almost from the first all those adherents of Freud who, following the example of the master, displayed original vigour and personal initiative in development were, one by one, compelled to leave the sect, when they were not actually kicked out.

From the Freudian point of view this was nonsense. Stekel, accepted by Ellis as a conventional analyst, was regarded by them as 'wild cat'. Whatever he wrote was suspect.

There followed a tribute from Ellis to Freud as too genuine a man of science (meaning art) to be the head of any narrow sect absurdly jealous of its preserves. 'The Freudians we may be sure will soon pass away. But Freud will not. . . .' In the event, Ellis proved as wrong there as he was in his next statement that Freud, like McDougall, had never been analysed, an omission which he regarded as ironical evasion of the doctor's own medicine. Ernest Jones wrote many years later, 'In the summer of 1897 . . . Freud undertook his most heroic feat – a psycho-analysis of his own unconscious.' Whether Ellis found self-psycho-analysis a contradiction in terms, is not clear, but he was unaware that Freud underwent analysis of any kind.

Ellis's *Forum* review set the dovecotes fluttering, and in no time, letters were ricochetting back from McDougall, Freud, Francis Wharton, Hirschfeld, Wittels and others. A triangular correspondence developed between Freud, McDougall and Ellis, each exchanging confidences about the other. Freud wrote a very long letter from which Ellis gathered that among other more important matters, the great analyst still strongly resisted the idea of being regarded as an artist, and was happy to remain a scientist. In his reply Ellis repeated what he had already said in other contexts that no man could be a great scientist without qualities which were indispensable to the artist – heightened imaginative insight for instance – and Freud was at some pains to explain the difference between scientific and aesthetic methodology. Thus in Ellis's view Einstein was a great artist. He referred to his *Forum* review saying that

Freud had misunderstood it and assured him that such misunder-standings were unavoidable, as if that in some way redeemed his attack. However he remained proud that he was one of the first in England to recognize the genius of Freud, a doubtful claim.[28] Freudians, at this point, saw Ellis's persistent application of the word 'artist' to Freud as identifying himself with the man who had solved the sexual problems which still baffled him.

In November 1925 Freud wrote once more to Ellis:[29]

My dear Sir,
    Your letter was an agreeable surprise to me. It is a long time since I last had heard from you, when you diagnosed me and found me to be an 'artist'; and as your reply to my proper 'self-portrait' did not come, I assumed – very hesitatingly – that your interest in, or your esteem for, psychoanalysis, had ceased. I am very pleased to understand that this is not the case.

There were, in fact, more similarities and in some cases identities between their two approaches than all this quibbling revealed. Ellis's general theory of sexual energy permeating many aspects of life and capable of sublimated expression was not so far removed from Freud's model of a closed energy system driven by libido and governed by a libidinal economy. They were both influenced by the positivistic aspects of nineteenth-century thinking and derived their models from biological bases. Artistic sublimation came through clearly in Freud and precisely the same idea was expressed by Ellis in *Sex in Relation to Society*: 'The stuff of the sexual life is the stuff of art; if it is expended in one channel it is lost for the other.'

Ellis had, for some time, referred to the approaching completion of the seventh supplementary volume of the *Studies in the Psychology of Sex*. In the winter of 1926–7 he did at last round off yet another volume which led to the final clash with the psycho-analytical school and Freud.

Most of the sections of the seventh volume – The Mechanism of Sexual Deviation, Eonism, A Case of Sexo-Aesthetic Inversion, The Synthesis of Dreams and The Conception of Narcissism – had been published as papers before, but 'Marriage Today and Tomorrow' was not published in *Forum* until 1928 and he poured into it what he regarded as the wisdom, distilled in his seventieth year from manifold experience, delivering his most mature judgment on the greatest problem of the age.

The limpid prose, the recondite learning were still very evident, but a new note ran through many chapters of the book which brought something resembling an attack in the *International Journal of Psycho-Analysis*. It was written by Ernest Jones and, making due allowance for his devotion to Freud, much of it remained valid:[30]

219

Into the dignity and serenity which have always distinguished his writings there has of late crept a somewhat personal querulousness which a little mars a character so many have come to love. To put the matter plainly, contact with psycho-analysis has revealed limitations that were previously imperceptible. It would have been better if Dr Ellis's career had either preceded the advent of psycho-analysis or else come after this had been assimilated by the general body of thought. An unhappy clash which has no other result than causing distress would then have been avoided to the benefit of both the author and his audience. . . .

Freud's work is at times depreciated by methods that it is hard to qualify as fair, and misleading innuendoes are made of a kind that evade criticism more successfully than direct assertion would. His lack of perspective, doubtless the result of working at second hand, leads him to designate all writers on the 'new psychology' as psycho-analysts and the authority whom he most cites in this field is Stekel.

In keeping with Ellis's opposition to a monosexual view of the universe, the seventh volume restricted sexual motivation, but it would have weathered publication better if the attempts to defeat sexual etiology had been more convincing. Ellis was not alone in rejecting sex as the major source of human behaviour. Adler's theories were rapidly finding acceptance in America, and Jung's Collective Unconscious, anima and animus, could no longer be called Freudian. But where Jung and Adler unfolded well-documented arguments reinforcing new theories, Ellis strained to protect old ones.

Renewing his attack on Freudian misuse of evidence Ellis said:

There are some psycho-analysts who when they see acknowledged signs of homosexuality, accept them, as most other people do, as the signs of homosexuality. But when they see the reverse, even a strong antipathy, they accept that also as a sign of homosexuality, the reaction of a suppressed wish. 'Heads, I win,' they seem to say; 'tails, you lose.'

With a patronage precisely matched by many analysts' regard for his own views he concluded: 'This is rather too youthful a method of conducting mental analysis.'

Dr Ernest Jones replied: 'I have analysed several typical cases of eonism for years and cannot but weigh the imposing mass of evidence showing the source of the anomaly in sexual inversion much heavier in the scale than this mere ipse dixit. . . .'

In 'The Synthesis of Dreams' – an uncomfortable picture emerged of a man advancing sometimes tortured, sometimes naïve justification for views which technical advances had superseded. Whether Ellis's mind had stiffened in the mould of his early thinking and he could no longer adjust himself to the swift revolutions of modern psychological thought, or whether he knew, deep inside himself, that to admit the validity of these philistine Freudians was to contribute to his own obsolescence, was not clear. Something of each combined in his mood.

If it was not difficult to demolish some of his conclusions, Ellis did not easily accept defeat. In the seventh volume under the heading 'Synthesis of Dreams' he contrasted Freud's method of dream analysis with his own.[31]

> A consideration of this group of dreams, I am now convinced, thus amply justifies a modification of the view I put forward in The World of Dreams, confining the causation of such dreams to disturbed or excited rhythm of the chest or heart. Accurately speaking, it is not so much a *modification* as an *extension* of that view which is required, for sexual activity also is ultimately a muscular rhythm. . . .

Confusions not only arose in dream interpretation. Ellis continued to write as if the *latent* and *manifest content* of dreams were one and the same thing. Freud had shown that all manner of displacement, secondary elaboration and symbolic substitution took place in dreams, which roughly meant that when someone dreamt of chopping down an elderly tree by stealth of night in a country quite remote from his own, it *might* indicate the repressed desire to murder's one's father in a community sufficiently alien not to level a charge of patricide. Hidden behind the tree-felling, might lie the wish-fulfilment which Freud said underlay every dream, once the jungle of confusion and deception was stripped aside. Yet Ellis now stated that there were food-dreams which could not be confused with any wish-fulfilment.

> They form a large and common group, and they are conveniently ignored by the writers who believe that wish-fulfilment is the key that will unlock all doors in the world of dreams. We find that 5 of the dreams of copious meals . . . occurred after partaking of a large meal. . . . It is evident that this group of dreams cannot be regarded as of wish-fulfilment. . . .

Certainly the whole wish-fulfilment principle has since been seriously qualified.

However, the seventh volume provided Freudians with a key word which some now used against Ellis – failure. Ernest Jones believed that he could not be said to have made any real contribution to the *science* of sex. Worse still, when Freud successfully achieved the aim which Ellis had set as his own, it was too much even for his noble nature. Thereupon he set himself a new aim – to prove that rival claims were unwarranted.

But the seventh volume of Ellis's *Studies* will not be remembered for the chapters on The Mechanism of Sexual Deviation, Eonism and The Synthesis of Dreams. The last chapter on The History of Marriage, a chapter as fresh and stimulating today as when it was written, will be the one to survive. Yet it, too, had very little to say which Ellis had not already made clear in earlier books.

Freud and Ellis remained in touch with one another and correspondence broke out afresh early in the summer of 1928. Freud wrote:[32]

My dear Friend,
    Thank you very much for your latest letter. I possess now the complete series of your precious works, including your dedication, up to volume IV ("Sexual Selection"). Is it, however, sensible at my age to look after the growth of my library? – Perhaps for the benefit of my heirs. My life has already become a burden and I do not see any advantage in having achieved so many years. I continue to attend to my professional duties, partly because it cannot be helped; but the material no longer lends itself to "constructions", no longer obeys dominating ideas. . . .
    Knowing little of each other, one is at liberty to think that the other person enjoys a perfect vigour and health. I know that only in 1929 can I congratulate you on reaching a spectacular number of years; if I am still alive then, I shall not miss the opportunity.
    Very sincerely Yours,
    (Freud).

In March 1930 Freud sent Ellis a copy of *Civilisation and Its Discontents*, a book which he did not settle down to study for some time. Meanwhile, articles and papers continued to underline their different views of love and aggression. A letter from Ellis to Freud in the spring of 1930 admitted that Ellis's religious mysticism might be the result of sublimated libido but had nothing to do with pseudo-intellectualism. He repeated his doctrine that primary aggression was matched by primary mutual aid. Aggression arose to protect those whom we loved – a very romantic concept.[33]

Ellis returned to the attack in his book *My Confessional*.[34] It was unfortunate that Freud and 'some other psycho-analysts' – sometimes showed 'a malicious pleasure in trying to give an evil aspect to human impulses' and 'regarded hate as a primary motive and love as a secondary derivative'. This was not easy to understand from the evolutionary point of view, Ellis said – 'the reverse order would be far more plausible . . . the human animal, so defenceless in early life, with an infancy of such unparalleled length (or only paralleled by the elephant) could not survive unless bathed in a perpetual atmosphere of love.' Regrettably, in all this welter of fragmented argument, Ellis never attempted a systematic critique of psycho-analysis which might have been very instructive.

When, at last, Ellis began to read *Civilisation and its Discontents* his qualifications about the book were immense. It was a book which saw man's attempts to realize happiness continually frustrated by three major forces: the hostility of nature, the ageing and decay of the human body and the appalling complexities of human relationships. It was a book which analysed the substitute gratifications pursued by so many people in the hope of deceiving reality. Some turned to drink, where the demons of reality were banished by alcohol, others retreated into forms of mysticism which brought peace at the price of blunted instincts, a third group disappeared into the world of art, and a fourth accepted the mass delusions of some form of religion. Even love itself, brought to the pitch which Ellis desired, was likely to become yet another surrogate, Freud said.

In the final analysis Ellis was so romantic about love as to open himself to the charge that he recreated the Pygamalion myth. The myth was central to the thinking of several French writers who influenced him, and his mystical flights sometimes encompass a love so idealized that it is far removed from time and place and belongs to the romantic love of the unattainable. Concealed somewhere within it was the splendidly handsome youth looking into the mirror to remove any imperfection from his countenance and searching in his life, through successive women, for the equivalent of his own narcissistic self-love.

When Freud asked why was it so tragically necessary that a large part of the human race could only face life armed with one or other of these self-deceptions, his answer was coldly realistic. The why and the wherefore of human existence was beyond our comprehension, and those boundaries we had so painfully uncovered, pushing back the romantic clouds amassed by our ancestors, told us that life was a harsh struggle, and in the long view, a tragic struggle, unrelieved by anything resembling divine compassion. Man stood on the summit of a colossal achievement. Man was supreme in all forms of life. But the spectacle revealed by his long climb out of the slime was overpowering in its icy majesty, and the chill of *knowing*, of facing the long chain of pitiless peaks, was only exhilarating if it brought forth a certain brand of courage.

Ellis's eyes had lifted to those selfsame peaks. He often lived among them for sustained periods. But they were for him sun-warmed, and the five surrogates were for him not completely valid. Drink he agreed was certainly a delusion, but the ageing of the human body need not be tragic, and the Indian summer of life was so much more serene and undemanding, as his own physical self now bore witness. As for mysticism, he smiled whenever he read Freudian references to it. They didn't understand; they didn't realize how artificial were the boundaries they imposed on themselves, how different from yoga or the teachings of Laotze was his own ability to yield to the oceanic feeling which Freud so accurately described and grossly misinterpreted. He should give more attention to Russell's book *Mysticism and Logic* and to the indefinable mysteries of the essence of personality, remembering that when a rose was dissected its essence vanished.

Turning to art, it seemed absurd to Ellis to term it a delusional transformation of reality 'using the libido-displacements that our mental equipment allows. . . .'. Art was for him at the very root of life. The energy which fired the aesthetic impulse might arise from sublimated sexuality, but the impulse itself was mysteriously part of the psychic constitution. If art for the artist was merely a beautiful course of psycho-therapeutic treatment, self-applied by specially constituted neurotics, what was it in their constitution which gave them the ability to achieve a cure, where the inartistic remained uncured? Art was not merely being neurotic. Neurotic energies seized upon special skills and dispositions which were still undefined. The significant differences between the dream life of an artist and that of a neurotic, lay in the artist controlling his dreams creatively.

So it was with love. When Freud stripped away what he thought a mask to reveal the features of hate, Ellis believed it possible to penetrate beyond *temporary* hate to another level of love, differing from the first by achieving greater depth.

But human relationships? There Ellis largely accepted Freud because once again his own emotional life had fallen into appalling disruption.

Chapter 18

Jealousy breaks in

The trouble really began in 1923. His close friend Hugh de Selincourt – referred to as Andrew Scott in Françoise Delisle's account – had become interested in Françoise. A vividly articulate devotee of Ellis's work, it might appear to anyone reading Mme Delisle's account of what followed that Hugh de Selincourt was the most irresponsible of lovers.[1] One might also conclude that the sanctions of Ellis's scholarship were as necessary to Selincourt as a number of love affairs, and this was said to explain the spontaneous enthusiasm with which he greeted every new book from the man now referred to by his intimate disciples as the 'King'. A quite different interpretation of Selincourt is given by friends still alive today, who insist that he was the very antithesis of Casanova. He was, in a sense, in love with many women, but that was because his warmth, understanding and vitality stirred quick responses and not because he desired to make every woman his mistress. It was Shelley who dominated his outlook, not Casanova.

It is not stated in Françoise Delisle's account that the first meeting between all three was arranged at Havelock Ellis's suggestion. In the end Ellis himself chose their old haunt the Monico Restaurant, Piccadilly. There, an amusing lunch first introduced Selincourt to Françoise Delisle and sent everyone away happy, quite unaware of what was to follow.

Over two years elapsed before Selincourt made any proposal of calling to see Mme Delisle in her own home. When at last he suggested the rendezvous, she at once consulted 'the Faun', explaining that she was a little embarrassed for a number of reasons. Havelock brushed aside her embarrassment. She must see him, he said. So, one day, late in 1922, Selincourt called upon Mme Delisle, and presently a relationship began which was to grow with alarming rapidity. A man of tremendous vitality, he could be the most fascinating companion, and his eloquence when he talked of Ellis thrilled Françoise Delisle. His high spirits were released into her workaday world with what presently amounted to

225

intoxication. The most attentive of admirers, he sometimes wrote two letters a day to Françoise Delisle. She was, he wrote, 'an exquisite Leonie Lamark rose flung on the rubbish heap of the East End. . .'. Extravagances of this kind had their own sanctions at the time but there was no mistaking the trend of his letters.

Françoise Delisle wanted to write a book, *What Woman Owes to Havelock Ellis*, and Hugh de Selincourt plunged in to help her. His visits became more frequent, his letters more intimate and then, one day they slept together. It would be absurd to suggest that Mme Delisle herself had no part in all this. She too – a prolific and accomplished letter writer – poured out pages to him.

At first Selincourt had seemed to her almost an alter ego of Havelock himself; but presently his comparative youth, virility and passion drove her over the edge into a state of trance-like rapture which she had never known before. It was Hugh de Selincourt's particular skill that he could sustain prolonged periods of intercourse by *coitus reservatus* which removed the need for the clumsy birth control devices then available and sustained the natural grace of passion. I was fortunate enough to know and stay with Hugh de Selincourt's widow for a short period in the 1950s during which she talked freely about her husband's affair with Françoise.[2] She gave me many of Françoise's letters to her husband and some to herself. Inevitably she discovered what had happened, but not from Françoise. The sexual convolutions between Mr and Mrs de Selincourt, Havelock and Françoise were of course partly the result of Janet de Selincourt herself having fallen in love with a man whose wife was said to be insane. Such was the inviolability of the marriage bond in some eyes that even when a wife had been certified, marriage to another woman remained morally impossible. So she too was involved in a love affair.

Correspondence between Havelock and Hugh de Selincourt continued unperturbed.[3] Many months passed before Havelock realized that something had changed between himself and Françoise, and then, an almost conventional characteristic in his otherwise original person, revealed itself sharply to everyone's distress.

There were, among his friends, disciples of Hinton who argued that it was not only possible to love two people at once, but that to do so was an enrichment; yet the philosopher of love, who encouraged so many relaxations in human relationships, recoiled from this one with some force. According to Françoise Delisle in *Friendship's Odyssey*, he 'explained' that Shelley and Hinton, 'both had beautiful visions of life, but when they tried to carry them out made a terrible mess of their lives and spread misery around them. Their ideas have always seemed fascinating to me, *but they are not my ideas*. Mine are absolutely the opposite to them.'[4]

In a sense, this attitude was in blank contradiction to the message he had just delivered to mankind on the shortcomings of marriage, but if he encouraged relaxations he did not, he said, believe in loving two people at the same time. Nevertheless there were resemblances between his own way of life and that of Hugh de Selincourt. Several women loved him and he returned their love.

Moreover it is very difficult to determine within the available evidence how far he carried certain relationships with men. For instance, D. H. Lawrence writing to Middleton Murry in February 1924 said: 'I met Lock-Ellis. Didn't like him. . . . And I very much dislike any attempt at an intimacy like the one you had with Lock-Ellis and others.' In the platonic meaning of the word, D. H. Lawrence had intimate relations with men and would not therefore have recoiled from such experiences. Did he mean the word intimacy in another sense? The widow of Middleton Murry strongly denies any homosexual experience between Ellis and her husband.

Ellis now warned Françoise that her new way of life might damage her nerves if not her health and in due course she did develop double pneumonia. Ellis took her to France to recuperate and there devised a test. Man Ray, the famous photographer, had taken a photograph of Françoise which Ellis particularly liked but she had only two copies. One she gave to Havelock and proposed sending the other to Hugh de Selincourt. Unaware that she was under close scrutiny, when Ellis said she ought to keep it for her children she rejected his advice and sent it to Hugh. That made Ellis suspect that Françoise and Hugh were lovers. While they were in France, a change in Havelock's attitude towards Françoise became apparent to her and she was very distressed. She no longer, it seemed to her, stirred the old response in him.

There were some ways in which Françoise Delisle undoubtedly resembled Edith Ellis and Olive Schreiner. Like them she was small, had an explosive, ebullient temperament and was not incapable of furious attack. Her mood now came close enough to attack to be indistinguishable from it, but Ellis received her outburst in silence. She had suffered a serious illnes and he felt that bad temper was permissible after such an experience. Whatever the reason, Françoise Delisle quickly decided that she had behaved badly, and was presently full of penitence, but both remained torn by the passionate relationship which had developed between herself and Hugh de Selincourt. It was doubly difficult for Ellis. A far younger man had roused his mistress to a new sexual fury and he felt that sense of age, disillusion and melancholy, inseparable from such an experience. Presently, his suffering was acute and he spoke vividly of the dance of life and the dancer whose 'slippers' were 'full of blood'.[5]

In a welter of sentimental letters which now passed between Havelock and Françoise two things became clear. Ellis seriously thought of breaking off the relationship with her and she as strongly resisted the idea. Another and more significant sidelight on his character emerged when he described his own powers as a lover as inadequate beside Hugh de Selincourt's. Mme Delisle would have none of it. He was a different kind of lover. He understood not merely the need for passion, but for so many mental, spiritual and psychic satisfactions. He was not the animal lover, he was the artist lover, and perhaps it was because most women looked for both in one man, that this trouble had come upon them. Without doubting the recorded protestations from either side, it was another very interesting link in the long chain of evidence pointing to impotence. For here was another woman Ellis could not satisfy as another person satisfied her. It is equally easy to conclude that a man nearly seventy years old could hardly be expected to compete with a man still in his forties, and might, in the normal course of nature, have reached a state of impotence. Letters continued to pass between Havelock and de Selincourt, and generally they did not read as if a volcano was about to erupt. De Selincourt, for his part, did not feel that he and Mme Delisle had betrayed Havelock's trust in them, and within his own philosophy, there were very good reasons for this.

In January 1923 Margaret Sanger decided to turn the February issue of her American periodical, the *Birth Control Review*, into a Havelock Ellis birthday issue. This was largely the result of a brilliant essay which de Selincourt had written about the 'King'. Margaret Sanger wrote from 18 Gramercy Park:[6]

> I want to say that the Havelock appreciation is simply *superb*! It's ringing truth is like the sun shining . . . through a clear blue sky. . . . While we have no right to print in a small propaganda magazine any one essay of nine printed pages, the staff was for dividing it in two and having the following five pages next month. But I've decided to make the 'King's' birthday number four more pages and so it all goes in together. . . .

Hugh de Selincourt replied that they should make every February issue from thence on a birthday issue. Ellis himself, rather overwhelmed by what he regarded as pure idolatry, expressed his appreciation of the February issue to Margaret but made no mention of his emotional troubles.

If he revealed nothing to de Selincourt or Margaret Sanger, inevitably with Françoise Delisle it was different. She protested, again and again that in her heart of hearts nothing had really changed between them, but Havelock, now away in Cornwall growing lonelier and more miserable, suddenly released his feelings in a letter as spontaneous as her own and full of despair. The detachment had gone, and the philosopher aware of the wisdom of all the ages was powerless in the grip of commonplace jealousy.

Françoise Delisle wrote a letter in which she claimed: 'Oh! my dear,

dear Faun, how I wish I could write to you clearly on these matters of life and death for you, for they are even more so for me. . . .'[7] With her strange twists of logic she insisted that she was still deeply in love with him, and this could, of course, have been true.

There now seemed as much substance in the threat of Françoise losing Havelock Ellis, as of his losing her. There were still many women who were devoted friends, two at least loved him deeply, and one might have made an ideal wife. If he suffered because he thought Françoise had left him for a younger lover, she dreaded the possibility that he might turn to another woman in his distress.

They continued to correspond, to meet sporadically, to love and argue, but for months afterwards all their attempts at reconciliation led to worse mutilation and a growing sense that two deeply experienced people remained inadequate when confronted by those forces which possess and twist the human spirit at the very moment when maturity gives the illusion of sanctuary.

In the summer of 1925 Ellis took a furnished cottage in the Chiltern Hills – Little Frieth – and there many friends visited him. Month after month the tensions with Françoise Delisle continued, and then at last she decided to tell Hugh de Selincourt that it must end. Whereupon, according to her own evidence, Hugh de Selincourt turned and attacked her. This bears no relation to other versions of the same event, but nerves were now jangled to breaking point. Delisle could bear no more. Distraught, unhappy and with a growing sense of illness overwhelming her, she wrote again to Havelock. Suddenly an operation became necessary. She was indeed ill.

It is clear from Hugh de Selincourt's unpublished letters, that the story ran far less against him than would appear from Delisle's book. The whole episode is truncated in her account. She makes no reference to de Selincourt's letters in October 1926 written in a spirit of genuine friendship.[8] Many details in her accounts have been passionately questioned by someone no less close to the situation than herself – de Selincourt's wife.[9] Confusingly, it seemed to her that all Ellis's torment notwithstanding, he stood up to the situation remarkably well. There was indeed, she said, a streak revealed in him rarely seen, a streak of toughness. Alternatively it could be interpreted as the masochist inevitably surviving his final hell-heaven. Whatever the truth, his attitude to Hugh de Selincourt remained restrained and slowly, as Delisle's relationship with de Selincourt relaxed, she saw more of Havelock again.

According to her book, Mme Delisle tried to patch up 'the friendship between the two men' but these chapters are so overwhelmed by a plethora of long drawn-out sentimental letters – some embarrassing to read – that the narrative is not clear. She also states that Hugh de

Selincourt was, in the long run, responsible for one blessing in her life. He had advised her to set up house with Havelock Ellis since everyone regarded their relationship as equivalent to marriage.

Unknown to Françoise Delisle, de Selincourt now wrote to their mutual and wealthy friend in America, Margaret Sanger. Within a few months Margaret Sanger offered to pay Delisle 'a salary just equivalent to what I received at school', in order to become Ellis's secretary.[10] A figure of £275 is quoted on page 405 of her book, but a different sum appears in some correspondence I have examined. Whatever the amount, it delighted Françoise Delisle.

The breach between Havelock Ellis and Françoise Delisle was finally resolved in 1928 when they went to live together at No. 24 Holmdene Avenue, a house leased once more with money provided by Margaret Sanger, as a letter to the present author made clear. Here Mme Delisle arrived in the summer (July 1928) with her two sons, thrilled to inhabit what they thought a fine spacious house with something like a father, after their bug-infested habitation in the East End of London. At the outset a not very propitious incident occurred. Ellis fell ill on the day appointed for his arrival and did not turn up. A severe attack of sciatica – said to be partly the result of repressed aggression – had temporarily crippled him. Clearly he was very torn about this new and major step. It must have required considerable courage for Ellis to break with a lifetime's independence or semi-independence to accept the complications of normal family life with children for the first time in fifty years, and the evidence of what actually took place is somewhat confused.

There were three stages in his surrender. First his Brixton address retained, then one part of the Holmdene Avenue house set apart exclusively for his use, and at last even that abandoned. Sometimes he now took his place at the head of the table with 'his family' gathered round him, giving some appearance of enjoying a novel experience. Whatever precise stages at last drew him completely out of his shell, the spectacle of his patriarchal figure at the head of the table with his vicarious family gathered about him, eating, became familiar. He responded to the demands of family life with considerable grace even, one Christmas, dutifully donning a paper hat from a Christmas cracker. Sometimes friends came to supper, sometimes they entertained in a modest way, but if the habits of a life-long recluse were radically changed, they could not be broken entirely. Much of his work, which continued apace, he did elsewhere. Expeditions to Cornwall were still considered necessary for Havelock's health, but memories of Edith persuaded him to accept sanctuary in a small house at Wivelsfield Green, Sussex, whither he repaired in the summer, for long periods. Without an indoor lavatory, lacking gas or electricity, it was far too primitive for some of his friends, but Ellis never tired of its odd quirks and crannies.

There, in a brilliant red sun-hut in the garden, he continued to write articles, to correspond and prepare a mass of material for yet another book, this time on illegitimacy. It wasn't long before Françoise invaded his sanctuary. According to Mme Delisle, her relationship with Hugh de Selincourt was over in any passionate sense by 1928 but a collection of over a hundred letters given me by Hugh de Selincourt's widow shows otherwise.[11] Janet de Selincourt confirmed this to me in great detail. She also claimed that Françoise was in the habit of deliberately torturing Havelock with doubts in order to extract greater reassurances of his love for her and these letters confirm that impression. The long-practising professional mosochist probably responded to this.

Françoise continued to write to Hugh de Selincourt in her rambling emotional style and in November 1929, came another passionate outburst of love[12] Not until December 1929 was she referring to their relationship as a friendship,[13] but no less than four years later once more she seemed to be in the grip of a fresh upsurge of love and according to Janet de Selincourt expressed it passionately once again. Janet de Selincourt bitterly resented the account given in *Friendship's Odyssey* of Françoise's relationship with her husband. She wrote to me:[14]

As you will see by Havelock's letter it was he who suggested the first meeting, without any request from my husband and eighteen months elapsed before his first visit to Forest Gate; so the *Odyssey* gives a false impression of that.

You would have to have known Hugh to realise how utterly false the interpretation of him and the relationship is. The fact that there *was* a close relationship between them, and that Havelock was deeply wounded is true, but the facts as given are so falsely and bitterly interpreted. Havelock, wise and good, as he was, did not understand Hugh fully, or he could not have written what he did about his letters. . . . A fantastic meaning to read if one knew Hugh. To think that his ideas of love were loose and easy or lightly treated. He had the deepest reverence for women and attracted them by his vitality and understanding; but he would *never* be possessed or made use of by any woman. . . .

Hugh also repudiates the report of conversations in the book. She completely misunderstands the Blake quotation on page 399 and twists what he meant in quoting it.

I wish you could have seen Margaret Sanger; she was a great friend of Hugh's and loved him deeply.

I saw her in London in Sept. and she spoke disgustedly of Françoise and does not want to see her. . . .

Two biographies of Ellis had, by now, appeared. The time was ripe for biography. Approaching seventy, he could not hope to escape at least one such book in his lifetime. Published in 1926, Isaac Goldberg's

Havelock Ellis was badly received. It took isolated fragments of Ellis's life up to 1925, and Ellis felt that sheer enthusiasm for his subject had overwhelmed Goldberg. None the less, he sent a copy of the book to Sigmund Freud who wrote a long reply in September 1926:[15]

> My dear Friend,
>   It sometimes is really good to act contrary to one's own adopted principles and habits. Had I subdued as usual the petty resentment I retained about your essay in the 'Forum', I certainly would have no right today to address you so cordially, nor would I have received the volume of your biography as a present which answered a long-cherished wish of mine, since I often desired to know more intimately about you. Well aware of the narrowness and limitations of my own being I look out for deeper and happier dispositions in others and ever since, I have understood that you had not been 'a beast of burden' as I have, but that a colourful and harmonious life has been yours. . . . I never could imagine myself being you, for your kindness is not mine. . . .
>   The picture representing St Hieronymus in his study is also dear to me, and always present before my eyes in my room. Thus, at least, we may have shared some of those ideals you have contrived to realize during your life.
>   I also find another proof of your philanthropy in the fact that you have disclosed so much of yourself to a biographer, a thing which I could not justify in myself. But it is senseless to carry on comparisons. . . .
>   Do not be surprised if you hear from me occasionally,
>   Yours very sincerely,
>   (Freud)

The London publication of a second biography, Houston Petersen's *Havelock Ellis, Philosopher of Love* in 1928, came as something of a surprise to Ellis. Petersen had returned from Russia, met Ellis at 14 Dover Mansions on 7 September and told him that the book was about to appear. Ellis had given Petersen access to a considerable amount of material and helped him extensively. The book examined Ellis's intellectual pilgrimage until 1926, but was forced to leave a large part of his personal life untouched. In the upshot Ellis liked the book but with serious reservations. It remains good reading today.

Goldberg and Petersen were both disciples of Ellis, moved by appreciation of his work to write about him. So it was with Joseph Wortis, a student of psychiatry from New York who met him for the first time in 1927 and was left with this impression:

> he appeared at once more robust and more aged than I had expected: there were dark lines beneath his eyes and his complexion seemed

rough and weather-beaten. His talk was perhaps somewhat pedantic and professional . . . never ponderous. He seemed disinclined to lock horns in discussion and liked to dispose of problems in the simplest possible terms. Of an anti-alcoholic congress in London he would say casually, for example, 'I don't believe in that sort of thing. Everybody knows that alcohol in excess is bad, and most people know that in moderation it is good.' And Wortis commented, 'One usually felt there was not much more to add.'[16]

His shyness, Wortis said, was no ordinary shyness. Behind his outward sensitivity he seemed fundamentally solid and thoroughly composed. Many times Ellis unburdened himself aphoristically to Wortis: 'The older I get the less sure I am of anything.' 'You have no great men in America because you have no leisure. You cannot have greatness without leisure!' 'Christianity used to be a very good idea until they put it into practice.' ' I have spent all my life among books but I have always had a contempt for them.'

Ellis told Wortis that he had tried to explain some less obvious truths about human nature to the readers of Hearst's newspapers without too much success. Within a year his salary had been cut for his pains. A new editor, less awed by the saintlike repute of Ellis, joined the *New York American* and proceeded to send back his articles for correction, making extravagant demands until at last, he rejected an article on Revolution outright.

Joseph Wortis underwent an analysis with Freud and in his book *Fragments of An Analysis* he revealed the very frank exchanges which went on behind the scenes between Ellis and Freud. He remarked to Freud one day how helpful Ellis had been to many of his 'patients'. 'Yes,' Freud said 'but that is superficial – it just gives you a kind of pleasant social standing.' Freud reminded Wortis that Ellis had severely critized psycho-analysis as unscientific. 'Now Ellis was doing great harm to psycho-analysis by treating it so unjustly. . . . It amounted to calling analysts a bunch of scoundrels (*Verbrocher*). . . .' Ellis, Freud added, simply did not know what he was talking about. Moreover, Freud said that when Ernest Jones attacked Ellis in the *International Journal of Psychoanalysis* for his 'falsifications', Ellis wrote a strong protest to Freud, but the latter felt bound to reaffirm Jones's criticism.

Wortis wrote to Ellis giving an account of these exchanges with Freud, and Ellis replied at once explaining that he had never written any such letter. He had glanced at Jones's review of his seventh volume, quickly recognized the familiar patronizing and supercilious note and brushed it aside. However, Françoise had taken it into her own hands, without consulting him, to write a letter to Freud explaining that Jones had misrepresented his [Ellis's] attitude towards him.

Another revealing description of Ellis in his seventieth year was left by

'John Cranston' who went to supper with Françoise Delisle and Havelock one evening in the spring of 1929 at their new house.[17]

> It was a happy occasion. We both laughed delightedly at the Bear's usual growls at the inadequacy of the exquisite meal, daintily served, which she had prepared. . . . To our mere English standards the food and service were delicious. But [she said] seriously in F*rrr*ance – this salad. . . . Of course she knew we were being dear and kind to put her at ease.
>
> In his eagerness to refute this base accusation, Havelock, very excusably, had a little accident with the fork-load of food he was putting into his mouth. An appreciable quantity missed and fell on to his beard and below. A deft movement with his fork to intercept it made matters worse. Françoise rose, and the growling bear gone, advanced upon him, napkin in hand, like a nurse obliged to leave her place to attend to a careless small boy. 'Ave-lock! she protested, and to my ill-concealed delight proceeded to clean his beard scrupulously up, to push his chair back and search in his lap. Then, satisfied at last that she had made a thoroughly good job of it, she tucked her napkin under her arm, combed her fingers gently through his beard, smoothed back his hair with both hands, and holding his head firmly, gave him two smacking kisses, one on either cheek, leaving him after much vain protestation, flushed with pleasure. As she returned to her place, our eyes met: and he, who rarely looked directly at anyone, kept his eyes on mine for five or six seconds. For we two men – with some one hundred and fifty years of rather wide experience between us – knew well that had some such little catastrophe happened to our dear hostess, we should have looked the other way and instantly become immersed in talk on any topic, while whatever damage there might be was seen to. . . .

Still upright, with a gleaming white beard, and the same glow in his eyes, increasing age added fresh grandeur to Ellis's magnificent appearance, and new disciples, coming upon him for the first time, were sometimes left breathless by the sheer spectacle of the man.

Seventy now, and the outside world he had so seldom troubled about suddenly ablaze with interest in his birthday. A dinner was organized to celebrate it. Letters, telegrams, postcards from all corners of the world poured in, complete strangers writing many pages to congratulate him. The *Nation* printed an article 'The Philosopher of the Middle Path', which seemed to mark him down for the kind of uninspired middle way which he intensely disliked. Newspaper reporters desperately tried to distil a message from the sage without success. A beautifully produced, hand-printed volume appeared, full of tributes from – Françoise Delisle, Elie Faure, Henry W. Nevinson, Clifford Bax, Edward Carpenter, M. J. Mencken, Waldo Frank, Bertrand Russell, Margaret

Sanger, Hugh de Selincourt and Dr B. Malinowski. There were many more tributes in the *Birth Control Review*. Some Ellis thought wildly extravagant. From the opposite point of view a book had lately appeared in America called *Sex Freedom and Social Control* which was an attack on Ellis made effective by selecting and combining one-sided passages from his books.[18] The author, automatically in favour of social control, equipped Ellis with the equivalent of a satyr's tail.

Seventy now, and the cloud of indecency largely dispersed in those places where the winds of literacy and learning blew. A not altogether justified sense of a moral revolution achieved in his life appeared in Ellis's writing. 'I cannot see now a girl walking along the street with her free air, her unswathed limbs, her gay and scanty raiment, without being conscious of a thrill of joy in the presence of a symbol of life that in my youth was unknown.'[19]

Seventy now, and the sense of Indian summer grown strong as the demands of the outside world multiplied. A cloud of letters sometimes burst through the letter box in the morning, from Europe, China, New Zealand, Africa and many corners of the United States. He sustained a prolonged correspondence with people in one kind of trouble or another and many of these – patients by post – continued to find reassurance in his replies.

Inevitably his correspondents included a remarkable number of women. Some, after years of correspondence, achieved that sense of intimacy where they sent photographs of themselves in the nude. Some corresponded with him from remote parts of America for fifteen years and died without ever reaching England and the Brixton flat.

And Marguerite Tracy, a woman friend living in Italy, was not alone in being driven to write: 'Dearest Havelock. . . . Oh, I love you so much . . . it sometimes seems as if I cannot NOT have to run up to England if only for one day. . . .'[20]

Josephine Walther then working in the Detroit Institute of Arts wrote many intimate letters to Ellis between 1923 and 1936. She journeyed to England several times, was invited to Wivelsfield and entered his personal circle. At one time these letters were undoubtedly love letters.

There are moments, among all this, when the last elements of the long trail pointing to impotence and a most complicated form of psychological disturbance emerge. It was almost as if above everything else he desired to be the great lover, a refined and enriched Casanova whose sensuality and depths of spiritual awareness drew women to him irresistibly, bringing to life a whole palace of love without any final sexual satisfaction. In his private diary for 26 December 1876 Ellis implied that he suffered from a similar malady to that diagnosed for Rousseau. Jean Starobinski has analysed Rousseau's complaint in some depth, with considerable ingenuity and states that 'bold commentators actually affirm that Rousseau was hypospadic.' Medically, hypospadic is defined as a deformity of the penis in which the urethra opens on its under surface. The autopsy on Rousseau showed this to be as untrue of Rousseau as it probably was of Ellis. Laforque, diagnosing Rousseau, came closer to Ellis: 'latent homosexuality with hysteriform obsessions and reactions.' None the less Rousseau did have difficulty in urinating and Ellis's preoccupation is now familiar to the reader. Starobinski comments: 'It can be seen that even if the urinary complaint [of Rousseau] had at the outset an organic cause Rousseau utilises it to express his refusal and his anguish. He seeks to retreat when confronted by normal sexuality and his illness providentially forces him to do so. . . .' There follows an analysis of Rousseau which could equally apply to Ellis. Thus we get a 'conversion of desire [which is] hostility turned against oneself. This accounts for [Rousseau's] passivity [and] masochism. . . . It leads too to the 'feminine' characteristics that have led some to speak of his 'latent homosexuality'.[21]

Letters from Radclyffe Hall appeared in his correspondence in the spring of 1928 when Ellis referred a case of female homosexuality to her for advice. Aware that *The Well of Loneliness* broke new ground, Radclyffe Hall was very anxious to have a foreword to her book from an authority like Ellis. He pleaded his rule of refusing all such requests, but having read the manuscript he admired the book so much that he agreed to write one. In June 1928 Radclyffe Hall wrote:[22]

> About D. . . . She writes in deep depression at the thought of your departure and I read between the lines that you have been to her a kind of salvation, a light wherewith to lighten her darkness. She openly refers to herself as an invert and although this sometimes brings a smile to my lips it more often brings a tear to my heart, because I divine the immense relief that she finds in being able to be quite frank – as I said in my book – 'How long oh Lord, how long!' . . .
>
> You have such a disconcerting way of disappearing. You hate being asked out to a meal so what am I to do? I can only hope you will ask us to Brixton to tea or something. . . .

The Well of Loneliness duly appeared, with the catastrophic results which have since gone down in literary history. A journalist named James Douglas launched a savage attack on it, and in the late summer of 1928, Radclyffe Hall wrote again to Ellis: 'Yesterday the Home Secretary demanded that no more copies be printed as the book was obscene by reason of its subject. . . .'[23]

In December 1928 Ellis wrote explaining his preoccupation with something in his own life. Louie, the sister closest to him, had died suddenly. It was a considerable blow. In his family she was the only person surviving who really understood his work.

Presently he met Radclyffe Hall and explained to her that it would be unwise for him to become a witness on her behalf for three reasons: (1) he had a very bad presence in front of an audience; (2) he was the author of *Sexual Inversion* and therefore biased; (3) he had himself been charged for a similar offence.

And finally in March 1929 Radclyffe Hall wrote again referring to the large circulation of *The Well of Loneliness*. 'You will never know my very dear friend,' she concluded 'what it has meant to me to feel that I have had your support throughout this time of real persecution . . . even my posts were tampered with by this disastrous government. . . .'[24]

Threading the mass of general correspondence ran scientific letters from people like Dr Herbert his psychologist friend, F. H. Perrycoste, John Samson, and Frederick Myers. They merely served to underline conclusions Ellis had drawn in other contexts about such complicated concepts as 'pain', 'consciousness', 'belief', 'narcissism' and 'shyness'. His attitude towards pain was explored in total solemnity when Dr Herbert's wife died a most unpleasant death from cancer. Dr Herbert wrote to Ellis: 'The inevitable has happened after great suffering. The only consolation I have is that she has at last peace. Seeing her immense agony has not reconciled me to any theory of pain. It seems to me that pain is nothing but the crude imperfection of this life on earth. It has to be borne, but seems to have no compensatory virtue.'[25]

Somewhat insensitively, Ellis chose his moment to reiterate his belief that pain was a means of guaranteeing survival, and insisted that Dr Herbert was too close to the problem to see it in perspective. Without pain there could be no life he said, a statement he had often made before with the same cryptic confusion. Dr Herbert thought this extraordinarily naïve for a thinker capable of such subtlety. Nature, as Dr Herbert vigorously reiterated, was not compassionate, and pain the embodiment of its indifference.

Built into Havelock's theory of the inevitable conflict of life, pain played a role as significant and indispensable as pleasure, but for him maturity consisted in the ability to see pain as a part of life no more ugly than pleasure. They were both part of consciousness, and he gave no particular stress to either. But, 'The people I have known who have most exquisitely tasted the joy and rapture of living are those who have known most of its discipline of pain.' Dr Herbert, witnessing the effect of the raw material of pain, rejected this Olympian theorizing. He could not know that a great part of Ellis's thinking was shot through with his own masochism. All unaware, Havelock himself was now on the verge of experiencing such pain as few people are called upon to bear, but for the moment life continued smoothly.

Chapter 19

A serious illness

He was approaching seventy-one. His energies diminished as his correspondence increased, his desire for intellectual conquest mounted as his mind showed signs of slackening. Many memories came back to him in the garden at Wivelsfield Green. Lying on the couch in his revolving sun-hut, he surrendered himself pantheistically to the rich autumn days. Mystically moved by every scent, sight and sound there were times when he felt himself freshly part of the timeless rhythm of the earth. His oneness with the world about him in moments of deepest reverie reached a new and sometimes self-annihilating pitch. Once the gardener found him in a state of trance, head back on the cushions, eyes shimmering.

He was happy in a way different from the past. As one appetite declined, he told Hugh de Selincourt, another less importunate had taken its place, until at last he wrote in that simplified English which marked much of his later writing: 'I have never been so happy as today when I have by my side a tender companion whose devotion and sympathy enfold me in radiance. . . . I am almost disposed to begin the narrative of a second and later life. I have never had so many lovely and loving friends.'[1] It was a statement about to be vulgarly shattered.

There had been two years of unbroken serenity. Moving between Holmdene Avenue and the cottage at Wivelsfield he and Françoise savoured, week after week, something resembling an Indian summer, but now a shadow broke across their path. Havelock's physical passion – if passion is the right word – for Françoise died away, and presently, they were faced with the last and crucial issue of any prolonged relationship whether in or out of marriage. Would the non-sexual elements in their relationship sustain them? Françoise's sexual relations with Hugh de Selincourt were over, and now Havelock, who knew so well the artistry of another kind of love, was the involuntary victim of age.

The whole long story of Ellis's sexual life can at last be seen in a certain pattern. It begins far back in the early days of family life, when Ellis, like many homosexuals, was forced into a one-sided relationship with his mother, his father spending long years at sea. Four sisters were added to the family over the next few years and no brother. The intensity of his mother's erotic reactions towards him were established by her urinary preoccupations which fixated one side of Ellis's erotic nature. Whether he, like many homosexuals, was sexually drawn to his mother one can only speculate, but in young manhood his nature and temperament bore all the signs of that soft femininity, completely lacking normal aggression, which might have resulted from a completely feminine upbringing. If, as modern psychology believed, we are all in some degree bisexual, every accident of environment in childhood accentuated that potential in Ellis. From early manhood he found the company of homosexuals sympathetic, becoming close friends with Edward Carpenter. When Olive Schreiner appeared she refused a lover relationship with him, according to Françoise, 'because he was not sufficiently virile. . .'.[2] He also told Olive Schreiner 'something' which he could not even bring himself to record in his private diary. When Edith followed, it is difficult to determine how far his inability to arouse or satisfy her was the result of her own lesbian nature, or his lack of virility. Again Mme Delisle commented: 'his wife Edith . . . being homosexual, prevented him from asserting his virility and thereby maimed it for years – it might have been for good',[3] implying what she more clearly stated in another context: 'On the first day I foolishly expected the marital act I had so far known. . . . There was, therefore, a slight dread when this did not happen.' More significant still '. . . On that bed . . . his hands and his kisses, never jerking me with fear, tenderly brought me to this delight.'[4]

Acknowledging the chief character in Edith's novel *Seaweed* – a miner rendered impotent by accident – as himself, Ellis added fresh links to the chain. There were also these phrases in a letter to Mme Delisle: 'But there is not one to whom I am a real lover. I don't ever want to be . . . as a lover or a husband you would find me very disappointing.[5] Hugh de Selincourt's evidence, as a man who knew Ellis intimately for twenty-five years, cannot easily be brushed aside. He stated categorically that Ellis was impotent.

The very lack of children fits the pattern. It became profoundly ironic for one who wrote so much of the necessity for reproducing the right kind of people, not to reproduce himself. There was also his extravagant shyness, and his own *Studies* said that persistent indigestion and impotence sometimes went together.

If Havelock Ellis's early environment encouraged the natural bisexuality of man to the point where homosexual inclinations troubled him, the picture falls into not unconvincing shape. However slight the homosexual impulse it would be reinforced by continued proximity and love of his mother. In flight from that fixation did he – in classical Freudian fashion – first retreat to self-love and then project that self-love on to men? The sexual desire he could not express with his mother would be transferred to men, but guilt at betraying his love for his mother would generate a sense of incapacity perfectly expressed in his lack of sexual virility. The homosexual component in the 'normal' person would be assimilated in adult life and taken over by hetero-sexuality, but in Ellis the conflict between the two sides of his nature persisted all his life. Turning away from the homosexual impulse, the taboo prohibiting incest would establish profound barriers against sleeping with anyone resembling his mother and yet drive him to search out her likeness or substitute. There was only one answer whenever a woman fell in love with him. Notoriously, homosexuals are often impotent when emotionally or sexually aroused by a woman. Yet Ellis was thrice damned on this thesis. Incapable of satisfying a woman in the 'normal' meaning of the term, he could not bring himself to practise homosexuality and so was driven to investigate not merely its nature, but the whole gigantic pattern of sexual behaviour. The contradictions of his own nature were the wellspring of his life's work, which fitted Adler's theory. Adler believed that each individual had 'some special point of weakness or inferiority', in body or mind which determined the direction of his search for power by an attempt to compensate. Beyond Adler it was also profoundly Freudian.

That one form of impotence sometimes overtook Ellis is certain, and there is considerable evidence for a wider generalization; that he was not normally potent. On the other hand, several people who knew Ellis intimately, categorically deny that he was homosexual.[6] What we seem to have in the final analysis is a repressed homosexual. The repression of the homosexual impulse became in Ellis a generalized repression which inhibited his normal self-assertiveness in life as well as sex and converted domination by others into a masochistic pleasure because it neurotically resolved the two conflicting sides of his nature. Reaffirming this analysis, he himself wrote in 1913 (*Sexual Problems Their Nervous and Mental Relations*):[7]

> Much the best result seems to be attained for the congenital invert, as modern society is constituted, when while retaining his own ideals, or inner instincts, he resolves to forgo alike the attempt to become normal and the attempt to secure the grosser gratification of his abnormal desires.

For Ellis in his seventy-first year, none of this mattered. His active sexual life was over. For Françoise Delisle it was otherwise. Still comparatively young, still freshly roused, she might have taken another lover. 'The Faun' had often told her, she said, 'that passion transcends

240

sex . . . the sexual impulse of physical attraction may pass and give place to a passion which is stronger than it. . . .'

So it transpired in their relationship. In the beginning there was conflict and quarrelling, but slowly they made the adjustment. Elements of autumn calm returned to their lives. Once again – sentimentally – they were Faun and Naiad to one another.

There were many visitors. Sometimes in the afternoons or evenings Suzanne Bloch would play music from another century on her virginal; sometimes Dr Herbert called and long hours vanished in talk and debate; sometimes Ted Shawn brought a troupe of dancers to perform privately for the man who had written *The Dance of Life*.

Among the visitors was Winifred de Kok who had known Ellis at Brixton, Herne Hill and now in Wivelsfield Green. She wrote:[8]

> The man who understood women and love and tenderness to a greater
> extent than any other person who has lived. . . . In a way – a very great
> way – Havelock was a father to my children. For without the vision he
> kindled in my soul I could not have given them the love and
> understanding I was able to do . . . that was the wonder of
> Havelock – he made one feel proud and wonderful in his presence,
> and never again could one lose that feeling of being worthwhile. . . .

There were others who shared that response.

According to Françoise Delisle, week now followed week in calm serenity. Then out of the blue came a blow worse than any they had known. The first small stir on the serene surface passed for nothing. It was a curious feeling of constriction which developed in Ellis's throat. One day he mentioned it to Françoise Delisle. They tried some minor remedies, but the difficulty persisted and at the end of a month still had not eased. Then, at last, breaking into their sanctuary with the effect of an earthquake, Havelock – impenetrably calm – diagnosed the trouble as cancer of the throat. He laid down the best diet for himself, refused to see another doctor, brushed aside the idea of X-rays and quietly pressed on with his work.

A thousand miles away in Vienna, the man who had come to dominate sex psychology was stricken down, almost simultaneously, in a similar way. It was a not very significant coincidence that Sigmund Freud should have suffered from cancer of the jaw at a time when Havelock diagnosed that disease in himself. They were both to face with stoic fortitude a slow disintegration, in the one necessitating the removal of his right jaw, fraction by surgical fraction, and in the other – well it turned out quite differently from the diagnosis Ellis gave.

On 9 May 1932 he made a will, revoking all former wills. In this will his sister Gertrude Ellis, Françoise Lafitte Cyon and Mneme Kirkland were appointed as executors, and the leasehold house at Holmdene Avenue bequeathed to Mme Lafitte Cyon.

Under heavy pressure Ellis at last saw two doctors. One said that the condition could be explained psychologically. Another had his throat examined by 'Abrams Box', now considered an eccentricity of medical experiment but taken seriously by Ellis and many others at that time. The instrument confirmed his own diagnosis of a growth. This was followed by an X-ray which brought to light some old tooth stumps, and slowly these were removed, a process which interfered still more with his eating and occasionally rendered his mouth one mass of pain.

Another year passed. Still a sense of pain and constriction accompanied swallowing, but there was no quick development of what he still thought a growth. As the months slipped past and his condition grew neither better nor worse, he began to revise his diagnosis. A cancerous condition, Ellis felt, should have revealed more definite symptoms in the span of a year. The medical books were rich in ailments of the throat, and it was easily possible to find similar symptoms indicating conditions well known to doctors. He, of course, knew the term cardiospasm. Hypertrophy and dilation were produced when the lower end of the oesophagus was obstructed, and 'dysphagia'[9] increased as the dilated gullet continued to hold undigested food and liquids. Classically there was occasional regurgitation, and the danger that 'carcinoma' if not already present might develop. Nothing quite so definite appeared in the early condition of Ellis's throat. Indeed, the disease remained so intangible that there were times when, anxiously watching him trying to eat the delicacies she had prepared, Mme Delisle wondered whether it wasn't all a psychological illusion. Ellis knew too well the profound powers of psychological disturbance, but if hidden conflicts were creating this illness in what did they consist and how had they arisen?

Ellis's friends noticed little difference in the 'King' himself. Many knew nothing of the throat trouble. If they came to dinner they were aware that he ate slowly, frugally, and that puzzled some who had known him as a very quick eater. He had never been a great talker and now, his long tradition of aloofness, reinforced the sense that all was well. Perhaps he seemed a little thinner, a little more preoccupied, but age, after all, exacted its toll. His friend Bernard Sleigh described him at this time. He had 'blue eyes, deep grey eyebrows, splendid hair white with a touch of gold lying in thick slabs over his wide forehead. . . . White-bearded with a moustache which hides his lips and tilting upwards gives a slight hint of irony to a face finely modelled.' The whole head reminded Bernard Sleigh of Michaelangelo's Moses.

He led me from room to room pointing out and remarking upon the loveliness of cherished drawings and paintings. . . . A Corot, a Gainsborough . . . and a good many ultra modern figures, landscapes, portraits, uncompromising in truth and vigour. . . . His

242

voice was . . . high pitched and an almost femine note crept into it when he spoke of his love of Cornwall. . . .

Still he worked, if the pace had slackened considerably. In June 1932 he joined with Adler, Freud, Glover, Jung and Wells to write a letter to the *Manchester Guardian* announcing the founding of The Association for the Scientific Treatment of Delinquency and Crime.[10]

[The Society] will secure contact and co-operation between all the authorities concerned – social, legal, medical and psychological. It will itself initiate and promote research along more comprehensive lines than are possible at the present. In short the Association may constitute the nucleus of a future National Institute of Criminology.

The *New York American* still published a weekly article based on one or other of the letters Ellis received from comparative strangers all over the world, and letters continued to pour into his letter-box. His fame in America had reached a new pitch. In February 1932 Marguerite Tracy wrote from Italy: 'speaking of the Bibliography which Jacob Schwartz is compiling . . . I'm puzzled how he can get all round it, that is in the U.S.A., where scarcely a review comes out without a familiar reference to Havelock Ellis.'[11]

In December 1932 he wrote an article for the *Daily Herald* entitled 'We Must Do More to Help Our Criminals', and a national newspaper, hearing that the Sage was ill, invaded his privacy to ask a number of not very profound questions. Ellis told the reporter, 'I spend much of my time now writing for complete strangers who write to me with their troubles, I do my best to answer them all. . . .' The interview threatened to become prolonged and Ellis suddenly said he was only permitted to talk for a few minutes at a time.

Reviewing Freud's brief essay in autobiography for the *New Statesman* he said that Freud's literary quality had always been undervalued. It was not true, however, as Freud suggested, that Jung and Adler's attacks on psycho-analysis had 'blown over'.

This was consistent with his now organized desire to put psycho-analysis in its place. In 1933 *The Psychology of Sex* appeared, a condensed introduction to the *Studies* for those without prolonged leisure to find their way through the six volumes. It took account of more advanced knowledge and showed how inexact it was to say that there were two 'definitely separated distinct and immutable sexes', the male bearing the sperm cell and the female the ovum. By now he put a different emphasis on the family in society. Originally a pioneer critic of the Victorian family and marriage system, in later works he put more stress on both. Basically Ellis remained a romantic, never losing his belief in love as the best foundation of sexual relations and monogamy as its chief expression, but he continued to criticize the Western concept of marriage, and in later works non-sexual ties played a greater part, reflecting his own experience.

Two more books were in process of production – *My Confessional*, which eventually appeared in 1934, and *Questions of Our Day* (1936). Neither contained anything more than a miscellaneous collection of essays mostly written in reply to letters for the weekly feature in the *New York American*, but some of the essays were newly astringent. As yet there was no diminution in his powers of writing but his troubles with the new editor of the *New York American* developed. Inordinate demands were now coming across the Atlantic.

'Flu attacked him late in 1935 and at once it was clear that his powers of resistance had been undermined by the mysterious throat trouble. When he should have recovered he did not. His desire for isolation suddenly rose with new force, and he insisted on sleeping alone in a separate room.

According to Mme Delisle's book, she presently developed sciatica and 'eventually went to pieces', the result as she put it of 'the nursing I undertook all by myself'. An extraordinary contradiction now arose. As Ellis showed signs of recovering from very serious 'flu, Mme Delisle herself became steadily less well. Presently her illness too was serious. Once more it was not only nursing Havelock which brought her close to a state of nervous breakdown: 'my sanity depended on a sorting out of my problems, and this I could only do in solitude.' What those problems were was not clearly stated, but her doctor also thought that she should go away. Havelock suggested revisiting Aix-les-Bains which had once before worked wonders with Edith's health, and at last she went.

Several weeks slipped away. Ellis grew steadily stronger. When Françoise Delisle returned to England she found him well enough to be driven to reflect, 'Perhaps it suited him best to have me away?'[12] It was an interesting thought.

At seventy-seven, Ellis still combined the intellect of the scientist, the emotions of a woman and the sensitivity of a child, with the scientist continuing to amass material for a book on illegitimacy, the artist writing an essay on Proust, and the child . . . well the child was especially interesting in this illness. Classically children subject to strain in relation to their parents reject their food and demand the attention of the family doctor if not psychiatrist. Ellis was now rather more of a child than he had been for sixty-five years.

However, Françoise Delisle's account remains confused. Within a paragraph of finding him better she wrote, 'The problem of how to diet him so that he retained his food was becoming acute.'[13] She tried many new dishes, some of them reasonably successful.

Another book appeared in 1936 – *From Rousseau to Proust*. Giving an analysis of Proust's work and personality, it drew attention to an

English writer whose vision of his beloved asleep, was even more effective, Ellis felt, than Proust's. Sir Kenelm Digby, 'a belated representative of the Renaissance, recorded in after years, like Proust drawing from memory, the picture of the famous beauty, Venetia Stanley, who afterwards became his wife, as he one day came upon her asleep on her bed.' The description was short, little more than a page, 'but it is marvellous in its direct freshness and intimacy and poetic symbolism, excelling Proust, though produced by the same method, one of a Temps Perdu. . . .'

Never infected by that idolatry which so easily swept seasoned critics away, Ellis held Proust in the highest esteem as an original writer with quite new vision, but 'many of Proust's characters . . . appear as a result of their confused complexity, thoroughly unsatisfactory and would hardly do much credit to a third rate novelist. . . .'[14] Ellis regarded Proust in person as a sort of beautiful human insect endowed with many-faceted eyes, moving by stealth of night, able to see in the dark and granted psychic insight of a kind which would paralyse any enemy encountered.

Sir Kenelm Digby apart, the essay revealed his powers of literary criticism as undiminished. There were others who thought his abilities to hold readers of a different calibre definitely failing. The *New York American* is now defunct and the exact history of Ellis's troubles with the paper obscure, but quite clearly his relations with its new editor had gradually worsened, and presently a letter came 'discontinuing his articles'.[15] The formal phase concealed a considerable blow. His income dropped by £25 a week. There were still articles in the *News Chronicle* and *Daily Herald* but they were not so well paid, and now, to complicate his illness, the threat of money troubles descended.

Another blow followed. Bessie, Françoise Delisle's maid, developed cancer of the breast in 1937. Over the next few months it was discovered to be inoperable, but an elaborate deception made her believe that it would eventually heal. When the pain became too great to bear, Delisle begged the doctors to put her to sleep. It was professionally impossible but the incident had repercussions. Havelock went to see Bessie and on the second occasion he came away and wrote an article pleading for euthanasia. His own throat was worse now. Sickness had become recurrent. Away in Vienna, another operation had been performed on the jaw of Sigmund Freud to prevent the spread of cancer. Like Ellis, he sometimes found talking painful and laborious.

Chapter 20

Last years and death

Ellis was now seventy-eight. The world about him, torn and traversed by new ideologies, saw Hitler trampling the last remnants of German democracy in the dust, Mussolini strutting the stage in Rome and the threat of yet another war grown to alarming proportions. Françoise Delisle talked long and passionately of her pacifist beliefs, while Havelock, his stock of small talk still further diminished by the painful effort now required to utter it, offered an occasional comment. Public recognition which so easily overtook those who worked in politics found its way at last to the recluse, but he was still so cut off from the world that when he was asked in May 1936 to receive a solitary honour, he nearly turned it down. The Royal College of Physicians, not without some dissent, had decided to make him a Fellow of the Royal College.[1] Simultaneously Clifford Bax tried to get the ear of Lord Vansittart with the object of recommending Ellis for the OM. There were three members of the Committee who advised the King – one of them Vansittart – and when the other two heard the proposal they were alleged to have said, 'but who is Havelock Ellis?'[2]

At last, under heavy persuasion, Ellis decided to go to the ceremonial dinner at the Royal College of Physicians which traditionally accompanied the FRCP. He wore a rusty old frock coat, dating from the days when he had first practised medicine, and with it a big black hat. Setting off down the road he looked like a frail old ship, under much canvas. It was the first public ceremony he had attended for over thirty years and it was some time before he could accustom himself to so many people all at once. There were a number of flattering speeches.

In the winter of 1937 another illness attacked him, this time pleurisy, with serious consequences. Constant sickness and difficulty in swallowing food had slowly reduced his strength, and as the pleurisy developed he was brought to a state of weakness bordering on collapse. At one point it seemed he must certainly die.

The doctor came every day. Havelock spoke to him one day of the constriction in his throat, and what followed should be carefully noted. The doctor said to Françoise Delisle, 'try to cure Dr Ellis of the idea that he has anything the matter with his throat. It is sheer fancy, a psychological problem.'[3]

There it was again. Had the psychological element in his nature risen to dominate him once more, or was this something with organic roots which the doctors could not detect?

Two people went to see him in the last years – Lord Horder, then the King's Physician, and Margaret Sanger. Both left a record very different from that given by Mme Delisle. According to Margaret Sanger a very distressed Madame Delisle burst out in anguish to her one day: 'I can't stand it any more. He won't seem to die'.[4]

Lord Horder told me that he called unexpectedly and found Havelock's room in a state of disorder with the curtains drawn and Havelock in semi-darkness. When he asked Havelock questions it was Mme Delisle who answered with the royal we – 'We don't think that it would do him any good. . . . We don't agree with you. . . .'

As a Harley Street consultant he gave her medical advice, but she refused to take it. 'I told her the right treatment', Lord Horder explained to me. 'But she would have none of it. In fact she tried to teach me my job.'[5] (I myself in my dealings with Mme Delisle found that she could swing from smiling sweetness to imperious declamation – all in a moment. Behind the charming façade was a person given to bursts of irrationality which could, occasionally, take the form of hysterical outpourings.)

Through the last stages of pleurisy, aggravated by his throat, Ellis showed the same stoical endurance. When Ellis had at last shaken off pleurisy, the knowledge that a more persistent illness was now inescapable still produced no marked flaw in what had become remarkably like impassivity.

Soon Françoise Delisle decided to let the house in Holmdene Avenue and the cottage at Wivelsfield Green. No. 24 had serious shortcomings and the cottage was no place to nurse a sick man. She began searching for a new house and at last hit on one at Hintlesham, near Ipswich. There she nursed him devotedly, preparing a succession of very light egg dishes which he managed to swallow.

His once full mouth tightened as the pain and discomfort grew. The effort required to write became considerable. But as his eyes dimmed, and the flesh of his face seemed literally to fall away, the lineaments of another stoical self, a self capable of silent endurance, began to emerge from the soft, serene, smiling Ellis. It was like a new embodiment. As the old self died, a new one grew from its decay. It was a frail, spiritualized self, looking out on the world with different eyes, now sometimes absent, but the personality retained its poise and his disinterested calm continued to dominate whatever the world chose to offer.

By 1938 he was losing grip of his affairs and correspondence. His power for work was seriously curtailed and he was suddenly very depressed by the reception given to the much revised *Sex in Relation to Society* published in England for the first time. No one, in fact, took much notice of it. It had no important review and a very small sale.

Still his brain was clear, his sheer power of writing undiminished and in the *Daily Herald* he vigorously rejected Spengler and all his works.[6] Still he was able to take walks, leaning on Françoise Delisle, and the beauty of the Suffolk landscape stirred the old joy in his dimmed eyes. Moments of dejection about his decaying body occurred. Sometimes he looked down on it with a gently mocking smile; the hands emaciated, the ribs showing through, the limbs fast becoming spindly, but he did not despair. Preserving his public image as best he could, he continued to reply to occasional letters in the same sprawling handwriting, touched now by shakiness. One such letter went to an un-named correspondent towards the end of August 1938. It maintained Havelock's later view of homosexuality that one must learn to live with it rather than repress it.[7]

A dark tide of evil rose on the continent of Europe as the harsh threat of guns, tanks and aeroplanes was matched by the overblown rhetoric of their master. Presently the tide broke. The Nazis marched into Vienna to find a frail old man of eighty-two, the inside of his right jaw almost eaten away by cancer, a man who had survived fifteen operations in fifteen years, sitting at the same desk in the same house which had been his home for forty-seven years. The Gestapo called to see the King of the intellectual Jews. His books were burnt, his money confiscated, but Sigmund Freud was too old and frail to concern them much further. Under persuasion from Ernest Jones, he at last boarded the Orient Express on 4 June 1938, and two days later a fragile death's-head figure, dressed almost gaily in a green hat and top-coat, walked, with the aid of a cane, into a house at Hampstead. One of the first things he did was to write to Havelock Ellis. He wished, very much, to see him, he said. Ellis replied in July 1938 regretting that it was very difficult to arrange a meeting with a permanent invalid.[8] Later, mutual friends explained the situation more exactly to Freud.

They never did meet. The two figures who had so deeply contributed to the moral revolution each desired to bring about were now within a few miles of one another but facing death. Freud, with the cold courage of the complete scientist, refusing any alleviation to the pain of cancer beyond the pitiful relief of an occasional aspirin. And Havelock Ellis reduced to easily absorbed foods like junket, beset at last with a deep distaste for his emaciated body; Havelock Ellis who suffered the continual temperature of the very weak, who was liable to fall down without warning, who presently sat in a big chair by the window and one June day in 1939, wrote a last letter to Freud. Visitors were now discouraged, he spoke very little and he never ventured beyond the garden.

Both men confronted death with the courage of reason. There were no evasions or rationalizations. The illusions of an after-life had no protection to offer, yet each brought such different persuasions to the last enactment. One who had thrown a cold northern light into the dark places of human nature, to emerge with no greater warmth or consolation to offer the bewildered human spirit than – a mild unhappiness is the common lot of Man. And the so much less harsh, more optimistic, Ellis, who had always insisted that men were not primarily driven by greed and destruction. His teeth were gone, his eyes were dim, his body a skeleton, the hand which held the pen shaky, pain his constant companion. Now he remembered with profound reaffirmation the words of Ninon de Lenclos: 'If I had known what my life was to be I would have killed myself.' But as a last gentle flourish in the face of fate, he added some words remarkable in a man dying from starvation: 'I see life whole, coldly, nakedly, all round and though I am glad it is over, though I would not live it again, yet now that I seem to view it whole I view it with joy.'[9] A last letter came from Freud sending a copy of *Moses and Monotheism*. Ellis replied that he was largely without mental or physical activity and had not strayed beyond his garden for months.[10]

In the spring of 1939 he reached the final stage. Even then, when the mask of his detachment had at last cracked, there was no collapse or self-pity. It was a reasoned and deliberate surrender. He saw the forces which were arrayed against him as overwhelming, and his body now threatened to disintegrate from starvation. It was ghost-thin. His strength had largely gone, his never very powerful voice had become a whisper.

The discussion which followed with Françoise Delisle preserved the same disinterested calm which he had brought to the spectacle of life but now concerned the best method for painlessly achieving death. He did not want to die the long drawn-out, clumsy death which nature had ordained for him. He believed in death control as much as birth control. Euthanasia carried out in the full light of reason, transcended that last tyranny of nature, outwitting decay which could become humiliating. We have, of course, no independent record of the conversations which Françoise now held with Havelock and in the light of confusing evidence from other quarters that is unfortunate. In her account she records that she said, 'I will do what you want if you will let me go too.' No one who knew Havelock would have expected anything but a vehement rejection of such a proposal. She was too young. Her time had not yet come. Joint suicide – anyway – did not appeal to him. In the end according to her account she decided that she would co-operate in his death.

Presently the strain was too much for Françoise Delisle. Once more she fell ill, but she went on nursing Havelock and day after day the question recurred at the back of her mind: how, when, where? Ironically fate had fastened on Ellis the kind of illness which made it difficult to swallow anything resembling a tablet. Suicide would not be easy for him.

In the devious and dismaying paths which Ellis's illness followed Françoise Delisle once more prepared to take a 'holiday'. Twice when the situation became too appalling, sciatica, neuritis or some similar complaint made her ill and drove her away from him. Now Ellis's doctor encouraged her to go away once more to be ready for the final day. Havelock himself added his persuasions. She left Havelock in the care of his two sisters, sixty-eight year old Edith and seventy-two year old Laura, with strict instructions about grinding up his vitamin pills and mixing them with his milk.[11]

The full glory of that summer of 1939 brought one sun-drenched day close on the heels of another, and Havelock Ellis sometimes watched through the windows as the first beams of sunlight thrilled across the earth in the dawn he was awake to greet. He would watch the flowers recover their colour, follow the deep shadow as it lifted from the garden, and smell the scent of the earth and plants as the sun distilled it anew. Such a glory unfolded in the outer world as made more appalling the desire for death in his mind. Willingly to cut oneself off from such a full-throated burgeoning, only revealed the depth of his despair.

But the outer world itself was deeply troubled. Planes rushed across the skies, men in uniform once again tramped the roads, great convoys moved through the night and all too soon, on the far coasts of Kent and Sussex, a cannonade of guns from France was to shake the English coastline, and an armada of ships to carry our defeated armies back to an embattled England. Already Churchill had sounded the first notes of that aggressive diapason which was to echo through a besieged and bewildered country. Ellis was largely unaware. He half inhabited another world. Dimly he knew that whatever moral revolution he had helped to set in motion, the immorality of war remained, immutable witness to man's inability to control his destiny.

Françoise Delisle had gone to Derbyshire for what was to be two weeks' holiday. There she received a message from Havelock asking her to return. She reached the Suffolk house at 11 a.m. on Saturday 8 July. The brief interval away had sufficed to change him deeply. Death was written in the slow pulse, the immense pallor, the voice so very faint that Françoise Delisle strained her ears to catch his words. The details of what had happened while she was away are conflicting. Arthur

Calder-Marshall states that the sisters gave Havelock the wrong pills for two weeks. Instead of vitamins they ground a brand of proprietary pills into Ellis's milk and Françoise claimed that this was responsible for his deterioration. However a chemist told Calder-Marshall that they could not have made any marked difference to his condition.[12]

Presently Ellis wrote on a pad with a pencil. The hand and writing shook. They were both ready for what Delisle described as 'our adventure'.

According to Françoise Delisle a heart attack came that evening. She spoke on the telephone to the doctor who reassured her and told her not to worry too much. She went back to Havelock's bedroom, saw that he was in pain and tried to relieve his breathing with ammonia. She thought of telephoning the doctor again but Havelock shook his head. He was, he knew, beyond the help of doctors. Shortly after eleven o'clock she switched off the light which troubled him and went into the kitchen to heat some water. Fifteen minutes later she returned. He seemed to be lying very still. She went over to him. She saw then that he had switched on the light and tried to . . . what? She would never know for certain. His breathing had ceased. The man who believed that life could be brought to such gracious perfection had almost certainly – connived at taking his own.[13]

Alternative interpretations of these events are possible but no corroborative documentary evidence is available. Consider the sequence from a different point of view. Madame Delisle had burst out to Margaret Sanger – he won't seem to die – and rejected Lord Horder's advice which, according to Horder, could have saved his life. At the crucial point of his prolonged illness Madame Delisle left Havelock to his sisters' care with instructions to administer certain pills. Confusion arose over the pills and when she arrived back she claimed that the wrong pills had been given.

Speculating about the motives of a dead person is a dangerous exercise but if Madame Delisle, consciously or unconsciously, wished him dead (an experience classic to psycho-analytic theory), then these events fall into a different pattern. They can be seen as conniving at his death in a sense different from straightforward suicide. However, the evidence of the death certificate contradicts this, but the term – exhaustion – is an oddly inexact clinical description.

Moreover, three other facts confuse the issue. A sudden outburst – he won't seem to die – might characterise a temporary mood of despair but need not imply a general attitude, and wishing a person dead is a common experience among those who are burdened with permanent invalids. Above all Ellis, reduced to the state of a helpless invalid, would almost certainly have connived at his own death whatever the circumstances which gave rise to it.

Epilogue

If it was characteristic of Havelock Ellis's creed that he reconciled opposing disciplines in the sweep of his vision, bringing science into mysticism and art into science, it never gave much satisfaction to rigorously analytical minds. Yet Ellis's language occasionally rose to those heights where it breaks through rational resistance, and a sense of communion with mystical realities momentarily defeats rational doubt. Ernest Jones remarked of *Little Essays of Love and Virtue* that it was 'a book to read and enjoy, not to criticise'. The quality of his spirit sometimes disarmed his worst critics.

Ellis developed that spirit of renaissance humanism which, first confined to re-interpretation of classical antiquities, grew deeper and richer as its boundaries extended. Like the renaissance humanists he pressed forward from man in society to the individual dominating society, but he went beyond that to the inner problems of man knowing himself. The romantic streak which ran through much of his thinking was re-affirmed by his scientific optimism but the new enlightenment of which he was clearly a part has only achieved partial realization. One classification always broke down with Ellis. There was an echo to every statement made about him.

Dr Kinsey pays frequent tribute to Ellis in his studies but rightly says, 'The monumental work of Havelock Ellis and of Freud . . . did not involve a general survey of persons . . .' without 'sexual problems which would lead them to professional sources for help. . . .'

But he remained a pioneer and it was pointless to complain that he lacked modern methods. In his day his approach was original enough, and similarities remained between his own work and Dr Kinsey's.

As a psychologist he had the scientific attitude but lacked the subtleties of the scientific method. He brilliantly charted a whole continent of sexual behaviour but did not sufficiently investigate motive. Freud not merely worked for years unravelling the tangled skeins of his patients' thoughts, conscious and unconscious; he saw that

252

they could hopelessly deceive themselves, he took little at its face value and detected unconscious patterns far below the surface.

Ellis had all the evidence. He wrestled with it for years. He identified the widespread permeation of sex in many unexpected areas, he apprehended infantile sexuality, religious sexuality and the element of sexual sublimation in art; but his theories were vague. He could not convincingly explain what he found. Freud could and did. His insight was of a different order. As a psychologist Freud succeeded where Ellis failed, but Ellis's benign influence was – in Victorian England – more persuasive than Freud's. He brought to the problems of human relationships a compassion which not merely marked him out in the cold world of science, but won the sympathetic hearing of people hostile to his beliefs. His books were strewn with findings on many basic human problems, and he established a rationale for sex reform which was a major achievement in his time. He stands as the leading English pioneer in the modernization of sex, and the renovation of the relations between the sexes, but women's liberation has now entered new conceptual fields which he would find dubious. The feminist movement today regards Ellis's *Sex in Relation to Society* as very old-fashioned with its admission of monogamy and the family as the best *social* basis for relations between the sexes. As for his lofty protestations about love, they consider them extravagantly romantic. Women's liberation would also take exception to his biologically based role prescription in which man is dominant and the woman submissive. Characteristically, a woman's passivity had, in Ellis's credo, to be aroused by a man, and the idea that a woman could herself assume the role of the man and take the sexual initiative would be alien to him. True fulfilment in a woman meant having at least one child in her lifetime and the responsibilites of the family were social and not individual. Each sex was clearly differentiated for Havelock Ellis and in the perfectly balanced society each would fulfil the different biological drives of its own nature, opening the way to the good and just community. Modern feminists find much of this unacceptable and when Ellis spoke of pregnancy as a woman's destiny which lifts her 'above the level of ordinary humanity to become the casket of an inestimable jewel', he simply incites them to ribaldry. However, as Jeffrey Weeks has said in his study of Havelock Ellis: 'Ellis's views on marriage and motherhood found their realisation in the idea of family allowances, the state supporting the family in the interests of healthy childhood and social stability.'[1] Moreover, in Western societies generally family patterns not only fulfil the implications of Ellis's much more traditional thinking, but the majority of women appear to sympathize with his outlook. Michael Young and Peter Willmott's book *The Symmetrical Family* is the logical outcome of Ellis's thinking.

As a mystic he did not undergo the austere discipline described by

Aldous Huxley. There was no first, second and third stage of annihilation leading to the incandescent core of contemplative life. Equally, the spirit informing the Cloud of Unknowing was not his. At first sight, his was a form of mysticism open to anyone. It had much in common with pantheism and he was most lost at the lyrical heart of life when the beauties of nature – the sound of the sea from a cliff-top, a bank of flowers on a summer day – worked magic with his senses.

His was not Brahmanic pantheism nor Buddhistic nihilism, both of which, rejecting the unreality of the apparent world, had something approaching contempt for the human personality. Neither was it Neoplatonic. The assumption that reason is capable of mapping all phenomena, except that of God, which being beyond reason must be assigned to the realms of mysticism, did not appeal to him. He was not Neoplatonic, because Neoplatonism too scorned the world of the senses. Even Plotinus was ashamed of the prison of his body, disliked naming his parents and in contradiction to Ellis said that moments of ecstatic union were so rare that 'I myself have realised it but three times as yet. . . .'

The literature of mysticism is full of irritating terms like The One and the Many, the Self and Not Self, and the Absolute Union. Ellis made little play with such jargon but there were many sources which had something in common with his own outlook. Sufism amongst the ninth-century Mohammedans of Persia delighted in a natural pantheism, where mystic awareness of all things heightened the intensity of being alive.

His mysticism did not in fact completely fit anywhere. The creeds of Meister Eckhart, John of the Cross, Henry More or Boehme, did not correspond; his feet remained too firmly on the ground for such thinkers. Always the whole man, Ellis reconciled, without any marked sense of effort, materialism and mysticism, and it was the essence of his creed that one could not exist without the balance of the other.

In this way he achieved a common-sense mysticism peculiar to twentieth-century man. Certainly it offered to those who shared his temperament an escape from everyday life, but many amongst his disciples were incapable of sustaining the self-sufficiency which it demanded. Modern psychology might speak of substitute gratifications, but Ellis believed that his mysticism brought him nearer to what he regarded as the heart of living. He was too much of a scholar not to know that mysticism derived from the Greek – to shut the eyes – but he insisted that his eyes were fully open.

As a literary critic, *The New Spirit, Affirmations* and *From Rousseau to Proust*, contained some good criticism in that particular school inspired by Taine. It was essentially a sane, down-to-earth, school. Taine, in constant intercourse with men like Renan, Sainte-Beuve, Gaultier and Flaubert – all regarded highly by Ellis – set out to study man in one of his pathological crises. He loved to abstract and classify as Ellis did, and if his positivist philosophy was too despairing for Ellis, and his condemnation of mankind too wholesale, he had the same preoccupation with the study of man. Ellis – who had read Taine extensively – was influenced by him in his early and middle years, which led him to follow a similar approach to literary criticism in the *New Spirit* and *Affirmations*. Taine believed that each great writer was a product of his race, environment and time. Whereas history had once been a frame to criticism, criticism, in his work, tended to become the frame, each writer epitomizing a certain epoch. In just such a manner, Ellis explained the *New Spirit* through selected persons, and his *Affirmations* through Nietzsche, Casanova, Zola, Huysmans, and St Francis.

Taine combined the roles of artist, *litterateur*, scientist and philosopher, and perfected a style which delighted in bold, highly coloured themes. Ellis matched most of these elements, but his style was distinguished in a different way. His *Essay on the Art of Writing* was a salutary experience in a world of literary criticism fast retreating into places unintelligible to the average reader. He even brought science into literary criticism when he wrote *The Colour Sense in Literature*, analysing the literary significance of colour in the work of different poets; psychology was invoked to analyse Proust; ethnography grammatical usage.

He regarded Croce as the most instructive literary critic of the time and believed with him that 'there are no objective standards of judgment', that 'we cannot approach a work of art with our laws and categories.' We had to comprehend the artist's own values, and only then were we fit to pronounce on his work – a complete contradiction of the intentional fallacy of today.

If literary criticism, in Ellis's day, had not fully explored those psychological subtleties which distinguished Richards, *Principles of Literary Criticism*, and the schools represented by Eliot, Leavis and Lionel Trilling might consider his simplicities naïve, in a sense he was a pioneer of the psychological approach. But his criticism today would be regarded as *belles lettres*.

Amongst his idolaters there were many who spoke with reverence of his poetry. The impulse to song seems to have died in modern poetry, and so many academic niceties have revolutionized verbal music that, once again, Ellis's work would appear absurd beside that of T. S. Eliot or Ezra Pound. Following every precept of his own critical creed, even when judged within his own period, values and form, his talents are not best represented by the sonnets he wrote in his lifetime. His poetry is a private poetry in a sense very different from Eliot's meaning of the term. It does not easily survive publication.

As a philosopher he merged something of Spinoza, Herbert Spencer,

Rousseau, Bergson and Jules de Gaultier with the little-known Castillian writer José Rodó. 'For Gaultier, the world is a spectacle', he wrote. 'It is only in Art that the solution of Life's problems can be found. Life is always immoral and unjust. It is Art alone which, rising above the categories of Morality, justifies the pains and griefs of Life. . . .' To see the world as beauty. . . . Could that be considered a philosophy?

It is clear that Ellis's philosophy did not fall into any category common to academic philosophy. It was not rationalist, positivist or analytical; terms like methodology would have irritated him, and the finer reaches of linguistic analysis remained for him, barren. Indeed, Ellis's philosophy, as with his religion, risked the charge that it was no philosophy at all. Plainly he invited this. He believed that every man who had reached that stage of development in which he enjoyed 'the philosophic emotion' would find 'his own philosophy. . . .'.

As unsophisticated a statement as ever encouraged donnish disdain. What followed was worse if one were a professor of philosophy. 'To be the serene spectator of the Absurdity of the world, to be at the same time the strenuous worker in the Rationalisation of the world – that is the function of the complete Man. But it remains a very difficult task, the supreme task in the Art of Living.'

In the last analysis Ellis's credo was best understood when personified in that type of human being which he considered ideal. But there a difficulty arose. Painfully creating around himself the contemplative life of the scholar, enriched by many friends and lovers, Ellis appeared to believe that his own capacities for love and aesthetic experience could be realized in large numbers of others. But Havelock Ellis was a rare human being.

Notes

Preface
1 *Psychiatry* (USA), 1940, vol. III, p. 145.

Prologue
1 Dr B. Malinowski, *In Appreciation*, 1929, p. 282.
2 Interview, *Daily Herald*, 24 April 1938.
3 Marie Stopes, *Literary Guide*, September 1939.
4 Ibid.
5 Havelock Ellis, *My Life*, 1940, p. 84. Interview, Françoise Delisle.
6 Oddly, there was an auxiliary police station immediately underneath Ellis's flat.
7 Interview, Francis Watson, 15 July 1952.
8 Isaac Goldberg, *Havelock Ellis*, 1926, p. 6.
9 Havelock Ellis, op. cit., p. 8.
10 Ibid.
11 Houston Petersen, *Havelock Ellis, Philosopher of Love*, 1930, p. 156.
12 Note left by his friend Hugh de Selincourt.
13 Havelock Ellis, op. cit., p. 84.
14 Ibid., p. 86.
15 24 January 1888.
16 Frederick Whyte, *Life of W. T. Stead*, vol. I, 1925, p. 162.
17 Havelock Ellis, *Impressions and Comments*, vol. III, 1924, p. 109.

Chapter 1: First beginnings
1 Houston Petersen, *Havelock Ellis,*

Philosopher of Love, 1930, p. 1.
2 Havelock Ellis, *My Life*, 1940, p. 42.
3 Havelock Ellis, *Studies in the Psychology of Sex*, vol. V, 1906.
4 Havelock Ellis, *My Life*, p. 37.
5 Houston Petersen, op. cit., p. 5.
6 Isaac Goldberg, *Havelock Ellis*, 1926, p. 18.
7 Houston Petersen, op. cit., p. 13.
8 Interview, Janet de Selincourt, widow of Hugh de Selincourt, 4 May 1953.
9 Hugh de Selincourt, notes.
10 Havelock Ellis, *Impressions and Comments*, vol. II, 1921, pp. 94–5.
11 Havelock Ellis, *Books I Have Read*, 16 April 1873.
12 Havelock Ellis, *Notebooks*, April 1873.
13 Ibid., April 1874.
14 Ibid.
15 J. B. S. Haldane, *The Causes of Evolution*, 1932.
16 Houston Petersen, op. cit., p. 52.
17 Havelock Ellis, *Books I Have Read*, Part Three.
18 Houston Petersen, op. cit., p. 40.

Chapter 2: Australian interlude
1 Shipboard Diary, 7 May 1875.
2 Ibid., 14 May 1875; also interviews with Françoise Delisle, during 1952–3.
3 Interviews with Françoise Delisle during 1952–3.
4 Ibid.
5 Letter to his mother, 20 December 1875.

6 Interview with Françoise Delisle, 14 January 1953.
7 Houston Petersen, *Havelock Ellis, Philosopher of Love*, 1930, p. 69.
8 Ibid.
9 Margaret Sanger, *Birth Control Review*, July / August / September 1923.
10 Diary, 31 December 1875; also interviews with Françoise Delisle during 1952–3.
11 Havelock Ellis, *Kanga Creek*, 1922, pp. 10–11.
12 Ibid., p. 28.
13 Diary, 6 August 1876.
14 Ibid., 6 August 1876; also interview with Françoise Delisle, 3 April 1952.
15 Diary, 26 December 1876; also, interview with Françoise Delisle, 3 April 1952.
16 Letter to his father, 14 February 1877.
17 Ibid.
18 Diary, 10 September 1877.
19 Ibid.
20 Ibid.
21 Letter to his father, 7 May 1877.
22 Havelock Ellis, *My Life*, 1940.
23 Diary, 1 February 1878.
24 Ibid.
25 Interview with Françoise Delisle, 3 April 1952.
26 Havelock Ellis, *Kanga Creek*, p. 14.
27 Ibid., p. 15.
28 Ibid., p. 22.
29 Havelock Ellis, *My Life*, p. 125.
30 Ibid., pp. 131–3.
31 Notebooks, March 1878.
32 James Hinton, *Life in Nature*, 1862, p. 217.
33 Havelock Ellis, *The Dance of Life*, 1923, p. 201.
34 J. Ellice Hopkins (ed.), *Life and Letters of James Hinton*, 1878.
35 Diary, 1 September 1878.

Chapter 3: Medical training and Olive Schreiner

1 Houston Petersen, *Havelock Ellis, Philosopher of Love*, 1930, p. 125.
2 James Hinton, *The Law-Breaker and the Coming of the Law*, 1884, p. 153.
3 *Modern Thought*, April 1881.
4 *Mind*, July 1884.
5 A. Calder-Marshall, *Havelock Ellis*, 1959.
6 Havelock Ellis, *My Life*, 1940, p. 147.
7 Letter to his father, 15 November 1882.
8 Havelock Ellis, *My Life*, p. 196.
9 Letter, Reginald Pound, close friend of Walter Gallicher, 10 February 1953.
10 Havelock Ellis, *Scientific Notes, Original and Selected*, 1881.
11 Houston Petersen, op. cit., p. 152.
12 S. C. Cronwright Schreiner, *Life of Olive Schreiner*, 1924, p. 156.
13 *Fortnightly Review*, December 1883.
14 Letter, 25 February 1884.
15 A. Calder-Marshall, op. cit., pp. 91–2.
16 Letter, 20 May 1884.
17 Letter, May 1884.
18 Interview with Françoise Delisle, 10 December 1952.
19 Ibid.
20 Diary, undated; also, interview with Françoise Delisle, 10 April 1952.
21 Ibid.; also, interview with Françoise Delisle, 10 April 1952.
22 Ibid.; also, interview with Françoise Delisle, 10 April 1952.
23 Interview with Françoise Delisle, 3 April 1952.
24 Diary, undated.
25 Interview with Françoise Delisle, 3 April 1952.
26 Françoise Delisle, *Friendship's Odyssey*, 1946, p. 408.

Chapter 4: His writing career begins

1 *Modern Thought*, April 1881.
2 *Westminster Review*, April 1883.
3 29 April 1883.
4 *Times*, December 1885.
5 *Indian Review*, February 1884.
6 *Mind*, July 1884.
7 *Today*, October 1884.
8 James Hinton, *The Law-Breaker and the Coming of the Law*, 1884.
9 Houston Petersen, *Havelock Ellis, Philosopher of Love*, 1930, p. 141.
10 Letter, 3 March 1927.
11 An abbreviated version of the *Harleian manuscript*, 6853 Fol: 320.
12 Introduction, *Christopher Marlowe's Plays*, 1887.
13 Philip Henderson examines the

detailed evidence, *Christopher Marlowe*, 1952, pp. 65–6.

14 Letter, 26 April 1885.

15 Karl Pearson Archive, University College, London. Schreiner letters, February 1887.

16 Letter, January 1886.

17 Letter, 14 December 1886. Karl Pearson Archive, University College, London.

18 Letter, 25 April 1887.

19 Havelock Ellis, *My Life*, 1940, p. 200.

20 Letter, Winifred Horrabin, 13 May 1952.

21 Letter to father, 11 June 1886.

22 Ibid., 11 December 1889.

23 Letter, Winifred Horrabin, 13 May 1952.

24 2 February 1889.

Chapter 5: Meets his wife-to-be

1 Havelock Ellis, *My Life*, 1940, p. 211.

2 Letter, 13 June 1891; see also Havelock Ellis, op. cit.

3 Vera Buchanan-Gould, *Not Without Honour*, 1924, pp. 119–20.

4 Interview with Janet de Selincourt, 4 May 1953.

5 Havelock Ellis, op. cit., p. 47.

6 Havelock Ellis, *The New Spirit*, 1890, p. 7.

7 Ernest Rhys, *Everyman Remembers*, 1930, p. 81.

8 Havelock Ellis, *The Criminal*, 1890, pp. 293–4.

9 Review of *From Rousseau to Proust*, *Observer*, 16 February 1936.

10 Houston Petersen, *Havelock Ellis, Philosopher of Love*, 1930, p. 189.

11 Author of *Histoire de la Litterature Anglaise*, 1863.

12 Arthur Symons, *Mes Souvenirs*, 1931, p. 5.

13 Ibid., p. 7.

14 Havelock Ellis, *From Rousseau to Proust*, p. 10.

15 Arthur Symons, op. cit., p. 10.

16 Havelock Ellis, *From Rousseau to Proust*, p. 12.

Chapter 6: Marriage to Edith

1 Letter to father, 28 December 1891.

2 Havelock Ellis, *My Life*, 1940, p. 220.

3 Letter from Janet de Selincourt, January 1954.

4 Margaret Sanger.

5 Havelock Ellis, *The Nationalisation of Health*, 1892, p. 227.

6 *The Chances of Death*, 1897. See also Ellis's letters, Karl Pearson Archive, University College, London, October 1897.

7 Houston Petersen, *Havelock Ellis, Philosopher of Love*, 1930.

8 Letter, Perrycoste, 29 August 1901.

Chapter 7: Studies in sex begin

1 Havelock Ellis, *Affirmations*, essay on Zola, 1897, p. 143.

2 Ibid.

3 Ibid., p. 130.

4 Unpublished notes.

5 Ibid.

6 Phyllis Grosskurth, *John Addington Symonds*, 1964, pp. 284–94.

7 Letter to Symonds, 10 July 1891.

8 Phyllis Grosskurth, op. cit., p. 287.

9 Copy of letter to Symonds, 1 July 1892.

10 Copy of letter, 19 February 1893; see also Phyllis Grosskurth, op. cit.

11 Copy of letter, 21 December 1892.

12 Copy of letter, 29 September 1892.

13 Copy of letter, 3 January 1893.

14 Letter to Houston Petersen, 15 March 1927.

15 Havelock Ellis, *Studies in the Psychology of Sex*, vol. 1, 1897, p. 129.

16 Ibid., p. 38.

17 Havelock Ellis, *Studies in the Psychology of Sex*, vol. II, 1924, pp. 355–6.

18 Havelock Ellis, *Studies in the Psychology of Sex*, vol. I, 1897, p. 77, footnote.

19 Ibid., p. 94.

20 John Sweeney, *At Scotland Yard*, 1905, p. 188.

21 *Adult*, September 1898.

22 John Sweeney, op. cit., p. 188.

23 *Lancet*, 19 November 1898.

24 Arthur Calder-Marshall, *Lewd, Blasphemous and Obscene*, 1972.

25 John Sweeney, op. cit.; see also *Cambridge Daily News*, 16 and 24 January 1902.

26 Havelock Ellis, *A Note on the Bedborough Trial*, 1898.

Chapter 8: His wife's lesbian experience
1 Much of the material in the following pages is based on the correspondence between Ellis and his wife and his autobiography, *My Life*, 1940.
2 Evidence from Olive Schreiner and Margaret Sanger.
3 *Bookman*, July 1918.

Chapter 9: Sex studies develop
1 *Lancet*, June 1897.
2 *Contemporary Review*, January 1898.
3 *Popular Science Monthly*, May 1902.
4 Houston Petersen, *Havelock Ellis, Philosopher of Love*, 1930, pp. 228–9.
5 Notebooks and 'St Francis and Others', 1897, pp. 241–2.
6 Havelock Ellis, *Studies in the Psychology of Sex*, vol. 1, preface, p. 6.
7 *British Medical Journal*, 14 June 1890.
8 *Dalton Journal of Asiatic Society*, Bengal, 4 January 1884, quoted by Ellis, *Studies in the Psychology of Sex*, vol. I, 1910, p. 14.
9 *Psycho-Analytic Review*, April 1927.
10 Havelock Ellis, *Studies in the Psychology of Sex*, vol. I, 1900, pp. 212–13.
11 Ibid.
12 J. P. West, *Transactions of the Ohio Pediatric Society*, 1895; see also abstract in *Medical Standard*, November 1895; Havelock Ellis, *Studies in the Psychology of Sex*, vol. I, 1900.
13 Moraglia, *Archivio di Psichiatria*, vol. XVI (fasc 4 & 5), p. 313; Havelock Ellis, *Studies in the Psychology of Sex*, vol. I, 1900, p. 238.
14 Dr Ernest Jones comments that it is a howler to speak of Freud's monosexual view of the universe. 'Freud never deviated from the dualistic view, there being a constant conflict between sexual impulses and various other ones.'
15 Havelock Ellis, *Studies in the Psychology of Sex*, vol. I, 1900, pp. 282–3.

16 Letter, Sigmund Freud to Wilhelm Fliess, 3 January 1899.
17 Havelock Ellis, *The Philosophy of Conflict*, 1919, p. 200.
18 Dr Ernest Jones commented: 'an innuendo which would be profoundly untrue of Freud'.
19 'The Synthesis of Dreams', *The Psycho-Analytic Review*, October 1925; January 1926.
20 *Journal of Medical Science*, April 1901.

Chapter 10: A typical 'perversion' case
1 J. Bronowski (ed.), *Ideas and Beliefs of the Victorians*, 1949, p. 352.
2 Samuel Butler, Notebooks.
3 J. Bronowski, op. cit., p. 168.
4 Havelock Ellis, *Studies in the Psychology of Sex*, vol. III, 1903, p. 128.
5 Ibid., p. 100.
6 Havelock Ellis, *Studies in the Psychology of Sex*, vol. VII, 1928, pp. 121 et seq.
7 Ibid., p. 191.
8 Ibid., pp. 197–8.
9 Sigmund Freud, *Collected Papers*, vol. II, 1924, pp. 191–2.
10 Mark Tellar, *A Young Man's Passage*, 1952, p. 242.
11 Ibid., pp. 310–11.
12 Letter to the author, 13 January 1953.

Chapter 11: Marital troubles
1 Havelock Ellis, *My Life*, 1940, p. 325.
2 The detailed print orders were: Vol. I 29,700; Vol. II 24,150; Vol. III 27,210; Vol. IV 21,750; Vol. V 23,650; Vol. VI 24,500; Vol. VII 10,000.
3 Havelock Ellis, *The Soul of Spain*, 1908, pp. 378–9.
4 Havelock Ellis. The following sequences are based on facts in *My Life*, 1940.
5 Ibid., p. 345. Houston Petersen made the same point differently, in a letter to the author, 15 June 1953.
6 Havelock Ellis, *My Life*, p. 345.
7 Edith Lees, *The Subjection of Kezia*.
8 Letter, Hugh de Selincourt, undated.
9 Letter, Edith Lees, 7 September 1909.

Chapter 12: Sex in relation to society

1 Jules de Gaultier, *De Kant à Nietzsche*, 1961, p. 303.
2 Havelock Ellis, *Studies in the Psychology of Sex*, vol. IV, 1905, p. 21.
3 Havelock Ellis, *Studies in the Psychology of Sex*, vol. V, 1906, pp. 57 et seq.
4 Marie Stopes, *Literary Guide*, September 1939.
5 Dean Inge.
6 Marie Stopes, op. cit.
7 Lancelot Hogben, *Dangerous Thoughts*, 1939, p. 188.
8 Havelock Ellis, *Studies in the Psychology of Sex*, vol. VI, 1910, p. 417.
9 Belfort Bax, *Outspoken Essays*, 1897, p. 6.
10 Rabelais, Book I, chapter LVII, p. 266.
11 Havelock Ellis, *Studies in the Psychology of Sex*, vol. VI, 1910, p. 429.
12 Diderot, vol. II, p. 20.
13 Havelock Ellis, *Studies in the Psychology of Sex*, vol. VI, 1910, p. 452.
14 Ibid., p. 453.
15 C. Booth, *Life and Labour of the People*, 1889, Appendix IV.
16 Havelock Ellis, *Studies in the Psychology of Sex*, vol. VI, 1910, pp. 488–9.
17 Ibid., p. 465.
18 Paul and Victor Margueritte, *Quelques Idées*, 1905, p. 3.
19 E. D. Cope, *The Marriage Problem*, 1890.
20 Tarde, *Archives d'Anthropologie Criminelle*, 1880.
21 Havelock Ellis, *My Life*, p. 363.

Chapter 13: Edith goes to America

1 Havelock Ellis, *The Nineteenth Century*, 1900, p. 119.
2 Ibid., p. 96.
3 Ibid., p. 97.
4 Houston Petersen, *Havelock Ellis, Philosopher of Love*, 1930, p. 288.
5 E. M. East, 'Havelock Ellis, Interpreter', *Birth Control Review*, February 1927.
6 Letter, Olive Schreiner, 30 June 1912.

7 Letter, Havelock Ellis to Freud, 5 April 1907.
8 Letter, 26 August 1907. Review, *Journal Mental Science*, vol. 53, October 1907.
9 Letter, 23 August 1910. Review, *Journal Mental Science*, vol. 47, April 1901.
10 Letter, 9 August 1911.
11 Letter, 27 June 1912.
12 First published in *The Nineteenth Century and After*, May 1906.
13 Havelock Ellis, *The Task of Social Hygiene*, 1912, p. 200.
14 Ibid., p. 206.
15 Based on facts in *My Life*, 1940.
16 Letter, Edith to Ellis, undated.
17 Unpublished account by Florence Mole.
18 Letter, Margaret Sanger, undated.
19 Letter to author, Mary McCall, undated.
20 Much of material in the following pages is based on facts from *My Life*.
21 Letter, Cronwright Schreiner to Ellis, 8 December 1927.
22 S. C. Cronwright Schreiner, *Life of Olive Schreiner*, 1924, pp. 303–4.
23 Letter, Olive Schreiner to Ellis, 16 March 1914.
24 Letter, 15 January 1914.
25 Letter, 28 April 1914.
26 Letter, Edith to Ellis, *My Life*, undated.
27 *Evening World*, 29 April 1914.
28 *New York Tribune*, 3 May 1914.
29 Ibid.
30 Ibid.

Chapter 14: Edith's attempted suicide and death

1 Havelock Ellis, *Impressions and Comments*, vol. II, 1914–20, pp. 59–60.
2 Letter to author, Margaret Sanger, 16 July 1952.
3 Ibid.
4 Ibid.
5 Letter, Edith to Ellis, 4 February 1915, *My Life*.
6 Letter to Margaret Sanger, 27 January 1915.
7 29 April 1915.
8 Margaret Sanger, letter, 3 December 1953.

9 Based on facts in *My Life*, 1940, pp. 462 et seq.
10 Letters to Edward Carpenter, 22, 27 and 31 March 1916.
11 Letter, Edward Carpenter to Ellis, 24 March 1916.
12 Interview with Françoise Delisle, 10 May 1953. Also, letters to Edward Carpenter, 22, 27 and 31 March 1916.
13 Françoise Delisle, *Friendship's Odyssey*, 1946, pp. 247–8.
14 Letter, Edith to Mme Delisle, 3 September 1916.
15 Havelock Ellis, *My Life*, pp. 507–11.
16 Ibid., p. 509.
17 Letter to Perrycoste, 17 November 1916.
18 Letter, Olive Schreiner to Ellis, 19 October 1918.
19 Ibid., February 1920.
20 Letter from Olive Renier (god-daughter of Olive Schreiner), 21 April 1954.

Chapter 15: A new love life
1 Letter to Perrycoste, 21 December 1918.
2 Ibid., 25 December 1918.
3 Letter from Ellis to Mme Delisle, 28 September 1916.
4 Françoise Delisle, *Friendship's Odyssey*, 1946, p. 256.
5 Arthur Calder-Marshall, *Havelock Ellis*, 1959, p. 244.
6 Based on interviews with Françoise Delisle; see also *Friendship's Odyssey*.
7 Ibid., p. 270.
8 Letter from Ellis to Françoise Delisle. *Friendship's Odyssey*.
9 Françoise Delisle, op. cit., pp. 278–9.
10 Ibid., p. 312.
11 Havelock Ellis, *Impressions and Comments*, second series, 1921, pp. 137–8.
12 Ibid., pp. 139–40.
13 Ibid., p. 233.
14 Ibid., p. 244.
15 Ibid., third series, 1924, pp. 54–5.
16 Ibid., pp. 87–8.

Chapter 16: *The dance of life*
1 *Evening Post* (USA), 24 September 1921.

2 Havelock Ellis, *The Dance of Life*, 1923, p. 33.
3 Ibid., p. 176.
4 Ibid., p. 211.
5 Based on *The Dance of Life*.
6 Ibid., pp. 230 et seq.
7 Ibid.
8 Ibid., p. 245.
9 Ibid., p. 131.
10 *Dial*, November 1923.
11 Ibid.
12 Ibid.

Chapter 17: Freud's relations with Ellis
1 Unpublished manuscript, Hugh de Selincourt.
2 Ibid.
3 Ernest Jones, *Life and Work of Sigmund Freud*, vol. I, 1953, p. 31.
4 Ibid., p. 63.
5 Ibid., p. 334.
6 Sigmund Freud, *Three Contributions to the Theory of Sex*, 1918, p. 43.
7 Ibid., p. 23 (footnote).
8 Ibid., p. 52.
9 Ibid., p. 82.
10 Ibid., p. 82 (footnote).
11 Ibid., p. 61.
12 Ibid., pp. 5–6.
13 Ibid., p. 6.
14 Ibid., p. 8.
15 Even four years later Freud was very aware of the gaps and obscurities in the first edition of *Three Contributions to the Theory of Sex*.
16 C. S. Ford and F. A. Beach, *Patterns of Sexual Behaviour*, 1951, p. 311.
17 Havelock Ellis, *The Philosophy of Conflict*, 1919, pp. 200–1.
18 Ernest Jones, *Life and Work of Sigmund Freud*, vol. I, 1953, p. 354.
19 J. P. West, *Transactions of the Ohio Pediatric Society*, 1895.
20 Havelock Ellis, *The Philosophy of Conflict*, p. 201.
21 Sigmund Freud, *Three Contributions to the Theory of Sex*, p. 43.
22 Havelock Ellis, *The Philosophy of Conflict*, pp. 214–15.
23 This view was later qualified. *My Life*, 1940, p. 141.
24 James Frazer, *The Golden Bough*, 1937.
25 Ellis to Freud, 20 April 1920.

26 *Forum*, February 1926.
27 Ibid.
28 Ellis to Freud, 31 August 1926.
29 Freud to Ellis, 8 November 1925.
30 *International Journal of Psycho-Analysis*, 1928, vol. IX, pp. 480–9.
31 Havelock Ellis, *Studies in the Psychology of Sex*, vol. VII, 1928, p. 327.
32 Freud to Ellis, July 1928.
33 Ellis to Freud, 24 March 1930.
34 Havelock Ellis, *My Confessional*, 1936, pp. 66–7.

Chapter 18: Jealousy breaks in
1 Françoise Delisle, *Friendship's Odyssey*, 1946.
2 Interview with Janet de Selincourt, 15 October 1953.
3 I have read this very long unpublished correspondence covering the period.
4 Françoise Delisle, op. cit., p. 367.
5 The following pages are based on *Friendship's Odyssey*.
6 13 January 1923.
7 Françoise Delisle, op. cit., pp. 387–8.
8 Scott to Delisle, October 1926.
9 Several interviews with Janet de Selincourt, summer 1953.
10 Interviews with Francoise Delisle, during 1952–3.
11 Letters, Delisle to de Selincourt, 1924–33.
12 27 November 1929.
13 The letters multiplied in this period.
14 Letter to author, Janet de Selincourt, 14 November 1953.
15 12 September 1926.
16 *American Scholar*, autumn 1939, vol. VIII.
17 Unpublished MS in my possession.
18 Charles W. Margold, *Sex, Freedom and Social Control*, 1926.
19 Havelock Ellis, *My Life*, 1940, p. 525.
20 This letter was in the possession of Françoise Delisle.
21 J. Starobinski, *Yale French Studies*, vol. 28, 1961–2, pp. 64–74.
22 Radclyffe Hall, 7 June 1928.
23 Ibid., 23 August 1928.
24 Ibid., 11 March 1929.
25 14 January 1930.

Chapter 19: A serious illness
1 Havelock Ellis, *My Confessional*, 1934, p. 129.
2 Françoise Delisle, *Friendship's Odyssey*, 1946, p. 408.
3 Ibid., p. 409.
4 Ibid., pp. 278–9.
5 Ibid.
6 Letter to the author, Margaret Sanger, 29 January 1954.
7 Havelock Ellis, *The Psychology of Sex*, 1946, p. 217.
8 Letter, probable date August 1947.
9 Difficulty in swallowing.
10 25 June 1932.
11 14 February 1932.
12 Françoise Delisle, op. cit., p. 472.
13 Ibid.
14 Havelock Ellis, *From Rousseau to Proust*, 1936, p. 367.
15 Joseph Wortis, *American Scholar*, autumn 1939, p. 505.

Chapter 20: Last years and death
1 Interview, Lord Horder, 10 June 1954.
2 Interview, Clifford Bax, 11 July 1953.
3 Françoise Delisle, *Friendship's Odyssey*, 1946, p. 474.
4 Interview, Janet de Selincourt, 11 August 1953.
5 Interview, Lord Horder, 10 June 1954.
6 *Daily Herald*, 24 April 1938.
7 British Museum MS 45498 f 153, 23 August 1938.
8 Ellis to Freud, 14 July 1938.
9 Havelock Ellis, *My Life*, 1940, p. 523.
10 4 June 1939.
11 A. Calder-Marshall, *Havelock Ellis*, 1959, p. 277.
12 Ibid., p. 281.
13 The cause of death given on the death certificate was: Exhaustion: Diverticulum of Oesophagus.

Epilogue
1 S. Rowbotham and Jeffrey Weeks, *Socialism and the New Life*, 1977, p. 180.

Bibliography

Main works of Havelock Ellis

Sexual Inversion, with J. A. Symonds, London: Wilson Macmillan, 1897. Withdrawn
  before publication at the request of Symonds's executors. German translation by
  Hans Kurella, *Das kontrare Geschlechtsgefuhl*, Leipzig: George H. Wigands
  Verlag, 1896.

Sexual Inversion (*Studies in the Psychology of Sex*, vol. I), Watford: The University
  Press, 1897 (reprinted from earlier edition excluding Symonds's contributions).
  2nd edition, revised, Philadelphia: F. A. Davis, 1901 (renumbered as vol. II,
  Studies in the Psychology of Sex). 3rd edition, revised and enlarged, 1915.

The Evolution of Modesty, The Phenomena of Sexual Periodicity, Auto-Erotism
  (*Studies in the Psychology of Sex*, vol. II), Leipzig: The University Press, 1899.
  2nd edition, revised and renumbered as *Studies in the Psychology of Sex*, vol. I,
  Philadelphia, F. A. Davis, 1900. 3rd edition, 1910.

*The Analysis of the Sexual Impulse, Love and Pain, The Sexual Impulse In
  Women* (*Studies in the Psychology of Sex*, vol. III), Philadelphia: F. A. Davis,
  1903. 2nd edition, revised and enlarged, 1913.

Sexual Selection in Man: I Touch. II Smell. III Hearing. IV Vision (*Studies in the
  Psychology of Sex*, vol. IV), Philadelphia: F. A. Davis, 1905.

Erotic Symbolism, The Mechanism of Detumescence, The Psychic State in Pregnancy
  (*Studies in the Psychology of Sex*, vol. V), Philadelphia: F. A. Davis, 1906.

Sex in Relation to Society (*Studies in the Psychology of Sex*, vol. VI), Philadelphia:
  F. A. Davis, 1910. The Mother and Child, Sexual Education, Sexual Morality,
  Marriage, etc. Abridged edition, London: Heinemann, 1937.

Eonism and Other Supplementary Studies (*Studies in the Psychology of Sex*, vol. VII),
  Philadelphia: F. A. Davis, 1928.

Psychology of Sex: The Biology of Sex – The Sexual Impulse in Youth – Sexual
  Deviation – The Erotic Symbolisms – Homosexuality – The Art of Love. A Manual
  for Students. London: William Heinemann (Medical Books), 1933.

Studies in the Psychology of Sex, 4 vols, New York: Random House, 1936.

The New Spirit, London: George Bell, 1890. 2nd edition, 1891. 3rd edition, 1892,
  Walter Scott. 4th edition, 1926, Constable.

The Criminal, London: Walter Scott, 1890. 2nd edition, 1895. 3rd edition, revised and
  enlarged, 1900. 4th edition, 1910.

The Nationalisation of Health, London: Fisher Unwin, 1892.

Man and Woman: A Study of Human Secondary Sexual Characters, London:
  Walter Scott, 1894. 4th edition, revised, 1904. 5th edition, revised, 1914. 6th edition,

1926, Black. 7th edition, 1929, Boston: Houghton Mifflin. 8th edition, 1934, Heinemann.

Affirmations, London: Walter Scott, 1898. 2nd edition, 1915, Constable. 3rd edition, 1926, Constable.

A Note on the Bedborough Trial, The University Press, Watford [London], 1898 (a privately printed pamphlet of 23 pages).

The Nineteenth Century: A Dialogue in Utopia, London: Grant Richards, 1900.

A Study of British Genius, London: Hurst & Blackett, 1904. 2nd edition, revised and enlarged, 1927, Constable.

The Soul of Spain, London: Constable, 1908. New edition, 1937 (with a new preface on the Spanish Civil War).

The World of Dreams, London: Constable, 1911.

The Problem of Race Degeneration, London: Cassell, 1911.

The Task of Social Hygiene, London: Constable, 1912. New edition, 1927.

Impressions and Comments, first series, London: Constable, 1914.

Essays in War-time, London: Constable, 1916.

The Erotic Rights of Women, and The Objects of Marriage. Two Essays, London: British Society for the Study of Sex Psychology, Publication No. 5, 1918.

The Philosophy of Conflict, second series, London: Constable, 1919.

Impressions and Comments, second series, 1914–20, London: Constable, 1921.

The Play-Function of Sex, London: British Society for the Study of Sex Psychology, Publication No. 9, 1921.

Kanga Creek: An Australian Idyll, Waltham St Lawrence: Golden Cockerel Press, 1922. New editions: New York, Black Hawk Press, 1935; Berkeley Heights, N.J.: The Oriole Press, 1938.

Little Essays of Love and Virtue, London: Black, 1920.

The Dance of Life, London: Constable, 1923. New edition, New York: Modern Library, 1929.

Impressions and Comments, third (and final) series, 1920–3, London: Constable, 1924.

Sonnets, with Folk Songs from the Spanish, Waltham St Lawrence: Golden Cockerel Press, 1925.

The Art of Life: Gleanings from the Works of Havelock Ellis, collected by Mrs S. Herbert (Constable's Miscellany), London: Constable, 1929.

Marriage To-day and To-morrow, San Francisco: Westgate Press, 1929.

Fountain of Life: Being the Impressions and Comments of Havelock Ellis, Boston: Houghton Mifflin, 1930 (three volumes in one with a new preface).

The Colour-Sense in Literature, London: Ulysses Book Shop, 1931.

Concerning Jude the Obscure, London: Ulysses Book Shop, 1931.

The Revaluation of Obscenity, Paris: The Hours Press, 1931.

More Essays of Love and Virtue, London: Constable, 1931.

Song of Songs: Ernest Renan, translated by Havelock Ellis. Berkeley Heights, N.J.: Oriole Press, 1932. City of Birmingham School of Painting College of Arts and Crafts, 1937.

Views and Reviews: A Selection of Uncollected Articles 1884–1932, first and second series, 2 vols, London: Desmond Harmsworth, 1932.

George Chapman, London: Nonesuch Press, 1934.

My Confessional: Questions of Our Day, London: John Lane, 1934.

From Rousseau to Proust, London: Constable, 1936.

Questions of Our Day, London: John Lane, 1936.

Selected Essays (Everyman's Library), London: Dent, 1936.

On Life and Sex: Essays of Love and Virtue, 2 vols in one, Heinemann, 1948.

Poems, Selected by John Gawsworth, London: Richards Press, 1937.

Morals, Manners and Men (Thinker's Library), London: Watts, 1939.

265

Bibliography

My Life, London: Heinemann, 1940.
The Genius of Europe, London: Williams & Norgate, 1950.
From Marlowe to Shaw, London: Williams & Norgate, 1950.
Sex and Marriage, London: Ernest Benn; New York: Random House, 1951.

Earlier biographical works
GOLDBERG, ISAAC, *Havelock Ellis, A Biographical and Critical Survey*, London: Constable, 1926.
PETERSON, HOUSTON, *Havelock Ellis, Philosopher of Love*, London: George Allen & Unwin, 1928.
HAVELOCK ELLIS, MRS, 'Havelock Ellis', an essay in *Essays*, N.J.: Free Spirit Press, 1924.
WORTIS, JOSEPH, M. D., *Fragments of an Analysis with Freud*, New York: Simon & Shuster, 1954. Dr Wortis's account of a short training analysis with Freud and Freud's comments on Ellis.
DELISLE, FRANÇOISE (FRANÇOISE LAFITTE CYON), *Friendship's Odyssey*, London: Heinemann, 1946. Autobiography of Françoise Delisle, giving a detailed account of her years with Havelock Ellis.
CALDER-MARSHALL, ARTHUR, *Havelock Ellis*, London: Rupert Hart-Davis, 1959.
COLLIS, JOHN STEWART, *An Artist of Life*, London: Cassell, 1959.
ISHILL, ROSE F., *Havelock Ellis*, Berkeley Heights, N.J.: Oriole Press, 1959.

Other published sources
MASTERS, W. H. AND JOHNSON, V. E., *Human Sexual Response*, Boston: Little Brown, 1966.
BRECHER, E. H., *The Sex Researchers*, London: Deutsch, 1971.
ROBINSON, PAUL A., *The Modernisation of Sex*, London: Elek, 1976.
ROWBOTHAM, SHEILA AND WEEKS, JEFFREY, *Socialism and the New Life*, London: Pluto Press, 1977.
KAPP, Y., *The Crowded Years*, London: Lawrence & Wishart, 1977.

Index

Index